Communications
in Computer and Information Science   1557

More information about this series at https://link.springer.com/bookseries/7899

Guojun Wang · Kim-Kwang Raymond Choo ·
Ryan K. L. Ko · Yang Xu · Bruno Crispo (Eds.)

Ubiquitous Security

First International Conference, UbiSec 2021
Guangzhou, China, December 28–31, 2021
Revised Selected Papers

Springer

Editors
Guojun Wang [ID]
Guangzhou University
Guangzhou, China

Kim-Kwang Raymond Choo [ID]
University of Texas at San Antonio
San Antonio, TX, USA

Ryan K. L. Ko [ID]
University of Queensland
Brisbane, QLD, Australia

Yang Xu [ID]
Hunan University
Changsha, China

Bruno Crispo [ID]
University of Trento
Trento, Italy

ISSN 1865-0929   ISSN 1865-0937 (electronic)
Communications in Computer and Information Science
ISBN 978-981-19-0467-7   ISBN 978-981-19-0468-4 (eBook)
https://doi.org/10.1007/978-981-19-0468-4

This Springer imprint is published by the registered company Springer Nature Singapore Pte Ltd.
The registered company address is: 152 Beach Road, #21-01/04 Gateway East, Singapore 189721, Singapore

Preface

The First International Conference on Ubiquitous Security (UbiSec 2021) was held in Guangzhou, China, between December 28 and 31, 2021, and hosted by Guangzhou University.

UbiSec builds on the success of three conference/symposium/workshop series, namely, the International Conference on Security, Privacy, and Anonymity in Computation, Communication, and Storage (SpaCCS), the International Symposium on UbiSafe Computing (UbiSafe), and the International Workshop on Cyberspace Security (IWCSS); however, it has a specific focus on the security, privacy, and anonymity aspects of cyberspace, the physical world, and social networks (collectively referred to as the metaverse).

UbiSec 2021 received a total of 96 submissions from authors in 17 different countries, and each submission was reviewed by at least three experts with relevant subject matter expertise. Based on the recommendations of the reviewers and subsequent discussions of the Program Committee members, 28 papers were selected for oral presentation at the conference and inclusion in this Springer CCIS volume (i.e., an acceptance rate of 29.2%). In addition to the technical presentations, the program included a number of keynote speeches by world-renowned researchers. On this note, we thank our distinguished keynote speakers, Ravi Sandhu, Vincenzo Piuri, Yang Xiao, My T. Thai, and Wanlei Zhou, for their time and willingness to share their knowledge with the conference attendees.

UbiSec 2021 was only possible because of the support and dedication of a large number of individuals and organizations worldwide. There is a long list of people who volunteered their time and energy to put together the conference and deserve special thanks. First and foremost, we would like to offer our gratitude to the Steering Committee Chairs, Guojun Wang from Guangzhou University, China, and Kim-Kwang Raymond Choo from the University of Texas at San Antonio, USA, for guiding the entire process of the conference. We are also deeply grateful to all the Program Committee members and reviewers for their time and efforts in reading, commenting, debating, and finally selecting the papers.

We would like to offer our gratitude to the General Chairs, Guojun Wang, Kouichi Sakurai, and Ravi Sandhu, for their tremendous support and advice in ensuring the success of the conference. Thanks also go to the Local Organizing Committee Chair, Hanpin Wang; the Publicity Chairs, Carlos Becker Westphall, Wenbin Jiang, Scott Fowler, Yulei Wu, Arcangelo Castiglione, Peter Mueller, and Shuhong Chen; and the Conference Secretariat, Wenyin Yang.

Finally, we thank the authors and all participants for your support and contribution; we hoped you found the conference a stimulating and exciting forum! Hopefully, you also enjoyed the beautiful city of Guangzhou, China!

January 2022

Ryan K. L. Ko
Yang Xu
Bruno Crispo

Organization

Local Organizing Chair

Hanpin Wang   Guangzhou University, China

General Chairs

Guojun Wang   Guangzhou University, China
Kouichi Sakurai   Kyushu University, Japan
Ravi Sandhu   University of Texas at San Antonio, USA

Program Chairs

Ryan K. L. Ko   University of Queensland, Australia
Yang Xu   Hunan University, China
Bruno Crispo   University of Trento, Italy

Program Vice Chairs

Cyberspace Security Track

Qin Liu   Hunan University, China
Simon Parkinson   University of Huddersfield, UK
Shajulin Benedict   Indian Institute of Information Technology,
                                 Kottayam, India
Wei Chang   Saint Joseph's University, USA
Wenjia Li   New York Institute of Technology, USA

Cyberspace Privacy Track

Wenjun Jiang   Hunan University, China
Radu Prodan   Klagenfurt University, Austria
Saqib Ali   University of Agriculture Faisalabad, Pakistan
Anish Shrestha   Sejong University, South Korea
Quazi Mamun   Charles Sturt University, Australia

Cyberspace Anonymity Track

Tian Wang	Beijing Normal University and United International College, China
Sergio Duarte Correia	Instituto Politecnico de Portalegre, Portugal
Dragan Perakovic	University of Zagreb, Croatia
Avinash Srinivasan	TDI Technologies, USA
A. S. M. Kayes	La Trobe University, Australia

Publicity Chairs

Carlos Becker Westphall	Federal University of Santa Catarina, Brazil
Wenbin Jiang	Huazhong University of Science and Technology, China
Scott Fowler	Linkoping University, Sweden
Yulei Wu	University of Exeter, UK
Arcangelo Castiglione	University of Salerno, Italy
Peter Mueller	IBM Zurich Research Laboratory, Switzerland
Shuhong Chen	Guangzhou University, China

Publication Chairs

Tao Peng	Guangzhou University, China
Fang Qi	Central South University, China

Registration Chairs

Xiaofei Xing	Guangzhou University, China
Pin Liu	Central South University, China

Conference Secretariat

Wenyin Yang	Foshan University, China

Web Chairs

Jiemin Huang	Foshan University, China
Yuming Xia	Foshan University, China

Steering Committee

Guojun Wang (Chair)	Guangzhou University, China
Kim-Kwang Raymond Choo (Chair)	University of Texas at San Antonio, USA

Saqib Ali	University of Agriculture Faisalabad, Pakistan
Valentina E. Balas	Aurel Vlaicu University of Arad, Romania
Md. Zakirul Alam Bhuiyan	Fordham University, USA
Jiannong Cao	Hong Kong Polytechnic University, Hong Kong
Aniello Castiglione	University of Naples Parthenope, Italy
Scott Fowler	Linkoping University, Sweden
Oana Geman	University of Suceava, Romania
Richard Hill	University of Huddersfield, UK
Ryan K. L. Ko	University of Queensland, Australia
Kuan-Ching Li	Providence University, Taiwan
Jianhua Ma	Hosei University, Japan
Gregorio Martinez	University of Murcia, Spain
Kouichi Sakurai	Kyushu University, Japan
Sabu M. Thampi	Indian Institute of Information Technology and Management, Kerala, India
Jie Wu	Temple University, USA
Yang Xu	Hunan University, China
Zheng Yan	Xidian University, China/Aalto University, Finland
Wenyin Yang	Foshan University, China
Haojin Zhu	Shanghai Jiao Tong University, China

Program Committee

Cyberspace Security Track

Mohiuddin Ahmed	Edith Cowan University, Australia
Raja Naeem Akram	University of Aberdeen, UK
Hussain Al-Aqrabi	University of Huddersfield, UK
Junaid Arshad	Birmingham City, UK
Man Ho Au	University of Hong Kong, Hong Kong
Eduard Babulak	National Science Foundation, USA
Tao Ban	National Institute of Information and Communications Technology, Japan
Abderrahim Benslimane	University of Avignon, France
Ana Calderon	Cardiff Metropolitan University, UK
Sudip Chakraborty	Valdosta State University, USA
Aldar C.-F. Chan	University of Hong Kong, Hong Kong
Lei Chen	Georgia Southern University, USA
Luca Davoli	University of Parma, Italy
Jose Maria de Fuentes	Universidad Carlos III de Madrid, Spain
James Dyer	University of Huddersfield, UK

Md.Sadek Ferdous	Shahjalal University of Science and Technology, Bangladesh
Eduardo B. Fernandez	Florida Atlantic University, USA
Elke Franz	Technische Universität Dresden, Germany
Jeff Garae	CERT Vanuatu, Vanuatu
Gerhard Hancke	City University of Hong Kong, Hong Kong
Michael Heinzl	Independent Security Researcher, Austria
Heemeng Ho	Singapore Institute of Technology, Singapore
Jie Hu	University of Electronic Science and Technology of China, China
Mike Johnstone	Edith Cowan University, Australia
Sokratis Katsikas	Norwegian University of Science and Technology, Norway
Saad Khan	University of Huddersfield, UK
Abigail Koay	University of Queensland, Australia
Vimal Kumar	University of Waikato, New Zealand
Nuno Laranjeiro	University of Coimbra, Portugal
Dawei Li	Montclair State University, USA
Jiguo Li	Fujian Normal University, China
Linsen Li	Shanghai Jiao Tong University, China
Kaitai Liang	Delft University of Technology, The Netherlands
Xin Liao	Hunan University, China
Jiagang Liu	Hunan Institute of Technology, China
Na Liu	University of Surrey, UK
Yuling Liu	Hunan University, China
Zhen Liu	Nagasaki Institute of Applied Science, Japan
Jonathan Loo	University of West London, UK
García Villalba Luis Javier	Universidad Complutense Madrid, Spain
Wissam Mallouli	Montimage EURL, France
Spiros Mancoridis	Drexel University, USA
Hafizah Mansor	International Islamic University Malaysia, Malaysia
Iberia Medeiros	University of Lisbon, Portugal
Weizhi Meng	Technical University of Denmark, Denmark
Aleksandra Mileva	Goce Delcev University, Macedonia
Reza Montasari	Swansea University, UK
David Naccache	ENS, France
Priyadarsi Nanda	University of Technology, Sydney, Australia
Jonathan Oliver	Trendmicro and University of Queensland, Australia
Pouya Ostovari	San Jose State University, USA
Francesco Piccialli	University of Naples Federico II, Italy

Josef Pieprzyk	Data61, CSIRO, Australia
Nikolaos Pitropakis	Edinburgh Napier University, UK
Vincenzo Piuri	University of Milan, Italy
Emil Pricop	Petroleum-Gas University of Ploiesti, Romania
Quan Qian	Shanghai University, China
Vinayakumar Ravi	Prince Mohammad Bin Fahd University, Saudi Arabia
Hassan Raza	Information Technology University, Pakistan
Sherif Saad	University of Windsor, Canada
Joshua Scarsbrook	University of Queensland, Australia
Amartya Sen	Oakland University, USA
Kewei Sha	University of Houston - Clear Lake, USA
Hossain Shahriar	Kennesaw State University, USA
Jiacheng Shang	Montclair State University, USA
Kashif Sharif	Beijing Institute of Technology, China
Dario Stabili	University of Modena and Reggio Emilia, Italy
Hung-Min Sun	National Tsing Hua University, Taiwan
Omair Uthmani	Glasgow Caledonian University, UK
Konstantinos Votis	Information Technologies Institute, Centre for Research and Technology Hellas, Greece
Lei Wang	Nanjing Forestry University, China
Wei Wang	Nanjing University of Aeronautics and Astronautics, China
Zumin Wang	Dalian University, China
Yehua Wei	Hunan Normal University, China
Chenshu Wu	University of Hong Kong, Hong Kong
Longfei Wu	Fayetteville State University, USA
Yulei Wu	University of Exeter, UK
Liang Xiao	Xiamen University, China
Anjia Yang	Jinan University, China
Baoliu Ye	Nanjing University, China
Chong Yu	University of Nebraska–Lincoln, USA
Nicola Zannone	Eindhoven University of Technology, The Netherlands
Mingwu Zhang	Hubei University of Technology, China
Yi Zhang	Sichuan University, China
Yuan Zhang	University of Electronic Science and Technology, China
Yongjun Zhao	Nanyang Technological University, Singapore
Xi Zheng	Macquarie University, Australia
Xinliang Zheng	Frostburg State University, USA
Yongbin Zhou	Nanjing University of Science and Technology, China

Congxu Zhu   Central South University, China
Liehuang Zhu   Beijing Institute of Technology, China

Cyberspace Privacy Track

Mamoun Alazab   Charles Darwin University, Australia
Flora Amato   University of Naples "Federico II", Italy
Rojeena Bajracharya   Incheon National University, South Korea
Salima Benbernou   LIPADE, Université de Paris, France
Jorge Bernal Bernabe   University of Murcia, Spain
Minh-Son Dao   National Institute of Information and
                                Communications Technology, Japan
Rajendra Dhakal   Sejong University, South Korea
Yucong Duan   Hainan University, China
Ramadan Elaiess   University of Benghazi, Libya
Philippe Fournier-Viger   Harbin Institute of Technology, China
Kambiz Ghazinour   Kent State University, USA
Sascha Hauke   HAW Landshut, Germany
Hai Jiang   Arkansas State University, USA
Gyanendra Prasad Joshi   Sejong University, South Korea
Ashad Kabir   Charles Sturt University, Australia
Vana Kalogeraki   Athens University of Economics and Business,
                                Greece
Waqas Khalid   Korea University Sejong, South Korea
Konstantinos Kolias   University of Idaho, USA
Miroslaw Kutylowski   Wroclaw University of Science and Technology,
                                Poland
Ruixuan Li   Huazhong University of Science and Technology,
                                China
Xin Li   Nanjing University of Aeronautics and
                                Astronautics, China
Dongxi Liu   CSIRO, Australia
Changqing Luo   Virginia Commonwealth University, USA
Yuxiang Ma   Henan University, China
Juan Pedro Munoz-Gea   Universidad Politécnica de Cartagena, Spain
Anand Nayyar   Duy Tan University, Vietnam
Zhan Qin   Zhejiang University, China
Manuel Roveri   Politecnico di Milano, Italy
Ricardo Seguel   Universidad Adolfo Ibañez, Chile
Jaydip Sen   Praxis Business School, Kolkata, India
Rakesh Shrestha   Yonsei University, South Korea
Junggab Son   Kennesaw State University, USA
Zhiyuan Tan   Edinburgh Napier University, UK

Muhhamad Imran Tariq	Superior University Lahore, Pakistan
Xiuhua Wang	Huazhong University of Science and Technology, China
Yunsheng Wang	Kettering University, USA
Lei Xu	University of Texas Rio Grande Valley, USA
Shuhui Yang	Purdue University Northwest, USA
Xuanxia Yao	University of Science and Technology Beijing, China
Ji Zhang	University of Southern Queensland, Australia
Youwen Zhu	Nanjing University of Aeronautics and Astronautics, China

Cyberspace Anonymity Track

Hamid Ali Abed AL-Asadi	Basra University, Iraq
Selcuk Baktir	American University of the Middle East, Kuwait
Fu Chen	Central University of Finance and Economics, China
Honglong Chen	China University of Petroleum, China
Ivan Cvitic	University of Zagreb, Croatia
Ke Gu	Changsha University of Science and Technology, China
Hasan Jamil	University of Idaho, USA
Aleksandar Jevremovic	Singidunum University, Serbia
Frank Jiang	Deakin University, Australia
Marko Krstic	Algolysis Ltd., Cyprus
Maryline Laurent	Telecom SudParis, Institut Polytechnique de Paris, France
Masahiro Mambo	Kanazawa University, Japan
Massimo Mecella	Sapienza University of Rome, Italy
Jose Andre Morales	Carnegie Mellon University, USA
Klimis Ntalianis	University of West Attica, Greece
Hao Peng	Zhejiang Normal University, China
Dapeng Qu	Liaoning University, China
Imed Romdhani	Edinburgh Napier University, UK
Zeyu Sun	Luoyang Institute of Science and Technology, China
Henry Tufo	University of Colorado Boulder, USA
Hongzhi Wang	Harbin Institute of Technology, China
Sherali Zeadally	University of Kentucky, USA
Chunsheng Zhu	University of British Columbia, Canada

Contents

A Backdoor Embedding Method for Backdoor Detection in Deep Neural Networks

Meirong Liu[1]ⓘ, Hong Zheng[1]ⓘ, Qin Liu[2]ⓘ, Xiaofei Xing[3]ⓘ,
and Yinglong Dai[4,5(✉)]ⓘ

[1] School of Physics and Electronics, Hunan Normal University,
Changsha 410081, China
[2] College of Computer Science and Electronic Engineering, Hunan University,
Changsha 410082, China
[3] School of Computer Science, Guangzhou University, Guangzhou 510006, China
[4] College of Liberal Arts and Sciences, National University of Defense Technology,
Changsha 410073, China
daiyl@hunnu.edu.cn
[5] Hunan Provincial Key Laboratory of Intelligent Computing and Language
Information Processing, College of Information Science and Engineering,
Hunan Normal University, Changsha 410081, China

Abstract. As the coming of artificial intelligence (AI) era, deep learning models are widely applied on many aspects of our daily lives, such as face recognition, speech recognition, and automatic driving. AI security is also becoming a burning problem. Because the deep learning model is usually regarded as a black box, it is susceptible to backdoor attacks that embed hidden patterns to impact the model prediction results. To promote backdoor detection research, this work proposes a simple backdoor embedding method to produce deep learning models with a backdoor for validating backdoor detection algorithms. Through conceptual embedding techniques, we decouple the backdoor pattern recognition function and the normal classification function in a deep learning model. One advantage is that the backdoor activation mechanism will not directly interfere with the normal function of the original DNN-based model. Another advantage is that the interference of the final prediction result can be more flexible. The backdoor pattern recognition phase and the model prediction interference phase can be developed independently. The aim is that the deep model needs to have an indistinguishable performance in terms of the normal sample classification while it can be triggered by the hidden backdoor patterns at the right time. The analysis and the experiments validate the proposed method that the embedding backdoor model can achieve almost the same prediction performance as the normal model while the backdoor mechanism can be activated precisely.

Keywords: Deep learning · Deep neural networks · Security · Backdoor attack · Backdoor embedding

ⓒ The Author(s), under exclusive license to Springer Nature Singapore Pte Ltd. 2022
G. Wang et al. (Eds.): UbiSec 2021, CCIS 1557, pp. 1–12, 2022.
https://doi.org/10.1007/978-981-19-0468-4_1

1   Introduction

Deep neural networks (DNNs) have shown impressive performance in complex machine learning tasks such as image classification or speech recognition. The rapid development of deep learning techniques has reduced the error rate of speech recognition and image recognition. One important application is classification. For the multi-layer DNNs, it is difficult to express it with specific mathematical expressions due to the complexity of its internal structure, that is to say, the model is a black box for people, lacking of explanation. Due to the lack of explanation, how to correctly classify is always a problem to be solved. Especially in some situations, such as in the application of image processing, certain secret information is added to the input image, which makes the DNNs confused to some degree. This kind of backdoor attack affects the decision of the system, and may produce fatal consequences. The backdoor attack of DNNs has strong concealment, so it plays a key role in the defense to correctly identify this concealed information. The ideal situation is that the neural network will make the right judgment even if there is a backdoor that can cause misclassification. For example, in an image recognition task, the neural network prediction model puts the input image into the right category while classifies the image with a backdoor pattern into a target category.

To promote the backdoor detection research, the preliminary work is to construct a backdoor model that can be used for backdoor detection test. A better backdoor model may promote a better backdoor detection algorithm. As the early research work of proactive attacks in DNN-based models, Gu et al. [3] proposed a backdoored neural network, termed BadNet, which incorporated the backdoor pattern recognition process in the original task-oriented DNN architecture. Liu et al. [5] proposed to make a general backdoor trigger, termed trojan trigger, by reverse engineering. They injected malicious behaviors to the DNN-based model through fine-tuning the pre-trained model with training data produced by reverse engineering. The backdoor mechanism is activated when the input sample has a trojan trigger. A DNN-based model with a hidden backdoor should keep the high accuracy with respect to the classification of normal samples. At the meantime, a sample with a backdoor pattern should trigger the model to target prediction. However, it would generally cause the performance reduction when we inject a backdoor to the DNN-based model, because the backdoor patterns and will inevitably change the weights of the DNN-based model.

In this paper, we propose to decouple the function of backdoor pattern recognition and the original task function. We construct a framework of the separated backdoor function for the DNN-based model with a hidden backdoor mechanism. It is a general backdoor embedding method that can be used for the existing models. The effectiveness of the framework is analyzed in Sect. 3. We also validate the proposed framework by some experiments in Sect. 4. Specifically, when a deep model has recognized the backdoor patterns, it will activate the specific hidden neurons, termed backdoor neurons, in the hidden layers of the DNN-based models. In this way, the backdoor pattern recognition network will not directly interfere the original classification results of the output layer. On the one hand, the approach can greatly reduce the performance interference of the normal sample prediction. On the other hand, with the hidden backdoor neurons, the backdoor triggering and prediction interference will be more flexible. We can easily change the model predictions to different target labels by fine-tuning a small part of neural network layers after the backdoor neurons.

In the following, we firstly introduce the related work of backdoor attack and detection in Sect. 2. And we mainly focus on the methods of backdoor attack mechanisms. Then, we introduce the backdoor embedding framework and propose the backdoor embedding method with some formalization analyses in Sect. 3. In Sect. 4, we take the experiments based on the FashionMNIST dataset and demonstrate the experimental results to validate the backdoor embedding method. Finally, we conclude the paper in Sect. 5.

2   Related Work

As the increasingly popular DNN-based models are widely deployed in our daily life, backdoor attacks become a urgent problem that a wrong classification rule is hidden in a seemingly correct model. The model is triggered by certain information hidden in the input data pattern, and wrong prediction output can be generated under certain backdoor mechanism. Many researchers begin to propose methods for backdoor detection of DNN-based models [4,6,12,14]. Typically, Wang et al. [11] analyzed the backdoor attacks and proposed a general detection framework for the backdoor attacks as prior work. They detected whether there is a backdoor in a DNN-based model by discovering the subtle variation among the output labels of the model. Specifically, they utilized a gradient descent strategy that can discover tiny backdoor patterns. However, if the subtle variation of the DNN-based model with backdoor is greatly reduced, the detection method may be failure. As the counterpart, the analysis of the backdoor attack mechanism may be another way to promote the backdoor attack detection field [1,7,15,16]. In this work, we focus on how to produce an effective backdoor in DNN-based models.

The backdoor attacks in deep learning can track back to the adversarial examples. Because the computing process of the DNN-based models is opaque and sensitive to small changes of parameters, Szegedy et al. [9] discovered that imperceptible perturbation of original samples could cause misclassification in DNN-based models. The adversarial examples can be regarded as bugs in DNN-based models and can also be regarded as backdoor. Backdoor attacks can use the characteristics to make backdoors in the DNN-based models. For the active backdoor attack, Shen et al. [8] proposed to poisoning the training dataset so as to make the DNN-based model misclassify to target label. However, their method would make the model performance have a noticeable reduce that can be detected easily. Our objective is to make the DNN-based model with a backdoor have the same performance with the original model in normal tasks while the backdoor model has high accuracy in backdoor pattern recognition.

Recently, Yao et al. [15] proposed a latent backdoor method, which is powerful and stealthy under transfer learning. But, it is not universal for normal training. Tang et al. [10] introduced an extra tiny backdoor network, termed TrojanNet, to escape the backdoor detection. The TrojanNet can be activated by tiny backdoor pattern while it will be concealed on the other conditions. Gu et al. [3] presented a clear DNN-based backdoor architecture that incorporated the backdoor pattern recognition network in the original DNN-based architecture. Therefore, there is a specific transformation function that can recognize the backdoor pattern and activate the backdoor mechanism. However, the backdoor pattern recognition network is coupled with the original network, so it is inevitable that the signals of the backdoor pattern recognition network interferes the normal computing process of the original network. In this paper, we propose a method to decouple the backdoor pattern recognition function to achieve better performance and flexibility.

3   Methods

In this section, the framework of backdoor embedding method in DNN-based models is introduced, including the formalization of the framework, and then the effectiveness of this approach is analyzed with respect to the model performance effect of the backdoor embedding.

3.1   The Framework of Backdoor Embedding Method in DNNs

The Mapping Function of DNNs. In essence, the DNN-based model can be regarded as an input-output mapping function. Assume a classification task $(X \mapsto Y)$, in which the input sample set is X and the prediction label set is Y. A specific sample $x \in X$ has a specific label $y \in Y$. In deep learning, we need to train a DNN-based model to fit a mapping function, represented as $f(\cdot)$,

$$y = f(x). \tag{1}$$

The training target is that the mapping function (1) can transfer a sample x in sample set X to its right label y.

Backdoor Pattern Recognition Network. For a DNN-based model with a backdoor, it should keep the model performance in terms of its original classification task, while the backdoor mechanism of the model should be activated when a sample contains a backdoor pattern. In this work, we will separate the function of the backdoor pattern recognition network and look into it. For any $x \in X$, we assume a micro-modified sample $x' = g(x)$ containing a backdoor pattern, whose label is $t \in \{0, 1\}$. We denote $t = 1$ when there is a backdoor pattern, and $t = 0$ when the sample is normal. For the function $g(\cdot)$, it may be a simple permutation as

$$x' = g(x) = x + \Delta x. \tag{2}$$

The backdoor pattern recognition network is to detect the backdoor patterns in the samples, represented as $h(\cdot)$,

$$t = h(x). \tag{3}$$

Specifically, for a normal sample $x \in X$, $h(x) = 0$ and $h(g(x)) = 1$.

Backdoor Neurons. The neurons of the DNN-based model activated by the backdoor patterns can be called backdoor neurons. More specifically, if the activation value of a neuron is strongly correlated with the backdoor pattern label t, we can call it backdoor neuron. It is worth noting that the backdoor neurons can be embedded in any layer of the DNN-based model using the conceptual alignment techniques [2], as illustrated in Fig. 1.

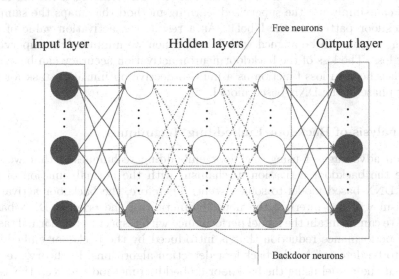

Fig. 1. The illustration of the DNN-based backdoor architecture with the embedding backdoor neurons. In the hidden layers of the architecture, the hidden neurons are divided into two categories, i.e. the backdoor neurons and the free neurons. The backdoor neurons are used for backdoor pattern recognition, and the free neurons are used for executing normal tasks. The backdoor neurons are trained by conceptual alignment techniques that the activation values are strongly correlated with the backdoor pattern labels.

Backdoor Embedding Network. The backdoor mechanism can be embedded in the original DNN-based model without change the original architecture. When the backdoor mechanism activated, the prediction result y' of the DNN-based model with a backdoor will depend on t, represented as,

$$y' = f'(x; t). \tag{4}$$

If there is no backdoor pattern, the prediction label will be the same as original label y, i.e. $y'(t = 0) = y$, and if there is a backdoor pattern, the prediction label can be changed to any target label $\tilde{y}$, i.e. $y'(t = 1) = \tilde{y}$. We can also formulate the mapping function as

$$y' = f'(x; t) = t\tilde{y} + (1 - t)f(x). \tag{5}$$

It is also worth noting that the numbers of backdoor neurons in each hidden layer are user-defined and their positions are not necessary ordered. Typically, we can simply embed a backdoor neuron in the last hidden layer whose activation value is strongly correlated with t. In other words, it introduces an extra task $(X \mapsto T)$ that maps the sample space X to the backdoor pattern label space T. When we want to change the prediction result of the output layer, we can only fine-tuning the last layer of the DNN-based model. The training of the backdoor neurons can simply use the supervised learning method that maps the samples with backdoor pattern to the label t. As a result, the activation value of the backdoor neuron will be aligned with label t when we minimize the supervised learning loss. The loss of the backdoor neuron activation accuracy can be added to the classification loss function as a multi-objective optimization task for the training phase of the DNN-based model.

3.2   Analysis of Backdoor Embedding Techniques

The main advantage of using backdoor embedding techniques is that we can separate the backdoor activation mechanism with the normal function of the original DNN-based model to some extent. Therefore, the backdoor activation mechanism will not interfere the normal function of the original DNN-based model. We maintain the model performance with respect to the normal tasks, and the performance reduction that is introduced by the backdoor embedding is hard to be detected by the backdoor detection algorithms. In theory, we can prove that the model using the backdoor embedding method can keep the same with the original DNN-based model.

Proposition 1. *If the model capacity of a DNN architecture without backdoor neurons is enough to fit the normal tasks, the performance of the backdoor embedding network in the normal tasks can keep the same with the original model.*

Proof. If the model capacity of a DNN architecture without backdoor neurons is enough to fit the normal tasks, we can train a same mapping function $y = f(x)$ with the original DNN-based model just employing the free neurons of the DNN architecture. In the normal tasks, i.e. the backdoor neurons are not activated that $t = 0$, we can use the original mapping function that the backdoor embedding network prediction y' will be the same with the original DNN-based model y, i.e. $y' = f(x) = y$, referring to Eq. (5). Hence, the performance of the backdoor embedding network in the normal tasks will not be reduced.

Proposition 1 demonstrates that we can use the backdoor embedding technique without any model performance reduction in normal tasks. Hence, if the backdoor detection algorithms try to discover the latent backdoor by detecting the model performance variation in normal tasks, the backdoor detection algorithms will be failure.

Through the backdoor embedding technique, on the other side, we can easily separate the backdoor pattern recognition phase $x \mapsto t$ that maps a sample x to backdoor pattern label t and the model prediction interference phase $t \mapsto y'$ that maps the backdoor pattern label t to malicious prediction y'. The backdoor neurons for backdoor pattern recognition can be concealed in the hidden layers of the DNN-based model. In this way, it brings the advantage that the interference of the final prediction result can be more flexible. The backdoor pattern recognition network can be trained independently with an extra loss function, and the backdoor malicious behaviour, i.e. $\tilde{y} = e(t)$, can be user-defined and can be changed more easily based on the backdoor neurons.

4 Experiments

In this section, we firstly introduce the experimental setup, including the dataset and the classification task. Then, we demonstrate the designed architecture of the DNN-based model with respect to this task. Finally, we show the experimental results and provide some analyses.

4.1 Experimental Setup

We use the classification task of FashionMNIST dataset [13] in our experiments. The FashionMNIST dataset is the improved version of the MNIST dataset. It has the same format as MNIST dataset, which contains 60,000 training examples and 10,000 test examples of 28×28 grayscale images. Different from MNIST, the image samples of FashionMNIST are ten categories of T-shirt, trouser, pullover, dress, coat, sandal, shirt, sneaker, bag, and ankle boot. So the classification task is more difficult than MNIST.

At first, we use the original dataset to train a normal DNN-based model for the FashionMNIST classification task. Then, we use a corresponding dataset with backdoor pattern labels to train a backdoor embedding DNN-based model with the same architecture with the normal model. In our experiments, we set a backdoor pattern that two pixels on the four corners of the original images are highlighted randomly, as illustrated in Fig. 2.

In the training phase, we embed the backdoor patterns in the original training samples and assign target labels for these modified samples. Then, the modified samples are mixed with the original samples for the training of deep neural networks. Our task is to make a backdoor embedding DNN-based model that can recognize the backdoor pattern and activate the backdoor neurons, while the performance of the normal classification task should not be reduced.

Fig. 2. An illustration of some images with a backdoor pattern. The images of the first line are the original samples, and the images of the second line are the corresponding samples with a backdoor pattern that two pixels on the four corners of the original images are highlighted randomly.

4.2   The Architecture of the Backdoor Embedding Network

In order to process the FashionMNIST classification task, we deploy a DNN-based model of five-layer architecture and embed a backdoor neuron in the architecture, as illustrated in Table 1.

Table 1. The backdoor embedding network architecture.

Layer no.	Layer type	Input dim.	Output dim.	Activation	Input layer
1	Convolution	$1 \times 28 \times 28$	$4 \times 14 \times 14$	ReLU	0
2	Convolution	$4 \times 14 \times 14$	$8 \times 7 \times 7$	ReLU	1
3	Fully-connected	392	256	ReLU	2
4-a	Fully-connected	256	127	ReLU	3
4-b	Fully-connected	256	1	Linear	3
5	Output	128	10	Softmax	4-a, 4-b

A backdoor neuron is set in the last hidden layer of the DNN architecture, and we add an extra loss of the backdoor neuron to the classification loss. The extra label t for the backdoor neuron is that the original samples are $t = 0$ and the modified samples are $t = 1$. The loss of the backdoor neuron activation b uses the mean square error $\|b - t\|$ to make the activation value of the backdoor neuron correlate with the backdoor pattern label. The total training loss function can be presented as

$$J = \|y' - y\| + \lambda\|b - t\|. \tag{6}$$

Where y' is the model prediction, y is the true label, and λ is the backdoor coefficient that can be used to adjust the backdoor effectiveness. When the λ is big, the optimization algorithm will trend to reduce the loss of the backdoor pattern recognition, i.e. $\|b - t\|$. To ensure the activation accuracy of the backdoor neuron, λ can be set a little large. We set $\lambda = 10$ in the experiments.

4.3   Experimental Results

The training process of the DNN-based model using the separated backdoor mechanism with an extra backdoor neuron loss is illustrated in Fig. 3. We use the model accuracy to demonstrate the whether the backdoor neuron embedding technique affect the model performance for the normal task. In the figure, the performance curve of the separated backdoor mechanism almost overlaps the performance curve of the normal training, and the performance curve of the non-separated backdoor mechanism has a obvious reduction compared with the normal training.

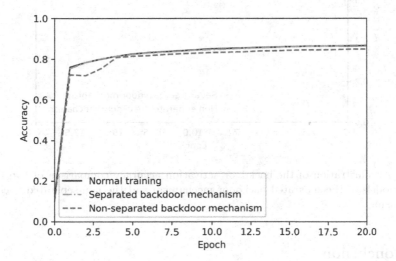

Fig. 3. An illustration of the normal task performance comparison of the normal DNN-based model and the two models of the separated backdoor mechanism with an extra backdoor neuron loss and the non-separated backdoor mechanism. The performance curve of the separated backdoor mechanism almost overlaps the performance curve of the normal training.

Although the backdoor embedding model is optimized with an extra loss objective, it almost has the same performance, an accuracy of 85%, compared with the normal model in the normal classification task, which can reach the accuracy about 85%. However, the traditional non-separated backdoor mechanism, whose accuracy of can only reach 80%, has an obvious performance reduction. That is to say, the proposed backdoor embedding method almost cannot be detected by the normal task performance variation.

On the other side, the backdoor activation accuracy of the backdoor pattern recognition is illustrated in Fig. 4. The backdoor activation accuracy of the separated backdoor mechanism is near 100% that the backdoor neuron can be activated perfectly if there is a backdoor pattern and vice versa. However, the non-separated backdoor mechanism has a noticeable loss in the backdoor pattern recognition function. The backdoor activation accuracy of the non-separated backdoor mechanism only reaches about 90%. That is to say, the backdoor mechanism may be activated wrongly sometimes or not activated even if there is a backdoor pattern in the sample.

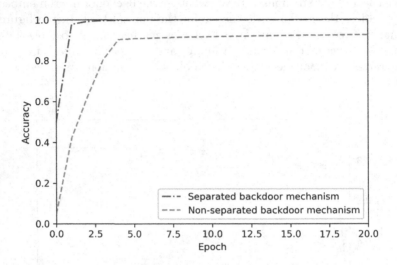

Fig. 4. An illustration of the backdoor activation accuracy comparison of two DNN-based models of the separated backdoor mechanism and the non-separated backdoor mechanism.

5   Conclusion

In this paper, we proposed a backdoor embedding method for backdoor detection in DNN-based models that separated the backdoor pattern recognition function and original classification function of the DNN-based model. We proved that the performance of the backdoor embedding network in the normal tasks can keep the same with the original model. Compared to the non-separated training approach, the proposed approach brought some benefits. The main advantage is that the backdoor activation mechanism will not directly interfere the normal function of the original DNN-based model and the backdoor model can achieve the same performance with original model. Another advantage of this approach is that the interference of the final prediction result can be more flexible. The backdoor pattern recognition phase and the model prediction interference phase can be developed independently, and the backdoor mechanism is easy to be embedded in a DNN-based model.

Acknowledgments. This work is partly supported by Hunan Provincial Natural Science Foundation under Grant Number 2020JJ5367, Project of Hunan Social Science Achievement Appraisal Committee in 2020 (No. XSP20YBZ043), Key Project of Teaching Reform in Colleges and Universities of Hunan Province under Grant Number

HNJG-2021-0251, Scientific Research Fund of Hunan Provincial Education Department under Grant Number 21A0599, and Scientific Research Innovation Project of Xiangjiang College of Artificial Intelligence, Hunan Normal University.

References

1. Chen, H., Fu, C., Zhao, J., Koushanfar, F.: Deepinspect: a black-box trojan detection and mitigation framework for deep neural networks. In: International Joint Conferences on Artificial Intelligence (IJCAI), pp. 4658–4664 (2019)
2. Dai, Y., Wang, G., Li, K.C.: Conceptual alignment deep neural networks. J. Intell. Fuzzy Syst. **34**(3), 1631–1642 (2018)
3. Gu, T., Liu, K., Dolan-Gavitt, B., Garg, S.: BadNets: evaluating backdooring attacks on deep neural networks. IEEE Access **7**, 47230–47244 (2019). https://doi.org/10.1109/ACCESS.2019.2909068
4. Liu, Y., Lee, W.C., Tao, G., Ma, S., Aafer, Y., Zhang, X.: Abs: scanning neural networks for back-doors by artificial brain stimulation. In: Proceedings of the 2019 ACM SIGSAC Conference on Computer and Communications Security, pp. 1265–1282 (2019)
5. Liu, Y., Ma, S., Aafer, Y., Lee, W.C., Zhai, J., Wang, W., Zhang, X.: Trojaning attack on neural networks. In: Proceedings of the 25th Network and Distributed System Security Symposium, pp. 1–15 (2018)
6. Qiu, H., Zeng, Y., Guo, S., Zhang, T., Qiu, M., Thuraisingham, B.: Deepsweep: an evaluation framework for mitigating DNN backdoor attacks using data augmentation. In: Proceedings of the 2021 ACM Asia Conference on Computer and Communications Security, pp. 363–377 (2021)
7. Saha, A., Subramanya, A., Pirsiavash, H.: Hidden trigger backdoor attacks. In: Proceedings of the AAAI Conference on Artificial Intelligence, Vol. 34, pp. 11957–11965 (2020)
8. Shen, S., Tople, S., Saxena, P.: AUROR: defending against poisoning attacks in collaborative deep learning systems. In: Proceedings of the 32nd Annual Conference on Computer Security Applications, pp. 508–C519. ACSAC 2016, Association for Computing Machinery, New York, NY, USA (2016). https://doi.org/10.1145/2991079.2991125
9. Szegedy, C., et al.: Intriguing properties of neural networks. In: 2nd International Conference on Learning Representations, ICLR 2014 (2014). https://arxiv.org/abs/1312.6199
10. Tang, R., Du, M., Liu, N., Yang, F., Hu, X.: An embarrassingly simple approach for trojan attack in deep neural networks. In: Proceedings of the 26th ACM SIGKDD International Conference on Knowledge Discovery & Data Mining, pp. 218–228 (2020)
11. Wang, B., et al.: Neural cleanse: identifying and mitigating backdoor attacks in neural networks. In: 2019 IEEE Symposium on Security and Privacy (SP), pp. 707–723 (2019). https://doi.org/10.1109/SP.2019.00031
12. Xiang, Z., Miller, D.J., Kesidis, G.: Revealing backdoors, post-training, in DNN classifiers via novel inference on optimized perturbations inducing group misclassification. In: ICASSP 2020–IEEE 2020 International Conference on Acoustics, Speech and Signal Processing (ICASSP), pp. 3827–3831. IEEE (2020)
13. Xiao, H., Rasul, K., Vollgraf, R.: Fashion-MNIST: a novel image dataset for benchmarking machine learning algorithms (2017). https://arxiv.org/abs/1708.07747

14. Xu, X., Wang, Q., Li, H., Borisov, N., Gunter, C.A., Li, B.: Detecting AI trojans using meta neural analysis. In: 2021 IEEE Symposium on Security and Privacy (SP) pp. 103–120 (2021). https://doi.org/10.1109/SP40001.2021.00034
15. Yao, Y., Li, H., Zheng, H., Zhao, B.Y.: Latent backdoor attacks on deep neural networks. In: Proceedings of the 2019 ACM SIGSAC Conference on Computer and Communications Security, pp. 2041–2055 (2019)
16. Zhai, T., Li, Y., Zhang, Z., Wu, B., Jiang, Y., Xia, S.T.: Backdoor attack against speaker verification. In: ICASSP 2021–2021 IEEE International Conference on Acoustics, Speech and Signal Processing (ICASSP), pp. 2560–2564. IEEE (2021)

Security and Privacy for Sharing Electronic Medical Records Based on Blockchain and Federated Learning

Wei Liu[1,2]([⊠]), Wenlong Feng[2], Benguo Yu[1], and Tao Peng[3]

[1] College of Biomedical Information and Engineering, Hainan Medical University,
Haikou 571199, People's Republic of China
[2] School of Information and Communication Engineering,
Hainan University, Haikou 570228, People's Republic of China
[3] School of Computer Science and Cyber Engineering, Guangzhou University,
Guangzhou 510006, People's Republic of China

Abstract. The sharing of Electronic Medical records (EMRs) has great positive significance for research of disease and doctors' diagnosis. However, patients' EMRs are usually distributed in the databases of multiple medical institutions. Due to the insecurity of the network environment and distrust of other parties, EMR owners worry about data insecurity and privacy leakage, which makes sharing with other parties difficult. Patients worry about the loose control of their health data as well. To solve this problem, we present a solution for the EMRs data sharing based on blockchain and federated learning, which will provide data security and patients' privacy. Firstly, we propose a method for EMRs data retrieval records and sharing records as transaction records adding to the blockchain, and design the two algorithm processes, respectively. Secondly, federated learning is used to help EMRs data owners to build a model based on the original data. The data owner only shares the model instead of the original data. Finally, by security and privacy analytics, we analyzed the advantages and influence of the proposed model. Overall, the evaluation shows that the proposed solution is significantly superior to the previous models and achieves reasonable efficiency for sharing EMRs data.

Keywords: Electronic medical records · Security sharing · Privacy · Blockchain · Federated learning

1 Introduction

With the rapid development of medical informatics, many medical institutions use Electronic Medical Records (EMRs) [1] to record patients' medical data. EMRs collect individuals' health-related information, which includes diseases, medication, medical images, and personal information such as name, age, gender, weight, and billing information. The sharing of EMRs has great positive significance for research of disease and doctors' diagnosis. Complete and accurate EMRs can be accessed by patients, which also can be used for warning of dangers, prompting of errors, and clinical decision support. The standardized templates and auxiliary tools provided by EMRs can make doctors free from medical record writing work, which is boring and repetitively, and focus on the diagnosis and treatment of patients. In addition, EMRs also provide a data source for doctors to prescribe and research data for research institutions. Hence, EMRs sharing between medical institutions can help improve medical diagnoses, treatment decisions, and enhance the overall patient experience.

However, the EMRs involve personal private information and individual vital signs of patients. Such data are generally sensitive and needed to be protected against unauthorized access. How to protect the data security and prevent the data privacy leak during sharing is insufficient and many problems have not been solved well. Blockchain [2]-based solution is a viable approach, which is a coordination mechanism and attribution, credit, proof, and reward incentive tracking method. It allows one to build upon cryptographic algorithms to ensure data integrity, standardized auditing, and some formalized contracts for data access. Moreover, to avoid directly sharing sensitive data, federated learning [3] is a prominent solution for multi-party machine learning. Participants train a shared model without revealing their underlying data or computation.

In our previous study [4], we proposed an optimized algorithm of PBFT, which improved C4.5 and introduced weighted average information gain to overcome the mutual influence between conditional attributes and improve the classification accuracy. We classified the nodes with improved C4.5 and selected the ones with a high trust level to form the main consensus group, and the integral voting mechanism was introduced to determine the leader node. Based on previous research, we will continue to invest in methods of security and privacy protection for sharing EMRs.

A novel solution for sharing EMRs based on blockchain and federated learning is proposed in this paper. The main contributions of this paper can be summarized as follows:

(1) We propose a new method of security and privacy protection for sharing EMRs based on blockchain and federated learning. Multi-party EMRs participants can share EMRs safely and reduce the risk of data leakage in a distributed environment. Through the proposed architecture, EMRs providers can control access to shared data as well.
(2) Both data retrieval records and data sharing records are designed as transaction records, which are written to the blockchain. Algorithms are designed for these two processes, to protect the security and non-tampering of transaction records.
(3) Furthermore, we suggest federated learning to build a model, and share the model instead of the original data, which can protect the privacy of patients. Finally, the effectiveness of the proposed solution is evaluated.

The rest of this paper is organized as follows. Related work is discussed in Sect. 2. The scenario, threat, and design goals are described in Sect. 3.

The proposed solution is presented in Sect. 4, and its analytics and performance evaluations are presented in Sect. 5. Finally, conclusions are drawn in Sect. 6.

2 Related Work

In recent years, both blockchain and federated learning have received extensive attention in the healthcare field. Medical data storage, sharing, and privacy protection have become hot research issues for scholars.

MIT [5] developed a prototype named MedRec, which is a blockchain-based decentralized record management system to handle EMRs, using blockchain technology. The MedRec platform is a practical way of exchanging EMRs through blockchain, which manages authentication, confidentiality, account-ability, and data sharing when handling sensitive information, and integrates modules with providers' existing, local data storage solutions. MedRec uses proof-of-work in its working process as a consensus algorithm. Roehrs A [6] proposed OmniPHR, a P2P Blockchain-based architecture for Personal Health Records. It allows a unified view, integrates patients' scattered health records, and promotes interoperability among different providers to access health records. Guo [7] proposed an attribute-based multi-authority signature scheme. Xu [8] proposed Healthchain, a large-scale health data privacy-preserving scheme based on blockchain technology, where health data are encrypted to conduct fine-grained access control. Users can effectively revoke or add authorized doctors by leveraging user transactions for key management. Both IoT data and doctor diagnosis cannot be deleted or tampered with to avoid medical disputes.

In the field of access control, [9–11] proposed to use an identity-based access control model for electronic medical record sharing. However, these methods only consider the use of privacy protection for access control mechanisms, but not the data itself. The security problems in data sharing still exist.

Cao [12] proposed a hybrid blockchain-based electronic medical records sharing scheme, which uses different sharing methods for different parts of medical big data. It shares privacy-sensitive couples on the consortium blockchain while sharing the non-sensitive parts on the public blockchain. In this way, authorized medical information control systems within the consortium can access the data on it for precise medical diagnosis. Institutions such as universities and research institutes can get access to the non-sensitive parts of medical big data for scientific research on symptoms to evolve medical technologies. Xiao [13] proposed HealthChain, which is built based on consortium blockchain technology. Hospitals, insurance providers, and governmental agencies form a consortium that operates under a governance model, which enforces the business logic agreed by all participants. Every peer node hosts an instance of the distributed ledger consisting of EHRs and an instance of chain code regulating the permissions of participants. Designated orders establish consensus on the order of EHRs and then disseminate blocks to peers. Qin [14] proposed a safe sharing scheme of stroke electronic medical records based on the consortium blockchain. It adopts the storage method of ciphertext of medical records stored in the cloud and index of medical records stored on the blockchain. The paper proposes a privacy protection mechanism, which combines proxy encryption and searchable encryption which supports patient pseudo-identity search, and proposes an improved Practical Byzantine Fault Tolerance mechanism to reach a consensus between consensus nodes.

However, in most existing solutions, the EMRs provider needs to share the original data with other participants, and the receivers can easy to infer the patients' privacy and the identity of the provider based on the received data, which increased the risk of data security and patients' privacy greatly. Currently, there are two main problems in the sharing of EMRs. One is that the centralized management server needs to process a large number of EMSs data from different parties, the other is that these parties do not trust each other fully. Each participant worries that the sharing EMRs data will be leaked to other unreliable participants.

To solve these problems, a novel solution for sharing EMRs based on blockchain and federated learning is proposed in this paper. This solution is facilitating different medical institutions to share EMRs securely. The work proposed in this paper focuses on security and privacy, and how they are applied to EMRs data sharing. Unlike traditional EMRs sharing methods, the new EMRs sharing mechanism, where private data can be trained at the owner's premises without revealing their underlying data or computation. Instead, a federated learning algorithm is used to map the original data to the corresponding model.

3   Scenario, Threat, and Design Goals

In this section, we introduce the distributed EMRs sharing scenario, threat analytics, and design goals of an EMRs sharing architecture based on blockchain and federated learning.

3.1   Distributed Scenario

This paper mainly considers a distributed EMRs sharing scenario involving multi-party participation and collaboration, in which medical institution as a participant has their EMRs data and is willing to share. Patients' EMRs are distributed in the databases of multiple different medical institutions. The medical institution is a data owner and provides the patient's EMRs. By querying the EMRs data saved by multi-party medical institutions, the query results are merged to realize the complete EMRs of the patient in collaboration. Figure 1 presents EMRs sharing scenario in a distributed environment.

3.2   Threat Analysis

In the scenario of distributed EMRs data sharing, multiple participants jointly complete the data sharing task. EMRs providers and EMRs requesters are considered untrustworthy, so the distributed EMRs data sharing model is vulnerable to three types of threats:

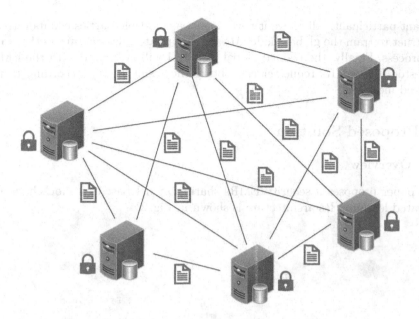

Fig. 1. EMRs sharing scenario in a distributed environment.

(1) The quality of the EMRs data. Dishonest EMRs providers may provide inaccurate results to EMRs requesters, thereby reducing the overall availability of shared data.
(2) Patients' data privacy. The EMRs providers and EMRs recipients, who participate in the sharing, may try to infer the privacy of the patient from the shared data, which may lead to the leakage of the patient's sensitive data.
(3) EMRs data authority management. Once the original data is shared, the EMRs owner will lose control of the data. EMRs data may be shared with other unauthorized entities.

3.3   Design Goals

We aim to achieve a security EMRs sharing solution, which can share EMRs data safely among distributed entities and protect patients' privacy.

Consider there are N participants, usually the participants are medical institutions, i.e., hospitals, which store EMRs data in their databases. The shared joint EMRs dataset is denoted as D. For any participant $P_i(1 \leq i \leq N)$, it owns a locally stored EMRs dataset $D_i(1 \leq i \leq N)$, D_i is a subset of D, $D_i \subseteq D$. N participants are willing to share their EMRs data without revealing the patient's privacy. Assume that $Req = req_1, req_2, \ldots, req_m$ represents the set of EMRs data sharing requests $R - i$ submitted by the EMRs requester. The EMRs owner P_i performs calculations on its data and the corresponding calculation model is M_i. Note that M_i is the calculated model instead of the original data. If a participant contains the data requested by the EMRs requester, it is regarded as a relevant participant. All relevant participants as multiple parties collaboratively construct to train the global model M, and no private is leaked during the training process. Finally, the trained global model M will be shared with the EMRs requester. The EMRs requester can obtain the result $R(M)$, according to the received model M.

4 Proposed Solution

4.1 Overview

This paper proposes a security EMRs sharing model based on blockchain and federated learning. Its architecture is shown in Fig. 2.

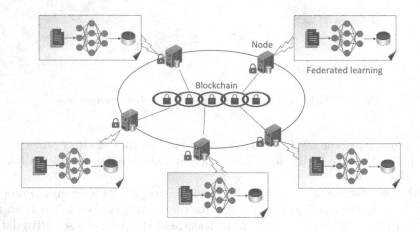

Fig. 2. Architecture of the proposed model.

It is composed of two modules: the blockchain module and the federated learning module.

The blockchain module is responsible for retrieving relevant data, managing data access mechanisms, recording data-sharing events, and tracking data usage. EMRs retrieval records and EMRs sharing records will be added to the blockchain as transactions records. The federated learning module is responsible for the retrieval request, which is sent by the EMRs requester, learning and calculating the original data locally, and sharing the calculation global model with the EMRs requester. The solution not only ensures that the original data will not be shared and protect patient privacy effectively but also return retrieval requests to meet the needs of the requesting party effectively. The EMRs retrieval records and EMRs sharing records are all added to the blockchain, which saves limited storage space and ensures the model is safe and effective.

It is assumed that all participating parties have already registered on the blockchain. Figure 3 describes the mechanism of the proposed model.

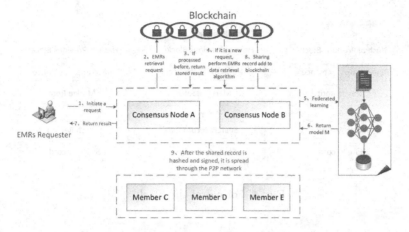

Fig. 3. Mechanism of the proposed model.

First, EMRs requester R_i initiates a EMRs sharing request $Req = \{req_1, req_2, \ldots, req_m\}$, which contains a set of query tasks $F(x) = \{f_1, f_2, \ldots, f_x\}$. After receiving the request, the node $N(req)$ searches the blockchain to confirm whether the request has been processed before. If the request has been processed before, the request Req will be forwarded to the node where the result is stored, and the corresponding node will send the stored result as a reply to the requester. If the request has not been processed, a multi-party EMRs data retrieval algorithm is performed to find the relevant EMRs provider based on the participant's registration record.

Then, the EMRs provider does not share the original data stored locally. Instead, multiple EMRs providers jointly train a global model M through federated learning, and the global model M will be shared with the EMRs requester R_i. The EMRs requester R_i takes $F(x) = \{f_1, f_2, \ldots, f_x\}$ as the input of the model M, and obtains the corresponding output result $M(req)$. The data model M can process any query f_x in the query set $F(x)$ and provide it with a calculation result $M(f_x)$.

Finally, EMRs retrieval records and EMRs sharing records will be added to the blockchain after reaching a consensus in the network.

4.2   Algorithm Design for EMRs Retrieval

When EMRs requester R_i initiates a EMRs sharing request $Req = \{req_1, req_2, \ldots, req_m\}$, EMRs retrieval algorithm will be executed. More details about the algorithm design process are given as follows.

When a new EMRs provider joins and participates, the blockchain needs to record its information. The participant's unique identification (ID) and the summary retrieval information of its EMRs data are added to the blockchain and verified by node through the Merkle tree. The format of the block is shown in Fig. 4. The EMRs retrieval algorithm process consists of the following steps:

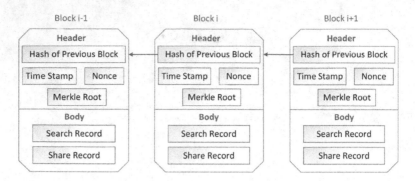

Fig. 4. Format of the block.

(1) System initialization. Suppose N EMRs providers P agrees to join the blockchain network to share their records. Each provider P_i will be generated its identification ID by calculating the hash value and will be associated with the data retrieval registration record based on summary information of the health records in its database. The EMRs providers node generates a new block with a timestamp and broadcasts it to other nodes on the blockchain for audit and verification.

(2) Sending EMRs retrieval requests. EMRs requester R_i initiates a EMRs sharing request $Req = \{req_1, req_2, \ldots, req_m\}$, which contains a set of query tasks $F(x) = \{f_1, f_2, \ldots, f_x\}$. Structurally, the request Req contains plaintext metadata (e.g., the unique identification ID of P_i, the type of data requested, the timestamp, and etc.). The request is signed (i.e., encrypted) using its private key SK_r can be verified (i.e., decrypted) by anyone with its public key PK_r.

(3) Uploading EMRs retrieval. After receiving the request, the node $N(req)$ verifies the identity of the EMRs requester R_i firstly. When verification is correct, the node $N(req)$ then searches the blockchain to confirm whether the request has been processed before.

(4) Returning result. If the same request has been processed, the previously saved model will be returned, otherwise, it is considered to be a new request, EMRs share algorithm will be executed.

The working procedures of the EMRs retrieval algorithm are described as Algorithm 1.

4.3   Algorithm Design for EMRs Sharing

For each EMRs sharing event, the participants and the transaction records will be added to the blockchain and verified by the node through the Merkle tree. The format of the block is shown in Fig. 4.

The EMRs sharing algorithm process consists of the following steps:

Algorithm 1. EMRs retrieval algorithm.

1: Initialization.
2: **while** true **do**
3:     Requester R_i initiates a request $Req = \{req_1, req_2, \ldots, req_m\}$
4:     **if** Ver($N(req) \leftarrow R_i$) is true **then**
5:         $Result(M) \leftarrow Sear(b)$
6:         **if** $Result(M)$ is $!NULL$ **then**
7:             return $Result(M)$
8:         **else**
9:             Jump to EMRs sharing algorithm
10:        **end if**
11:    **end if**
12: **end while**

---

(1) New request. When EMRs requester R_i initiates an EMRs sharing request $Req = \{req_1, req_2, \ldots, req_m\}$ is considered to be a new request, the blockchain will search the relevant participants that own the data.

(2) Training model. After the relevant participant P_j receives request Req, it will calculate the corresponding local model M_j based on the original data, and then forwards request Req to other relevant participants according to its local retrieval table. The process is repeated until all relevant participants have been traversed to completion. The training set is based on the local original data D and the corresponding query result in $f_x(D)$, the training data DT = <fx, fx(D)>.

(3) Sharing data. All relevant participants as multiple parties collaboratively construct to train the global model M, which will be shared with the EMRs requester. The EMRs requester can obtain the result $R(M)$, according to the received model M. Model M is saved by relevant nodes for use in subsequent sessions.

The working procedures of the EMRs sharing algorithm are described as Algorithm 2.

Algorithm 2. EMRs sharing algorithm.

1: $Req = req_1, req_2, \ldots, req_m$ is a new request.
2: Search relevant participants, suppose k participants $P_j (1 \leqslant j \leqslant k)$.
3: **for** $j = 1$ **to** k **do**
4:     Training data $DT_j \leftarrow < f_x, f_x(D_j) >$
5:     Model $M_j \leftarrow < DT_j, fx(D_j) >$
6: **end for**
7: **return** Global model $M \leftarrow < k, \sum_{j-1}^{k} M_j >$

4.4   Consensus Mechanism

The EMRs sharing event between the EMRs requester R_i and the relevant participants P_i generates as a transaction record and broadcasts it to the blockchain. All transaction records are collected by the nodes in the blockchain and cryptographically signed.

We choose the consensus mechanism of proof-of-work to select a core relevant participant node to aggregate transaction records. The winning then broadcasts its block to the other nodes in the network to validate the block. Each node stores blocks of transaction records that have been validated. The blocks cannot be deleted or tampered with to avoid medical disputes.

In summary, the proposed solution, which combines blockchain and federated learning in the distributed EMRs sharing scenario, can retrieve and share the requested EMRs data safely, and protect patients' privacy.

5   Analysis and Evaluation

5.1   Security and Privacy Analysis

The blockchain establishes a secure collaboration mechanism between multiple parties who do not trust each other. And adding federated learning to the consensus protocol process of blockchain, some existing security risks can be alleviated. As analyzed above, there are three threats to sharing EMRs data in a distributed environment, and our proposed solution can reduce the risks of these threats effectively.

(1) The quality of the EMRs data. The consensus mechanism verifies the quality of the models learned by other EMRs providers, and only qualified models will be retained and trained to a global model, to prevent dishonest EMRs providers provide inaccurate results to EMRs requesters.

(2) Patients' data privacy. The proposed solution does not share original data. Instead, a federated learning algorithm is used to map the original data to the corresponding model. The EMRs requester obtains the retrieval result, according to the received model. It is impossible to guess who provided the data and from whom this piece of data came.

(3) EMRs data authority management. Only the retrieval information of the EMRs data will be added to the blockchain, and the original data will be stored in the database by the EMRs provider locally. EMRs owners can control their data permissions by changing the retrieved information. In addition, the blockchain uses a series of cryptographic algorithms, i.e., Elliptic Curve Digital Signature Algorithm (ECDSA) and asymmetric algorithms, to ensure data security.

(4) Decentralization management. The proposed solution use blockchain to replace a trusted centralized management server and connect multiple participants through EMRs data retrieval. There is no longer a need for a centralized trust entity to exist, which reduces the risk of data leakage caused

by a centralized trust. The blockchain is a growing list of EMRs retrieval records and sharing records, which are interconnected by utilizing cryptography. Each block contains a cryptographic hash of the previous block, a time stamp, and exchange information. Blockchain will track all information trade called ledger and it uses a distributed system to verify every exchange.

5.2 Evaluation

To evaluate the proposed sharing EMRs architecture based on blockchain and federated learning, we compared it with the existing models based on blockchain technology. Table 1 shows the differences among these models in 4 aspects. The evaluation shows that the proposed method outperforms the state-of-the-art methods in terms of EMRs sharing in a distributed environment. Therefore, according to the analysis and evaluation above, it can be concluded that our proposed solution ensures data security and protect patient privacy effectively.

Table 1. Comparison with different models.

	Based on blockchain	Without the third party	Alleviating the size of data in blockchain	Not share local data
MedRec,2016	✓	✓	✗	✗
OmniPHR,2017	✓	✓	✗	✗
Healthchain,2019	✓	✓	✓	✗
HealthChain,2021	✓	✓	✓	✗
Proposed solution	✓	✓	✓	✓

6 Conclusions

In this paper, we addressed the problem of sharing EMRs transaction security and privacy without reliance on a trusted third party. We proposed a decentralized EMRs sharing solution that enables requesters to obtain retrieval models instead of original data and perform sharing transactions securely. We used blockchain technology to provide certain levels of privacy and security. Our method uses federated learning where multiple parties collaboratively construct to train a global model, which will be shared with the EMRs requester instead of original data. In addition, the consensus mechanism of proof-of-work, as in Bitcoin, authenticates the sharing data to prove the work and allows the system to overcome Byzantine failures.

We performed security and privacy analysis and evaluation. Overall, we found that the appropriate combination of blockchain technology and federated learning presents a feasible and reliable direction towards decentralized EMRs sharing with higher privacy and security compared to the traditional centralized sharing solutions.

Acknowledgments. This work was supported in part by Hainan Provincial Natural Science Foundation of China under Grant Number 620RC620 and 619MS057, in part by the National Key Research and Development Project under Grant 2018YFB1404400, and in part by the National Natural Science Foundation of China under Grant 62062030.

References

1. Miller, R.H., Sim, I.: Physicians' use of electronic medical records: barriers and solutions. Health Aff. **23**(2), 116–126 (2004)
2. David, B., Safa, O., Nikolas, S., Dylan, P., Yaser, J.: A survey on blockchain for information systems management and security. Inf. Process. Manage. **58**(1), 102397 (2021)
3. Cheng, K., et al.: SecureBoost: a lossless federated learning framework. IEEE Intell. Syst. **36**(6), 87–98 (2021)
4. Zheng, X., Feng, W., Huang, M., Feng, S.: Optimization of PBFT algorithm based on improved c4.5. Math. Prob. Eng. **2021**, 5542078 (2021)
5. Azaria, A., Ekblaw, A., Vieira, T., Lippman, A.: MedRec: using blockchain for medical data access and permission management. In: 2016 2nd International Conference on Open and Big Data (OBD), pp. 25–30. IEEE (2016)
6. Roehrs, A., Da Costa, C.A., da Rosa Righi, R.: OmniPHR: a distributed architecture model to integrate personal health records. J. Biomed. Inf. **71**, 70–81 (2017)
7. Guo, R., Shi, H., Zhao, Q., Zheng, D.: Secure attribute-based signature scheme with multiple authorities for blockchain in electronic health records systems. IEEE Access **6**, 11676–11686 (2018)
8. Xu, J., et al.: Healthchain: a blockchain-based privacy preserving scheme for large-scale health data. IEEE IoT J. **6**(5), 8770–8781 (2019)
9. Zhao, Y., et al.: Research on electronic medical record access control based on blockchain. Int. J. Distrib. Sens. Netw. **15**(11), 1550147719889330 (2019). https://doi.org/10.1177/1550147719889330
10. Hang, L., Choi, E., Kim, D.-H.: A novel EMR integrity management based on a medical blockchain platform in hospital. Electronics **8**(4), 467 (2019)
11. Tanwar, S., Parekh, K., Evans, R.: Blockchain-based electronic healthcare record system for healthcare 4.0 applications. J. Inf. Secur. Appl. **50**, 102407 (2020)
12. Cao, Y., Sun, Y., Min, J.: Hybrid blockchain-based privacy-preserving electronic medical records sharing scheme across medical information control system. Meas. Control **53**(7–8), 1286–1299 (2020)
13. Xiao, Y., Xu, B., Jiang, W., Wu, Y.: The HealthChain blockchain for electronic health records: development study. J. Med. Internet Res. **23**(1), e13556 (2021)
14. Qin, Q., Jin, B., Liu, Y.: A secure storage and sharing scheme of stroke electronic medical records based on consortium blockchain. BioMed Res. Int. **2021**, 6676171 (2021)

A Fine-Grained Access Control Scheme for Electronic Health Records Based on Roles and Attributes

Shaobo Zhang[1,2,3]($\boxtimes$), Shuo Yang[1,2], Gengming Zhu[1,2], Entao Luo[4],
Jiyong Zhang[1,2], and Desheng Xiang[1,2]

[1] School of Computer Science and Engineering,
Hunan University of Science and Technology, Xiangtan 411201, China
shaobozhang@hnust.edu.cn
[2] Hunan Key Laboratory of Service Computing and New Software Service
Technology, Xiangtan 411201, China
[3] College of Computer, National University of Defense Technology,
Changsha 410073, China
[4] School of Information Engineering, Hunan University of Science and Engineering,
Yongzhou 425199, China

Abstract. The electronic medical cloud system has shown its potential to improve the quality of medical care and personal life. At present, there are mainly two forms of access control to electronic medical cloud systems: role-based access control (RBAC) and attribute-based access control (ABAC). But RBAC cannot achieve fine-grained access control, and ABAC cannot achieve the role of RBAC to manage resource functions. This paper proposes a patient-centric access control model that combines RBAC and ABAC in response to this problem. We use the Linear Secret Sharing Scheme (LSSS) access control structure to implement attribute-based access control, and the Casbin access control framework to implement role-based access control. The patient first uses the ciphertext strategy attribute-based encryption algorithm (CP-ABE) on the client to encrypt the electronic health record (EHR), then the patient stores the encrypted EHR data in the cloud. When a data user wants to access patient EHR data, the cloud will determine whether the user role or user attribute meets the access request. After the request is passed, the user can obtain the ciphertext and the plaintext after two decryption steps. Finally, we conduct an extensive safety analysis and performance evaluation, which confirmed the effectiveness and efficiency of our program.

Keywords: Attribute-based access control · Role-based access
control · CP-ABE · Cloud computing

1 Introduction

Electronic healthcare provides timely, accurate and low-cost healthcare services, and has shown its potential to improve the quality of healthcare and personal life.

© The Author(s), under exclusive license to Springer Nature Singapore Pte Ltd. 2022
G. Wang et al. (Eds.): UbiSec 2021, CCIS 1557, pp. 25–37, 2022.
https://doi.org/10.1007/978-981-19-0468-4_3

Electronic health care uses digital electronic records, such as electronic medical records (EMR), electronic health records (EHR), personal health records (PHR) and electronic health data (EHD) [1]. Compared with traditional paper records, electronic health records have apparent advantages in workforce, time and physical storage. However, there are still some challenges in the storage and sharing of electronic health records [2].

Cloud computing has become a vital computing paradigm and is being widely used in the healthcare industry [3]. Cloud computing not only enhances the coordination between multiple healthcare stakeholders, but also ensures the continuous availability and scalability of medical information [4,5]. However, security and privacy will hinder the widespread deployment and application of electronic medical cloud systems. The fundamental reason is that once sensitive EHR data is outsourced to the cloud, the data owner will lose control of it. Therefore, protecting the security and privacy of EHR data stored in the electronic medical cloud system is very important [6].

At present, domestic and foreign scholars have proposed some methods for privacy protection and access control of EHR data in the cloud. Xie M *et al.* [7] proposed an original hybrid cloud multi-authority ciphertext-policy attribute-based encryption (HCMACP-ABE) scheme. They use the LSSS access structure to achieve secure access control, while the private cloud is responsible for maintaining the user's authorization list and authenticating users. This solution implements fine-grained access control in a hybrid cloud environment. Chen E *et al.* [8] integrates attribute-based access control/extensible access control markup language (ABAC/XACML) model and CP-ABE into cloud file sharing. To improve the performance of CP-ABE, the author uses an optimization method to convert the ABAC/XACML strategy into a small strategy matrix. Ezhilarasan E *et al.* [9] designed a framework called Secure and Robust Data Access Management (SRDAM) algorithm, which aims to maintain enhanced privacy, secure data transmission and access management. The algorithm integrates the verification of cloud service providers and considers the necessity of the attributes of cloud users and cloud service providers (CSP). Zhang W *et al.* [10] proposed a two-layer encryption scheme. In the first layer of encryption, the frequency of appearance of role attributes in EHR is hidden, saving a lot of encryption time. In the second layer of encryption, the first layer of the access policy is combined, and noise is added to the combined access policy. Mazhar A *et al.* [11] proposed a method called SeSPHR for the secure sharing of PHR in the cloud. The patient stores the encrypted PHR in an untrusted cloud server and selectively grants access to different types of users in other parts of the PHR. This method can resist internal threats.

Although the above methods can effectively protect the security of EHR data in the cloud, there are still the following challenges to design an efficient electronic medical cloud system with fine-grained access control:

1) Which access control mechanism is more effective for the secure transmission of EHR? At present, there are mainly four access control mechanisms: Discretionary Access Control (DAC), RBAC, ABAC and Personal Identity Authentication Access Control (IBAC). It is challenging to design a new access control model to make EHR transmission more secure and effective.

2) How to effectively share health data among multiple healthcare providers?
3) Since the cloud owns all the EHR data and is responsible for returning the accessed data, ensuring that the cloud returns the data attributes correctly and efficiently without knowing which data attributes are returned is also a challenging problem.

In response to the above challenges, this paper proposes a patient-centered access control model that combines RBAC and ABAC. We use the LSSS access control structure to implement ABAC, and the Casbin access control model to implement RBAC. The main contributions of this paper are as follows:

1) We propose a patient-centered access control model based on the combination of RBAC and ABAC. The LSSS access control structure is used to implement attribute-based access control, and the Casbin access control model is used to implement role-based access control. Besides, the patient can set read and write, download, upload and delete permissions for the data user.
2) We use the CP-ABE algorithm to encrypt the EHR data, and store the encrypted EHR data in the cloud, and then perform secondary encryption in the cloud to ensure the security of the EHR data.
3) Theoretical analysis proves the privacy and usability of the method, and the experimental results on real data sets show that this method makes EHR transmission more secure and effective.

2   Preliminaries

2.1   Bilinear Map

Suppose that G_1 and G_2 are two multiplicative cyclic groups of order p, where p is any large prime number, and g is the generator of G_1. For the bilinear mapping $e : G_1 \times G_1 \rightarrow G_2$, the following properties need to be satisfied:

1) Bilinearity: $\forall G_1, G_2 \in G_1, a, b \in Z_P, e\left(G_1{}^a, G_2{}^b\right) = e\left(G_1, G_2\right)^{ab}$;
2) Non-degeneracy: $\forall G_1, G_2 \in G_1$, there is an efficient polynomial-time algorithm to calculate $e\left(G_1, G_2\right) \neq 1$;
3) Computability: $\forall g, h \in G_1$, there are polynomial-time algorithms to calculate $e\left(g, h\right)$.

2.2   Linear Secret Sharing Scheme (LSSS)

If a secret sharing scheme $\prod$ in the participant set P satisfies the following two conditions, it can be called a linear secret sharing scheme on Z_P.

1) The vector on Z_P is composed of the secret share of each entity.
2) For each secret sharing scheme $\prod$, there is a corresponding generator matrix $M\left(l \times n\right)$, mapping $\rho : \{1, 2, \cdots, l\} \rightarrow P$ put each row of matrix M $i = 1, 2, \cdots, l$ are all mapped to the participant $\rho\left(i\right)$, where ρ is an injective function. Introduce the vertical vector $v = \left(s, y_2, \cdots, y_n\right)$, which is called the secret sharing vector. Randomly select $y_2, \cdots, y_n \in Z_P$ to hide the shared secret s and $s \in Z_P$, then the vector $\lambda_i = \left(Mv\right)$ represents the sub-secret of the shared key s held by l participants $\rho\left(i\right)$.

According to the linear reconstruction of the LSSS, assuming that $\prod$ is a linear secret sharing in the access strategy T, let $S \in T$ be an access authorization set, and $I = \{i : \rho(i) \in S\}$, if $\{\lambda_i\}$ is a valid sub-secret to the secret s, then a set of constants $\{\omega_i \in Z_P\}_{i \in I}$ can be found in polynomial time, so that the equation $\sum_{i \in I} \omega_i \lambda_i = s$ is established.

2.3   Decisional Bilinear Diffie-Hellman Assumption (DBDH)

Suppose that G_1 and G_2 are two multiplicative cyclic groups of order p, where p is any large prime number, and g is the generator of G_1. For the bilinear mapping $e : G_1 \times G_1 \rightarrow G_2, R \in G_2$. $\forall a, b, c \in Z_P$, given $\left(g, g^a, g^b, g^c, R\right)$, determine whether $e\left(g, g\right)^{abc}$ equals R.

3   System Model and Security Model

In this section, we introduce our system model and security model. We first introduce the symbols in Table 1.

Table 1. The annotation of parameters.

Parameter	Annotation
PK	The system public key
MSK	The master secrete key
T	Access policy
S	The set of attributes
ψ	Secret parameter
PCT	The partially decrypted ciphertext
SK	The private key
AA_key	Attribute secret key

3.1   System Model

The system model we proposed involves five entities, as shown in Fig. 1, including data owner (DO), data user (DU), electronic medical cloud (EMC), attribute authority (AA), and proxy server (PS). AA is responsible for the generation of public parameters such as the system public key (PK) and master key (MSK), as well as the user's attribute key (AA_Key). DO is the person who outsources his EHR data to the cloud. To protect data privacy, DO needs to encrypt EHR data before outsourcing EHR data. EMC is responsible for storing encrypted electronic health records and generating private keys (SK). PS is responsible for performing part of the decryption operation. DU is for those who want to access EHR data. When the user role or attribute meets the access request, the data can be obtained after two steps of decryption.

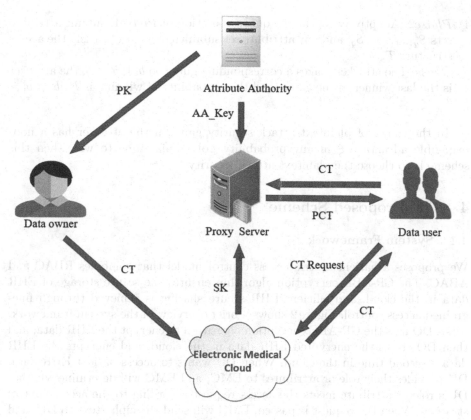

Fig. 1. Electronic medical cloud system model.

3.2 Security Model

The security model inherits the assumptions of [12], and we create a game between the opponent and the challenger.

1) *Setup*: The challenger selects the corresponding parameters and then runs the initialization algorithm to realize the generation of the system public key PK and the master key MSK, and sends the system public key PK to the attacker, but retains the master key MSK.

2) *Phase*1: The attacker wants to query as many private keys as possible from the challenger, so he provides the challenger with a set of attributes $S_1, S_2, \cdots, S_{q1}$ associated with the private key. After the challenger receives the attacker's query request, he obtains the private key SK by running the key generation algorithm and sends it to the attacker.

3) *Challenge*: The attacker submits two plaintexts M_0 and M_1 of equal length and the access structure T to the challenger, and randomly throws a coin b, then randomly determines the value of $b = \{0, 1\}$, uses the access structure T encrypt M_b and sends the generated ciphertext CT to the attacker.

4) *Phase*2: Adaptively repeat the query operation of *Phase*1, submit attribute sets $S_{q1+1}, \cdots, S_q$, and any attribute set submitted does not satisfy the access structure T.
5) *Guess*: The attacker makes a corresponding guess on b. If $b' = b$, the attacker is the last winner in the game, and the probability of winning is $P_r[b' = b] = \frac{1}{2} + \xi$.

In the choice of plaintext attack security game, if the attacker has a non-negligible advantage ξ in any probability polynomial time to win, then this scheme is to choose the plaintext attack security.

4   The Proposed Scheme

4.1   System Framework

We proposes a patient-centric access control model that combines RBAC and ABAC. The CP-ABE encryption algorithm ensures the secure storage of EHR data in the cloud, and efficient EHR secure sharing is achieved through fine-grained access control. Figure 2 shows a brief overview of the system framework. First, DO uses the CP-ABE encryption algorithm to encrypt the EHR data, and then DO stores the encrypted EHR data in the cloud, and encrypts the EHR data a second time in the cloud. When DU wants to access patient EHR data, DU provides their role or attributes to EMC, and EMC will determine whether DU's role or attribute meets the access request according to the access control strategy. When the request is passed, EMC will send the ciphertext to DU, and DU can get the plaintext after two steps of decryption. Next, the safety structure will be demonstrated step by step.

4.2   ABAC

Setup. $Setup(\lambda) \rightarrow (PK, MSK)$: executed by AA, taking the security parameter λ as input, the system public key PK and master key MSK as output.

Select two multiplicative groups G_1 and G_2 of order p, let g be a random generator of G_1, let $e : G_1 \times G_1 \rightarrow G_2$ denote bilinear mapping, and define the public mapping $H\{0, 1\} \rightarrow G_2$. AA randomly selects $\alpha, \beta \in Z_P$, the system public key PK and master key MSK are calculated as follows:

$$PK = \left(H, g, h = g^\beta, f = g^{1/\beta}, e(g, g)^\alpha\right) \tag{1}$$

$$MSK = (\beta, g^\alpha) \tag{2}$$

Encrypt. $Encrypt(PK, M, (M, \rho)) \rightarrow CT$: executed by DO, with system public key PK, plaintext M and LSSS access policy as input, where LSSS access control structure $T = (M, \rho)$, M is a matrix of $l \times n$. Then, the algorithm constructs a vector $v = (s, q_2, \cdots, q_n) \in Z_{P}{}^n$, where s is the shared secret.

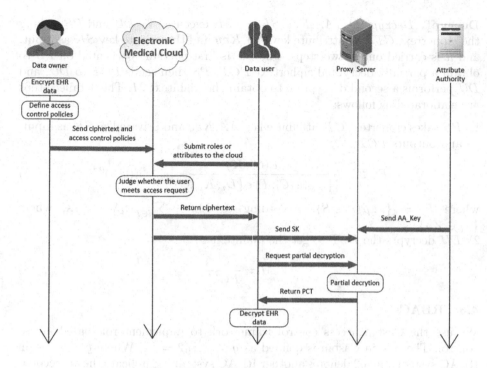

Fig. 2. Electronic medical cloud system framework.

Subsequently, the algorithm selects a set of random numbers $r_1, \cdots r_l \in Z_P$ and outputs the ciphertext.

$$CT = \left\{ C = M \cdot e\left(g, g\right)^{\alpha s} ; C' = g^s ; C_i = g^{\beta \lambda_i} \cdot H\left(\rho\left(i\right)\right)^{-r_i} ; D_i = g^{r_i} \right\} \quad (3)$$

where λ_i is the effective secret share of secret $s, i \in \{1, 2, \cdots l\}$.

Keygen. $Keygen\left(PK, S, \psi\right) \rightarrow \left(SK, AA\_Key\right)$: executed by AA and EMC, taking system public key PK, user attribute set S and secret value ψ as input, private key SK and attribute key AA_Key as output.

Randomly select $\psi \in Z_P$, the private key SK is calculated as follows:

$$SK = \left(K = g^\alpha \cdot g^{\beta \psi} = g^{\alpha + \beta \psi} ; T = g^\psi \right) \quad (4)$$

AA first generates AA_i_Key for each attribute in attribute set S, and then aggregates AA_i_Key to generate AA_Key. The attribute key AA_i_Key and AA_Key is calculated as follows:

$$AA_i\_Key = \left(\forall i \in S : K_i = H\left(i\right)^\psi, T = g^\psi\right) \quad (5)$$

$$AA\_Key = \{AA_1\_Key, AA_2\_Key, \cdots, AA_i\_Key\} \quad (6)$$

Decrypt. $Decrypt\,(CT, AA\_Key, SK) \rightarrow M$: executed by DU and PS, taking the ciphertext CT, the attribute key AA_Key and the private key SK as input, and it is carried out in two steps. The CT is first partially decrypted on PS to obtain a partially decrypted ciphertext PCT. PS then sends PCT to DU, and DU performs a second decryption to obtain the plaintext M. The detailed steps are elaborated as follows:

1) PS takes ciphertext CT, attribute key AA_Key and private key SK as input, and outputs PCT:

$$PCT = \frac{e\,(C', K)}{\prod_{i \in I} \left(e\,(C_i, T)\,e\,\left(D_i, K_{\rho(i)}\right)\right)^{\omega_i}} = e\,(g,g)^{\alpha s} \tag{7}$$

where $I = \{i : \rho\,(i) \in S\}$. According to LSSS, $\sum_{i \in I} \omega_i \lambda_i = s$, where $\{\omega_i \in Z_P\}_{i \in I}$.

2) DU decrypts the PCT to get the plaintext M:

$$M = \frac{C}{PCT} \tag{8}$$

4.3   RBAC

We use the Casbin access control framework to implement role-based access control. The role in Casbin is defined as $g = \_, \_; g2 = \_, \_$. Where g denotes an RBAC system, and $g2$ denotes another RBAC system. $\_, \_$ indicate the antecedent and subsequent items of the role inheritance relationship; that is, the antecedent inherits the permissions of the subsequent role. Casbin's RBAC supports the role hierarchy function. If Alice has role1 and role1 has role2, then Alice will also own role2 and inherit its permissions. The RBAC role in Casbin can be global or domain-based. The role of a specific domain means that when users are in different domains/tenant groups, users' roles are also different. This is very useful for large systems like cloud services, because users usually belong to other tenant groups.

In our RBAC, the *Setup* and the *Encrypt* are the same as in our ABAC. In the *Keygen*, only SK is generated. The generation process of SK is the same as in our ABAC. The decrypt will be introduced below.

$Decrypt\,(CT, SK) \rightarrow M$: executed by DU and PS, with the ciphertext CT and the private key SK as input, and it is carried out in two steps. The CT is first partially decrypted on PS to obtain a partially decrypted ciphertext PCT. PS then sends the PCT to DU, and DU performs a second decryption to obtain the plaintext M. The detailed steps are elaborated as follows:

1) PS takes ciphertext CT and private key SK as input, and outputs PCT:

$$PCT = \frac{e\,(C', K)}{e\,(C'^{\beta}, T)} = e\,(g,g)^{\alpha s} \tag{9}$$

2) DU decrypts the PCT to get the plaintext M:

$$M = \frac{C}{PCT} \tag{10}$$

4.4   Security Analysis

Assuming that there is an adversary A who can win the plaintext attack game with a non-negligible advantage ξ, a simulator χ is constructed to use the ability of the adversary A and solve the DBDH hypothesis with a non-negligible advantage $\frac{\xi}{2}$.

1) Setup: Adversary A controls a group of attacked attribute authority $AA_k \in AA$ (at least two attributes in AA are not controlled by adversary A), and the simulator χ controls the remaining attributes. The adversary A creates a challenge access structure $T = (M^*, \rho^*)$, and then the simulator χ initializes the authorization attribute set. The simulator χ sets $a = \sum d_k, b = \frac{\sum v_k}{\sum c_k}, c = s_0$, where $d_1, d_2, \cdots, d_n, v_1, v_2, \cdots, v_n, s_0 \in Z_P$ is randomly selected. Simultaneously, the simulator χ sets the public parameter $Y = e(g, g)^{ab}$, and sends the public parameter to the adversary A.

2) Phase1: The adversary A wants to query as many attribute keys AA_Key as possible through the simulator χ, and multiple AA_k manages the corresponding attribute set, none of which satisfy the access structure T. For the key query request of adversary A, the simulator χ calculates the key component to respond the request of adversary A. For all attributes $i \in S$, the simulator χ selects a random number $\psi \in Z_P$ to calculate $K_i = H(i)^{\psi}, T = g^{\psi}$. Then the simulator χ sends the calculated attribute key AA_Key to the adversary A.

3) Challenge: After the adversary A submits two challenge messages m_0 and m_1 to the simulator χ, the simulator χ randomly throws a coin b, calculates the ciphertext $CT^* = \left\{ (M, \rho); E = m_b \cdot Z; C' = g^s; C_i = g^{\beta \lambda_i} \cdot H(\rho(i))^{-r_i}; D_i = g^{r_i} \right\}$, and sends the obtained ciphertext to the adversary A. If $b = 0$, $Z = e(g, g)^{abc}$, then $Z = e(g, g)^{abc} = \left(e(g, g)^{ab} \right)^c = Y^{s_0}$, and $E = m_0 \cdot e(g, g)^{abc}$, so CT^* is a valid ciphertext of the message m_b. On the contrary, if $b = 1$, $Z = e(g, g)^z$, then $E = m_b \cdot e(g, g)^z$. So from the point of view of the adversary A, the E calculated from the random element $z \in Z_P$ is a random element in G_2, so CT^* is an invalid ciphertext that does not include information about m_b.

4) Phase2: Repeat the query operation in *Phase1* adaptively.

5) Guess: The adversary A makes a related guess b' on b. If $b = b'$, the simulator χ will output the result of $b = 0$. On the contrary, if $b \neq b'$, the simulator χ will output the result of $b = 1$. When $b = 0$, the adversary A gets a valid ciphertext m_b, and the probability of the adversary $A's$ success in this case is $P_r = [b = b'|b = 0] = \frac{1}{2} + \varepsilon$. When $b = 1$, the adversary A does not know any information about b. In this case, the probability of success is $P_r = [b \neq b'|b = 1] = P_r[b = b'|b = 1] = \frac{1}{2}$.

In summary, it can be seen that if the adversary A wins the game with a non-negligible advantage ε in any polynomial time, the advantage $\frac{\xi}{2}$ of the simulator χ is also non-negligible. Since this scheme can solve the DBDH problem in any polynomial time, this scheme is safe for selecting plaintext attacks.

5 Performance Evaluation

5.1 Experimental Setup

The experiment mainly uses two real data sets. One data set comes from the public data of the IPUMS website, from which 50,000 census data from the USA are selected. The other is the Adult data set in the UCI database commonly used in privacy protection research. After deleting the invalid records, there are 30162 records in total.

The hardware environment of the experiment is: Intel(R) Core(TM) i5-7300HQ CPU @2.50 GHz 2.50 GHz, 8.00 GB memory. The software environment is: Microsoft Windows 10. It adopts GoLand development platform and is implemented in Golang programming language.

5.2 Efficiency Analysis

Figure 3 and Fig. 4 show the time cost of key generation, EHR encryption and decryption. We use KGT, ENC and DEC to represent the key generation, encryption and decryption time in this scheme, and use TRKGT, TRENC and TRDEC to represent the key generation, encryption and decryption time in [13]. It can be seen from Fig. 3(a) that the key generation time of our scheme is significantly better than [13]. Since the complexity of the access strategy in the encryption phase is related to the number of attributes, the higher the complexity of the strategy, the longer it takes. In Fig. 3(b), it can be observed that the time spent in the encryption phase increases linearly with the number of attributes. The encryption time of this scheme and [13] both increase with the increase of the number of attributes, but the advantage this scheme shows is better than [13]. Figure 4(a) and Fig. 4(b) show the time overhead of decryption in our ABAC and RBAC, respectively. Since the decryption stage of this scheme consists of two parts: PS part decryption and DU decryption, PS undertakes most of the decryption calculation work. As we have seen, compared with [13], this scheme significantly reduces the user decryption time overhead.

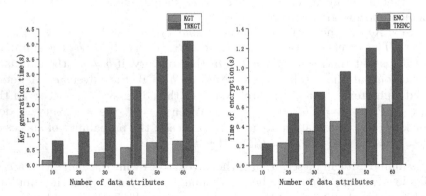

Fig. 3. (a) Time cost of key generation (b) Time cost of encryption.

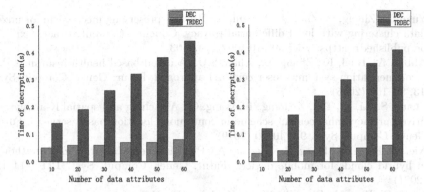

Fig. 4. (a) Time cost of decryption in ABAC (b) Time cost of decryption in RBAC.

6 Conclusion

In this paper, we propose a new scheme combining RBAC and ABAC to realize fine-grained access control of EHR in the cloud. CP-ABE encryption algorithm ensures the secure storage of EHR data in the cloud, and fine-grained access control realizes efficient EHR security sharing. In our scheme, we focus on reducing the computational overhead of DU. We introduce PS, which undertakes a large number of decryption operations, so the computational overhead of DU is greatly reduced. In addition, we use LSSS and Casbin access control models to implement access control of attributes and roles, which not only greatly improves efficiency, but also is essential for DU. Finally, extensive security analysis and performance evaluation also confirm the effectiveness and efficiency of our scheme.

Acknowledgments. This work was supported in part by the National Natural Science Foundation of China under Grant number 62172159, the Hunan Provincial Education Department of China under Grant number 21A0318, the Research project on Teaching Reform of Ordinary Colleges and Universities in Hunan Province under Grant Number HNJG-2021-0651, and the Research Project of Degree and Postgraduate Education Reform of Hunan University of Science and Technology under Grant Number G71922.

References

1. Guo, H., Li, W., Nejad, M., Shen, C.C.: Access control for electronic health records with hybrid blockchain-edge architecture. In: 2019 IEEE International Conference on Blockchain (Blockchain), pp. 44–51. IEEE (2019)
2. Zhang, S., Mao, X., Choo, K.K.R., Peng, T., Wang, G.: A trajectory privacy-preserving scheme based on a dual-K mechanism for continuous location-based services. Inf. Sci. **527**, 406–419 (2020)
3. Yi, X., Miao, Y., Bertino, E., Willemson, J.: Multiparty privacy protection for electronic health records. In: 2013 IEEE Global Communications Conference (GLOBE-COM), pp. 2730–2735. IEEE (2013)

4. Yuan, L., Zhang, S., Zhu, G., Alinani, K.: Privacy-preserving mechanism for mixed data clustering with local differential privacy. Concurr. Comput. Pract. Exp. (to be published). https://doi.org/10.1002/cpe.6503
5. Abbas, A., Bilal, K., Zhang, L., Khan, S.U.: A cloud based health insurance plan recommendation system: a user centered approach. Futur. Gener. Comput. Syst. **43**, 99–109 (2015)
6. Zhang, S., Li, X., Tan, Z., Peng, T., Wang, G.: A caching and spatial K-anonymity driven privacy enhancement scheme in continuous location-based services. Futur. Gener. Comput. Syst. **94**, 40–50 (2019)
7. Xie, M., Ruan, Y., Hong, H., Shao, J.: A CP-ABE scheme based on multi-authority in hybrid clouds for mobile devices. Futur. Gener. Comput. Syst. **121**, 114–122 (2021)
8. Chen, E., Zhu, Y., Zhu, G., Liang, K., Feng, R.: How to implement secure cloud file sharing using optimized attribute-based access control with small policy matrix and minimized cumulative errors. Comput. Secur. **107**, 1–20 (2021)
9. Ezhilarasan, E., Dinakaran, M.: Privacy preserving and data transpiration in multiple cloud using secure and robust data access management algorithm. Microprocess. Microsyst. **82**, 1–8 (2021)
10. Zhang, W., Lin, Y., Wu, J., Zhou, T.: Inference attack-resistant e-healthcare cloud system with fine-grained access control. IEEE Trans. Serv. Comput. **14**(1), 167–178 (2018)
11. Ali, M., Abbas, A., Khan, M.U.S., Khan, S.U.: SeSPHR: a methodology for secure sharing of personal health records in the cloud. IEEE Trans. Cloud Comput. **9**(1), 347–359 (2018)
12. Sandor, V.K.A., Lin, Y., Li, X., Lin, F., Zhang, S.: Efficient decentralized multi-authority attribute based encryption for mobile cloud data storage. J. Netw. Comput. Appl. **129**, 25–36 (2019)
13. Bouchaala, M., Ghazel, C., Saidane, L.A.: TRAK-CPABE: a novel traceable, revocable and accountable ciphertext-policy attribute-based encryption scheme in cloud computing. J. Inf. Secur. Appl. **61**, 1–13 (2021)
14. Islam, M.S., Kuzu, M., Kantarcioglu, M.: Inference attack against encrypted range queries on outsourced databases. In: Proceedings of the 4th ACM Conference on Data and Application Security and Privacy (CODASPY), pp. 235–246. ACM (2014)
15. Guo, L., Zhang, C., Sun, J., Fang, Y.: A privacy-preserving attribute-based authentication system for mobile health networks. IEEE Trans. Mob. Comput. **13**(9), 1927–1941 (2013)
16. Keshta, I., Odeh, A.: Security and privacy of electronic health records: concerns and challenges. Egyptian Inform. J. **22**(2), 177–183 (2021)
17. Kanwal, T., Anjum, A., Malik, S.U., Khan, A., Khan, M.A.: Privacy preservation of electronic health records with adversarial attacks identification in hybrid cloud. Comput. Stand. Interfaces **78**, 1–16 (2021)
18. Qin, X., Huang, Y., Yang, Z., Li, X.: A Blockchain-based access control scheme with multiple attribute authorities for secure cloud data sharing. J. Syst. Architect. **112**, 1–11 (2020)
19. Hong, H., Sun, Z.: A flexible attribute based data access management scheme for sensor-cloud system. J. Syst. Architect. **119**, 1–9 (2021)
20. Unal, D., Al-Ali, A., Catak, F.O., Hammoudeh, M.: A secure and efficient Internet of Things cloud encryption scheme with forensics investigation compatibility based on identity-based encryption. Futur. Gener. Comput. Syst. **125**, 433–445 (2021)

21. Ayfaa, B., Apa, C.: LMAAS-IoT: lightweight multi-factor authentication and authorization scheme for real-time data access in IoT cloud-based environment. J. Netw. Comput. Appl. **192**, 1–20 (2021)

22. Karati, A., Amin, R., Mohit, P., Sureshkumar, V., Biswas, G.P.: Design of a secure file storage and access protocol for cloud-enabled Internet of Things environment. Comput. Electr. Eng. **94**, 1–15 (2021)

23. Hozhabr, M., Asghari, P., Javadi, H.H.S.: Dynamic secure multi-keyword ranked search over encrypted cloud data. J. Inf. Secur. Appl. **61**, 1–12 (2021)

24. Najafi, A., Bayat, M., Javadi, H.H.S.: Fair multi-owner search over encrypted data with forward and backward privacy in cloud-assisted Internet of Things. Futur. Gener. Comput. Syst. **124**, 285–294 (2021)

25. Saravanan, N., Umamakeswari, A.: Lattice based access control for protecting user data in cloud environments with hybrid security. Comput. Secur. **100**, 1–9 (2020)

26. Khan, R., Tao, X., Anjum, A., Kanwal, T., Maple, C.: θ-sensitive k-anonymity: an anonymization model for IoT based electronic health records. Electronics **9**(5), 716–740 (2020)

27. Sabitha, S., Rajasree, M.S.: Access control based privacy preserving secure data sharing with hidden access policies in cloud. J. Syst. Architect. **75**, 50–58 (2017)

28. Rafique, A., Van Landuyt, D., Beni, E.H., Lagaisse, B., Joosen, W.: CryptDICE: distributed data protection system for secure cloud data storage and computation. Inf. Syst. **96**, 1–23 (2021)

29. Chen, M., Qian, Y., Chen, J., Hwang, K., Mao, S., Hu, L.: Privacy protection and intrusion avoidance for cloudlet-based medical data sharing. IEEE Trans. Cloud Comput. **8**(4), 1274–1283 (2016)

30. Kanwal, T., et al.: A robust privacy preserving approach for electronic health records using multiple dataset with multiple sensitive attributes. Comput. Secur. **105**, 1–21 (2021)

Active Malicious Accounts Detection with Multimodal Fusion Machine Learning Algorithm

Yuting Tang[1], Dafang Zhang[1(✉)], Wei Liang[1], Kuan-Ching Li[2], and Nitin Sukhija[3]

[1] Hunan University, South of Lushan Road, Changsha 410082, China
{yuting_tang,dfzhang,weiliang99}@hnu.edu.cn
[2] Providence University, Taiwan Road, Taiwan 43301, China
kuancli@pu.edu.tw
[3] Slippery Rock University of Pennsylvania, Slippery Rock, PA 16057, USA
nitin.sukhija@sru.edu

Abstract. This paper presents a multi-modal fusion machine learning algorithm to detect active malicious accounts in social networks. First, we use the XGBoost algorithm to rank features' importance and reduce the impact of redundant features. Then, we use density detection algorithms to monitor malicious accounts according to the actual situation and the cooperative behavior of malicious accounts. Finally, we employ neural network algorithms to make secondary judgments on the results obtained in the previous step based on the periodic activity characteristics of active malicious accounts. We evaluate our approach on a real-world social network dataset. We have conducted experiments that demonstrate that the XGBoost algorithm aids in obtaining better results than other feature selection algorithms. Moreover, the comparison with other malicious account detection algorithms is also illustrated by extensive experiments. The result concludes that our proposed model is more efficient, more accurate, takes less time, and has a certain degree of scalability, thus performing well in practical applications.

Keywords: Malicious accounts detection · XGBoost · Feature selection · Online social networks · Quadratic-estimation

1 Introduction

The rapid development of Internet technology has created good conditions for Online Social Networks (OSN). User-centric social networks provide different information content and network services, and their lightweight and convenience have also contributed to the proliferation of malicious users. The number of social network users increases daily, making online social networks (OSN) such as Facebook, Weibo, Twitter, or Instagram also popular targets for cyber-attacks. Attackers create fake users [1, 2] or destroy existing user accounts to perform illegal operations such as zombie fans, network water stickers, advertising, and phishing websites [3], which brings a poor user experience to normal users and is often accompanied by considerable economic losses to normal users.

G. Wang et al. (Eds.): UbiSec 2021, CCIS 1557, pp. 38–52, 2022.
https://doi.org/10.1007/978-981-19-0468-4_4

Netizens have criticized the abovementioned behavior at home and abroad. In the face of malicious users spreading false and harmful information, driving public opinion and other issues, and enhancing anti-reconnaissance capabilities of malicious users, their behavior has become concealed and confusing, making detection more and more complex. However, for malicious users The process of user identification and governance has been ongoing, and many scholars have conducted relevant testing and research on such problems.

Most previous studies have directly identified false or compromised accounts controlled by attackers [4]. There are two broad methods. One method is based on user behavior [5, 6], which judges malicious accounts by constructing a machine learning model. This method can effectively identify malicious accounts with known malicious characteristics but may miss many malicious accounts with unknown characteristics [7]. The other method is based on the relationship between users. By analyzing the relationship between users, fake accounts that have little connection with real social networks can be identified, but well-maintained fake accounts cannot be identified.

Based on the above challenges, G. Wang [8] explored a new method to detect malicious accounts. By analyzing the overall behavior pattern of social network accounts, it is found that malicious accounts show a kind of aggregation synchronization in time. For example, malicious accounts tend to perform consistent operations on a particular user or event in a short period of time, and propose copycatch Algorithms to detect such malicious accounts. The density monitoring algorithm [9] proposed by Kijung Shin can also be used to detect malicious accounts with this feature and has good performance.

This article presents a Multimodal Fusion machine learning (MFML) algorithm that can detect many malicious accounts that act synchronously. We face many unique challenges when designing the MFML algorithm, which makes this algorithm different from previous work in this field (D-cube). First, we use the XGBoost algorithm to filter and combine user features. XGBoost is an efficient machine learning model that has the advantages of saving resources, less training time, and high accuracy. Therefore, we use it to sort and filter the importance of features. Secondly, the goal of our algorithm is to be used on real-world OSNs, so the algorithm must be able to process several terabytes of data per day, and many anomaly detection algorithms in the past cannot handle this magnitude of data. At the same time, to further improve the accuracy, we used the neural network model to make a second judgment on the detected malicious accounts.

Our research contributions include: (1) We conducted experiments on real user behavior data of a famous domestic social networking site, and we implemented an automated malicious user detection algorithm for feature extraction, static analysis, feature selection, and malicious accounts Recognition; (2) We apply the feature selection algorithm based on XGBoost to rank and combine the importance of features, and evaluate the effectiveness of different feature selection algorithms in malicious account identification; (3) The Multimodal Fusion machine learning algorithm is used to detect malicious accounts in social networks, which verifies the algorithm's good design efficiency and recognition accuracy.

2 Related Work

2.1 Feature Selection

In the field of machine learning and data mining, it may be necessary to process high-dimensional data containing a large number of irrelevant features [10]. These irrelevant features will lead to the sparseness of the data distribution in the feature space and hinder the data analysis. If you directly process high-dimensional data [11] (such as text, DNA microarrays, and medical images), it will not only increase the amount of calculation and quickly consume memory but also affect the performance of the classifier [12]. Feature selection as a dimensionality reduction technology has been widely used in various fields, such as pattern recognition, multivariate statistical analysis, computer vision, and data mining [13]. Feature selection is a meaningful data preprocessing method that reduces the negative impact of irrelevant data and provides a solution for determining the most relevant or valuable features [14].

Feature selection as a common dimensionality reduction method is one of the research hotspots in pattern recognition. It refers to selecting a feature subset that optimizes a specific evaluation criterion from the original feature set. Its purpose is to make the classification or regression model constructed by the selected optimal feature subset achieve the prediction accuracy similar to or even better before the feature selection, which not only improves the generalization ability, comprehensibility, and computational efficiency of the model but also can reduce the frequency of "dimension disasters" [15].

In order to build models with good performance, many feature selection methods have been proposed in the past few decades. The early feature selection is mainly considered in the case of full supervision. Fully supervised feature selection methods include Relief-based methods [16] and Fisher criteria-based methods [17]. The Relief-based method optimizes the objective function to obtain feature weights by calculating the sample interval. The basic principle of the method based on the Fisher criterion is to find a projection axis, and the cross part of the sample project on this axis is as tiny as possible to obtain a clear classification limit. However, fully supervised methods may encounter mislabeled data, which will mislead such methods to delete some relevant features and retain irrelevant features. Furthermore, fully supervised feature selection requires a large amount of difficult-to-obtain label data in the process of feature selection. One challenge of this method is that the label is given by external knowledge, and its correctness cannot be verified [18], exacerbating the risk of over-fitting learning in fully supervised feature selection by unintentionally deleting many relevant or discriminative features.

Compared with the fully-supervised feature selection method, unsupervised feature selection is a more complex problem and faces more significant challenges [19] due to the lack of label assistance. Because the processed data does not have the label information, researchers have defined criteria related to features. A commonly used criterion is to select features that best retain the manifold structure of the original data [20]. Another less commonly used method is where the clustering algorithm labels the data, and then the unsupervised feature selection is converted to the fully-supervised framework [21]. However, unsupervised methods ignore the possible connections between features and tasks without the guidance of prior knowledge. Therefore, the obtained feature subset may not be optimal for the actual discrimination task. Moreover, unsupervised relies on certain hypothetical principles, but it does not guarantee that these hypothetical principles are common to all data sets.

In contrast, semi-supervised feature selection has better applicability. When the number of labeled data is limited, semi-supervised feature selection methods can make full use of unlabeled data to select features. For example, in the semi-supervised feature selection algorithm, labeled data is used to maximize the margins between samples of different categories, while unlabeled data is used to discover the geometric structure of the feature space. Common semi-supervised methods are based on Laplacian operators, such as semi-supervised discriminant analysis (SDA) [22].

However, the construction of graphs is time-consuming and inefficient when processing large-scale data sets. Based on the constraints, Zhang et al. proposed an effective dimensionality reduction method, called Semi-Supervised Dimensionality Reduction (Semi-Supervised Dimensionality Reduction, SSDR), which uses constraint information to preserve the local structure of the data. Benadeslem and Hindawi [23] explored another semi-supervised method based on constraints, called Constrained Laplacian Score (CLS). CLS can obtain similar and dissimilar samples through pre-set "must link" constraints and "unlinked" constraints, and then use the obtained information can be used to construct neighboring graphs and calculate the Laplacian scores of features. According to the scoring result, CLS eliminates redundant features in the data. But in this case, the CLS algorithm depends on user-defined links. Therefore, if the user redefines the constraint set, the corresponding feature score will also be modified. Zhao et al. proposed a Locality Sensitive Discriminant Feature (LSDF), which uses labeled samples to maximize the interval between samples of different categories, and uses unlabeled data to discover the geometric structure of the data. However, LSDF has a high complexity problem, and it is not easy to deal with the situation where two sampling points are adjacent to each other. In addition, some methods consider selecting feature subsets from the perspective of feature relevance and redundancy. For example, semi-supervised feature selection based on max-Relevance (Semi-supervised feature selection based on max-Relevance, and Min-Redundancy, Semi-mRMR) and methods based on Pearson's criterion [24] (max-Relevance and min-Redundancy criterion based on Pearson's Correlation coefficient, RRPC), these methods are the expansion of the fully-supervised method in the semi-supervised field.

Based on the advantages and disadvantages of the abovementioned feature selection methods, we have employed the XGBoost algorithm to rank the importance of features in this research. After obtaining essential features, they are combined with being used in subsequent algorithm models.

2.2 The Malicious Account Detection Algorithm

Feature selection and analysis methods for malicious users can be mainly divided into user content, behavior, and relationship characteristics. For malicious user detection methods, there are mainly classification-based technologies, clustering-based technologies, statistics-based technologies, combination-based technologies, information-based technologies, and graph-based technologies [25].

Most scholars focus on studying malicious users on Twitter, the most prominent social platform. According to Twitter's official policy [26], malicious users are defined as following a large number of users in a short period of time, or their tweets are mainly composed of URL or "#" symbols, or they are posting irrelevant information or reposting similar tweets. Velammal et al. [27] started with Twitter and proposed two categories of user-based and content-based features that can distinguish spammers from ordinary users, and they are used in support vector machines, naive Bayes, k-NN, and classification of the four classifiers of random forest. The results show that the random forest classifier achieves the best results and verifies the excellent performance of the random forest classifier on the imbalanced data set. In order to help people effectively identify the people interacting with them, Ravanmehr et al. divided Twitter users into humans [28], robots and cyborgs, and proposed to use time entropy measures and some user attributes (such as URL ratio) to distinguish them. Different users use machine learning methods to test the effectiveness of recognition. Aswani [29] proposed a spam detection system to identify suspicious users on Twitter and proposed content-based and graph-based features to facilitate detection; the results prove that the Bayesian classifier measures F1 Has the best performance. However, under the combination of functions selected in this article, each experimental classifier has a high accuracy rate and a low recall rate. To detect malicious users, we should focus more on how many malicious users are identified, the recall rate.

We summarize the previous research on malicious users and raise the following aspects: First, it is about the collection aspect. Most researches propose a series of characteristics based on experience, and most of them are behavioral characteristics, content characteristics, and attribute characteristics, often ignoring the time period characteristics of malicious users and normal users when they perform different behaviors. According to the behavioral habits of malicious users and normal users, deep mining of period feature information is beneficial to identifying malicious users and enriches the diversity of detection features.

Second, we focus on feature selection. Most of the literature did not analyze the importance of the feature after the feature was proposed, and some literature only adopted the artificial method of combining and comparing different feature values without considering the feature redundancy. A large number of features will bring challenges to data storage and model calculations. At the same time, as time goes by and malicious users continue to upgrade and change, some classic features will not be suitable for malicious users for a long time. Therefore, it is indispensable to select essential features for feature engineering before model training. Selecting significant features for model training reduces the computing time and storage complexity and makes the identification features of malicious users more straightforward. At the same time, it also reduces Noise, or irrelevant data is improved, and the recognition performance of the model is improved.

Third, in terms of model selection. In recent years, most researchers have adopted and verified that the random forest algorithm represented by Bagging is superior to other models in malicious user identification, but few people consider using Boosting integrated related algorithms to identify malicious users. In recent years, the XGBoost algorithm has shined in the field of data mining, so consider applying the algorithm to malicious user identification to compare the performance of other models. At the same time, there is little literature to design models based on the relevance of features, and they are often all input to model training after the features are proposed. For example, when deep neural networks are used for training, the increase in the number of features will significantly affect the complexity of the model. It is also necessary to consider the adverse effects of missing data in some models. Therefore, it is necessary to design a flexible and accurate malicious account detection model to correlate features.

3 Methodologies

3.1 Machine Learning Framework

The purpose of the machine learning model in this article is to first extract the most crucial feature combinations from the multi-dimensional features, then use the extracted feature combinations to build a multi-dimensional tensor block. Next, detect the tensor density block with a density more remarkable than the threshold, so finally, use the machine learning algorithm to the detected density block is judged twice to improve the accuracy of the model. The model integrates feature selection based on machine learning and a semi-supervised malicious account detection algorithm.

The model uses XGBoost as the key algorithm for feature selection. XGBoost is the abbreviation of eXtreme Gradient Boosting, proposed by Chen and Guestrin (2016) [30]. XGBoost is an optimized gradient tree boosting system with some algorithm innovations (approximate greedy search, parallel learning) and hyperparameters to improve learning and control overfitting. Chen and Guestrin (2016) have a detailed introduction.

Our proposed model aims to establish a semi-supervised machine learning model based on a small amount of labeled data, to judge the massive amount of user data in social networks and detect malicious accounts. It consists of four modules: data preprocessing, feature engineering, density block detection, and neural network secondary judgment. The core algorithm model diagram is shown in Fig. 1. The feature engineering part uses the XGBoost algorithm. The model's performance is evaluated separately using recall and precision, and the area under the precision-recall curve (AUC) is calculated as a comprehensive metric. At the same time, we also compared related algorithms in terms of model robustness and timeliness. The experimental data we use is representative real user data of a large domestic social networking site.

3.2 XGBoost-Based Feature Selection

The connection between user behavior characteristics and user categories is established using XGBoost. First, configure hyper-parameters to construct an appropriate XGBoost model for feature importance ranking. After the model is trained, the segmentation weight and average gain of each feature are generated, and they are normalized to calculate the weight-based and gain-based relative importance scores, respectively. Scores measure the usefulness of features in constructing boost trees in XGBoost. The higher the score, the greater the relative importance. A series of score thresholds are defined for fast feature filtering. In each iteration, the features whose importance scores are more significant than the threshold are retained, and the learning performance is estimated through 10-fold hierarchical cross-validation.

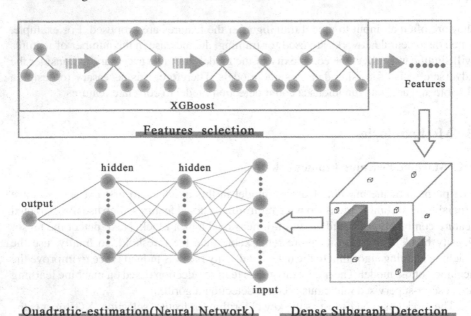

Fig. 1. The algorithm framework consists of three parts.

The process of recursive feature elimination is used here. The main idea of recursive feature elimination is to repeatedly build the model, then select the best (or worst) feature (selected according to the coefficient), place the selected feature aside, and then repeat the process on the remaining features. Until all the features are traversed, the order eliminated in this process is the ordering of features.

From a practical point of view, identifying essential features guides data collection, mining, and understanding. For example, when we analyze the actual problems, we see that user behavior is the most informative variable involving malicious accounts. At the same time, the integration of multiple perspectives and multiple features increases the robustness and fault tolerance of the system and makes the model more interpretable.

XGBoost, a gradient boosting decision tree, uses regularized learning and cache-aware block structure tree learning for ensemble learning. L represents the loss function; f_t represents the t-th tree and $\Omega(f_t)$ is the regularized term. The second-order Taylor series of L at the t-th iteration is:

$$L^{(t)} \simeq \sum_{i=1}^{k} \left[l\left(y_i, y_i^{(t-1)}\right) + g_i f_t(x_i) + \frac{1}{2} h_i f_t^2(x) \right] + \Omega(f_t) \tag{1}$$

where g_i, h_i denotes the first and second-order gradients. During our training of XGBoost, we use gain to determine the optimal split node:

$$gain = \frac{1}{2} \left[\frac{\left(\sum_{i \in I_L} g_i\right)^2}{\sum_{i \in I_L} h_i + \lambda} + \frac{\left(\sum_{i \in I_R} g_i\right)^2}{\sum_{i \in I_R} h_i + \lambda} - \frac{\left(\sum_{i \in I} g_i\right)^2}{\sum_{i \in I} h_i + \lambda} \right] \tag{2}$$

where I_L and I_R represent samples of the left and right nodes after the segmentation, respectively. $I = I_L \cup I_R$. λ, γ are the penalty parameters. Gain represents the gain score for each split of a tree, and the final feature importance score is calculated by the average gain. The average gain is the total gain of all trees divided by the total number of splits for each feature. The higher the feature importance score of XGBoost is, the more important and influential the corresponding feature is. We obtain the top-ranked features based on descending order of feature importance to characterize the PPIs. XGBoost feature selection method has been used in the area of bioinformatics, and it achieves good performance. The number of boosting trees and the max depth is set as a parameter, and the loss function is binary: logistic, and the others use default parameters.

3.3 Dense Subgraph Detection

We propose a density measure that has proven helpful for anomaly detection in past researches and is used throughout this article.

The average arithmetic quality (Definition 1) and geometric average quality (Definition 2) used to detect network intrusions and collaborative activities [31] of malicious accounts are an extension of the density measurement that is widely used in graphs [32]. The Table 1 is the table of symbols.

Table 1. Table of symbols.

Symbol	Definition
$\mathcal{R}(A_1, \cdots, A_N, X)$	Relation representing an N-way tensor
N	Number of dimension attributes in $\mathcal{R}$
A_n	n-th dimension attribute in $\mathcal{R}$
X	Measure attribute in $\mathcal{R}$
$t[A_n](or t[X])$	Value of attribute A_n (or X) in tuple t in $\mathcal{R}$
$\mathcal{B}$	A block in $\mathcal{R}$
$\rho(\mathcal{B}, \mathcal{R})$	The density of block $\mathcal{B}$ in $\mathcal{R}$
$\mathcal{R}_n(or \mathcal{B}_n)$	Set of distinct values of A_n in $\mathcal{R}(or \mathcal{B})$
$M_{\mathcal{R}}(or M_{\mathcal{B}})$	Mass of $\mathcal{R}(or \mathcal{B})$
$\mathcal{B}(a, n)$	Set of tuples with attribute $A_n = a$ in $\mathcal{B}$
$M_{\mathcal{B}(a,n)}$	Attribute-value mass of a in A_n
k	Number of blocks we aim to find
[x]	$\{1, 2 \cdots, x\}$

Definition 1 (Arithmetic Average Mass ρ_{ari}) [31]. The arithmetic average mass of a block B in a relation R is

$$\rho_{ari}(\mathcal{B}, \mathcal{R}) = \rho_{ari}\left(M_{\mathcal{B}}, \{|\mathcal{B}_n|\}_{n=1}^{N}, M_{\mathcal{R}}, \{|\mathcal{R}_n|\}_{n=1}^{N}\right) = \frac{M_{\mathcal{B}}}{\frac{1}{N}\sum_{n=1}^{N}|\mathcal{B}_n|} \quad (3)$$

Definition 2 (Geometric Average Mass ρ_{geo}) [31]. The geometric average mass of a block B in a relation R is.

$$\rho_{geo}(\mathcal{B}, \mathcal{R}) = \rho_{geo}\left(M_{\mathcal{B}}, \{|\mathcal{B}_n|\}_{n=1}^{N}, M_{\mathcal{R}}, \{|\mathcal{R}_n|\}_{n=1}^{N}\right) = \frac{M_{\mathcal{B}}}{\left(\prod_{n=1}^{N}|\mathcal{B}_n|\right)^{\frac{1}{N}}} \tag{4}$$

3.4 Quadratic-Estimation Based on Neural Network

The analysis of data visualization and actual application scenarios shows that malicious account behaviors are concentrated in time and have concentrated disease behaviors in a short period of time. On the other hand, the behaviors of most normal users last longer and have discrete distributions. However, malicious accounts often have an intensive cluster of illnesses, and it is judged from the time characteristic that the malicious account will not perform secondary operation behaviors for a long time. Therefore, through the long-term behavior analysis of users, the selected users can be made quadratic-estimation.

As the neural network can analyze a large amount of nonlinear data and complete discrete trend analysis, it is especially suitable for constructing data prediction models, so this article will use the neural network to do the second judgment method. We can use artificial neural network algorithms to make secondary judgments on user categories based on the number of behaviors in the user's time period.

BP neural network (Back-Propagation) usually refers to a multi-layer forward neural network based on an error direction propagation algorithm. It was researched and designed by Rumelhart and his colleagues in 1985 and realized Minsy's multi-layer network design. It is currently the most widely used type of neural network.

The basic idea of the BP neural network algorithm is the forward propagation of the signal and the backward propagation of the error. The threshold of each node in the network and connection weight of each layer are adjusted layer by layer from back to front. When the signal is propagating in the forward direction, the sample signal is calculated through the input, hidden, and output layers. When the output does not match the expectation, the signal is transmitted back. In the process, the error is obtained by apportioning the error to all neurons in each layer. The error signal of each layer of neurons is used to correct the weight of each neuron. This process is until it is satisfied that the output error of the neural network is less than a particular set value, or the number of learning reaches the preset value. In this process, the weight of each node is constantly adjusted, which is the process of continuous learning and optimization of the network.

We use the number of user behaviors in a period of time as an input, and output as a user label, to train the neural network. Through the trained neural network model, we can prejudge the malicious accounts screened out for the second time to improve the judgment accuracy of the model further.

4 Experiments

4.1 System Configuration

In order to verify the effectiveness of our proposed algorithm for detecting malicious accounts in social networks, we conducted experiments on a user behavior data set of a well-known representative social networking site. This data set is a non-public data set provided by a well-known domestic artificial intelligence technology company that provides intelligent risk control and supervision for financial institutions. The data set consists of 5.38 million behavioral data of 1.38 million users. Moreover, we also compared the algorithms on other data sets, as mentioned in Sect. 4.3. Finally, we implement the proposed algorithm by executing a server composed of one Xeon 4-core CPU, 8G memory, CentOS 7.2.6 OS, and network bandwidth 200Mbps, and used the open-source M-Zoom1 [31] and HoloScope [33] Java implementation in order to compare the performance of all aspects of our proposed algorithm.

4.2 Ranking of Feature Importance

In this section, we analyze the sample set, preprocess the data, and use the selection algorithm of XGBoost to obtain the importance of features. This step uses 70% of the labeled sample data as the training set and 30% of the labeled data as the test set. Here, we present a data instance of the dataset, as shown in Table 2.

Table 2. A data instance of the dataset.

ip	ip_city	email_prefix	email_provider	event_type	resource_category
119.28.62.29	Hongkong	39694	33	1	107
mobile_profix_3	mobile_city	time_stamp	user_name	user_agent	os_version
139	Yantai	2017/10/12 18:49:51	1556152	0	0
resourse_owner	register_type	category	status	resource_type	
49936	3	0	4	1515	

The parameters of the algorithm need to define specific values when building the tree model. We define the number of trees as the estimator, and the depth of the tree is set to Table 3 lists the accuracy rates corresponding to different parameters and the ranking results of feature importance. We list the top 5 features. It can be seen from Table 3 that when the number of trees is $N = 30$, the accuracy rate is the highest. We numbered 17 features, and numbers represented selected features.

At the same time, we compared XGBoost with several other commonly used feature selection (FS) methods. As shown in Table 4, it is the feature importance ranking (top 5) obtained by other FS algorithms. We can see that some features appear in multiple In the result of the feature selection algorithm, these features will be used in the following model evaluation part for comparison experiments.

Table 3. Feature selection with different parameters.

Estimator	Threshold	Accuracy	Features
N = 20	0.6	0.57	3, 4, 6, 8, 10
	0.5	0.69	3, 5, 6, 9, 11
	0.4	0.66	2, 3, 7, 9, 15
N = 30	0.6	0.63	1, 4, 6, 9, 14
	0.5	0.77	1, 3, 6, 8, 13
	0.4	0.72	2, 3, 6, 8, 9
N = 40	0.6	0.60	2, 4, 7, 9, 10
	0.5	0.70	3, 5, 9, 13, 16
	0.4	0.65	2, 8, 11, 13, 15

Table 4. Feature selection with different algorithms.

Algorithms	Features
Weight by Gini	3, 5, 7, 8, 15
Weight by Chi-square	3, 5, 7, 9, 15
Hierarchical variable clustering	1, 3, 6, 9, 13
Weight by correlation	3, 5, 8, 12, 16
Weight by information	3, 5, 7, 8, 16

4.3 Model Evaluation

We compared various methods' speed, accuracy, and recall rate in detecting malicious accounts in this data set.

Features Selection. Through the feature selection process, the useless features were first screened out in multiple experiments, and the number of features was reduced in dimensionality. We use the essential features selected by various FS algorithms in the last part to compare them in the subsequent algorithm part. Each FS algorithm filters out the top five features, and we combine them, and every 3 features are one. Combining the features of the group, a total of 10 groups of feature combinations will be generated. We numbered them and used them in the subsequent algorithm, which result is shown in Fig. 2. We can see that the crucial features obtained through the XGBoost algorithm are more prominent in the follow-up core algorithms.

Speed and Accuracy. Compared with other machine learning algorithms, as shown in Fig. 3 and Fig. 4, compared with the MAF algorithm, our algorithm is mainly better than or equal to it in accuracy and recall. However, MAF requires more time in larger dimensions, especially in finding suitable parameters in terms of training time.

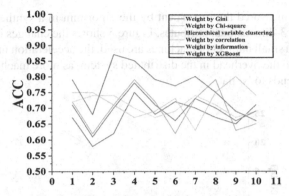

Fig. 2. Different feature selection algorithms.

Our algorithm provides the best trade-off between speed and accuracy. Specifically, our algorithm is about 30% faster than the second-fastest method M-Zoom. In addition, our algorithm consistently finds malicious accounts more efficiently, while the accuracy of other methods varies from data to data. In particular, the results given in the SMS, Android, and EnWiki data sets have an accuracy rate of 3% higher than that of CPDs.

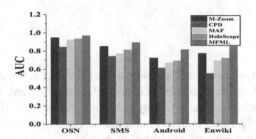

Fig. 3. Different datasets with different algorithms in AUC.

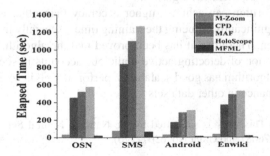

Fig. 4. Different datasets with different algorithms in elapsed time.

Scalability. We also evaluated the machine scalability of the MapReduce implementation of the algorithm. When we increased the number of machines running in parallel from 1 to 20, we measured the time spent by the algorithm in a synthetic tensor with 30,000 tuples and 3-dimensional attributes. Figure 5 shows the changes in running time and speed. When a small number of machines are used, the acceleration increases almost linearly, and due to the overhead in the distributed system, as more machines are added, the acceleration tends to be flat.

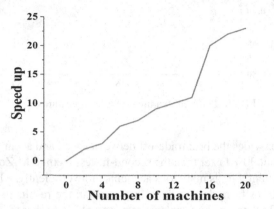

Fig. 5. Speed up with the number of machines.

5   Conclusion

In this paper, we propose a multimodal fusion model to detect active malicious accounts in social networks. First, we use the XGBoost algorithm to rank the importance of features, which can achieve dimensionality reduction. At the same time, we use a density block detection algorithm to detect malicious accounts with cooperative behavior. Finally, we use a neural network algorithm to make a second judgment on the result to improve the algorithm's accuracy. The above three parts constitute the Multimodal Fusion machine learning (MFML) algorithm.

The MFML algorithm can achieve higher accuracy than other algorithms in the experiment while significantly reducing the training time, especially in feature selection and density detection. Therefore, it has been proved that the algorithm is beneficial to the practical application of detecting active malicious accounts in social networks. At the same time, the algorithm has good scalability, performs well in social networks, and shows good performance in other data sets.

Acknowledgements. This work is supported by the National Natural Science Foundation of China (Grant No. 61976087 and Grant No. 62072170),

References

1. Sheikhi, F.: An efficient method for detection of fake accounts on the Instagram platform. Rev. D Intell. Artif. **34**(4), 429–436 (2020)

2. Dover, Y., Goldenberg, J., Shapira, D.: Uncovering Social Network Structures Through Penetration Data. Social Science Electronic Publishing, Rochester (2009)
3. Schuetz, S.W., Wei, J.: When your friends render you vulnerable: a social network analysis perspective on users' vulnerability to socially engineered phishing attacks. In: ICIS 2019 (2019)
4. Stein, T., Chen, E., Mangla, K.: Facebook immune system. In: Proceedings of the 4th Workshop on Social Network Systems, pp. 1–8 (2011)
5. Lyu, C., et al.: Predictable model for detecting sybil attacks in mobile social networks. In: 2021 IEEE Wireless Communications and Networking Conference (WCNC), pp. 1–6. IEEE (2021)
6. Lobo, A., Mandekar, Y., Pundpal, S., Roy, B.: Detection of sybil attacks in social networks. In: Chellappan, S., Choo, K.-K., Phan, N. (eds.) CSoNet. LNCS, vol. 12575, pp. 366–377. Springer, Cham (2020). https://doi.org/10.1007/978-3-030-66046-8_30
7. Xu, E.H.W., Hui, P.M.: Uncovering complex overlapping pattern of communities in large-scale social networks. Appl. Netw. Sci. 4(1), 1–16 (2019). https://doi.org/10.1007/s41109-019-0138-z
8. Wang, G., Konolige, T., Wilson, C., Wang, X., Zheng, H., Zhao, B.Y.: You are how you click: clickstream analysis for sybil detection. In: 22nd USENIX Security Symposium ({USENIX}Security 13), pp. 241–256 (2013)
9. Shin, K., Hooi, B., Kim, J., Faloutsos, C.: D-cube: dense-block detection interabyte-scale tensors. In: Proceedings of the Tenth ACM International Conference on Web Search and Data Mining, pp. 681–689 (2017)
10. Tang, B., Zhang, L.: Local preserving logistic i-relief for semi-supervised feature selection. Neurocomputing 399, 48–64 (2020)
11. Chen, J., Tang, G.: A feature selection model to filter periodic variable stars with data-sensitive light-variable characteristics. J. Signal Process. Syst. 93(7), 733–744 (2021)
12. Liu, H., Motoda, H.: Computational Methods of Feature Selection. CRC Press, Boca Raton (2007)
13. Selvalakshmi, B., Subramaniam, M.: Intelligent ontology based semantic information retrieval using feature selection and classification. Clust. Comput. 22(5), 12871–12881 (2018). https://doi.org/10.1007/s10586-018-1789-8
14. Ndaoud, M.: Contributions to variable selection, clustering and statistical estimation in high dimension (2019)
15. Wang, X., Wang, Z., Zhang, Y., Jiang, X., Cai, Z.: Latent representation learning based autoencoder for unsupervised feature selection in hyper-spectral imagery. Multimedia Tools Appl. 1–15 (2021). https://doi.org/10.1007/s11042-020-10474-8
16. Zhang, L., Huang, X., Zhou, W.: Logistic local hyperplane-relief: a feature weighting method for classification. Knowl.-Based Syst. 181, 104741 (2019)
17. Klein, A., Melard, G.: Invertibility condition of the fisher information matrix of a varmax process and the tensor sylvester matrix. In: Working Papers ECARES (2020)
18. Kl, A., Xy, A., Hy, A., Jm, B., Pwb, C., Xc, A.: Rough set based semi-supervised feature selection via ensemble selector. Knowl.-Based Syst. 165, 282–296 (2019)
19. Li, J., et al.: Feature selection: a data perspective. ACM Comput. Surv. 50(6), 1–45 (2016)
20. Zeng, X., Zheng, H.: CS sparse k-means: An algorithm for cluster-specific feature selection in high-dimensional clustering (2019)
21. Jza, B., Hp, A., Jt, A., Ql, A.: Generalized refined composite multiscale fuzzy entropy and multi-cluster feature selection based intelligent fault diagnosis of rolling bearing. ISA Trans. (2021)
22. Li, K., Zhang, J., Fang, Z.: Communication emitter identification based on kernel semi-supervised discriminant analysis. In: 2019 IEEE International Conference on Power, Intelligent Computing and Systems (ICPICS) (2019)

23. Benabdeslem, K., Hindawi, M.: Efficient semi-supervised feature selection: constraint, relevance, and redundancy. IEEE Trans. Knowl. Data Eng. **26**(5), 1131–1143 (2014)
24. Fang, H., Tang, P., Si, H.: Feature selections using minimal redundancy maximal relevance algorithm for human activity recognition in smarthome environments. J. Healthc. Eng. **2020**(1), 1–13 (2020)
25. Rastogi, A., Mehrotra, M.: Opinion spam detection in online reviews. J. Inf. Knowl. Manag. **16**(04), 1750036 (2017)
26. Gayo-Avello, D., Brenes, D.J.: Overcoming spammers in Twitter-a taleof five algorithms (2010)
27. Velammal, B.L., Aarthy, N.: Improvised spam detection in twitter datausing lightweight detectors and classifiers. Int. J. Web-Based Learn. Teach. Technol. (IJWLTT) **16**, 12–32 (2021)
28. Mojiri, M.M., Ravanmehr, R.: Event detection in Twitter using multi timing chained windows. Comput. Inf. **39**(6), 1336–1359 (2020)
29. Aswani, R., Kar, A.K., Ilavarasan, P.V.: Detection of spammers in Twitter marketing: a hybrid approach using social media analytics and bioinspired computing. Inf. Syst. Front. **20**(3), 515–530 (2018)
30. Youlve, C., Kaiyun, B., Jiangtian, C.: Credit decision system based on combination weight and extreme gradient boosting algorithm. J. Phys. Conf. Ser. **1955**, 012081(2021)
31. Shin, K., Hooi, B., Faloutsos, C.: M-zoom: fast dense-block detection in tensors with quality guarantees. In: Frasconi, P., Landwehr, N., Manco, G., Vreeken, J. (eds.) ECML PKDD 2016. LNCS (LNAI), vol. 9851, pp. 264–280. Springer, Cham (2016). https://doi.org/10.1007/978-3-319-46128-1_17
32. Charikar, M.: Greedy approximation algorithms for finding dense components in a graph. In: Jansen, K., Khuller, S. (eds.) APPROX 2000. LNCS, vol. 1913, pp. 84–95. Springer, Heidelberg (2000). https://doi.org/10.1007/3-540-44436-X_10
33. Jiang, M., Beutel, A., Cui, P., Hooi, B., Yang, S., Faloutsos, C.: A general suspiciousness metric for dense blocks in multimodal data. In: 2015 IEEE International Conference on Data Mining, pp. 781–786. IEEE (2015)

Evaluation of an Anomaly Detector for Routers Using Parameterizable Malware in an IoT Ecosystem

John Carter$^{(\boxtimes)}$ and Spiros Mancoridis

Drexel University, Philadelphia, PA 19104, USA
jmc683@drexel.edu

Abstract. This work explores the evaluation of a machine learning anomaly detector using custom-made parameterizable malware in an Internet of Things (IoT) Ecosystem. It is assumed that the malware has infected, and resides on, the Linux router that serves other devices on the network, as depicted in Fig. 1. This IoT Ecosystem was developed as a testbed to evaluate the efficacy of a behavior-based anomaly detector. The malware consists of three types of custom-made malware: ransomware, cryptominer, and keylogger, which all have exfiltration capabilities to the network. The parameterization of the malware gives the malware samples multiple degrees of freedom, specifically relating to the rate and size of data exfiltration. The anomaly detector uses feature sets crafted from system calls and network traffic, and uses a Support Vector Machine (SVM) for behavioral-based anomaly detection. The custom-made malware is used to evaluate the situations where the SVM is effective, as well as the situations where it is not effective.

Keywords: Internet of Things · Malware · Routers · Malware detection · Linux · Machine learning · Anomaly detector

1 Introduction

Malware detection on small, resource-constrained devices has emerged as an important area of research, as IoT devices have grown in popularity. Since these devices have limited resources [8], malware detection software running on them must be efficient and lightweight, yet accurate and useful. This work focuses on creating and deploying custom-made parameterizable malware on a router in an IoT ecosystem to evaluate an anomaly detector's effectiveness in detecting the presence of malware. The parameterization of the malware enables the conditions on the router to vary, which provides a variety of data with which to train and test the anomaly detector. We show that while the SVM is incredibly effective and practical as an anomaly detector on IoT devices due to its low resource consumption and high accuracy, the parameters of the malware can be adjusted to decrease the effectiveness of the SVM.

G. Wang et al. (Eds.): UbiSec 2021, CCIS 1557, pp. 53–65, 2022.
https://doi.org/10.1007/978-981-19-0468-4_5

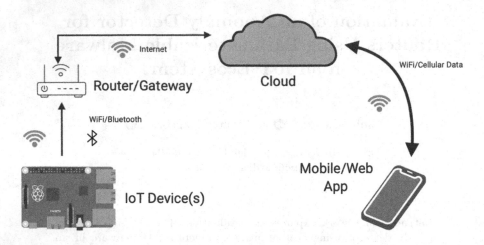

Fig. 1. The IoT ecosystem

Routers can be described as IoT devices that do not require constant human oversight, and have limited behavioral patterns and resources. Their limited behavior make anomaly detection simpler, but the anomaly detection we describe in this work could likely be ported to non-IoT devices as well. Since routers are used to connect devices on a local area network (LAN) to the Internet, their security is critical. If a router is infected with malware, there is a high probability that the malware can spread quickly to other devices on the network. This idea underpins one of the important reasons to work on the topic of securing routers. If it is possible to make a router resilient to malware, then it is possible that the router could act as a firewall to prevent malware from infecting devices connected to the router's network. In this work, the router we are working with is a Raspberry Pi 3, called Pi-Router, that has been configured to work as a router using the *hostapd* package. This package allows the Raspberry Pi to work as a wireless access point. The Raspberry Pi gives a realistic picture of working on an IoT device due to its own limited resources, and the fact that it runs on a Linux distribution. This provides a useful environment in which to develop lightweight malware detection systems that can be ported to similar Linux-based IoT devices.

In order to have a diverse set of fully-functional and parameterizable malware samples, we have created three types of malware for this work: ransomware, cryptominer, and keylogger, all with remote exfiltration capabilities. Some of these malware samples, such as the keylogger, may not be commonly found on routers, but including it in this research demonstrates the breadth of different malware examples that could infect any IoT device. Often, malware caught "in the wild" fails to run well, or at all, for a variety of reasons. These can include outdated code, attempts to connect to a server that no longer exists, and other reasons. This situation can make malware samples from the wild less useful to train and test a malware detector, which creates a need for custom-made malware that emulates how different malware families behave.

The malware created all have parameterizable exfiltration rates, which means they can be tuned to attempt to elude the anomaly detector. These degrees of freedom on the malware samples are essential to emulate the adversarial relationship between the malware and the malware detection software. The parameterization of the malware is depicted on the right side of Fig. 2. The specific functionality and capabilities of each of the malware samples will be discussed further in Sect. 3.

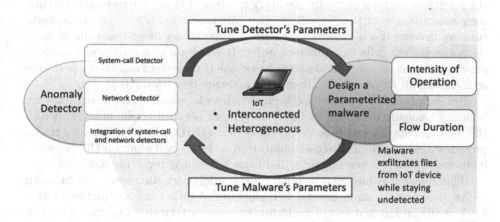

Fig. 2. Parallel development of an anomaly detector and malware samples

A SVM is used for router behavioral anomaly detection. The SVM was chosen because it can be trained effectively with less data than other machine learning models, such as neural networks, and it is more efficient to run on a resource-constrained IoT device. The detector was trained on three types of data. The rest of the paper demonstrates how it is possible to detect malware running on the Pi-Router by first training the anomaly detector on kernel-level system call data, training the detector on network traffic data, and lastly, training the detector on a combination of the two, which is depicted on the left side of Fig. 2, [10]. Each of these anomaly detectors are accurate in classifying data, but we will show that the detector trained on the combination of data generally performs the best.

2 Related Work

This work draws on prior research in the areas of anomaly detection and malware detection on IoT devices. Previous work focused on specific IoT devices with predictable behavior, such as Amazon's Alexa running on a Raspberry Pi.

This work approaches the problem more broadly in the context of routers infected with custom-made parameterizable malware [9,10].

It has been shown that sequences of system calls and network traffic data provide useful and explanatory feature sets for classifiers, as they provide insight to the programs running on a machine and can often be used to differentiate between a period of benign behavior, and a period of malware infection [10].

System call sequences have been shown to be effective as a feature set in many architectures due to the fact that they are one of the best indicators of what is happening on a machine at runtime [2,10]. Each process running on a machine uses system calls to request resources from the OS kernel, which means the programs running normally are likely to make similar system calls each time they run. Because of this, it will be more obvious when a new program starts running because it will likely either issue a different set of system calls or issue the same system calls in a different order. It has been suggested, by results in prior work, that an anomaly detector based solely on system call traces performs well enough on its own to be effective in malware detection [10].

Network traffic data have also been shown to be effective as a feature set for behavior anomaly detection [6,12]. This type of network traffic analysis is also the basis of network intrusion detection systems (NIDS) [3,5,7]. Network traffic provides insight into all the communication a device is having on the network, including where it is sending data and from where it is receiving data [10].

This research is intended to build on the prior work discussed, and broaden its application to a more general IoT platform. Another key distinction of this work is the design and use of custom-made parameterizable malware to aid in the evaluation of behavioral-based anomaly detectors.

3   Malware

Three types of malware are used in the experimentation, which together provide a variety in the breadth of the malware. Some of the malware are more computationally expensive on the device and issue many system calls, while others issue fewer system calls but exfiltrate more information at varying speeds, which contributes to higher overall network traffic. All of the malware used in this research are custom-made, which provides more freedom to create interesting types of malware that are diverse in their execution behavior, yet stay true to behaviors that would be exemplified in real malware samples. In addition, the malware used in this research each have varying degrees of freedom, that include the rate of data exfiltration, as well as the size of the data exfiltration. These degrees of freedom are important because they enable the malware to adapt to changing conditions on the host prompted by malware detection software, as well as provide a better basis to show situations where the malware detection is successful, and situations where it is less successful.

3.1 Keylogger

The first type of malware used in this research is a keylogger, which tracks all of the key presses on the device, and saves them to a buffer. The key presses can then be exfiltrated to another machine. The speed and the size of the exfiltration are set by user-defined parameters, which means an adversary can adjust the malware to attempt to avoid detection by an anomaly detector. The speed of the exfiltration refers to the rate of exfiltration, which can be defined as the interval at which the buffer of key presses, or a subset of them, are removed from the buffer and sent to a remote machine. The size of the exfiltration, in this case, refers to the number of key presses to send with each exfiltration packet to a remote machine. This allows the adversary to adapt the malware in order to evade detection and possible mitigation strategies implemented by the malware detection. Although a keylogger is not usually deployed on a router, this malware family was included in this work to provide a larger breadth of malware behaviors with which to train a more effective IoT behavioral anomaly detector.

3.2 Ransomware

The ransomware malware uses the Python cryptography library to encrypt a file system, and exfiltrate the contents to a remote host on the network. The exfiltration happens during the encryption process. An encryption key is created, and then the malware traverses the file system. For each file it finds, it first sends a copy of it to the remote host using secure copy (scp), and then encrypts it and continues to the next file. The decryption functionality is also provided. The location to save the file on the remote host is user-specified. The user can also provide an exfiltration interval, which will insert a delay in between exlfiltrating individual files. Similar to the rate of exfiltration on the keylogger, this allows an adversary to become more inconspicuous, since copying and sending files at a slower rate will likely draw less attention to the malware than performing the same process rapidly.

3.3 Cryptominer

Lastly, the cryptominer malware is a simple coin mining script, that runs a mining simulation to emulate the computational cost of a real cryptominer. The user specifies a remote host to send the new hash that was mined on the host after the completion of the mining process. Similar to the ransomware, the user can specify an exfiltration interval, which will insert a delay between the mining process and the exfiltration of the calculated hash. While the behavior of the two previous malware discussed is often easily traceable by both system call data and network traffic data, the cryptominer malware is more easily traceable by system call data, due to the heavy computation cost of the mining process, and the relatively few packets being sent over the network as a result of its execution.

4   Anomaly Detection Model

The feature sets for the anomaly detection model are extracted from sequences of system calls and network traffic flows on the Pi-Router. This includes any system calls executed on the Pi-Router during data collection, as well as any packets sent to or from the Pi-Router during its execution.

4.1   System Calls

System calls indicate the activity of each running process on the machine. Therefore, when a malware sample starts to execute, its process will likely make different system calls than previously seen and will be useful in detecting an anomaly present on the machine.

The pre-processing step for system calls is similar to [2], where a sequence of system calls collected in a window size of length L is treated as an observation. Then, a bag-of-n-grams approach [1,4,11] is used to group the system calls and create the feature vector $\mathbf{x} \in \mathbb{R}^p$. This can be described as the number of times a system call n-gram sequence was observed in an observation window of length L, [10]. An n-gram length of $n = 2$ was used when the results of the classifier were compiled, although this is another parameter of the data processing code that can be changed by the user. Other values of n, such as $n = 3$, were used in the experimentation phase as well, but did not yield significantly better results.

4.2   Network Traffic

Network traffic features are extracted from network flows collected by CICFlowMeter. CICFlowMeter is a package in the Python Package Index (PyPi) that listens to network traffic on a device, generates bidirectional network flows, and then extracts features from these flows. In the network traffic data collected, one packet sent or received by the Pi-Router counts as one observation.

One issue that arises when using network traffic as a feature set is that many of the packets that are sent by normal non-malicious applications on the Pi-Router are also included in the malware dataset. This results in these benign packets being labeled as malicious data, which yields an inseparable dataset [10]. This issue is resolved by grouping the network traffic data into m-second intervals, which results in more finely-grained malware traces that distinguish them from the benign traces [10]. The key idea here is to find the optimal value of m so that the bin is large enough to collect enough packets to determine their source or destination program, but small enough so that packets from other programs are excluded, making each packet sequence more distinct. As with the bag-of-n-grams approach used in the system call processing, the value of m is a tunable parameter that can be adjusted by the user. During the experimentation phase of this work, a few different values of m were used, and it was found that smaller values of m are better for classifying our malware samples.

4.3   Principal Component Analysis

After the pre-processing mentioned above was applied to the datasets, approximately 2600 features were extracted from the system call dataset, and 237 features were extracted from the network traffic dataset. Combining these features brings the total number of features in the feature set to approximately 2800 features. Principal Component Analysis (PCA) was then used to reduce the dimensionality of the created feature space, similar to work by [10]. The number of components to use was determined by calculating the explained variance of the components, and selecting the number of components that explain at least 95% of the variance in the dataset. Figure 3 depicts the number of components needed to explain 95% of the variance for the Cryptominer combined feature set, which in this specific case is four components.

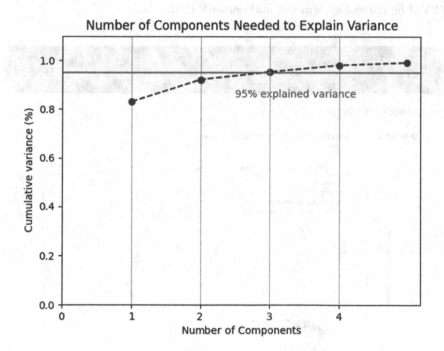

Fig. 3. Explained variance for the cryptominer combined feature set

The anomaly detection model uses a Support Vector Machine (SVM), which finds a hyperplane that separates the training data from origin with the largest possible margin. The objective function is thus maximizing the margin, or the distance from the origin to the hyperplane.

5   Experimental Setup

5.1   Pi-Router

Most of the setup for the experiments conducted is focused on the Pi-Router. The Pi-Router is a Raspberry Pi 3 running Raspberry Pi OS (formerly Raspbian), which is based on the Debian Linux distribution. This Raspberry Pi has been configured to act as a wireless access point by using the software package *hostapd*, which is a user-space daemon that allows the network interface card (NIC) to act as an access point. A Flask web server running as a Linux service was created on the Pi-Router to act as a portal for users to configure the router and track the health of the network by running the malware detection software and showing the results. Figure 4 shows how the Network Health section might look to the user on the Pi-Router web server, where the graphs show the results of running the SVM on current system call and network traffic data.

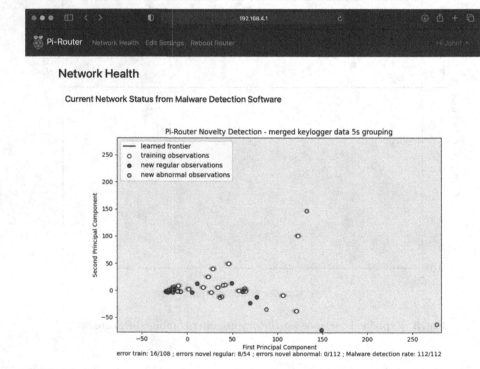

Fig. 4. Example screenshot of the Pi-router UI

The web server presents the essence of the usability of this system, in that it allows users to monitor the behavior and overall health of their network and track anomalous behaviors caused by malware.

5.2 Pi-Network and Connected Devices

The Pi-Router's network is the Pi-Network, which has two other hosts connected to it currently: a Pi-Camera and the attacker machine. The Pi-Camera in this work is simply another host on the network that generates traffic unrelated to the router. The attacker is a laptop running Ubuntu 20.04 and is responsible for receiving all of the exfiltrated data sent by the malware. This includes key presses sent from the keylogger, files copied by the ransomware, and hashes sent by the cryptominer. As a result, the relevant network traffic would often originate from the Pi-Router or the attacker, and be received by the other. Most of the exfiltration communication was one-way, from the Pi-Router to the attacker.

6 Experimental Results

The classification experiments were conducted with the three types of malware, each with different window sizes, or values of L, used in the SVM. Each of these was carried out for the three types of features: system calls, network traffic, and a combination of the two. In Fig. 5, we show a visualization of the classification process using the SVM, in which the first two principal components derived from PCA are shown. In this example, the SVM is classifying keylogger data using a five-second window size. The goal is to have as many new abnormal observations outside of the learned frontier as possible, because they will be easier to identify and isolate from the benign data and thus be better indicators of a possible malware infection.

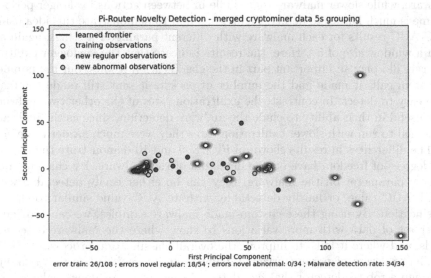

Fig. 5. Visualization of first two principal components on cryptominer data using a 5 s window size

After some experimentation, it was found that a $L = 5$ s window size was optimal for classification accuracy. Other window sizes yielded suboptimal results for each feature set. Figure 6 shows the comparison between F1 score and window size for the three types of malware, in which we see that for all three types of malware, a $L = 5$ s window size had the best classification performance of the 6 different window sizes.

In addition, we found that using a classifier trained on both the system call feature set and network traffic feature set generally outperformed classifiers trained on each type of data individually. While system call data can provide a lot of information relating to the behavior of a process, the network traffic data often augments that behavior data and makes the classification results more conclusive. Figure 7 shows an example of the merged data providing better features than system call and network traffic data individually using cryptominer data with a five second window size. In this case, both the classifier trained on system call data and the classifier trained on network traffic data each only had a mean AUC value of 0.75 or less, while the combined data had a mean AUC value of 0.98, which is a significant improvement.

In all three types of malware, the combined dataset of system calls and network traffic generally outperformed the system call and network traffic classifiers individually.

The parameters provided in the malware samples greatly affect the classification effectiveness of the SVM. Specifically, the rate of exfiltration parameter in each malware sample is instrumental in its detection. In general, as one might expect, the faster the exfiltration rate, the easier the detection process becomes. Rapidly issuing system calls and sending packets results in more conspicuous malware, while slower malware that is idle in between actions for longer periods of time is much harder to detect. Figures 8, 9 and 10 demonstrate this idea using ROC-AUC results for each malware with different parameter settings, again all with a window size of 5 s. Here, the results indicate that the keylogger exfiltration rate did play an important part in the classification results, but the number of system calls it made and the number of packets it sent still made the malware easy to detect. In contrast, the exfiltration rates of the other two malware were useful in their ability to elude the malware detection, since as the malware continued to run with slower exfiltration rates they were much harder to detect.

The differences in results shown in Figs. 8, 9 and 10 demonstrate the impact the degrees of freedom have on the detection of the malware. By changing one tunable parameter on the malware, they can be either easily detectable with a high AUC value, or hardly detectable, with an AUC value similar to chance classification. By using these custom-made malware samples, we can provide a larger set of data with more variations to show where the malware detection excels, and where it fails, to improve the overall classification process.

The co-design of parameterizable malware and anomaly detectors is useful to design a robust detector that can detect elusive, inconspicuous, malware.

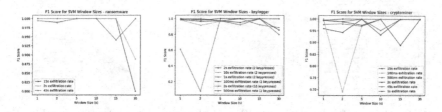

Fig. 6. A comparison of F1 scores using different window size values (values of L)

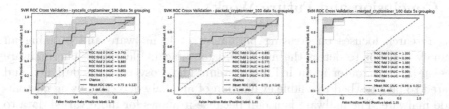

Fig. 7. As with the other types of malware, the combined feature set outperforms the feature sets comprised of system call data and network traffic data individually. Here, we demonstrate this using the cryptominer malware with a Window Size of 5 s and an exfiltration rate of 100 ms. The first figure uses system call features, the second uses network traffic features, and the third uses both types of features.

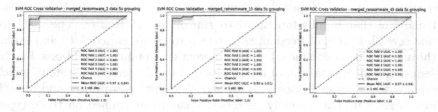

Fig. 8. ROC curves for ransomware with a window size of 5 s and a 2 s exfiltration rate, a 15 s exfiltration rate, and a 45 s exfiltration rate.

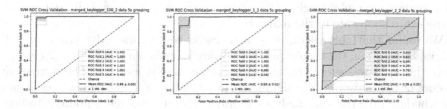

Fig. 9. ROC curves for keylogger with a window size of 5 s and a 100 ms exfiltration rate, a 1 s exfiltration rate, and a 2 s exfiltration rate.

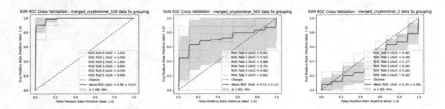

Fig. 10. ROC curves for cryptominer with a window size of 5 s and a 100 ms exfiltration rate, a 500 ms exfiltration rate, and a 2 s exfiltration rate.

7   Conclusion and Future Work

This research focuses on creating parameterizable malware and building an anomaly detector to detect the malware using machine learning. The malware lives on a Linux router in an IoT Ecosystem. The ecosystem was designed and created to be a testbed to enable evaluation of anomaly detectors using custom-made malware. The malware is useful because it allows for more varied data to be generated while still emulating its respective malware family. This method of malware detection is useful for IoT devices because it does not rely on prior knowledge of the environment of the device, and is also very resource efficient, which is essential if the malware detection is going to run on the IoT device itself.

In this research, we created a real IoT Ecosystem, which in this work focuses primarily on the Pi-Router. The Pi-Router is a fully-functional wireless access point that provides a network that devices can connect to locally. We also created malware that is fully-functional to run on the Pi-Router. The malware provide several degrees of freedom with which to create varied data and evaluate the anomaly detection model under different environment conditions. Lastly, we demonstrated the creation of a behavioral anomaly detection system, which is designed to detect malicious software running on the Pi-Router and on IoT devices in general. The anomaly detection system was trained on three types of data: system call sequences, network traffic data, and a combined dataset comprised of system calls and network traffic data. Our results indicate that a classifier trained on the combined data with a window size of $L = 5$ s generally outperformed the other classifiers that were used. We also found that the ability of the malware samples to elude the anomaly detector was generally dependent on the exfiltration rate of the malware.

We found that this classifier is very useful for malware detection on IoT devices. In addition, the custom-made malware is useful for identifying situations where the SVM was successful and situations where it was not. The degrees of freedom of the malware were significant in providing a way to quickly generate different data from the same malware family to test the classifier's ability to adapt to changing malware behavior. We plan to continue and expand on this research by using the data obtained from the IoT Ecosystem to train a generator and a discriminator in a Generative Adversarial Network (GAN) [7]. Feeding the real data to the GAN initially will save training time, at which point the generator will have a useful benchmark from which to start creating realistic but fake data. We hope that this will provide an even better classifier to detect malware running on IoT devices.

The anomaly detection code is available on GitHub. The README file in the repository has instructions on how to run the code used to generate the graphs and results discussed in this paper.

Acknowledgments. The work was funded in part by Spiros Mancoridis' Auerbach Berger Chair in Cybersecurity.

References

1. An, N., et al.: Behavioral anomaly detection of malware on home routers. In: 2017 12th International Conference on Malicious and Unwanted Software (MALWARE), pp. 47–54 (2017). https://doi.org/10.1109/MALWARE.2017.8323956
2. An, N., et al.: Malware anomaly detection on virtual assistants. In: 2018 13th International Conference on Malicious and Unwanted Software (MALWARE), pp. 124–131 (2018). https://doi.org/10.1109/MALWARE.2018.8659366
3. Bhuyan, M.H., Bhattacharyya, D.K., Kalita, J.K.: Network anomaly detection: methods, systems and tools. IEEE Commun. Surv. Tutor. **16**(1), 303–336 (2014). https://doi.org/10.1109/SURV.2013.052213.00046
4. Canzanese, R., Mancoridis, S., Kam, M.: System call-based detection of malicious processes. In: 2015 IEEE International Conference on Software Quality, Reliability and Security, pp. 119–124 (2015). https://doi.org/10.1109/QRS.2015.26
5. Chalapathy, R., Chawla, S.: Deep learning for anomaly detection: a survey. CoRR, abs/1901.03407 (2019). http://arxiv.org/abs/1901.03407
6. Doshi, R., Apthorpe, N., Feamster, N.: Machine learning DDoS detection for consumer internet of things devices. In: 2018 IEEE Security and Privacy Workshops (SPW), May 2018. https://doi.org/10.1109/spw.2018.00013. http://dx.doi.org/10.1109/SPW.2018.00013
7. García-Teodoro, P., et al.: Anomaly-based network intrusion detection: techniques, systems and challenges. Comput. Secur. **28**, 18–28 (2009). https://doi.org/10.1016/j.cose.2008.08.003
8. Hadar, N., Siboni, S., Elovici, Y.: A lightweight vulnerability mitigation framework for IoT devices. In: Proceedings of the 2017 Workshop on Internet of Things Security and Privacy, IoTS&P 2017, pp. 71–75. Association for Computing Machinery, Dallas (2017). https://doi.org/10.1145/3139937.3139944. ISBN 9781450353960
9. Noorani, M., Mancoridis, S., Weber, S.: Automatic malware detection on an Alexa-Pi IoT device. In: 35th Annual Computer Security Applications Conference (ACSAC 2019) (2019)
10. Noorani, M., Mancoridis, S., Weber, S.: On the detection of malware on virtual assistants based on behavioral anomalies (2019)
11. Sekar, R., et al.: A fast automaton-based method for detecting anomalous program behaviors. In: Proceedings 2001 IEEE Symposium on Security and Privacy, S P 2001, pp. 144–155 (2001). https://doi.org/10.1109/SECPRI.2001.924295
12. Terzi, D.S., Terzi, R., Sagiroglu, S.: Big data analytics for network anomaly detection from NetFlow data. In: 2017 International Conference on Computer Science and Engineering (UBMK), pp. 592–597 (2017). https://doi.org/10.1109/UBMK.2017.8093473

PUFloc: PUF and Location Based Hierarchical Mutual Authentication Protocol for Surveillance Drone Networks

Aiswarya S. Nair[1,2]([✉]) and Sabu M. Thampi[3]

[1] Indian Institute of Information Technology and Management-Kerala (IIITM-K), Trivandrum, Kerala, India
aiswarya.res19@iiitmk.ac.in
[2] Cochin University of Science and Techology (CUSAT), Cochin, Kerala, India
[3] Kerala University of Digital Sciences, Innovation and Technology (KUDSIT), Technocity Campus, Trivandrum, Kerala, India
sabu.thampi@duk.ac.in

Abstract. The security hazards in the digital sky of drones urges for lightweight and secure defense mechanisms against several cyber-attacks on drone networks. The main issues in a surveillance drone network are identification of valid drones, maintaining boundaries and information security along with physical security. To address these issues we are proposing a lightweight and secure drone-to-ground station and drone-to-drone mutual authentication protocol, PUFloc, using Physical unclonable functions (PUFs) and drone location data. PUFloc ensures attack resiliency and fail safe operation and uses only hash functions, XOR operations, PUF and random number generators. This is the first work that addresses physical security along with location validation of drones for mutually authenticating the drone with the ground station with minimum resource overheads and maximum security. Formal security analysis is done using random oracle model and ProVerif tool and informal security analysis also proves the resistance of our protocol against several possible attacks. FPGA implementation of the major cryptographic operations to estimate the power consumption and resource utilization show that the operations are lightweight to be implemented on drones. The analysis of performance and security and their comparison with existing works showcase the merit of PUFloc over other protocols.

Keywords: Drone authentication · PUF · Location validation · Impersonation · PUFloc · FPGA

1 Introduction

The invention of drones or unmanned aerial vehicles (UAVs) has created a flying revolution of drones making them a common sight nowadays. They play promising roles in search and rescue, disaster management, pandemic surveillance, military surveillance, wars, traffic monitoring, goods and medicine delivery

G. Wang et al. (Eds.): UbiSec 2021, CCIS 1557, pp. 66–89, 2022.
https://doi.org/10.1007/978-981-19-0468-4_6

[10,15]. A drone network can expand the application horizon and render more productive and fail-safe services through inter-drone communications, reduced computational complexity on individual drone, increased operational coverage area and more data that increase the reliability of the system. The Federal Aviation Administration (FAA) and NASA operates an Unmanned aircraft system Traffic Management (UTM) for monitoring the traffic at low altitudes using drone networks [1]. Apart from these enchanting applications, UAV networks also confront with many threats and challenges including data security and privacy, path planning, fleet communication and coordination, physical security, lightweight design, energy management, swarm intelligence, device fingerprinting and network and communication security.

Insecure open environments, resource limitations and the free availability of drones are the major vulnerabilities in the system that can lead to an array of attacks such as eavesdropping, masquerade, man-in-the-middle, replay, node tampering, physical capture and session key disclosure. Hacking of US drones by Russia in 2014 [28], spoofing of navigation signals of US drones by adversaries in 2015 [34] and capture of video feeds from Israeli UAVs by British and US in 2016 [22] are a few cyber attacks on drones in the recent past. In a border surveillance application, it is necessary to ensure that the messages received at the ground station are from valid drones belonging to a particular service area and not from impersonating drones that are outside the prescribed borders. Drone hijack and impersonation are very dangerous attacks that expose the secret data stored in drones causing serious security issues. The use of device specific features and drone location information for authentication will thwart drone impersonation attacks and will also validate position of drones before establishing secure communication with it. Hence, identifying the real drone and authenticating it based on its location and device specific features is an indispensable part of securing the drone network. In this work, we focus on mutually authenticating the drones with the GCS with thrust on the physical security and location validation of drones using a combination of physical unclonable functions and drone location data. To highlight the importance of the proposed method, consider a border surveillance system as in Fig. 1, where a drone may be captured and impersonated at the country border or an illegitimate drone from outside the boundary try to access the data at the country borders leading to calamities and distress. This reiterates the fundamental and critical need for location based drone authentication mechanisms in border surveillance systems.

Physical unclonable functions will produce challenge-response pairs that are device specific and unique for a device using the intrinsic manufacturing variations. Drones embedded with PUFs can generate unique hardware fingerprints that can be used for drone authentication and it also makes the system attack resilient by storing zero secrets in drone memory. Even though there are several authentication protocols in the area of UAV networks for mutual authentication [8,9,16,30,31,35,37], user authentication [32,36] and device authentication, these works have not considered the physical security of the drones. There are also a very few authentication protocols based on PUF that address this aspect

Fig. 1. A surveillance drone network

as in [4,5,13,23,29] but they have several drawbacks. None of these works have addressed the problem of validating the location of drones to ensure that the communicating drones are within the service area. This also prevents the drones in other regions from communicating with the GCS. This is the first mutual authentication protocol that addresses both physical security and location validation of drones using the hardware fingerprints from physical unclonable functions (PUFs) on drones and the location data from the drone GPS/NavIC or any other navigation receivers respectively to mutually authenticate the drone with the ground control station. When drones are equipped with PUF circuits, impersonating or replicating the drone is never possible for an attacker. Verifying the location data from the drone navigation receivers will ensure that the drone is authentic with respect to position, has not violated the boundaries and is communicating from the allotted operational area. The major contributions of this paper are listed below:

1. We propose a hierarchical PUF and location based drone-to-GCS and drone-to-drone mutual authentication protocol (PUFloc) using only hash functions, XOR operations, PUF, location data and random number generators.
2. Server-less drone-to-drone mutual authentication protocol with zero storage of secrets in drone memory.
3. We have also made the system fail-safe by considering the cases of drone failure and assigning one of the drones as redundant.
4. We provide formal security verification using ProVerif tool and random oracle model and informal security analysis using theoretical and logical analysis.
5. We have also implemented the major operations such as hash functions, PUF and random number generators using Xilinx Vivado tool for Artix-7 field programmable gate arrays (FPGA) to evaluate the power consumption and resource utilization.
6. The protocol has been compared with the existing works in this domain and proves to be lightweight and secure.

The organization of this paper is as follows. Section 2 discusses the related works in the area of UAV authentication protocols. The network model, assumptions and threat model are discussed in Sect. 3. In Sect. 4 the proposed mutual authentication protocol is presented. Formal and informal analysis are described in

Sect. 5. FPGA implementation and performance evaluation in Sect. 6. Section 7 concludes the paper.

2   Related Works

Recently there have been several works in the area of authentication in UAV networks that include both user authentication and drone authentication protocols. User authentication protocols in UAV networks include TCALAS [32], iTCALAS [3], elliptic curve based [25] and Lake-IoD [33]. TCALAS is a temporal credential based three factor user authentication protocol in an internet of drones (IoD) environment proposed by Srinivas et al. [32]. The protocol was not resistant to stolen verifier attack and user traceability. Nikooghadam et al. in [25] proposed an elliptic curve cryptography (ECC) based user authentication protocol for a system with users, drones and control server. However, the physical security of drones was not considered in the work. Tanveer et al. in [33] proposed a mutual authentication protocol between a mobile user and drone in a flying zone using hash function, bitwise XOR and an authenticated encryption scheme. Zhang et al. [38] proposed a user drone authentication protocol in IoD using only hash functions and bitwise XOR operations. User id and password are used as the user credentials but Gope et al. [14] has pointed out that this protocol is insecure against forgery attacks. But all these protocols focus on user authentication in a drone network.

Drone authentication protocols in IoD have also gained momentum in the past one year. Rodrigues et al. in [30] modified the ECC based mutual authentication protocol in wireless sensor networks into drone-to-drone and drone-to-ground mutual authentication protocols. But they have designed server based drone-to-drone mutual authentication and have not considered physical security. Tian et al. in [35] has proposed a lightweight offline/online signature generation mechanism for a system of network connected UAVs with mobile edge centres (MEC), drones and a trusted authority (TA). They have not considered the mutual authentication of the entities and attack resiliency of the protocol as secret data are stored on the drones increasing the storage cost as well. Chen et al. in [8] proposed another elliptic curve based drone authentication protocol with privacy protection using ECC, hash function and digital signature. The protocol uses key and signature exchanges between the entities which may increase the communication and computation overheads. Another drone authentication protocol is SENTINEL, proposed by Cho et al. [9] which discusses about the security issues and detection of unauthorized drones in a particular fly zone. Drones with an approved flight plan from the ground station obtains the flight session key but the physical security of the drones is not considered in their protocol. Jan et al. [20] proposed an authentication framework as an extension of [9] for a network with drone service provider, the ground station, drones, and external user with dynamic drone addition and revocation phases and have handled stolen verifier attack, insider attack and transmission flaws with higher computation costs.

Recently, a few authors have used PUFs for drone authentication. A two stage PUF based drone authentication protocol was developed by Alladi et al. [4]. A mini drone initiates the communication with the nearest leader drone and the leader in turn authenticates with the ground station. But the protocol has not considered location validation of drones and leader drone failure and also requires ground station for mutual authentication between leader drone and mini drone. Pu et al. [29] has also proposed a drone authentication protocol using PUF and chaotic system. Duffing map chaotic system is used to shuffle the message eliminating the need for other cryptographic mechanisms but they have not considered inter-drone communications and location validation. A similar work is SecauthUAV by Alladi et al. [5] in which an initial challenge is stored on the UAV which reduces the attack resiliency of the system. But they have designed server based mutual authentication between drones. Gope et al. [14] has proposed a PUF based mutual authentication scheme for RFID enabled UAVs between server and drone tag unit. But there may be range issues and application restrictions for an RFID UAV. Gope et al. [13] has also proposed a double PUF based authentication scheme for a network with UAVs, UAV service provider and MEC operators. This protocol cannot be used in highly critical areas where MEC is unavailable. The integrity of the hardware and software are verified and PUF fingerprint is extracted from every unit inside a drone by Vishal Pal in [27] consisting of a network of service provider, service client, drone identity provider, user identity provider and domain security manager. Their protocol, adopted from Hussain et al. [17], depend on drone identity provider and domain security manager for drone authentication and moreover, they have not considered anonymity issues and location validation of drones. A Chinese residual theorem and PUF based optimized identity authentication protocol for IoD is proposed by Lei et al. [23] for a network of sensors, drones, access points and servers. The UAV stores the public key in its memory which reduces the attack resiliency of the system. Moreover, the performance is not compared with state of the art PUF based authentication protocols and also they have not considered insider attacks and location validity. Another PUF based mutual authentication was proposed by Nyangaresi et al. [26], but the protocol depends on an intermediary service provide for mutual authentication between drone and drone service provider. In addition, they have not evaluated man-in-the-middle attacks and insider attacks and they have also not considered the authentication of intermediary service providers.

From the above review, it can be noted that there are several drawbacks for the existing drone authentication protocols including high communication and computation costs, secret data storage on drones, server based drone to drone authentication and lack of location based drone authentication and fail-safe system operation. To overcome these drawbacks we have proposed PUFloc, a PUF and location based mutual authentication protocol between drone-to-ground and drone-to-drone providing drone physical security, location validation, attack resiliency and fail-safe operation. This work, on top of the work in [4] considers a hierarchical network with a master drone, patrol drones, a redundant drone and a GCS and our protocol ensures fail-safe operation in cases of master failure, stores absolutely no secrets in the drone memory making it attack resilient and performs drone-drone mutual authentication without the intervention of a server.

3 Network Model, Threat Model and Security Goals

3.1 Network Model

The proposed system consists of a GCS that communicates with a master drone which in turn communicates with the patrol drones as shown on Fig. 2. One among the patrol drones is configured as a redundant drone before deployment and is ideally a patrol drone and if the master fails to communicate with the patrol drones within a fixed timeout, the redundant drone becomes the new master drone. All the drones are equipped with PUF circuits and navigation receivers. The registration of drones is through secure communication channels and GCS is considered as a trusted authority. Every drone has an embedded tamper-resistant and reliable PUF circuit and any attempt to physically access the drone and tampering it will render the PUF useless and the authentication fails. The PUFs in master, patrol and redundant drones are designed in such a way that the average inter-chip hamming distance of the master and patrol PUF responses are fixed to be within a threshold. Similarly, the average inter-chip hamming distance of the redundant and patrol PUF responses are also within the fixed threshold. The master communicates with the patrol drones in fixed intervals of time and failure of communication within timeout shows master failure.

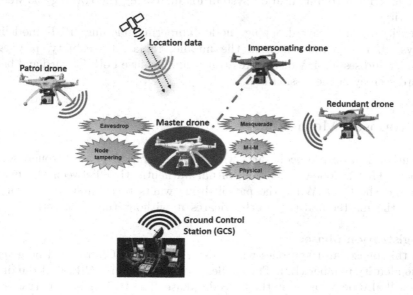

Fig. 2. Network architecture

3.2   Threat Model and Security Goals

The threat model considered is the Dolev-Yao threat model in which the adversary can eavesdrop into the communication channel, spoof the location data, modify, tamper and replay the messages communicated. The attacker may impersonate or clone the drones and place duplicate ones or capture the drones. The main motive of the adversary drone is to pass the authentication process and establish secure connection with the GCS to get the secret data at the borders. The security goals addressed in this work are:

- Endpoint security of the drones and protection from impersonation, cloning attacks and node tampering.
- Ensuring the location of the drones while establishing secure communication channel. This is the only work that addresses this issue and this helps in validating the location of drones before establishing a secure channel with the GCS and transfer of secret information. This data in combination with PUF provides a unique and secure drone authentication mechanism for the drones in a surveillance drone network, especially in a border surveillance scenario. This prevents the drones in the other boundary regions from communicating securely with the GCS.
- Drone-to-drone mutual authentication without the intervention of ground control station.
- Attack resiliency even if the drone is captured by storing zero secrets in drone memory.
- A unique session key for every communication session.
- A hierarchical communication system for increasing the coverage as well as security.
- Security against eavesdropping, node tampering, cloning, PUF modeling, physical, masquerade, man in the middle, replay, traceability, privileged insider and session key disclosure attacks and achieve both forward and backward secrecy of the session key.

4   Proposed Methodology

The authentication protocol starts with the registration phase through secure channels. This is followed by the mutual authentication between the master drone and the GCS. When the patrol drone wants to communicate with the master, the master mutually authenticates it without the intervention of the GCS.

i) Registration phase:

In this phase, all the drones will register with the GCS and will be given a unique identity number (ID). The challenge-response pairs (CRPs) of the drone PUFs will also be recorded in the GCS database. The PUF in each patrol drone is configured in such a way that the average inter-chip hamming distance of the responses between the master and patrol drone PUF is within a fixed preset

Table 1. Notations

Notations	Description
IDMD, IDG, IDS, IDR	Master drone, GCS, Patrol drone and redundant drone identity
⊕, ‖	XOR and Concatenation operation
H(), Rot()	Hash and Rotate function
PUFm, PUFp, PUFr	PUF at master, patrol and redundant drones
lm, L	Location data of master and Hash of location data of GCS
Nm, Nm1, Nm2, Ng, Ng1, Ng2, Na, Nb, Np, Nr, Ns, Ns1	Nonces
d1, d, M, g, g1, M′, M1, M2, M4, M3, M5, M6, OK, outm, M7, s1, s2, M8, M9, M10, Z, X	Message parameters
Chs, Chs′, Rs, Rs′, R, Res	PUF challenges and responses
Sk1, Sk2	Session keys

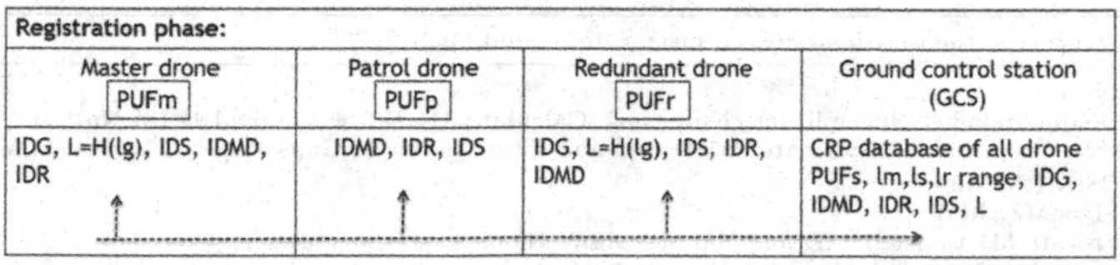

Registration phase:			
Master drone PUFm	Patrol drone PUFp	Redundant drone PUFr	Ground control station (GCS)
IDG, L=H(lg), IDS, IDMD, IDR	IDMD, IDR, IDS	IDG, L=H(lg), IDS, IDR, IDMD	CRP database of all drone PUFs, lm,ls,lr range, IDG, IDMD, IDR, IDS, L

Fig. 3. Registration phase

value or threshold before deployment. The altitude, latitude, longitude and range which denotes the location data of the drones are allocated and registered with the GCS. The registration phase is depicted in Fig. 3 showing the data stored in different entities. The notations used in the protocol are given in Table 1.

ii) Mutual authentication between master drone and GCS:

1) The master drone initiates the communication with the GCS by generating a random number Nm and splits into Nm1 and Nm2, it also fetches the location data lm and L to compute $d1 = Nm1 \oplus lm$, $d = d1 \oplus L \oplus Nm1$, $M = d \oplus Nm2$ and $M2 = H(M)$. M1 is formed by rotating the concatenated message (IDMD and Nm) nibble of M times (rightmost four bits of M), M1 = Rot(IDMD‖Nm, nibble(M)). Finally M1, M, M2 is sent to the GCS.

2) The GCS on receiving this message verifies if $H(M) = M2$ and then reverse rotates M1 to obtain IDMD‖Nm and checks the ID of the master drone and if satisfied, performs the reverse operations as $Nm1‖Nm2 = Nm$, $d = M \oplus Nm2$, $d1 = d \oplus L$, $lm = d1 \oplus Nm1$ and verifies if lm is within the range, if yes, generates the nonce Ng and chooses a random Ch from the GCS database. GCS then computes $L = L1‖L2$, $Ng = Ng1‖Ng2$, $g1 = Ch \oplus Ng2$, $g = g1 \oplus$

L2, $M' = g \oplus Ng1$, $M4 = H(M'\|L)$, $M3 = Rot(IDG \|Ng, nibble(M'))$ and GCS sends back M3, M', M4 to the master drone.

3) The master drone in turn verifies if $H(M' \|L) = M4$, and then reverse rotates M3 to obtain $IDG \|Ng$. It checks the ID of the GCS then computes $L = L1\|L2$, $Ng1\|Ng2 = Ng$, $g = M' \oplus Ng1$, $g1 = g \oplus L2$, $Ch = g1 \oplus Ng2$ and $R = PUFm(Ch)$. Master drone generates a nonce Na and calculates M5 as $H(R\|Na\|IDMD)$ and sends M5 and Na to the GCS.

4) The GCS retrieves the CRP from database and verifies if the hash of $Res\|Na\|IDMD$ is same as the hash received. If yes, then master drone is authenticated and sends back OK= $H(Res)$ to the master drone.

5) The master drone verifies the received hash and generates the session key, Sk1 $= H((R\|Ng2) \oplus H(Nm\|Ng1))$. The GCS also calculates the same session key as, $Sk1 = H((Res\|Ng2) \oplus H(Nm\|Ng1))$.

The GCS calculates the time difference between sending of the challenge and reception of the response. Similarly the master drone also calculates the time difference between the sending of M1 and reception of M4 and that between M1 and M5 and OK message will be sent by GCS only if these time differences fall within a threshold proportional to the height of deployment of the master drone.

Algorithm 1 Mutual authentication between master drone and GCS

```
1:  procedure MASTER
2:      Generates random number Nm, split into Nm1,Nm2, Calculate d1=Nm1⊕ lm, d=d1⊕ L⊕ Nm1 and M=d ⊕ Nm2.
3:      Calculate M2=Hash of M, Concatenate IDMD, Nm and rotate nibble M times to get M1, Send M,M1,M2 to GCS
4:  procedure GCS(M1,M,M2)
5:      if hash of M = M2 then
6:          Reverse rotate M1 to get IDMD and Nm and verify ID of master drone
7:          Calculate d=M⊕ Nm2 and d1=d ⊕ L, lm=d1 ⊕ Nm1
8:          if lm = True then
9:              Generate Ng and choose a random Ch from database
10:             Compute g=g1 ⊕ l2 and M'=g ⊕ Ng1, M4= hash of M' concatenated with L.
11:             Concatenate IDG with Ng and rotate it nibble of M' times to get M3, Send M3,M'and M4 back
12:         else
13:             Authentication failed
14: procedure MASTER(M3,M',M4)
15:     if hash of M' concatenated with L = M4 then
16:         Reverse rotate M3 to get IDG and Ng
17:         Verify IDG split L into L1,L2,Ng into Ng1,Ng2
18:         Compute g=M' ⊕ Ng1, g1=g ⊕ L2, Ch=g1 ⊕ Ng2, also get the PUF response for Ch as Res
19:         Generate nonce Na, hash of concatenation of R,Na and IDMD is M5, Send Na and M5 to GCS
20:     else
21:         Authentication failed
22: procedure GCS(Na, M5)
23:     if hash of concatenation of Res,Na and IDMD = M5 then
24:         Master drone is authentic, hash of response is OK
25:         GCS sends OK to master drone
26:     else
27:         Authentication failed
28: procedure MASTER(OK)
29:
30:     if hash of R = OK then
31:         Generate session key as Sk1=H(R ‖ Ng2) XOR (H(Nm and Ng1))
```

---

iii) Mutual authentication between master and patrol drone:

When a patrolling drone wants to communicate with the master drone, they have to perform mutual authentication.

1) The patrol drone generates a nonce, Ns and sends its identity IDS and Ns to the master drone as Message = $Rot(IDS, nibble(Ns))\|Ns$.

2) The master drone retrieves the nonce Ns and reverse rotates the received Message and checks the ID of the patrol drone. It feeds Ns to its PUF and

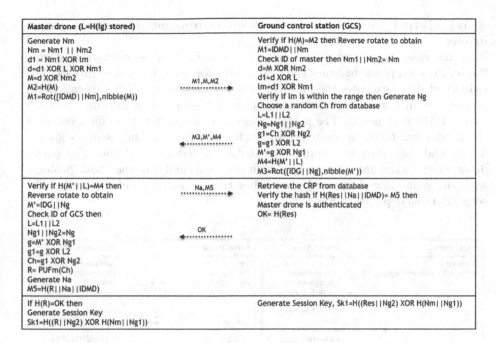

Master drone (L=H(lg) stored)		Ground control station (GCS)
Generate Nm Nm = Nm1 || Nm2 d1 = Nm1 XOR lm d=d1 XOR L XOR Nm1 M=d XOR Nm2 M2=H(M) M1=Rot({IDMD||Nm},nibble(M))	M1,M,M2 ·············▶	Verify if H(M)=M2 then Reverse rotate to obtain M1=IDMD||Nm Check ID of master then Nm1||Nm2= Nm d=M XOR Nm2 d1=d XOR L lm=d1 XOR Nm1 Verify if lm is within the range then Generate Ng Choose a random Ch from database L=L1||L2 Ng=Ng1||Ng2 g1=Ch XOR Ng2 g=g1 XOR L2 M'=g XOR Ng1 M4=H(M'||L) M3=Rot({IDG||Ng},nibble(M'))
	M3,M',M4 ◀··············	
Verify if H(M'||L)=M4 then Reverse rotate to obtain M'=IDG||Ng Check ID of GCS then L=L1||L2 Ng1||Ng2=Ng g=M' XOR Ng1 g1=g XOR L2 Ch=g1 XOR Ng2 R= PUFm(Ch) Generate Na M5=H(R||Na||IDMD)	Na,M5 ·············▶ OK ◀··············	Retrieve the CRP from database Verify the hash if H(Res||Na||IDMD)= M5 then Master drone is authenticated OK= H(Res)
If H(R)=OK then Generate Session Key Sk1=H((R||Ng2) XOR H(Nm||Ng1))		Generate Session Key, Sk1=H((Res||Ng2) XOR H(Nm||Ng1))

Fig. 4. Proposed master-to-GCS and master-to-patrol drone mutual authentication

generates the response Chs and also generates a random number Nb. The master then computes M6 = Chs XOR H(Ns||Nb), M7 = H(M6||IDMD) and outm = M6|| Nb and sends outm, M7 to the patrol drone.

3) The patrol drone on receiving M6 and M7, verifies if Hash of (M6||IDMD) is equal to the received M7 and also verifies the identity IDMD. It then feeds Ns to its PUF to obtain Chs', computes Chs as M6 ⊕ H(Ns||Nb) and checks if Chs and Chs' are within the limits and then obtains Rs = PUFp(Chs). The patrol drone then generates Ns1 and estimates s1 = Rs ⊕ Ns1, s2 = s1 ⊕ IDS, M8 = s2 || Ns1, Z = H(M8 || Chs), M9 = H(Z) and sends M8, M9 to the master drone.

4) The master drone in turn performs X = H(M8 || Chs) and verifies if the hash of X is equal to M9 then determines s2||Ns1 = M8, s1 = s2 ⊕ IDS, Rs = Ns1 ⊕ s1 and Rs' = PUFm(Chs). If Rs and Rs' is within inter-chip hamming threshold then patrol drone is authenticated and sends the message M10 = X to the patrol drone.

5) Patrol drone verifies if Z is equal to X and then generates the session key as Sk2 = H(H(Nb||IDMD) ⊕ (Rs XOR Ns1)). The master also generates the same key for further communication.

The master drone calculates the time difference between the sending of Message and reception of M8. The slave drone also calculates the time difference between Message and M7 and that between Message and M8.

iv) Mutual authentication between redundant drone and patrol drone:

If in any case the master drone fails, the redundant drone configured during the registration phase becomes the new master for the other patrol drones. The redundant drone executes the protocol similar to master-to-GCS authentication protocol as in Fig. 4 and using the generated session key it informs the GCS that it is the new master. The patrol drones after a specified time finds out that the master has failed to communicate within the timeout and assumes master failure and they start to communicate with the redundant drone. The patrol drone executes the mutual authentication protocol similar to the above protocol with the redundant drone and establishes the session key before sending the secret data as depicted in Fig. 5.

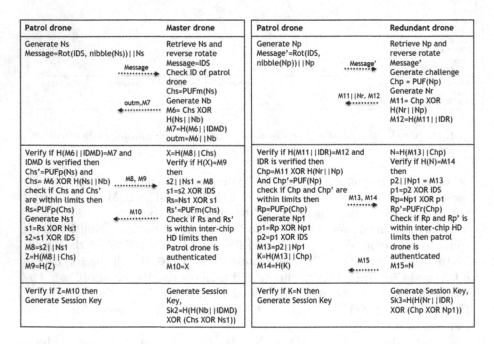

Fig. 5. Master-to-patrol drone and patrol-to-redundant drone mutual authentication protocol

5   Security Analysis

In this section, the formal and the informal security of the proposed protocol are verified. Formal security verification is done using Real-or-Random oracle model (RoR) and ProVerif analysis tool. Informal security verification against various known attacks is also discussed non-mathematically to demonstrate the security of PUFloc.

5.1 Formal Security Analysis Using Real-or-Random Model

In this section, we analyze the security and indistinguishability of the generated session key using the Real-Or-Random model (ROR), originally proposed by Abdalla et al. in [2]. ROR also has been used for security verification in several lightweight user authentication protocols [7,12,14].

ROR Model Description

1. **Participants**: The participants are the master drone, GCS and patrol drone. Their instances are termed as oracles denoted by π_M^{t1} π_G^{t2} and π_P^{t3} at t1, t2 and t3 respectively.
2. **Partnering**: Two instances are partnered if they are mutually authenticated and share a common session identity.
3. **Freshness**: π_M^{t1} and π_G^{t2} are fresh if the session key between them are not disclosed to an adversary.
4. **Adversary**: The ROR model uses the Dolev-Yao threat model in which the adversary, A can eavesdrop, inject, modify and even delete the communicated messages using the following queries:
   - *Execute(π^{t1}, π^{t2})*: This query is modelled as an eavesdropping attack from which the adversary gets to know the messages transmitted between legitimate participants π^{t1}, π^{t2}.
   - *Reveal(π^{t1})*: By executing this query, the current session key between π^{t1} and its partner are revealed to the adversary.
   - *Send(π^{t1} and Msg)*: In this query, the adversary models an active attack by sending a message Msg, to the participant instance π^{t1} and receives a reply message corresponding to the transmitted one.
   - *CorruptDevice(π^{t1})*: This query is modelled as an active attack and the secret data stored in the device are extracted by the adversary.
   - *Test(π^{t1})*: This query is to test the semantic security of the session key. Semantic security of the session key ensures that the session key is secure from adversaries. The adversary, A executes repeated number of Test queries to distinguish between a random key and real key. A initially flips an unbiased coin c and its outcome is known only to A and it is used to decide the result of the Test query. After executing this query, if the session key is fresh, π^{t1} returns SK if c = 1 or if c = 0, it returns a random number.

Before the game ends, A guesses a bit c′ and A wins if c = c′. Let W be the event that A wins the game. The advantage of A in breaking the semantic security of the protocol is defined as $Adv_{PUFloc} = |2P(W)-1|$ [2]. Any protocol is secure if the advantage of breaking the semantic security by A or the advantage of success of A, is very less and is represented as, $Adv_{PUFloc} \le \varepsilon$ where ε is very small and is greater than zero.

Preliminaries

1. Collision resistant one way hash function: Hash collision refers to having same hash for two different inputs. The collision resistance of hash functions is related to the birthday paradox. The number of queries required to find a hash collision is proportional to the square root of the total range of the hash function. As the range of the hash function increases, the advantage (Adv) of finding hash collisions by A decreases. Thus, birthday paradox derivation in terms of hash collision is $Adv_{PUFloc} = q^2/(2 \times 2^{l_H})$ where l_H is the range of the hash function.

2. Physical unclonable function: Similar to the hash collision problem, the responses of different PUFs for the same challenge may show collision. When the same challenge is applied to two PUFs, the hamming distance between their responses should be above a threshold value for collision resistance. The advantage of adversary in winning the game depends on the correct guess of the PUF responses and it is inversely proportional to the CRP space of the PUF.

ROR Security Proof *Theorem:* The advantage of an adversary A in breaking the semantic security of PUFloc protocol 1 in polynomial time is given by:

$$Adv_{P1}^{PUFloc}(t) \leq \frac{(q_h)^2}{2^{l_H}} + \frac{(q_p)^2}{|PUF|} + \frac{q_{send}}{2^{l_g-1}} Adv^{PUF}.$$

where q_h, q_p, q_{send} are the number of hash, PUF and send queries respectively; 2^{l_H}, $|PUF|$, 2^{l_g} and Adv^{PUF} denote the range space of hash function, PUF challenge-response pair (CRP) range space, range space of location data and advantage of PUF respectively.

Proof: There are a sequence of five games denoted by G_0, G_1, G_2, G_3 and G_4 in this proof.

Game G_0: This game is an active attack on the protocol in which A randomly guesses a bit c in the beginning. Then by definition we have,

$$Adv_{P1}^{PUFloc}(t) = |2P(W_0) - 1|. \tag{1}$$

Game G_1: This game simulates an eavesdropping attack by the adversary using $Execute(\pi^{t1}, \pi^{t2})$ query followed by $Test(\pi^{t1})$ query. A intercepts the messages Message1, Message2 and Message3 transmitted between the participants and at the end of the game executes $Test(\pi^{t1})$ query to determine if it is the real session key or a arbitrary one. In PUFloc, SK1 is calculated as H((Res||Ng2) XOR H(Nm||Ng1)) and the adversary needs to correctly guess the nonces and Res which cannot be obtained directly by eavesdropping the messages transmitted. These parameters are transmitted in mathematically transformed states and the CRP database is available only to the GCS hence eavesdropping will not increase the chance of winning the game. So we have,

$$P[W_0] = P[W_1]. \tag{2}$$

Game G_2: In this game the adversary tries to fool the participants by sending modified messages using Send and Hash queries. A can send multiple Send queries and checks for collisions in the hash digest. If the messages are altered, the location information changes and A fails in authenticating. Since each of the transmitted messages are associated with random nonces, location data and long term secrets, the probability of winning the game by hash collisions is negligible. Hence we get,

$$|P[W_1] - P[W_2]| \le \frac{q_h^2}{2(2^{l_H})}. \tag{3}$$

Game G_3: This game is similar to game 2 where the adversary performs Send and PUF queries to find the CRP match. So we can write in the same line as,

$$|P[W_2] - P[W_3]| \le \frac{q_{PUF}^2}{2(|PUF|)}. \tag{4}$$

Game G_4: This game is an active attack using the CorruptDevice query in which A captures the drone and gets the secrets stored. But in our protocol, only IDs and hash of the location data are stored in the drone (L) which cannot help in session key calculation as they are not involved in it; $Sk1 = H((Res\|Ng2)$ XOR $H(Nm\|Ng1))$. However, A tries to guess the location of GCS with a probability of $1/2^{l_g}$. The temporary secrets are protected by PUF as the device is rendered useless on trying to corrupt the device. Moreover if the drone is captured, the location data sent will not match with the GCS database location and hence session key generation fails. Hence the advantage of winning Sk1 is negligible and depends on these two factors.

$$|P[W_3] - P[W_4]| \le \frac{q_{send}}{2^{l_g}} Adv^{PUF}. \tag{5}$$

Now the only possibility of winning the game is to guess the bit c after the Test query, so we get,

$$P[W_4] = \frac{1}{2}. \tag{6}$$

From Eq. (1) and (2),

$$\frac{1}{2} Adv_{P1}^{PUFloc}(t) = |P(W_1) - \frac{1}{2}| \tag{7}$$

Combining Eqs. (3), (4), (5) and applying triangular inequality,
$$|P[W_1] - P[W_4]| \le |P[W_1] - P[W_2]| + |P[W_2] - P[W_3]| + |P[W_3] - P[W_4]|,$$

$$|P[W_1] - P[W_4]| \le \frac{q_h^2}{2(2^{l_H})} + \frac{q_{PUF}^2}{2(|PUF|)} + \frac{q_{send}}{2^{l_g}} Adv^{PUF}$$

Applying (6), $|P[W1] - \frac{1}{2}| \le \dfrac{q_h^2}{2(2^{l_H})} + \dfrac{q_{PUF}^2}{2(|PUF|)} + \dfrac{q_{send}}{2^{l_g}} Adv^{PUF}$

From (7),

$$\frac{1}{2} Adv_{P1}^{PUFloc}(t) \leq \frac{q_h^2}{2(2^{l_H})} + \frac{q_{PUF}^2}{2(|PUF|)} + \frac{q_{send}}{2^{l_g}} Adv^{PUF}$$

Thus we prove, $Adv_{P1}^{PUFloc}(t) \leq \frac{q_h^2}{(2^{l_H})} + \frac{q_{PUF}^2}{(|PUF|)} + \frac{q_{send}}{2^{l_g-1}} Adv^{PUF}$.

5.2 Formal Security Analysis Using ProVerif

ProVerif is an automated security tool used for verifying the security of the mutual authentication protocol based on applied pi calculus. Here, the attacker is modelled using Dolev-Yao model and the tool shows the resistance of the protocol against the various attacks in this threat model. The simulation script contains variables, functions, queries and process definitions. The master drone and GCS processes and the results of protocol 1 and protocol 2 are shown in Fig. 6.

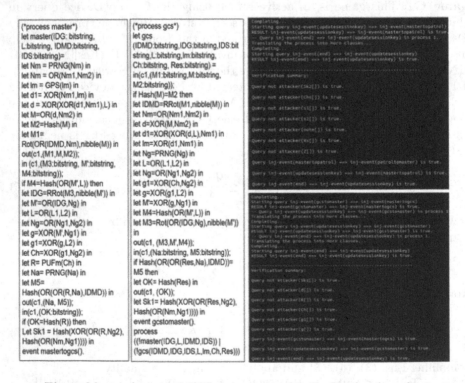

Fig. 6. Master drone and GCS processes used in ProVerif and results

5.3 Informal Security Analysis

In this section we will prove that PUFloc is resistant to several attacks through theoretical and logical analysis of the protocol. The security features are compared with the other existing authentication protocols in the area of drone networks in Table 2 and it is evident that PUFloc outperforms the existing works.

i) Resistant to masquerade attack:

The attacker may try to masquerade the master drone or patrol drone or the GCS. Masquerading the drones is not possible since the drones are equipped with PUFs. The proposed authentication protocol is based on the PUF responses that are unique and have varied inter-chip hamming distances. Hence impersonating the drones is not possible. If the adversary has to masquerade the ground station, it has to know the entire CRP database of all the drones in the network. This will be possible only if the ground station is invaded but we have assumed GCS as a trusted entity.

ii) Resistant to Man-in-the-middle attack:

An adversary can eavesdrop, modify and manipulate the messages communicated. For example, if the adversary modifies the message M6 or outm $=$ M6$\|$Nb that is communicated from master to patrol drone, then message M7 will get modified because M7 is hash of (M6$\|$IDMD). When the patrol drone checks the hash, it will show mismatch. If both M6 and M7 are modified, the hash comparison may match and proceeds to the extraction of challenge. But it will not pass the inter-chip hamming distance criteria since it is a modified one. This is applicable to the next pair of messages also, M8 and M9. Another example between master and GCS is the message M1,M,M2 and if the attacker modifies M1, then IDMD is modified and authentication fails because M1 $=$ Rot(IDMD$\|$Nm,nibble(M)). If M is modified, then M2 will not match because M2 $=$ H(M). If both M1 and M2 are modified then when computing lm, the value may go out of the range of lm that is the drone will shown to be outside the country border as lm $=$ d1 XOR Nm1. If the next message M3, M′, M4 is modified, Ch $=$ g1 XOR Ng2 will result in a different value of Ch and response. Hence, the system is completely resistant to M-i-M attacks.

iii) Resistant to Node tampering and cloning attack:

The system is completely resistant to node tampering and cloning attacks as the drones are equipped with PUFs which when tampered become function-less. If the drone is captured and any attempt to tamper the PUF makes it unusable and since no secrets are stored in the drone memory, attacks are not useful. The PUF in drones will make the drones unclonable and no other PUF can be manufactured with the same CRPs.

iv) Resistant to PUF modeling attack:

The challenge for the drone PUF are enclosed and protected by multiple XOR, concatenation, rotate and hash functions; L $=$ L1$\|$L2, Ng $=$ Ng1$\|$Ng2, g1 $=$ Ch XOR Ng2, g $=$ g1 XOR L2, M′ $=$ g XOR Ng1, M4 $=$ H(M′$\|$L) and M3 $=$ Rot(IDG$\|$Ng, nibble(M′)). Hence the challenge cannot be guessed and also the response is sent as a hash value; M5 $=$ H(R$\|$Na$\|$IDMD). Hence the attacker is completely blind to the CRP space and PUF modeling attacks are rendered impossible.

v) Resistant to physical attacks/attack resiliency:

The master drone stores only IDG, L (hash of ground station location lg), IDS and IDMD. The patrol drone stores IDMD, IDR and IDG and the redundant drone stores IDG, H(lg), IDS, IDR and IDMD. These data are insufficient to calculate the session key and hence even if physically captured, the attackers cannot deduct the session key from these IDs because the Sk consists of random nonces and PUF responses. Moreover, for the master drone authentication, the location data is also verified for device authentication. If captured, the location data changes and authentication fails. In the same way if the patrol drone is captured, the session key cannot be deduced from IDs and due to the unique properties of PUF, any manipulations on the device will lead to PUF failure and authentication failure.

vi) Forward secrecy:

As it can be seen from Fig. 4, even if the session key is captured in a particular session, the session key for the next upcoming session cannot be guessed as it is dependent on non-recurring challenge, response and nonces. If the adversary gets the challenge alone, he will not be able to predict the next session key and hence forward secrecy is achieved.

vii) Backward secrecy:

The session keys in PUFloc depends on hash functions and XOR and concatenation operations on IDMD, fresh nonces, challenges and responses. Hence it is impossible to get the previous session key from the current session key and moreover the previous session key cannot be used for the other sessions, achieving backward secrecy.

viii) Resistant to replay and desynchronization attack:

The communication messages contain fresh nonce and the entities check the freshness of the nonce during any communication. If a message is replayed at a later time, then the nonce will not be fresh and hence the message will be discarded. In the case of master-to-GCS mutual authentication, message M contains lm (location data of master) which has the timestamp information which can be used for verifying the replay and this time is later compared with the time of reception of M5 by the GCS. Similarly it also checks the time difference between the sending of challenge and reception of response from the master. Only if both these values are within a threshold, OK message is sent from the GCS confirming the identity of the master preventing replay of messages. The master also verifies the time difference between sending of request M2 and reception of M4 and that between sending M5 and reception of OK to confirm the identity of the GCS and prevention of replay attack. A similar strategy is undertaken for the master-to-patrol and patrol-to-redundant drone mutual authentication. The time threshold chosen is proportional to twice the height at which the drones are placed strengthening the system security. This method also reduces the communication cost of sending timestamps and also prevents desynchronization attacks.

ix) Resistant to traceability:

The master sends the message $M1 = \text{Rot}(\text{IDMD}\|\text{Nm}, \text{nibble}(M))$ in which the ID of the master is concatenated with nonce and rotated by $M's$ nibble. This leaves the adversary with no information about the sender of the message.

Similarly the GCS also sends $M3 = Rot(IDG\|Ng, nibble(M'))$ after rotating the concatenated GCS ID and nonce with the nibble of M'. This provides perfect untraceability between the master and GCS. The patrol drone sends the message $= Rot(IDS, nibble(Ns))\|Ns$ and master sends $M7 = H(M6\|IDMD)$ which again proves untraceability.

x) Resistant to Privileged-Insider Attack:

If an insider gets to know the credentials during the registration phase, he/she cannot guess the session key because it is dependant on random nonces generated by the drones at the time of mutual authentication as $Sk1 = H((R\|Ng2)$ XOR $H(Nm\|Ng1))$.

xi) Resistant to Session-key disclosure Attack:

To calculate the session key, the attacker should be aware of the internal random challenge, random nonces and the real identities of the entities. According to the above defenses to various attacks, it implies that the proposed protocol is also resistant to session key disclosure attack.

xii) Resistant to master-failure:

The registration phase allots a redundant drone for the system to replace the master drone in cases of low battery issues, master capture or any other undefined failures. If the master drone is captured it cannot be duplicated because of the unclonability of PUFs and the session keys cannot be deduced as the session keys are composed of PUF response values and location data of the master. The master sends a signal to all the patrol drones in fixed and regular intervals of time. If the master fails, after a time out the patrol drones will assume that some problem has occurred and the patrol drone configured as redundant takes over the functions of the master making the system fail-safe. The redundant drone communicates and informs the GCS of the change and continues surveillance.

Table 2. Security comparison with existing works

Attack resiliency	Authors								
	[9]	[20]	[4]	[5]	[29]	[24]	[26]	[23]	PUFloc
Masquerade attack	✓	✓	✓	✓	✓	✓	✓	✓	✓
Man-in-the-middle attack	✓	✓	✓	✓	✓	✓	×	✓	✓
Node tampering and cloning	×	×	✓	✓	✓	×	×	×	✓
PUF modeling attack	–	–	×	×	×	–	×	×	✓
Physical attack	×	✓	✓	✓	✓	✓	✓	✓	✓
Forward secrecy	✓	✓	✓	✓	✓	✓	✓	✓	✓
Backward secrecy	✓	✓	✓	✓	✓	✓	✓	✓	✓
Replay and desynchronization attack	✓	✓	✓	✓	✓	✓	✓	✓	✓
Untraceability	✓	✓	✓	✓	×	×	×	✓	✓
Privileged-insider attack	×	✓	×	×	×	×	×	×	✓
Session-key disclosure attack	✓	✓	✓	×	×	✓	×	×	✓
Master fail-safe operation	–	–	×	–	–	–	–	–	✓

6   FPGA Implementation and Performance Analysis

6.1   FPGA Implementation

The major operations used in the protocol are hash functions, random number generation and physical unclonable functions. We have implemented and simulated these functions using Xilinx Vivado tool mapped to Artix-7 FPGA board with 50 MHz on-board clock. The lightweight and secure hash function selected for this protocol is Spongent hash function [6,19,21]. It has higher security and throughput when compared to other lightweight hash functions. Pseudo random number generators (PRNG) are of two types; chaos and linear feedback shift register (LFSR) based. Chaotic PRNG are more random and unpredictable than LFSR. They produce random numbers for fractional changes in input. Here we have implemented Bernoulli chaos as the random number generator on FPGA that generates 52 bit random number. It is lightweight and of high performance and throughput [11]. Physical unclonable functions are of many types; ring oscillator, arbiter, hybrid, memory, configurable, acoustic, optical and so on. Configurable ring oscillator (CRO) PUFs [18] with more output ports and less hardware requirements is used here for the testing purposes to generate 52 bit response from a 52 bit challenge. The percentage utilization of the slices, registers, LUTs and slice LUTs of these three implementations and the power consumed are shown in Table 3. All the operations consume very less resources and have utilization below 25%.

Table 3. Total on-chip power and percentage utilization of resources for different operations on Artix-7 FPGA

Operation	Total on-chip power
CRO-PUF	12.88 W
Spongent Hash	87 mW
Bernoulli chaos	285mW
PUFloc total power	66.7 W

6.2   Performance Analysis

The performance of PUFloc in terms of computation cost, communication cost and storage cost are evaluated and compared with the state-of-the art works and is shown in Table 4. The computation cost of individual entities is given in Table 4 and let T_p, T_h, T_c, T_x, T_{hmac}, T_{puf} and T_r be the computation time for random number generation, hash, concatenation, XOR, HMAC, PUF, rotation and fuzzy extractor operations respectively. According to the work in [5], the execution time in C for the main operations on Raspberry Pi are 0.253 μs for T_p, 4.63 μs for T_h, 0.4 μs for T_{puf} and 23 μs for T_{hmac} and negligible execution time for T_c, T_x and T_r. The computation time of PUFloc is only slightly higher than [29] and [23] but it offers more security features as depicted in Table 2 when compared to these works.

The communication cost is represented in bits and in our protocol we have used standardised values as given in [5] and [23]. Device ID, random number, hash outputs are represented by 160 bits, PUF responses are 256 bits and ECC manipulations are 320 bits. The total communication cost for protocol1 is 1856 bits and 1312 bits for protocol2 and it is very less compared to other existing works in this domain. This is only slightly higher than [5] and [23] whereas they do not consider location validation, fail-safe operation, insider attacks and session key disclosure attacks. The differences in performance parameters are very negligible when compared to the features and security in PUFloc.

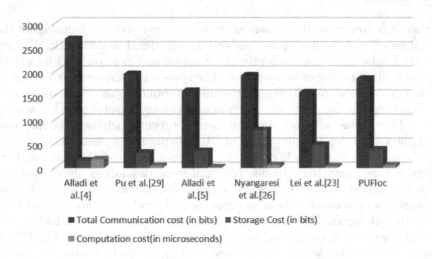

Fig. 7. Performance comparison with existing works

Storing secrets in memory help the attackers to capture the drone and extract secrets from memory. In our protocol, only IDs are stored in memory which cannot reveal the secret session key and any other secret information about the network/system. The total storage cost in PUFloc is 384 bits and it is very less when compared with other existing works. The storage cost of the separate entities are 728 bits (91 bytes) for the master and redundant drone and 384 bits (48 bytes) for the patrol drone. The comparison of communication cost and storage cost of PUFloc with the existing works is shown in Fig. 7. Thus the performance attributes of PUFloc prove that it is a suitable authentication protocol for drone networks in terms of both security and performance.

Table 4. Performance comparison with existing works

Author	Total communication cost	Storage cost at Drone	Total computation cost	Total execution time (µs)
Alladi et al. [4]	2680 bits	ID	$4T_p + 8T_{hmac} + 26T_x$	185
Pu et al. [29]	1952 bits	320 bits	$5T_p + 6T_c + 2T_{hmac} + 2T_{puf}$	48.065
Alladi et al. [5]	1600 bits	352 bits	$2T_p + 3T_h + 11T_c + 8T_x + 2T_{puf}$	15.196
Nyangaresi et al. [26]	1920 bits	786 bits	$13T_h + 6T_{puf}$	62.59
Lei et al. [23]	1568 bits	480 bits	$8T_h + T_{puf}$	37.84
PUFloc protocol1	1856 bits	384 bits	$3T_p + 12T_h + 17T_c + 4T_r + 15T_x + 1T_{puf}$	56.71
PUFloc protocol2	1312 bits	384 bits	$3T_p + 12T_h + 10T_c + 2T_r + 10T_x + 4T_{puf}$	57.919

7 Conclusion

A drone-GCS and drone-drone mutual authentication protocol focusing on the physical security of the drones in a network is considered in this work. We have proposed a lightweight approach using PUF and drone location data for identifying the legitimate drones in a network. The system has a master drone, patrol drones, a ground control station and a redundant drone to ensure fail-safe operation. The drones do not store any secrets in memory and ensures attack resiliency and the drone-drone authentication protocol is executed without the intervention of the GCS using the properties of PUFs deployed on them. The security verification of the protocols is done using ProVerif tool and the mathematical analysis is done using ROR model. Informal security analysis shows that the system is resistant to several possible attacks. Performance is estimated from the computation, communication and storage costs and are compared with the state-of-the-art works. The major operations are implemented on FPGA and the total power consumption is analysed and they also utilize very less FPGA resources. PUFloc outperforms the other existing works in terms of security, attack resiliency, fail-safe operation and provides an efficient and low power drone authentication mechanism for a surveillance UAV network.

References

1. What is Unmanned Aircraft Systems Traffic Management? https://www.faa.gov/uas/research_development/traffic_management/
2. Abdalla, M., Fouque, P.-A., Pointcheval, D.: Password-based authenticated key exchange in the three-party setting. In: Vaudenay, S. (ed.) PKC 2005. LNCS, vol. 3386, pp. 65–84. Springer, Heidelberg (2005). https://doi.org/10.1007/978-3-540-30580-4_6
3. Ali, Z., Chaudhry, S.A., Ramzan, M.S., Al-Turjman, F.: Securing smart city surveillance: a lightweight authentication mechanism for unmanned vehicles. IEEE Access 8, 43711–43724 (2020)

4. Alladi, T., Chamola, V., Kumar, N., et al.: PARTH: a two-stage lightweight mutual authentication protocol for UAV surveillance networks. Comput. Commun. **160**, 81–90 (2020)
5. Alladi, T., Naren, N., Bansal, G., Chamola, V., Guizani, M.: SecAuthUAV: a novel authentication scheme for UAV-base station scenario. IEEE Trans. Veh. Technol. **69**, 15068–15077 (2020)
6. Bogdanov, A., Knezevic, M., Leander, G., Toz, D., Varici, K., Verbauwhede, I.: SPONGENT: the design space of lightweight cryptographic hashing. IEEE Trans. Comput. **62**(10), 2041–2053 (2012)
7. Chang, C.C., Le, H.D.: A provably secure, efficient, and flexible authentication scheme for ad hoc wireless sensor networks. IEEE Trans. Wireless Commun. **15**(1), 357–366 (2015)
8. Chen, C.L., Deng, Y.Y., Weng, W., Chen, C.H., Chiu, Y.J., Wu, C.M.: A traceable and privacy-preserving authentication for UAV communication control system. Electronics **9**(1), 62 (2020)
9. Cho, G., Cho, J., Hyun, S., Kim, H.: SENTINEL: a secure and efficient authentication framework for unmanned aerial vehicles. Appl. Sci. **10**(9), 3149 (2020)
10. Devi, M., Maakar, S.K., Sinwar, D., Jangid, M., Sangwan, P.: Applications of flying ad-hoc network during COVID-19 pandemic. In: IOP Conference Series: Materials Science and Engineering, vol. 1099, p. 012005. IOP Publishing (2021)
11. de la Fraga, L.G., Torres-Pérez, E., Tlelo-Cuautle, E., Mancillas-López, C.: Hardware implementation of pseudo-random number generators based on chaotic maps. Nonlinear Dyn. **90**(3), 1661–1670 (2017). https://doi.org/10.1007/s11071-017-3755-z
12. Gope, P., Das, A.K., Kumar, N., Cheng, Y.: Lightweight and physically secure anonymous mutual authentication protocol for real-time data access in industrial wireless sensor networks. IEEE Trans. Industr. Inf. **15**(9), 4957–4968 (2019)
13. Gope, P., Millwood, O., Saxena, N.: A provably secure authentication scheme for RFID-enabled UAV applications. Comput. Commun. **166**, 19–25 (2021)
14. Gope, P., Sikdar, B.: An efficient privacy-preserving authenticated key agreement scheme for edge-assisted internet of drones. IEEE Trans. Veh. Technol. **69**(11), 13621–13630 (2020)
15. Hassanalian, M., Abdelkefi, A.: Classifications, applications, and design challenges of drones: a review. Prog. Aerosp. Sci. **91**, 99–131 (2017)
16. He, S., Wu, Q., Liu, J., Hu, W., Qin, B., Li, Y.-N.: Secure communications in unmanned aerial vehicle network. In: Liu, J.K., Samarati, P. (eds.) ISPEC 2017. LNCS, vol. 10701, pp. 601–620. Springer, Cham (2017). https://doi.org/10.1007/978-3-319-72359-4_37
17. Hossain, M., Noor, S., Hasan, R.: HSC-IoT: a hardware and software co-verification based authentication scheme for internet of things. In: 2017 5th IEEE International Conference on Mobile Cloud Computing, Services, and Engineering (MobileCloud), pp. 109–116. IEEE (2017)
18. Huang, Z., Wang, Q.: A PUF-based unified identity verification framework for secure IoT hardware via device authentication. World Wide Web **23**(2), 1057–1088 (2020)
19. Jaffal, R., Mohd, B.J., Al-Shayeji, M., et al.: An analysis and evaluation of lightweight hash functions for blockchain-based IoT devices. Cluster Comput. **24**, 1–20 (2021)
20. Jan, S.U., Qayum, F., Khan, H.U.: Design and analysis of lightweight authentication protocol for securing IoD. IEEE Access **9**, 69287–69306 (2021)

21. Jungk, B., Lima, L.R., Hiller, M.: A systematic study of lightweight hash functions on FPGAs. In: 2014 International Conference on ReConFigurable Computing and FPGAs (ReConFig 2014), pp. 1–6. IEEE (2014)
22. Lamothe, D.: U.S. and Britain hacked into feeds from Israeli drones and fighter jets, according to report (2015). https://www.washingtonpost.com/news/checkpoint/wp/2016/01/29/u-s-and-britain-hacked-into-feeds-from-israeli-drones-and-fighter-jets-according-to-report. Accessed 29 Jan 2016
23. Lei, Y., Zeng, L., Li, Y.X., Wang, M.X., Qin, H.: A lightweight authentication protocol for UAV networks based on security and computational resource optimization. IEEE Access **9**, 53769–53785 (2021)
24. Li, S., Zhang, T., Yu, B., He, K.: A provably secure and practical PUF-based end-to-end mutual authentication and key exchange protocol for IoT. IEEE Sens. J. **21**, 5487–5501 (2020)
25. Nikooghadam, M., Amintoosi, H., Islam, S.H., Moghadam, M.F.: A provably secure and lightweight authentication scheme for internet of drones for smart city surveillance. J. Syst. Architect. **115**, 101955 (2021)
26. Nyangaresi, V.O., Petrovic, N.: Efficient PUF based authentication protocol for internet of drones. In: 2021 International Telecommunications Conference (ITC-Egypt), pp. 1–4. IEEE (2021)
27. Pal, V., Acharya, B.S., Shrivastav, S., Saha, S., Joglekar, A., Amrutur, B.: PUF based secure framework for hardware and software security of drones. In: 2020 Asian Hardware Oriented Security and Trust Symposium (AsianHOST), pp. 01–06. IEEE (2020)
28. Porche, I.R.: Cyberwarfare Goes Wireless (2015). https://www.usnews.com/opinion/blogs/world-report/2014/04/04/russia-hacks-a-us-drone-in-crimea-as-cyberwarfare-has-gone-wireless. Accessed 4 April 2014
29. Pu, C., Li, Y.: Lightweight authentication protocol for unmanned aerial vehicles using physical unclonable function and chaotic system. In: 2020 IEEE International Symposium on Local and Metropolitan Area Networks (LANMAN), pp. 1–6. IEEE (2020)
30. Rodrigues, M., Amaro, J., Osório, F.S., Branco Kalinka, R.L.J.C.: Authentication methods for UAV communication. In: 2019 IEEE Symposium on Computers and Communications (ISCC), pp. 1210–1215. IEEE (2019)
31. Semal, B., Markantonakis, K., Akram, R.N.: A certificateless group authenticated key agreement protocol for secure communication in untrusted UAV networks. In: 2018 IEEE/AIAA 37th Digital Avionics Systems Conference (DASC), pp. 1–8. IEEE (2018)
32. Srinivas, J., Das, A.K., Kumar, N., Rodrigues, J.J.: TCALAS: temporal credential-based anonymous lightweight authentication scheme for internet of drones environment. IEEE Trans. Veh. Technol. **68**(7), 6903–6916 (2019)
33. Tanveer, M., Zahid, A.H., Ahmad, M., Baz, A., Alhakami, H.: LAKE-IoD: lightweight authenticated key exchange protocol for the internet of drone environment. IEEE Access **8**, 155645–155659 (2020)
34. Thompson, C.: Drug traffickers are hacking US surveillance drones to get past border patrol (2015). https://www.businessinsider.com/drug-traffickers-are-hacking-us-border-drones-2015-12?IR=T. Accessed 30 Dec 2015
35. Tian, Y., Yuan, J., Song, H.: Efficient privacy-preserving authentication framework for edge-assisted internet of drones. J. Inf. Secur. Appl. **48**, 102354 (2019)
36. Wazid, M., Das, A.K., Kumar, N., Vasilakos, A.V., Rodrigues, J.J.: Design and analysis of secure lightweight remote user authentication and key agreement scheme in internet of drones deployment. IEEE Internet Things J. **6**(2), 3572–3584 (2018)

37. Won, J., Seo, S.H., Bertino, E.: Certificateless cryptographic protocols for efficient drone-based smart city applications. IEEE Access **5**, 3721–3749 (2017)
38. Zhang, Y., He, D., Li, L., Chen, B.: A lightweight authentication and key agreement scheme for internet of drones. Comput. Commun. **154**, 455–464 (2020)

Smart Search over Encrypted Educational Resources in Cloud Storage

Qiang Zhang[1,2], Guihua Duan[3]([✉]), and Shukun Liu[4]

[1] School of Computer Science and Engineering, Hunan University of Science
and Technology, Xiangtan 411201, China
qzhang@csu.edu.cn
[2] Hunan Key Laboratory for Service Computing and Novel Software Technology,
Hunan University of Science and Technology, Xiangtan 411201, China
[3] School of Computer Science and Engineering, Central South University,
Changsha 410083, China
duangh@csu.edu.cn
[4] College of Information Science and Engineering, Hunan Women's University,
Changsha 410004, China
liu_shukun@csu.edu.cn

Abstract. With the development of education, educational big data is
taking shape, and the cloud has a natural advantage of storing big data.
Data is usually stored in the cloud server in the form of ciphertext for
the sake of privacy protection. However, this is against the use of data.
Currently, although the search schemes under ciphertext are primarily
based on keywords, these schemes fail to reflect the actual needs of users
well. Moreover, the quality of educational resources varies. Therefore,
ensuring users' privacy protection while providing high-quality educational resources is challenging. In order to solve this problem, a Smart
Search over Encrypted Educational Resources (SSEER) in cloud storage
was proposed in this paper. The contribution of this paper is mainly
reflected in two aspects: First, SSEER introduces a trusted third party
(TTP) server to obtain a large number of educational resources through
crowdsourcing. Second, the index is updated based on the user's use of
educational resources, through which high-quality educational resources
can be identified, thus increasing the probability for users to access quality resources. As a result, the educational resource graph can screen out
the educational resources related to the user search.

Keywords: Personalized search · Resource graph · Searchable
encryption · Cloud computing · Crowdsourcing

1 Introduction

In order to reduce the storage and management costs of educational data, educational organizations tend to store vast amounts of educational resources in
the cloud. However, the cloud server is an honest but curious entity that may

G. Wang et al. (Eds.): UbiSec 2021, CCIS 1557, pp. 90–101, 2022.
https://doi.org/10.1007/978-981-19-0468-4_7

cherish the value of educational resources and the use of resources by users. This threatens the security of data and the privacy of users. Therefore, data owners tend to encrypt the data and then outsource the ciphertext to the cloud server [16,24,26]. However, the availability of encrypted data is degraded. In order to solve this problem, researchers have proposed many searchable encryption schemes [6,13,18].

Knowledge graph brings search into a new era. Knowledge graph shows the relationship between entities. Through knowledge graph, users can find the most desired information, make search deeper and broader, and greatly improve the user's search experience. There are also various links between educational resources stored on cloud servers. How to tap the relationship between resources, and then use the relationship between resources to provide users with smart search results, so that users can not only get high-quality educational resources related to current learning, but also recommend the educational resources most needed by users is a very challenging problem.

Educational resources require a high degree of coverage. The amount of educational resources is very large. How to build a massive educational resource library is a huge challenge, and crowdsourcing can make full use of the power of the general public [5] to build an educational resource library at a lower cost. However, the quality of educational resources provided by contributors is uneven. How to select quality resources among vast educational resources to improve the user's search experience is a topic worthy of study. In order to achieve this goal, we propose SSEER scheme, compare literature [2,9,14,20,25], the main contributions of the paper are as follows:

1) By introducing a TTP server, it is possible to collect resources contributed by the masses of contributors, thereby constructing educational resource big data, and ensuring data security and searchability by encrypting resources and indexes.
2) Through the use of educational resources, the user sends an index corresponding to the boutique resource to the TTP. The TTP updates the index according to the usage of the user and sends it to the cloud server, Thus, through the power of the general public, the fine resources are selected from the vast resources which increased the probability that users will receive quality educational resources.

2   Related Work

2.1   Crowdsourcing

Ever since Jeff Howe proposed the concept of crowdsourcing [12] in 2006, it has attracted the attention of many scholars. Crowdsourcing is the outsourcing of a company's task to an unspecified group of people, rather than assigning it to designated employees [11]. Crowdsourcing is different from the company's employment model. For example, through the crowdsourcing platform Amazon Mechanical Turk (AMT), a task can be completed by a large number of Internet workers by paying a small amount of compensation, and Internet workers can choose the platform to issue tasks according to their own circumstances and get paid for completing these tasks [5].

2.2 Searchable Encryption

For data privacy considerations, data is usually encrypted before the encrypted data is uploaded to the cloud server. However, the availability of encrypted data deteriorates. In order to solve the search problem in the ciphertext environment, Song [18] put forward the first symmetric searchable encryption scheme. Subsequently, researchers continue to promote the development of searchable encryption. For example, multi-keyword searchable encryption schemes [4,7]. Boneh [8] et al. first proposed a searchable encryption scheme based on public key cryptography. Subsequently, in order to make searchable encryption schemes practical, researchers [10,19] proposed schemes that support various functions. However, the above schemes ignore the user's personalized search needs. In response to this problem, the literature [9] has integrated the user's interest into the user's query keywords through the construction of the user model, and realized the personalized search in the ciphertext environment purpose.

3 Problem Formulation

3.1 System Model

The system model is shown in Fig. 1. The system consists of four types of entities: resource contributors, users, the trusted third-party (TTP) server, and the cloud server.

Contributors: Contributors made up of the general public provide their own resources to TTP servers. To build an educational resource pool and form big data on educational resources.

Trusted Third-Party Server (TTP): TTP is responsible for generating keys and is responsible for the construction and encryption of educational resource indexes. It also encrypts educational resources in order to ensure data security. TTP is also responsible for collecting the probability distribution of influential users using related resources after using a certain high-quality resource, constructing a resource graph according to the probability distribution between resources, and finally uploading the resource graph to the cloud server.

Cloud Server: The cloud server is responsible for storing ciphertext, encrypted indexes, and resource graph, and is responsible for the user's query processing.

User: On the user side, the user inputs the corresponding query keyword according to his own needs, and the query keyword is converted after the interest model, and generates a query matrix with user interest information. In turn, the user can obtain query results related to both the user query and the user interest.

The query matrix is encrypted, along with the parameters K and K_g sent to the cloud server to complete the query process. In the scheme, the user also plays an important role, and the user sends the index I_A corresponding to the good resource to the TTP server according to the query result returned by the cloud server and according to the situation in which the educational resource is used by the user. The TTP server updates the index based on the index I_A and sends the updated index I' to the cloud server after a certain time.

A summary of notations used in the scheme is presented in Table 1.

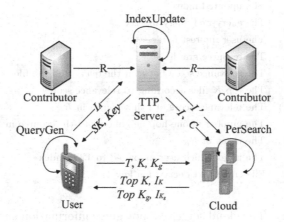

Fig. 1. System model.

3.2 Design Goals

In order to ensure that our scheme works well under the security model, our scheme must meet two requirements: smart search and privacy protection based on educational resource graph.

- **Index update:** The quality of educational resources contributed by the general public is mixed. In order to enable users to obtain quality educational resources, SSEER can use the power of the general public to update the index by using the user's usage, thus filtering out high-quality resources.
- **Smart search:** Smart search based on educational resource graph means that the cloud server will not only return Top K search results based on the user's search, but also return Top K_g smart search resource list based on Top K search results and educational resource graph which improve the user's search experience.
- **Data privacy:** Cloud servers are honest but curious entities that can jeopardize the value of data and therefore need to encrypt data to ensure data privacy. Symmetric encryption technology has the characteristics of small computational overhead and high security [17]. In this paper, we use symmetric encryption to encrypt data before uploading it to the cloud server.

Table 1. Summary of notations

Notation	Description
F	The plaintext file set, $F = (F_1, F_2, ..., F_m)$
C	The encrypted file set, $C = (C_1, C_2, ..., C_m)$
q	The query matrix of a user
p	The plain index for F
T	The trapdoor of the query of a user
I	The encrypted index p
I'	The updated index
Q	The encrypted query matrix q
U	The user interest model
RG	The resource graph
$R(i,:)$	The relevance score between the query and the file
R_K	The top-K files according to relevance scores
$R_K(i,:)$	The relevance score of i-th resource in R_K
h_i	The number of one-hop neighbors of i-th resource in R_K
I_K	The index of R_K
I_A	The index which user uploaded to TTP index
Key	File ciphertext decryption key

- **Index privacy:** The cloud server cannot guess information such as keywords in the index.
- **The non-linkability of the search trapdoor:** the cloud server will get the user's search trapdoor for the query process. We need to ensure that for the same query, different search trapdoors are generated, so that the cloud server cannot guess the relationship between multiple queries based on the search trapdoor.

3.3   Related Concepts

Google Knowledge Graph (GKG): In 2012, Google proposed the concept of knowledge graph, whose main purpose is to convert keyword-based search to semantic-based search. KG can be used to better query complex associations and understand user intent from the semantic level, thus improving user search quality.

Influential Users: What are influential users, there is no consensus yet. Some literatures refers to influential users as opinion leaders and innovators [3]. Some literatures classify influential users based on their content and permissions [22]. Influential user predictions are not the focus of this paper. Interested readers can refer to the relevant literature [1, 15, 23].

User Model: The user model can well represent the user's interest preferences. This paper builds the user model based on the user's search history, as described in the literature [9]. According to the user's query keyword and user interest model, the user can obtain personalized search results and improve the user's search satisfaction.

A user interest model of user i is denoted by U_i:

$$U_i = (k_{i,1} : m_{i,1}, k_{i,2} : m_{i,2}, ..., k_{i,n} : m_{i,n}) \tag{1}$$

Let the value represent the user interest model. We obtain a user interest model as follows:

$$U_i = (m_{i,1}, m_{i,2}, ..., m_{i,n}) \tag{2}$$

When a user submits a query, the SSEER scheme uses the user's query to update the user interest model. For example, when the user's query matrix $q = (1, 1, 0, 1, 0, 1, 1, 0, 0)$, the user interest model $U_i = (4, 0, 2, 5, 0, 0, 3, 2, 0)$. Then, the updated user interest model is $U_i = (5, 1, 2, 6, 0, 1, 4, 2, 0)$.

Relevance Score: The relevance score reflects the degree of relevant between the user query and the file index. The higher the relevance score, the more the file needs to be returned to the user first.

Secure Inner Product [21,27]: The algorithm computes the inner product of the two encrypted matrices $E(p)$ and $E(q)$ without knowing the actual values of p and q. We can obtain $E(p) \cdot E(q) = p \cdot q$.

3.4 The Example of Resource Graph

The resource graph shows the interrelationships between resources. For ease of understanding, we present an example of a resource graph, as shown in Fig. 2: According to the resource graph, users can get more satisfactory search results.

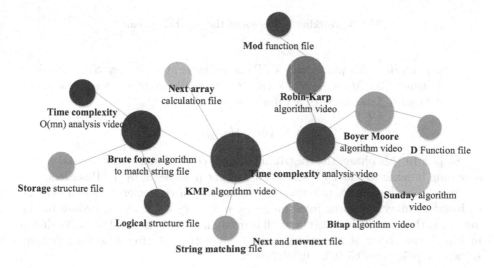

Fig. 2. The example of resource graph

4 Construction of the Scheme

The amount of educational resources obtained through crowdsourcing is huge, and the quality is mixed. How to make users get the high-quality resources they need when searching, thus improving the user's search experience is a question worth considering. To address this problem, we have proposed a smart search scheme in the encryption education resource, through the use of educational resources by the user, and according to the feedback result of the user, updates the index of the educational resource, thereby improving the exposure rate of the high-quality resource. According to the resource graph, the user can not only obtain the search result of Top K, but also obtain the Top K_g result related to the Top K result (Fig. 3).

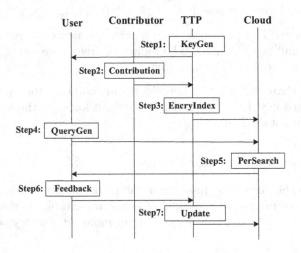

Fig. 3. Working processes of the SSEER scheme

Step 1: During this phase, the TTP server generates the key SK according to Eq. 3, where M_1, M_2 is $(n + t) \times (n + t)$ reversible matrices. s is a matrix of $1 \times (n + t)$ with elements with a value of 0 or 1.

$$SK = \{M_1, M_2, s\}. \tag{3}$$

Step 2: In this phase, the contributors send educational resources and corresponding indexes to the TTP server for further processing by TTP servers.

Step 3: In this phase, to enhance the security of the scheme, it is necessary to insert dummy keywords into the index $p(j,:)$ $(j \in [1, m])$ according to the matrix s, the sum of the weights of all dummy keywords is equal to 0. As shown in Fig. 4, the index of file $p(1,:) = (0.5, 0.3, 0.2)$, and after inserting dummy keywords, $p(1,:) = (0.5, 0.3, -0.3, 0.3, 0.2)$.

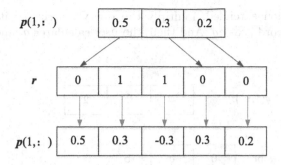

$p(1,:)$ | 0.5 | 0.3 | 0.2

r | 0 | 1 | 1 | 0 | 0

$p(1,:)$ | 0.5 | 0.3 | -0.3 | 0.3 | 0.2

Fig. 4. Insert dummy keywords into the file index

After dummy keywords are inserted into the index, the dimension expansion process is completed. Next, according to Eq. 4, the p' and p'' can be obtained.

$$p'(j,g) = p''(j,g) = p(j,g), \ if \ s(g) = 0, (g \in [1, n+t])$$
$$p'(j,g) + p''(j,g) = p(j,g), \ if \ s(g) = 1. (g \in [1, n+t]) \tag{4}$$

Subsequently, the TTP will obtain the encrypted index I according to $I = [p' * M_1^T, p'' * M_2^T]$ and upload it to the cloud server.

Finally, the cloud server saves the index I from the TTP server and the encrypted file C.

Step 4: Query conversion is performed on the client side, as described in Algorithm 1, when $q[j] \times U[j] > 0$, $q[j] = U[j]$; otherwise the value of $q[j]$ is unchanged. For example, when $q = (1, 0, 1, 0, 1, 0, 0, 1, 1)$, $U = (6.5, 2, 3, 1, 4, 0, 5, 3, 0)$, after the query conversion, $q = (6.5, 0, 3, 0, 4, 0, 0, 3, 1)$.

Algorithm 1 : Query conversion

Require: q, U.
Ensure: q.
 1: **for** $j = 1 : n$ **do**
 2:     **if** $(q[j] \times U[j] > 0)$ **then**
 3:         $q[j] = U[j]$;
 4:     **else**
 5:         $q[j] = q[j]$;
 6:     **end if**
 7: **end for**
 8: **return** q

Query Encryption: The length of the dictionary is longer due to the insertion of dummy keywords in the dictionary. In q, the weights of all dummy keywords is set to choose the same random number b $(b \neq 0)$ according to the matrix r, as shown in Fig. 5, since only $r(1,2) = r(1,3) = 1$, so after dimension expansion, $q(1,2) = q(1,3) = b$.

After dimension extended, multiply the query matrix q with the random number a and record it as aq. And then, the user calculates q' and q'' according to Eq. 5.

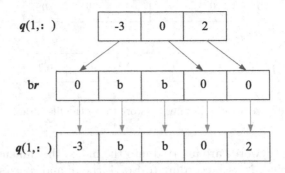

Fig. 5. Insert dummy keywords into the query matrix

$$q'(1,g) = q''(1,g) = aq(1,g), \; if \; s(g) = 1,$$
$$q'(1,g) + q''(1,g) = aq(1,g), \; if \; s(g) = 0. \tag{5}$$

The user calculate $T = [aq' * M_1^{-1}, aq'' * M_2^{-1}]$. Finally, the user uploads T and the parameter KK_g to the cloud server to obtain query results.

Step 5: When the user uploads T and the parameter K to the cloud server, the cloud server uses the security inner product to calculate the correlation score of each file index with T according to the Eq. 6, get a list of results for Top K.

$$R(i,:) = dot(I(i,:),T)$$
$$= I(i,:) \cdot T \tag{6}$$
$$= ap(i,:) \cdot q$$

Finally, the cloud server returns the top K ciphertext with the highest relevance score and the corresponding index I_K to the user, and according to the Algorithm 2, the Top K_g ciphertext obtained by the resource graph and the corresponding index I_{K_g} are returned to the user.

In Algorithm 2, $P_{i \to j}$ is probability of the i-th resource to the j-th one-hop resource t in Top K.

After the user obtains the K ciphertexts, he only needs to use the file decryption key key for decryption to obtain corresponding plaintext information, thereby obtaining smart search results.

Algorithm 2 : Top K_g Result List Acquisition

Require: RG; R_K.
Ensure: R_{K_g}.
 1: **for** $j = 1 : K$ **do**
 2:    **for** $j = 1 : h_i$ **do**
 3:       $S(i, t) = R_k(i, :) \times P_{i \to j}$;
 4:    **end for**
 5: **end for**
 6: **if** There existence resource t is a one-hop neighbor of multiple resources in R_K **then**
 7:    Take the maximum value of $S(i, t)$ as the score of resource t;
 8: **end if**
 9: Sort resource scores S(:,t);
10: Record the top K_g resources with the highest score as Top K_g;
11: **return** Top K_g;I_{K_g}.

Step 6: After obtaining the ciphertext, the user only needs to use the file decryption Key to decrypt, and then obtain the corresponding plaintext information. In order to select excellent resources from a large number of resources, SSEER allows the user to feedback the usage, and it will evaluate the acquired resources which the user used. The user can send the encrypted index I_A corresponding to the good resource he thinks to the TTP server.

Step 7: After the TTP obtains the encrypted index I_A of the recommended of the user, it will multiply the keyword weight of the plaintext index of the corresponding file by a factor, such as multiplying by 1.01, thereby increasing the corresponding keywords weight in the file. After a period of feedback, TTP encrypts the index using the EncryIndex algorithm and uploads it to the cloud server, which completes the index update process. This will further achieve the refinement of basic education resources to fine one.

5   Conclusion

This paper constructs large data of educational resources by crowdsourcing, and solves the problem of high coverage of educational resources. According to the user's use of educational resources, the index is updated to increase the probability of acquiring high-quality resources, so as to achieve the purpose of screening out high-quality resources from mass resources.

However, the theme of influential users is not fully taken into account in the construction of resource graph in this paper. The next research work can build resource graph under the consideration of influential user themes in order to better reflect the relationship between resources.

Acknowledgments. This work is supported in part by the National Natural Science Foundation of China under Grants 61632009 & 61472451, in part by the Guangdong Provincial Natural Science Foundation under Grant 2017A030308006, in part by Scientific Research Fund of Hunan Provincial Education Department under Grants 19B208

& 20C0809 & 21A0599, in part by Project of Hunan Social Science Achievement Appraisal Committee in 2020 under Grant XSP20YBZ043, and High-Level Talents Program of Higher Education in Guangdong Province under Grant 2016ZJ01.

References

1. Bouguessa, M., Romdhane, L.B.: Identifying authorities in online communities. ACM Trans. Intell. Syst. Technol. (TIST) **6**(3), 30 (2015)
2. Cao, N., Wang, C., Li, M., Ren, K., Lou, W.: Privacy-preserving multi-keyword ranked search over encrypted cloud data. IEEE Trans. Parallel Distrib. Syst. **25**(1), 222–233 (2013)
3. Chai, W., Xu, W., Zuo, M., Wen, X.: ACQR: a novel framework to identify and predict influential users in micro-blogging. In: PACIS, p. 20 (2013)
4. Chang, Y.C., Mitzenmacher, M.: Privacy preserving keyword searches on remote encrypted data. In: International Conference on Applied Cryptography and Network Security, pp. 442–455 (2005)
5. Chittilappilly, A.I., Chen, L., Amer-Yahia, S.: A survey of general-purpose crowdsourcing techniques. IEEE Trans. Knowl. Data Eng. **28**(9), 2246–2266 (2016)
6. Cui, B., Liu, Z., Wang, L.: Key-aggregate searchable encryption (KASE) for group data sharing via cloud storage. IEEE Trans. Comput. **65**(8), 2374–2385 (2016)
7. Curtmola, R., Garay, J., Kamara, S., Ostrovsky, R.: Searchable symmetric encryption: improved definitions and efficient constructions. J. Comput. Secur. **19**(5), 895–934 (2011)
8. Dan, B., Crescenzo, G.D., Ostrovsky, R., Persiano, G.: Public key encryption with keyword search. In: International Conference on the Theory and Applications of Cryptographic Techniques, pp. 506–522 (2004)
9. Fu, Z., Ren, K., Shu, J., Sun, X., Huang, F.: Enabling personalized search over encrypted outsourced data with efficiency improvement. IEEE Trans. Parallel Distrib. Syst. **27**(9), 2546–2559 (2016)
10. Golle, P., Staddon, J., Waters, B.: Secure conjunctive keyword search over encrypted data. In: Jakobsson, M., Yung, M., Zhou, J. (eds.) ACNS 2004. LNCS, vol. 3089, pp. 31–45. Springer, Heidelberg (2004). https://doi.org/10.1007/978-3-540-24852-1_3
11. Howe, J.: Crowdsourcing: A definition (2006)
12. Howe, J.: The rise of crowdsourcing. Wired Mag. **14**(6), 1–4 (2006)
13. Huang, Q., Li, H.: An efficient public-key searchable encryption scheme secure against inside keyword guessing attacks. Inf. Sci. **403**, 1–14 (2017). 403C404
14. Li, H., Liu, D., Dai, Y., Luan, T.H., Yu, S.: Personalized search over encrypted data with efficient and secure updates in mobile clouds. IEEE Trans. Emerg. Top. Comput. **6**(1), 97–109 (2018)
15. Li, J., Peng, W., Li, T., Sun, T., Li, Q., Xu, J.: Social network user influence sense-making and dynamics prediction. Expert Syst. Appl. **41**(11), 5115–5124 (2014)
16. Liu, Q., Tan, C.C., Wu, J., Wang, G.: Towards differential query services in cost-efficient clouds. IEEE Trans. Parallel Distrib. Syst. **25**(6), 1648–1658 (2014)
17. Singh, S.P., Maini, R.: Comparison of data encryption algorithms. Int. J. Comput. Sci. Commun. **2**(1), 125–127 (2011)
18. Song, D.X., Wagner, D., Perrig, A.: Practical techniques for searches on encrypted data. In: 2000 IEEE Symposium on Security and Privacy, S&P 2000. Proceedings, p. 0044 (2002)

19. Wang, C., Cao, N., Li, J., Ren, K., Lou, W.: Secure ranked keyword search over encrypted cloud data. In: 2010 IEEE 30th International Conference on Distributed Computing Systems, pp. 253–262. IEEE (2010)
20. Wang, Q., He, M., Du, M., Chow, S.S., Lai, R.W., Zou, Q.: Searchable encryption over feature-rich data. IEEE Trans. Dependable Secure Comput. **15**(3), 496–510 (2018)
21. Wong, W.K., Cheung, D.W., Kao, B., Mamoulis, N.: Secure KNN computation on encrypted databases. In: ACM SIGMOD International Conference on Management of Data, pp. 139–152 (2009)
22. Xiao, F., Noro, T., Tokuda, T.: Finding news-topic oriented influential twitter users based on topic related hashtag community detection. J. Web Eng. **13**(5&6), 405–429 (2014)
23. Yin, Z., Zhang, Y.: Measuring pair-wise social influence in microblog. In: 2012 International Conference on Privacy, Security, Risk and Trust and 2012 International Conference on Social Computing, pp. 502–507. IEEE (2012)
24. Zhang, Q., Liu, Q., Wang, G.: A privacy-preserving hybrid cooperative searching scheme over outsourced cloud data. In: International Conference on Security, Privacy and Anonymity in Computation, Communication and Storage, pp. 265–278 (2016)
25. Zhang, Q., Liu, Q., Wang, G.: PRMS: a personalized mobile search over encrypted outsourced data. IEEE Access **6**, 31541–31552 (2018)
26. Zhang, Q., Wang, G., Tang, W., Alinani, K., Liu, Q., Li, X.: Efficient personalized search over encrypted data for mobile edge-assisted cloud storage. Comput. Commun. **176**, 81–90 (2021)
27. Zhang, S., Choo, K.K.R., Liu, Q., Wang, G.: Enhancing privacy through uniform grid and caching in location-based services. Futur. Gener. Comput. Syst. **86**, 881–892 (2018)

SDGen: A Scalable, Reproducible and Flexible Approach to Generate Real World Cyber Security Datasets

Abigail M. Y. Koay[1]([⊠]), Miao Xie[2], Ryan K. L. Ko[1], Charles Sterner[2], Taejun Choi[1], and Naipeng Dong[1]

[1] University of Queensland, Brisbane, QLD 4067, Australia
{a.koay,ryan.ko,taejun.choi,n.dong}@uq.edu.au
[2] Australian Academic Research Network, Chatswood, NSW 1515, Australia
{miao.xie,charles.sterner}@aarnet.edu.au

Abstract. Real world cyber security datasets are essential for developing and evaluating new techniques to counter cyber attacks. Ideally, these datasets should represent modern network infrastructures with up-to-date cyber attacks. However, existing datasets commonly used by researchers are either synthetic, unscalable or easily outdated due to the dynamic network infrastructure and evolving nature of cyber attacks. In this paper, we introduce a security dataset generator (SDGen) which focuses on a scalable, reproducible and flexible approach to generate real world datasets for detection and response against cyber attacks. We implement SDGen within a virtual environment using DetectionLab, ELK (Elasticsearch, Logstash, Kibana) stack with Beats and AttackIQ (a security control validation platform). This implementation in fact provides a proof-of-concept (POC) of SDGen to demonstrate the dataset generation of an organisation being compromised by several types of Ransomware. We showcase that our proposed dataset generator, SDGen, provides scalability, reproducibility and flexibility in generating cyber security datasets by modifying the configurations in DetectionLab, VagrantFiles and launching different types of attacks in AttackIQ.

Keywords: Dataset generation · MITRE ATT&CK framework · Application security

1 Introduction

Since the 1990s, public cyber security datasets have helped researchers develop and evaluate approaches for detecting and countering cyber attacks. In recent years, and at the time of writing, cyber security research has been increasingly data-driven. This consequently increases the demand for representative cyber security datasets [27]. One of the earlier work in this area saw datasets being generated in simulated network environment with background traffic and synthetic attacks [9,12]. Despite a relatively large interest from the machine learning and cyber security communities, these datasets were usually criticized for

G. Wang et al. (Eds.): UbiSec 2021, CCIS 1557, pp. 102–115, 2022.
https://doi.org/10.1007/978-981-19-0468-4_8

their unrealistic (and unreproducible) scenarios, duplicate records and out-of-date attacks.

Newer datasets tried to address the problems by using realistic testbeds and newer attacks, however, they are unscalable. Setting up a real testbed can be costly, hence researchers often employ a scaled down version of the real systems for dataset generations. Also, most datasets used in cyber security research are not made public to the community due to privacy issues [27]. The inability of being reproducible prevents replication of results and development of new innovations based on the datasets. On the other hand, the few publicly available datasets are only specific to a certain set of attack scenarios and do not come with any flexibility to include other types of attacks [20,22]. These limitations hinder researchers efforts to produce accurate analysis and develop innovative cyber security tools.

These limitations are mainly caused by the lack of a dedicated approach for generating high quality datasets that are scalable, reproducible and contain up-to-date cyber attacks. Researchers often use data collection tools that can only accommodate a single type of data such as network traffic or system logs. For example, at the time of writing and to our best knowledge, we have not observed the existence of public datasets with new attacks that are based on the increasingly popular MITRE ATT&CK Framework [25]. The framework consists of tactics, techniques and procedures that model the attack pathways of modern day cyber-attacks commonly used by threat hunters and cyber defenders.

To address the aforementioned limitations, there is a need to have standardised guidelines to facilitate high-quality dataset generation. In this paper, we propose a framework that integrates multi-source data collectors, attack simulators and an automated network environment builder that are scalable, reproducible and flexible. Specifically, we demonstrate the feasibility of our proposed framework using the Elasticsearch, Logstash and Kibana (ELK) stack with Beats, DetectionLab and AttackIQ platforms in generating datasets containing popular ransomware attacks.

The paper provides the following contributions.

- A dataset generation framework that is scalable, reproducible and flexible.
- A proof-of-concept of the proposed framework that generates and collects realistic data from multiple sources including not only network and system logs but also application logs with up-to-date attacks that are in sync with the MITRE ATT&CK Framework.

2   Existing Dataset Generation

A cyber security dataset is a collection of network, system or application data mostly in the form of time series or flow records. Researchers have proposed several criteria for generating high quality datasets such as wide attack diversity, complete labeled dataset and high data heterogeneity [2,11,21]. These criteria are important to ensure the research community are able to carry effective development and evaluation of cyber security tools.

Most datasets are compiled from real data, synthetic data or a mixture of both. For example, UNSW-NB15 [19] dataset was generated using a synthetic network environment with attack and normal traffic generator tool. It contains more than two millions records collected across a 16 h simulation period. The ISCX/CIC datasets [22,23] are generated using a controlled physical testbed environment with real devices and traffic generators to generate desired data based on customised traffic profiles. Unlike the prior datasets, the KYOTO dataset [24] contains real network traffic data collected from a diverse sets of distributed honeypots. It consists of more than 93 millions records of normal, attack and unknown sessions across three years. A list of other cyber security datasets can be found in a survey by Ring et al. [20].

A common flaw of existing datasets is the inability to evaluate scalability. Scalability is an important component in cyber security tools to handle different volumes of data. At the time of writing, researchers either rely of multiple datasets of different data volume and attack variety or splitting a single large dataset into different sizes manually to evaluate scalability of their proposed tools [14,17].

3   SDGen

SDGen is a cyber security dataset generation framework for generating realistic datasets that are scalable, reproducible, and flexible. SDGen is intended to allow researchers to generate cyber security datasets in a structured but flexible way. Dataset generation exercise can be scaled up or down to represent various network sizes or reproduced to include other types of cyber attacks in the MITRE ATT&CK Framework. Also, the testbed environment are flexible in accommodating various types of devices. In essence, SDGen integrates three key technologies:

A: ELK Stack with Beats. The ELK stack originally comprises of three main open-source engines; Elasticsearch, Logstash and Kibana. Recently, a fourth element, called Beats, is added to the stack. These four components (Elasticsearch, Logstash, Kibana and Beats) provide data gathering, pipeline, data search, and visualization of the data and processed result as shown in Fig. 1. In SDGen, ELK stack is used to compile data collected by Beats, parse data into selected features and label data according to information provided by the AttackIQ platform.

Elasticsearch: *Elasticsearch* is a distributed and analytics search engine for a variety of different types of data including unstructured data [4]. The engine provides near real-time big data search capability and high relevance of search results from various factors.

Logstash: As introduced in [6], *Logstash* is a server-side data processing pipeline. The delivered data from *Beats* are ingested in this pipeline component. Using its library of filters, it is able to ingest data from various types of data sources regardless of format or complexity. Using the filters, this software component could output a structured data set to *Elasticsearch* or desired destinations.

Kibana: Using *Kibana*, we were able to monitor the generated attack data via querying to *Elasticsearch*. As [5] introduces it as a window of ELK stack, the compiled data could be shown on monitoring screens via the visualization of *Kibana*. Its provision of user interactions for ELK stack covers from navigating data to intuitively tracking them.

Beats: *Beats* is data shippers [3]. Each Beats has its own purpose, such as file activities logs or windows logs, for gathering data. After collecting data, it documents them with metadata to ship them to the next pipelined process, which is normally *Logstash*.

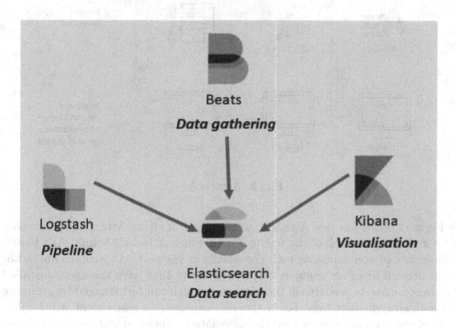

Fig. 1. ELK stack with Beats Process Flow

B: AttackIQ. AttackIQ is a security optimisation platform which is originally designed to deliver a continuous validation of an enterprise's security controls. While a bunch of cyber attacks are simulated via AttackIQ agents against the victim (testing) networks and hosts, it collects the responses from various security programs such as firewalls, data loss prevention (DLP), intrusion detection systems (IDS), endpoint detection and response (EDR), network detection and response (NDR), SIEM and etc. In particular, due to the integration with the MITRE ATT&CK framework, AttackIQ almost can simulate any adversary tactics, techniques and procedures (TTPs) (approx. 3000 attack scenarios in the latest version) and, by reshuffling a bit, can constitute other more complex intrusion campaigns or advanced persistent threats (APTs) such as ransomware [1]. A report will be generated once an assessment is completed, which details how the attacks are prevented and/or detected and indicates the overall security posture and incident response capabilities.

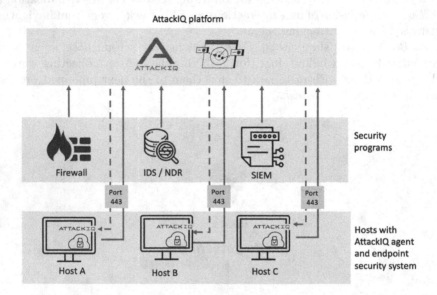

Fig. 2. AttackIQ

Figure 2 illustrates how AttackIQ works. First of all, an AttackIQ agent needs to be installed into each of the testing hosts. Since AttackIQ is fully API based, the agents can communicate with the platform via port 443 without any additional firewall or proxy configurations. The hosts that have the agent installed then become assets available in the platform, which can be managed by grouping and assigning distinct tags. For a specific use case, an assessment will be created, where it requires setting up the associated assets and test scenarios. If the assessment is created from a template, there will be some built in test scenarios loaded; otherwise the test scenarios can be selected from the library sorted in line with the MITRE ATT&CK framework. Furthermore, in some test scenarios, it allows the user to configure the attack strategy or even replace the built-in malicious payload, making the simulated attack more customised and targeted. Normally, an assessment can be kicked off straight away once everything is set up but, if it is simulating a persistent penetration, there is an option to schedule the assessment to be run at different times. Finally, the platform will collect the responses from the deployed security programs, and compile a report indicating whether each of the test scenarios has been passed (prevented/detected) or not. The detailed execution logs are also collected from the agent, by which it can find out the root causes of failing in a test scenario.

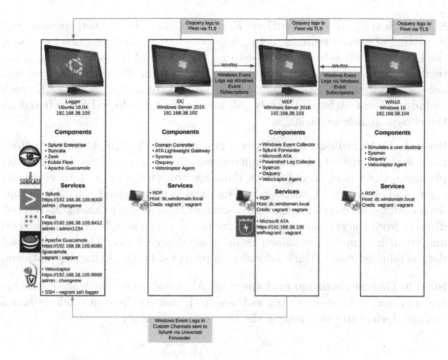

Fig. 3. DetectionLab setup as illustrated by Chris Long [10]

D: DetectionLab. DetectionLab is a repository that allows users to create a virtual network environment on various platforms using automated scripts [10]. The automated scripts can be used to customise the network environment by adding or removing hardware and software as required. In addition, the flexibility of installing software tools maximizes researchers to secure visibility and introspection. As Fig. 3 shows it, four different purposed hosts, DC/WEF/Win10/Logger, consist of the lab. DC simulates a domain controller and WEF simulates Windows 2016 server managing Windows Event Collection. To collect non-server data, Win10 is set up and a represented simulation of a SIEM system is Logger [16].

3.1 Generation of Dataset

Figure 4 shows the architecture of our framework. We divide the dataset generation process into three steps.

Step 1: Setting up the Testbed Environment. The testbed environment consisting of various systems, network devices and applications is set up using the DetectionLab automation repository. The size and types of devices in the testbed can be customised by editing the *VagrantFile*. Once the systems, network devices and applications are set up and connected to the ELK stack including Beats, AttackIQ agents will be installed in selected hosts based on the chosen attack scenarios.

Step 2: Data collection and pre-processing. After the testbed environment is set up, the attack simulation process can be executed via the AttackIQ platform. Both normal and attack data are collected as raw data via Beats agent and stored in ElasticSearch. The data is then parsed into XX format with customised number of features. Some of these features are extracted out directly from the raw data and some are newly constructed features based on analytical information obtained from Elasticsearch tools. Then, the parsed data is labelled using attack information provided by the AttackIQ platform.

Step 3: Dataset storage and sharing. After data is labelled, the dataset is sent to a server for storage such as Hadoop. It can also be sent to cloud-based storage devices to share among the research community.

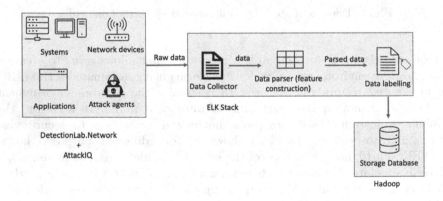

Fig. 4. Architecture design of SDGen

3.2   Scalability, Reproducibility and Flexibility

SDGen is featured with scalability, reproducibility and flexibility, which will be discussed in the following paragraphs respectively.

Scalability, in the context of dataset generation, refers to how easily to scale up a network infrastructure that consists of multiple hosts, servers (e.g., DNS,

Database, Email and etc.) and network devices (e.g., firewall, proxy, router and etc.). Essentially, the complexity and diversity of network infrastructure determine the cyber attacks' variety and cyber kill chain [26] and, more importantly, how likely it has represented a real world setting. In SDGen, the dynamic adjustment of the network infrastructure is achieved by DetectionLab by modifying the *Vagrantfile* [13]. Namely, a new virtual machine can be spined up and added into an existing network with the some parameters configured in the *Vagrantfile*, such as function (domain controller, window event forwarder and etc.), operating system (Windows, MacOS or other Unix/Linux distributions), pre-installed software, and network setting (e.g., IP address and sub-netting). The above modification is simply overwriting a configuration file and, thus, building a virtual network at any scale is possible as long as resource is adequate.

Reproducibility is also an important feature for a dataset generation approach. Firstly, we can validate the effectiveness or correctness by reproducing the dataset rather than having to access its publicly available data feeds. Furthermore, when conducting comparative research, multiple datasets can be generated with a few minor settings changed, for example testing an algorithm with datasets being affected by different sets of cyber attacks. SDGen comes with excellent reproducibility as its underlying DetectionLab is fully Vagrant based [13], which enables users to create and manage various development environments effectively and efficiently. As a result, publishing and reproducing datasets can be as simply implemented as transferring a bunch of *Vagranfiles*.

Flexibility is the largest gain from the integration of AttackIQ into SDGen. While most of the existing datasets are unchanged in terms of cyber attack scenarios, a dataset with dynamically adjustable testing scenarios is very attractive. As mentioned in the above, AttackIQ has more than 3000 built-in test scenarios arranged in line with MITRE ATT&CK framework. Intuitively, an attack procedure can be easily constructed by selecting test scenarios from corresponding techniques and tactics. In addition, each test scenario is configurable, such as choosing Python/Powershell script or specifying target folder, and some even allow users to upload a customised malicious payload. Therefore, we can not only simulate known attack vectors, but also deal with any previously unseen variants.

4 Implementation

In this section, SDGen will be implemented to generate some datasets. As a proof-of-concept (POC), it is aimed to demonstrate the configuration of an AttackIQ assessment and the attack scenarios, the security data collection within the DetectionLab and ELK stack with Beats, and the potential of how the collected data can be leveraged to facilitate cyber security research.

Particularly, we focus on generating ransomware [18] affected datasets in this paper. Ransomware is a typical example of an advanced persistent threat (APT) - a type of malware that encrypts the victim's personal data (or threatens to publish it) to demand a ransom payment. Since the encryption is often realised via symmetric and asymmetric cryptographic algorithms (e.g., AES and RSA) and even their hybrid, recovering the data encrypted by ransomware is almost impossible without the decryption key. This makes ransomware extremely hazardous to the victim organisations and draws increasing interest among cyber security researchers.

4.1 Configuration

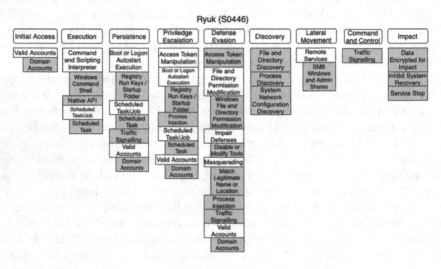

Fig. 5. An snippet of Ryuk ransomware attack vector according to the Enterprise MITRE ATT&CK framework. The full list can be found at [8].

While the attack vector might be different, all ransomware eventually takes malicious actions through 'command and control' and 'impact' from the MITRE ATT&CK framework's perspective. Hence, intuitively, two assessments will be created: 1) the first is only comprised of attack scenarios that belong to 'command and control' and 'impact' but tests against several popular ransomware and, 2) the second focuses on a specific ransomware and its entire attack vector from 'initial access' to 'impact'. In particular, the first assessment tests 3 attack scenarios regarding malware delivery, command and control and the encryption of victim's data, and the second assessment covers the entire attack vector of RYUK ransomware [7]. Figure 5 illustrates RYUK ransomware attack vectors within a MITRE ATT&CK framework navigator layer and Tables 1 and 2 list the attack vectors for the two assessments respectively.

Furthermore, we can configure each attack scenario individually to customise the attack vector. For example, it has the option to choose different methods/scripts to deliver the malicious payload and/or execute the attack pattern, and even upload the customised malicious payload. However, in this paper, most attack scenarios are set by default, with only the ransomware file encryption path configured as "C:\Users".

Table 1. Assessment 1 - list of attacks

Test	Tactic	Attack scenario
Locky	Command and Control	Download Locky to Memory
	Command and Control	Save Locky to File System
	Impact	Locky File Encryption
NotPetya	Command and Control	Download NotPetya to Memory
	Command and Control	Save NotPetya to File System
	Impact	NotPetya File Encryption
Ryuk	Command and Control	Download Ryuk to Memory
	Command and Control	Save Ryuk to File System
	Impact	Ryuk File Encryption
SamSam	Command and Control	Download SamSam to Memory
	Command and Control	Save SamSam to File System
	Impact	SamSam File Encryption

With everything configured properly, we executed the assessments a few times to "contaminate" the data we are about to collect. As shown in Figs. 6 and 7, the assessment 1 was repeated three times between 28/08/2021 and 29/08/2021 and the assessment 2 was conducted twice on 29/08/2021.

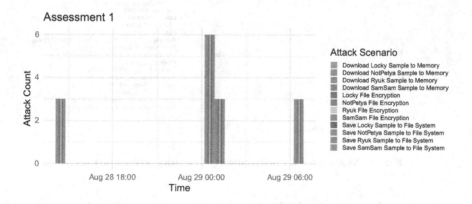

Fig. 6. Assessment 1 - distribution of attacks based on time

4.2 Security Data Collection and Descriptive Statistics

In general, security data is categorised as network-based, host-based or contextual, each of which can find a number of use cases in addressing cyber security detection problems [15]. Some commonly seen network-based data include logs

Table 2. Assessment 2 - list of attacks

Test	Tactic	Attack Scenario
Ryuk	Initial Access	Process Discovery via Native API
	Execution	Regsvcs/Regasm Script
	Execution	Persistence Through Scheduled Task
	Persistence	Persistence Through Registry Run and RunOnce Keys
	Privilege Escalation	Access Token Manipulation
	Privilege Escalation	Code Injection
	Defense Evasion	Access Token Manipulation
	Defense Evasion	Stop Windows Defender Service Script
	Defense Evasion	Masquerading Script
	Discovery	File and Directory Discovery Script
	Discovery	Process Discovery
	Discovery	System Network Configuration Discovery
	Lateral Movement	Lateral Movement Through WMI
	Impact	Ryuk File Encryption
	Impact	File Deletion Script

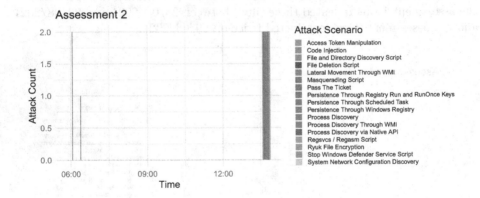

Fig. 7. Assessment 2 - distribution of attacks based on time

collected from Proxy, DNS, VPN, Firewall, etc.; the host-based data can be represented by system calls, file operations, EDR logs, etc.; and, the contextual data often contains the background information, such as LDAP and HR data.

In the environment built with DetectionLab, technically, all the previously mentioned data can be collected by using various Beats such as Filebeat, Winlogbeat, Auditbeat, Functionbeat, Heartbeat, Metricbeat, Packetbeat and so on. As a starting point, we collect Winlogbeat and Auditbeat which contain really useful information about the hosts' and operating systems' behaviours. Figure 8 illustrates the data distribution for Winlogbeat data, which is consistent with

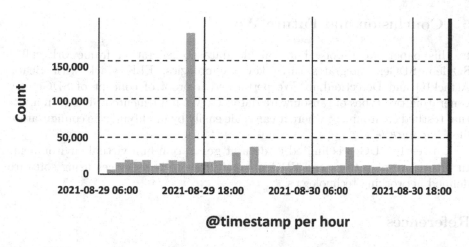

Fig. 8. Data distribution collection using winlogbeats

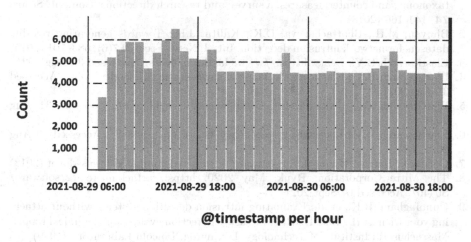

Fig. 9. Data distribution collection using auditbeats

the timeline that the attacks are executed. In addition, it can be observed that there are approximately 8,000 events every 30 min but once some hosts are being attacked the volume can easily reach to 30,000+ events, which indicates intense noise resulted from the attacks. However, since this is a virtual lab environment where there are no active users interacting with the hosts, that noise does not necessarily represent an indication of being attacked or compromised. Looking at the data collected from Auditbeat which are shown in Fig. 9, it does not present a similar pattern with the attacks in terms of timeline. That is, ransomware attack scenarios may not impact the auditing significantly, but Auditbeat may contribute insights in some other ways. In the future works, we will continue explore the characteristics of the collected security data sets and attempt modelling various behaviours to identify the attacks.

5   Conclusion and Future Work

In this paper, we proposed a scalable dataset generation framework called SDGen. SDGen integrates three key technologies; ELK stack with Beats, AttackIQ and DetectionLab. We performed a proof of concept of SDGen by generating two types of ransomware datasets. We implemented SDGen in a virtual testbed environment where it can scale easily by modifying the configuration file (*VagrantFile*).

Currently, SDGen is limited to dataset generation in a virtual environment. In future, we plan to extend SDGen capabilities to real-devices using software defined networking technologies.

References

1. Al-rimy, B.A.S., Maarof, M.A., Shaid, S.Z.M.: Ransomware threat success factors, taxonomy, and countermeasures: a survey and research directions. Comput. Secur. **74**, 144–166 (2018)
2. Bhuyan, M.H., Bhattacharyya, D.K., Kalita, J.K.: Towards generating real-life datasets for network intrusion detection. Int. J. Netw. Secur. **17**(6), 683–701 (2015)
3. Elasticsearch B.V.: Beats. https://www.elastic.co/beats/. Accessed 30 Aug 2021
4. Elasticsearch B.V.: Elasticsearch. https://www.elastic.co/elasticsearch/. Accessed 31 Aug 2021
5. Elasticsearch B.V.: Kibana. https://www.elastic.co/kibana/. Accessed 31 Aug 2021
6. Elasticsearch B.V.: Logstash. https://www.elastic.co/logstash/. Accessed 30 Aug 2021
7. Cohen, I., Herzog, B.: Ryuk ransomware: a targeted campaign break-down (2018)
8. The Mitre Corporation: Ryuk, May 2020. https://attack.mitre.org/software/ S0446/. Accessed 07 Sept 2021
9. Cunningham, R.K., et al.: Evaluating intrusion detection systems without attacking your friends: the 1998 DARPA intrusion detection evaluation. Technical report, Massachusetts Institute of Technology, Lexington, Lincoln Laboratory (1999)
10. DetectionLab. https://detectionlab.network
11. Gharib, A., Sharafaldin, I., Lashkari, A.H., Ghorbani, A.A.: An evaluation framework for intrusion detection dataset. In: 2016 International Conference on Information Science and Security (ICISS), pp. 1–6. IEEE (2016)
12. Haines, J.W., Lippmann, R.P., Fried, D.J., Zissman, M., Tran, E.: 1999 DARPA intrusion detection evaluation: design and procedures. Technical report, Massachusetts Institute of Technology, Lexington, Lincoln Laboratory (2001)
13. Hashimoto, M.: Vagrant: Up and Running: Create and Manage Virtualized Development Environments. O'Reilly Media Inc., Sebastopol (2013)
14. Kozik, R., Choraś, M., Ficco, M., Palmieri, F.: A scalable distributed machine learning approach for attack detection in edge computing environments. J. Parallel Distrib. Comput. **119**, 18–26 (2018)
15. Liu, L., De Vel, O., Han, Q.L., Zhang, J., Xiang, Y.: Detecting and preventing cyber insider threats: a survey. IEEE Commun. Surv. Tutor. **20**(2), 1397–1417 (2018)
16. Long, C.: Introducing: Detection Lab. https://medium.com/@clong/introducing-detection-lab-61db34bed6ae

17. Mighan, S.N., Kahani, M.: A novel scalable intrusion detection system based on deep learning. Int. J. Inf. Secur. **20**(3), 387–403 (2020). https://doi.org/10.1007/s10207-020-00508-5
18. Mixon, E.: Top 10 ransomware attacks of 2021 (so far) - blumira. https://www.blumira.com/ransomware-attacks-2021/
19. Moustafa, N., Slay, J.: UNSW-NB15: a comprehensive data set for network intrusion detection systems (UNSW-NB15 network data set). In: 2015 Military Communications and Information Systems Conference (MilCIS), pp. 1–6. IEEE (2015)
20. Ring, M., Wunderlich, S., Scheuring, D., Landes, D., Hotho, A.: A survey of network-based intrusion detection data sets. Comput. Secur. **86**, 147–167 (2019)
21. Sharafaldin, I., Gharib, A., Lashkari, A.H., Ghorbani, A.A.: Towards a reliable intrusion detection benchmark dataset. Softw. Netw. **2018**(1), 177–200 (2018)
22. Sharafaldin, I., Lashkari, A.H., Ghorbani, A.A.: Toward generating a new intrusion detection dataset and intrusion traffic characterization. In: ICISSP, vol. 1, pp. 108–116 (2018)
23. Shiravi, A., Shiravi, H., Tavallaee, M., Ghorbani, A.A.: Toward developing a systematic approach to generate benchmark datasets for intrusion detection. Comput. Secur. **31**(3), 357–374 (2012)
24. Song, J., Takakura, H., Okabe, Y., Eto, M., Inoue, D., Nakao, K.: Statistical analysis of honeypot data and building of Kyoto 2006+ dataset for NIDS evaluation. In: Proceedings of the First Workshop on Building Analysis Datasets and Gathering Experience Returns for Security, pp. 29–36 (2011)
25. Strom, B.E., Applebaum, A., Miller, D.P., Nickels, K.C., Pennington, A.G., Thomas, C.B.: MITRE ATT&CK: design and philosophy. Technical report (2018)
26. Yadav, T., Rao, A.M.: Technical aspects of cyber kill chain. In: Abawajy, J.H., Mukherjea, S., Thampi, S.M., Ruiz-Martínez, A. (eds.) SSCC 2015. CCIS, vol. 536, pp. 438–452. Springer, Cham (2015). https://doi.org/10.1007/978-3-319-22915-7_40
27. Zheng, M., Robbins, H., Chai, Z., Thapa, P., Moore, T.: Cybersecurity research datasets: taxonomy and empirical analysis. In: 11th USENIX Workshop on Cyber Security Experimentation and Test (CSET 2018) (2018)

Towards a Location-Aware Blockchain-Based Solution to Distinguish Fake News in Social Media

Wahid Sadique Koly[1], Abu Kaisar Jamil[1], Mohammad Shahriar Rahman[2], Hanif Bhuiyan[3], Md Zakirul Alam Bhuiyan[4], and Abdullah Al Omar[1]([✉])

[1] Department of Computer Science and Engineering, University of Asia Pacific, Dhaka, Bangladesh
[2] United International University, Dhaka, Bangladesh
msr@ieee.org
[3] Data61, CSIRO, Canberra, Australia
hanif.bhuiyan@data61.csiro.au
[4] Department of Computer and Information Sciences, Fordham University, New York, NY 10458, USA
bhuiyan3@fordham.edu

Abstract. Nowadays, social media is the main source of all global and local news in this generation. But the propagation of fake news and misleading information through social media has become a major concern. Fake news and misleading information often cause crucial damage to human life and society. Moreover, social media has become a source of news, views, and facts for its user. Through social media, a piece of news or information can reach every corner of the world within seconds. It is quite hard for a general social media user to distinguish fake news from real one. Even sometimes social media users cannot distinguish the fake news while residing in the same location of that real news. Hence, in this paper, we have proposed a location-aware blockchain-based news validation system that can be integrated with social media in order to distinguish fake news and misleading information from real ones.

Keywords: Fake news · Location-aware · Blockchain · Consensus

1 Introduction

In this era of technology, social media has brought everyone closer. We can be more interconnected to each other than before through social media. At present, news of any incident propagates throughout the world within a second through social media. Though it has made our life easier, it has some demerits too.

People tend to believe everything they saw on social media [1]. Generally, we are not in a critical mindset whenever we scroll the news-feed of a social platform. Thus, we do not bother to cross-check the veracity of that particular news and often make it viral by sharing without thinking. Moreover, a survey ran

G. Wang et al. (Eds.): UbiSec 2021, CCIS 1557, pp. 116–130, 2022.
https://doi.org/10.1007/978-981-19-0468-4_9

by Pew Research Center in 2020 [2] stated that about 52% of Americans prefer digital platforms as their source of news. So if a piece of misleading information gets viral on social media, it might cause much more damage.

In 2012, a series of assaults conducted by the local mob on Buddhists minority in Ramu, Bangladesh [3,4]. 22 Buddhist temples along with two Hindu temples and 100 houses were destroyed [5] over a false allegation of posting a photo of burned Quran by a Buddhist male on Facebook. In 2020, a rumor propagated through Facebook that, a certain amount of human heads are needed to be sacrificed for the Padma Bridge Bangladesh [8], and children are being kidnapped for that purpose [9]. This rumor eventually caused some major violent events. There were mob killings of eight people [7] on suspicion of child kidnapping, but none of them were child kidnappers. Later in that year, a clash between police and a religious group caused 4 deaths and several injuries [6,9]. The violent protest started in the first place when a screenshot containing a hate conversation about the holy prophet of Muslims got viral on Facebook. Later the police confirmed the alleged Facebook account got hacked and, the hacker intentionally made those conversations to create riots between the two religious groups.

Misleading information often puts risks to public health and security [10]. In 2020, a piece of misleading news got viral that Methanol can cure Covid-19 [12]. Around 700 people in Iran died [11] due to Methanol poisoning after consuming Methanol, believing that information. Sometimes scammers/hackers put fake offers or advertisements with attractive headlines on social media. Naive users often got scammed by responding to those offers.

Nowadays, it is hard to decide whether a news is fake or real. If the task to validate a news is given to any organization, there is no guarantee that the organization will be unbiased. As that certain organization will have the authority and responsibility to certify a news, in some extreme cases, the government or some influential organizations might pressurize them or they can be easily corrupted. In Blockchain, we can build a system where the fake news validation can be done anonymously. In our proposed system, the system will be integrated with social media in such a manner that the users of any social media will act as validators of a particular news. As their identity will be unknown, they can certify any facts or stories without any outside influences. Hence, they can remain unbiased nor forced by any other organization or individual.

Organization of the Paper: The remainder of the paper is organized as follows: Sect. 2 explains the background study. Related work is described in Sect. 3. Section 4 explains property comparison between our proposed system and other related work. Section 5 outlines the preliminaries. The working methodology of our system is discussed in Sect. 6. Section 7 briefly analyses the features of the protocol. In Sect. 8, we have analyzed the blockchain based performance of our proposed system. Lastly, conclusion is included in Sect. 9.

2 Background

Though our proposed system can be implemented with any other technology, we choosed to implement this idea with blockchain technology which is way more complicated but secure than any other traditional technologies [25, 26].

Blockchain is a chain of blocks that interface with each block through a cryptographic approval called hashing function. Blockchain is also known as distributed ledger as it is customized to record monetary exchanges and to store the record in a decentralized manner [23, 24].

In our proposed architecture, we proposed to store our validation records in a distributed Blockchain. For this, no hacker can harm the system or tamper with the record, as copies of all the transactions will be stored in the computer of every participant node. In order to tamper with information, the hacker will have to recalculate all the hash values and will have to change more than 50% of copies of the chain that are distributed in the network. Also, in this way, decentralization of the database moves trust from the central authority as every node connected with the system has all the records and, if changes are needed, all have to change their record, else the system will not work. In our proposed architecture, we also promised transparency as in this blockchain technology, each and everything is visible to start to end. Also, the decentralized organization makes it an open innovation where nothing is covered up and diminishes the opportunity of discrepancy.

Blockchain technology ensures the freedom of speech as there is no central governing body, and it's completely decentralized [18, 22]. Any individual can reclaim their opportunity. Transfer values and administration only can occur on an overall scale of utilizing a decentralized organization at a worldwide level, which also can eliminate any prerequisites from any administration.

3 Related Works

In [13], T. W. Jing and R. K. Murugesan discussed the likeliness of implementing Blockchain technology and advanced AI in social media to prevent fake news from roaming around social media. Also, they discussed the possible research methodology and the research direction for building a trusted network through Blockchain and AI as well as the research problems and limitations.

In a later study [14], authors elaborately reviewed the impacts of fake news along with the amenities of implementing Blockchain technology with advanced AI algorithms in social media to improve mutual trust and prevent fake news. In that paper, they provided a basic overview of Blockchain in terms of privacy, security, validity, transparency and freedom of speech. In an article [15], A. Qayyum et al. proposed a Blockchain-based news publishing framework where news publishers can join and publish their news through a publisher management protocol that registers, updates, and invalidates their identities. The news can be validated by the honest miners using consensus mechanism and upon validation, the news can be added to the chain. In a research [16], I. S. Ochoa et al. proposed a system based on centralized Blockchain to detect fake news in social media. In their proposed architecture they defined the news sources as full nodes and the validators as miner nodes. When a piece of news deploys as a block in the chain, the miner nodes can validate the block, and using the *PoS* algorithm the reliability of that block can be increased or decreased. In another research [17], Paul et al. proposed a similar architecture with a decentralized approach. There are several related research based on technologies other than Blockchain. M. Granik et al. [20] proposed a model to detect fake news using naive Bayes classifier, in 2017. They used a data set collected by BuzzFeed News to train their model. They split the data set into three parts, the first one for training the classifier model, the second one to calibrate the model, and the third one to test the performance of the model. In 2018 [19], D. Vedova et al. proposed a novel machine learning based approach to detect fake news in social media. In another research [21], J. C. S. Reis et al. proposed a supervised learning based approach to detect fake news in social media. In their method, they explored different attributes extracted from the news content, source, and social media and classified these attributes through various classifiers (i.e., KNN, Random Forests, Naive Bayes).

4 Comparison Between Our Architecture and the Related Works

In this section, we show the results in the eight properties of our architectures. If a particular architecture has the property in it then we marked it with 'Y' otherwise marked with 'N'. Here, Table 1 compares our architecture with other existing architectures. With the careful analogy of the systems, a conclusion can be drawn that our architecture has greater advantages than the other systems in this table.

Table 1. Comparison table

Metric	Qayyum et al. [15]	Ochoa et al. [16]	Granik et al. [20]	Tee et al. [14]	Our architecture
Social media integration	N	Y	Y	Y	Y
Anonymity	N	N	N	N	Y
Transparent	N	N	N	Y	Y
Truthfulness indicator	Y	N	Y	N	Y
Reliability indicator	N	Y	N	N	Y
User evaluation	N	Y	N	N	Y
Area factor	N	N	N	N	Y
Blockchain based	Y	Y	N	Y	Y

5 Preliminaries

In this section, we initially discussed each properties shortly that our system achieved. Afterthat, we discussed about the blockchain technology for our proposed system.

5.1 Properties

Our system's key focus points are anonymity, integrity, privacy, and reliability. Some key points of security and privacy are briefly described below:

Anonymity: Anonymity is ensured by generating an unique hash address for each validator of our system. The real identity of each validator will remain hidden.

Integrity: Blockchain ensures the data integrity of our system by storing the validation value of a particular news.

Privacy: In our system, privacy is ensured by keeping the validator's information confidential.

Reliability: The weighting factors and the reliability indicator ensures the reliability during validation process of a particular news in our system.

6 Working Methodology

The proposed system is a blockchain based solution to distinguish the widespread of fake news in social media platform. In our system, verified users of any social media platform will act as validators of a particular news. When a news got viral on social media platform, it will be stored in the chain and after that two indicators, and two reaction buttons will be shown under that news on the news-feed of that social media platform. Whenever a verified user validates a news using our reaction button, our system starts generating the validation value of that news through some process. Two indicators will indicate whether the news is true or false after going through some evaluations.

Figure 1 portrays the whole architecture of our proposed system. All the sections and their functionalities of the architecture are briefly described below.

6.1 Validator Creation

As our system will be integrated with a social media platform, every verified user of that platform will be appointed as a validator. Figure 2 shows the validator creation of our proposed system. A social media user (U_s) will be identified with an unique hash address, therefore user's identity will remain hidden. A user (U_s) will have a rank (U_r) on a scale of 1 to 10 and a reliability value on a scale of 50–100. 1 carries the lowest rank and 10 carries the highest rank in this system. Initially, each user (U_s) will be assigned with a rank (U_r) of 1 and a reliability value (U_{rv}) of 50. Upon their evaluation, their Reliability value (U_{rv}) and rank (U_r) will be increased or decreased.

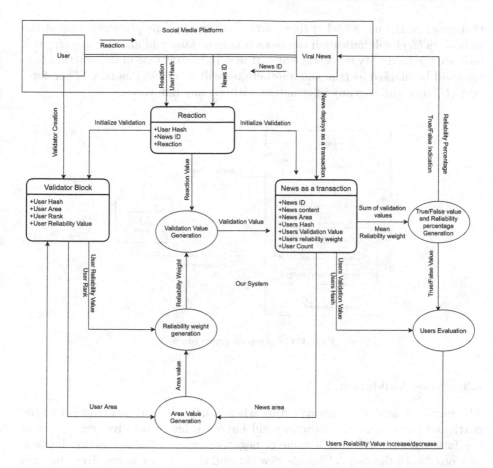

Fig. 1. Architecture of our proposed system.

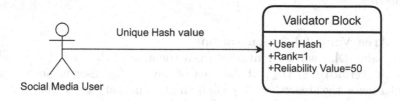

Fig. 2. Validator creation

6.2   News as a Transaction (N_w)

If a piece of news or information got viral on that particular social media platform, that means if it reaches a certain amount of shares, it will be added on
the chain as a transaction. This transaction shown in Fig. 3 will contain news
id, news area (N_a) information and the news itself. After a news (N_w) has been
added to the chain, two indicators, and two reaction buttons will be shown under

that news on the news-feed of that particular social media platform. One of the indicators (I_{tf}) will indicate if the news is true or false and another one (I_r) will indicate the reliability percentage of that first indicator. One of the reaction buttons will be marked as true and another one will be marked as false. Therefore, user (U_s) can validate any information without any influences.

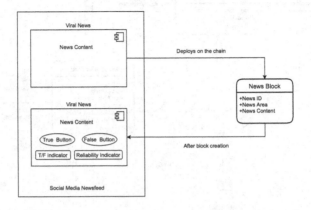

Fig. 3. Creation of news block

6.3   News Validation

The news validation process will start when a user (U_s) gives a reaction to the particular news. The True reaction will have a value of positive one $(+1)$ and the false reaction will have a value of negative one (-1). The reaction block is generated with the user (U_s) hash, news id and the reaction value. To generate a final validation value (U_v) from a user towards a news, system needs to undergo some process.

6.3.1   Area Value (A_v) Generation
An area value (A_v) will be generated from the area of the news (N_a) and the area of the verified user (U_a). If the area of any verified user is closest to any particular news, the area value (A_v) will be highest in that case. Figure 4 displays the process of generating the area value (A_v) of this system. As the distance between news and user increases, the area value (A_v) will be proportionally decreased. Thus, the nearest user will have the highest area value (A_v) and the farthest user will have the lowest area value (A_v). After generating the area value (A_v), it will be converted into a value between 1 to 100.

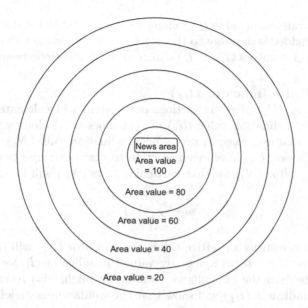

Fig. 4. Area value generation

6.3.2   Reliability Weight (R_w) Calculation

Reliability weight (R_w) is very important in our validation process as it indicates, how much reliable is a user to validate a particular news on a scale of 1 to 100. Reliability weight (R_w) will be calculated based on area value (A_v), user rank (U_r), and reliability value (U_{rv}) of a user using the following formula.

$$R_w = \frac{A_v + (U_{rv} \times U_r)}{11}$$

We can see a user with a higher area value (A_v), higher rank (U_r), and higher reliability value (R_w) will generate higher reliability weight (R_w). Besides, user with lower values tends to generate a lower reliability weight (R_w).

6.3.3   Validation Value (U_v) Generation

After reliability weight (R_w) generation, it will be multiplied with the reaction value (R_v) to generate the validation value (U_v) towards the particular news.

$$U_v = R_v \times R_w$$

As the true reaction will have a value of +1 and the false reaction will have a value of -1, therefore if a user gives a true reaction to a news (N_w) a positive validation value (U_v) will be added to that news (N_w), and if the user gives false reaction, a negative validation value (U_v) will be added to the news (N_w). User with higher reliability weight (R_w) will contribute a higher value (U_v) and user with lower reliability weight (R_w) will contribute a lower value (U_v) in both cases (Positive or Negative). Therefore, we can see when a user (U_s) gives a reaction to any news, a validation value (U_v) along with a reliability weight (R_w) will be generated and added separately to the news. These two value will contribute to achieve the two indicators $(I_{tf}$ & $I_r)$ which we have mentioned earlier.

6.3.4   True/False Indicator (I_{tf})

Each time a user (U_s) gives a reaction, our system will calculate the sum of all previous user validation value (U_v) of that news (N_w) along with the value generated from that user to generate the news validation value (N_v). That means, if n number of users (U_s) have given reaction to that particular news (N_w), the news validation value (N_v) for that particular news (N_w) will be as follows,

$$N_v = \sum_{k=1}^{n}(V_v)_k$$

If the summation returns a positive value, the indicator (I_{tf}) will show that the news is true, and if it returns a negative value the indicator (I_{tf}) will show that the news is false. On the other hand, summation might also return a zero. In that case, the indicator (I_{tf}) will show that the validation is undefined.

$$I_{tf} = f(N_v) = \begin{cases} \textbf{True,} & N_v > 0 \\ \textbf{False,} & N_v < 0 \\ \textbf{Undefined,} & N_v = 0 \end{cases}$$

6.3.5   Reliability Indicator (I_r)

As we have mentioned earlier, there will be an another indicator (I_r) under the news to show the reliability percentage of the True/False indicator. To do so, we need to first calculate the reliability percentage (R_p) of that particular news. Reliability percentage (R_p) will be calculated using the mean reliability weight (R_w) added to that news. As the reliability weight (R_w) is generated on a scale of 1–100, the mean value itself will be the reliability percentage (R_p). That means, if n number of users have given reaction to that particular news, the reliability percentage (R_p) of the True/False indicator (I_{tf}) of that particular news (N_w) will be as follows,

$$R_p = \frac{\sum_{k=1}^{n}(R_w)_k}{n}$$

Here, we can see if any news (N_w) gets reactions mostly from the users (U_s) of higher reliability, the reliability indicator (I_r) will show a higher value. Besides, if the news (N_w) gets most of its reaction from the users (U_s) of lower reliability, the indicator (I_r) will show a lower value.

6.4   User (U_s) Evaluation

To make our system more reliable, our system needs to evaluate each user continuously. Through continuous evaluation, rank (U_r) and reliability value (U_{rv}) of a user can be increased or decreased.

6.4.1 Reliability Value (U_{rv})

Each time a user (U_s) gives a reaction to any news (N_w), the system will update the news validation value (N_v) for that particular news (N_w) and will start the evaluation process. Our system will compare the news validation value (N_v) with all the users validation value (U_v) added on that news. If the sign ($+/-$) of these two value don't match for a particular user, his (U_s) reliability value (U_{rv}) will be decreased. Besides, if the sign of these two values match, the reliability value (U_{rv}) of that particular user (U_s) will be increased. The system will skip evaluation process if the news validation value (N_v) is zero.

$$U_{rv} = f(U_v) = \begin{cases} \textbf{Increments,} & \frac{U_v}{|U_v|} = \frac{N_v}{|N_v|} \\ \textbf{Decrements,} & \frac{U_v}{|U_v|} \neq \frac{N_v}{|N_v|} \\ \textbf{No change,} & N_v = 0 \end{cases}$$

6.4.2 Rank (U_r)

As we have stated earlier, a user will have a rank between 1 to 10 where 1 will be the lowest rank and 10 will be the highest. In each rank, the reliability value (U_{rv}) will be between 50–100. That means the lower reliability limit (L_l) will be 50 and the upper reliability limit (L_u) will be 100. If Reliability value (U_{rv}) of any user decreased lower than the lower reliable limit (L_l), his rank (U_r) will be downgraded. On the other hand, if his reliability value (U_{rv}) increased higher than the upper reliable limit (L_u), his rank (U_r) will be upgraded.

$$U_r = f(U_{rv}) = \begin{cases} \textbf{Upgrade,} & U_{rv} > L_u \\ \textbf{Downgrade,} & U_{rv} < L_l \end{cases}$$

In the continuous evaluation, if the rank of a user is downgraded to 0, then that user will be removed from our system as a validator.

7 Protocol Analysis

In this section, our protocols are described in terms of security parameters.

- **Anonymity:** Our system provides anonymity by generating the hash for each validator. As an unique hash address will be used to identify and track each validator, the real identity of each validator will remain hidden in our system. Thus the validators can validate any information anonymously without any influences. Moreover, users who are connected with our system are not capable to identify any user (U_s) during interaction with our system or blockchain transaction which provides pseudonymity too.
- **Data integrity:** Data integrity of our system is ensured by storing data transaction records in the blockchain. When a user (U_s) gives any reaction on a particular news (N_w) a validation value (U_v) will be generated through some process. This validation value (U_v) can not be altered when it once stores into the blockchain.

- **Privacy:** Privacy is provided by keeping the validator's information confidential as validator block contains an unique hash. Moreover, the code is immutable once it gets deployed, and all the data blocks are encrypted which makes the system more secure.
- **Reliability:** Our system ensures the reliability by maintaining the weighting factors and the reliability indicator. The reliability weight (R_w) plays an important role in our validation process as a user's reliability to validate a particular news depends on it. Besides, there will be a reliability indicator (I_r) under the news (N_w) which shows the reliability percentage of the True/False indicator.

8   Experimental Analysis

We simulate our proposed system in this section to evaluate the feasibility through graph and proper description.

Experimental Setup: To evaluate the effectiveness and performance efficiency of our proposed system, we setup an environment using the following configurations:

- Intel(R) Core(TM) i5-7200U 2.50 GHz
- 8.00 GB of RAM, Windows 10 (64-bit) OS

In our evaluation, we have written the programs using languages: Solidity, Web3.js, HTML and CSS. Software: atom, browser, Remix-Ethereum IDE to write the smart contract using solidity language to form a simulated Ethereum network locally. Wi-Fi connection is required in the setup.

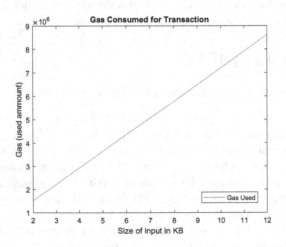

Fig. 5. Gas used for transaction in blockchain

8.1   Gas Used for Transaction in Blockchain

The amount of computational effort required to perform any operations in the Ethereum blockchain network is referred to as Gas. Here, we've calculated the amount of Gas used to complete transactions with different data sizes for our system. Figure 5 depicts the trends of gas used for each transaction occurs in our proposed system. In order to analyze the consumption of Gas of different size of data, we have taken 2 to 12 KB of data. In the resulting graph, we find that with the increase size of input data, Gas increases. As a result, the graph shows a linear trend.

8.2   Transaction Time

Here, we have observed the transaction time taken in seconds to complete the transaction of varying data sizes of our proposed system. The time required to complete any transaction in blockchain is considered as transaction time. Our system's transactions show the tends in Fig. 6 with regards to time. Initially the transaction time increases from 2 KB to 4 KB data and then suddenly starts decreasing with the data from 4 KB to 8 KB. We notice that transaction time again starts increasing with the increase of data sizes from 8 KB. From the resultant graph, the highest transaction time was found for 4 KB data due to inconsistencies in the testing environment.

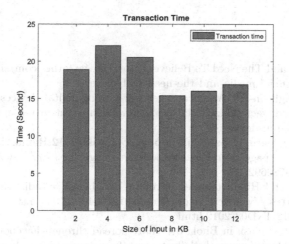

Fig. 6. Blockchain transaction time

9   Conclusion

In our proposed method, we tried our best to utilize the core benefits of Blockchain technology (immutability, decentralization, security, ease of use) to reduce the widespread of fake news in social media. As fake news in social media often mislead people and turn them against each other and often result in violent incidents, it is a concerning issue. Individuals or organizations often deceive people by propagating fake or misleading information to gather profits. Hackers often propagate fake or misleading information over social media and convince a gullible user to click on harmful links or install harmful programs in their system and stole their personal data. Moreover, in a traditional validation system, users might not validate news freely because of the pressure created by some influential organizations. To address the problems, we proposed a location-aware blockchain based solution to reduce fake news in social media platform. In our system, any verified user of a particular social media platform can play the validator role for a particular news. Whenever a user validates a news which got viral in social media platform using our reaction button, our system starts generating the validation value of that news through some process. We introduced two indicators which will indicate whether the news is true or false after going through some evaluations. There may be some limitations. Being biased, some or a major portion of the validators may validate a fake news as real one during validation. Yet we hope if we can integrate this system into mainstream social media, all or some of the issues can be reduced.

References

1. Social Media and The Need To Believe. https://www.forbes.com/sites/petersuciu/2019/11/11/social-media-and-the-need-to-believe/
2. More than eight-in-ten Americans get news from digital devices. https://www.pewresearch.org/fact-tank/2021/01/12/more-than-eight-in-ten-americans-get-news-from-digital-devices/
3. 2012 Ramu violence. https://en.wikipedia.org/wiki/2012_Ramu_violence/
4. Bangladesh rampage over Facebook Koran image. https://www.bbc.com/news/world-asia-19780692
5. 24 Buddhist and Hindu temples burnt in Bangladesh - India and UN urged to intervene. https://web.archive.org/web/20121004004231/. http://www.achrweb.org/press/2012/IND08-2012.html
6. Police-protesters clash in Bhola over hate spread through Facebook ID: 4 Killed, 100 Injured. https://www.thedailystar.net/frontpage/clash-in-bhola-4-killed-100-injured-1816540
7. Children being sacrificed, heads used for bridge project: social media rumour sparks spate of Bangladesh lynchings. https://www.straitstimes.com/asia/south-asia/children-being-sacrificed-heads-used-for-bridge-project-social-media-rumour-sparks
8. Padma Bridge. https://en.wikipedia.org/wiki/Padma_Bridge

9. Bangladesh: Fake news on Facebook fuels communal violence. https://www.dw.com/en/bangladesh-fake-news-on-facebook-fuels-communal-violence/a-51083787

10. Naeem, S.B., Bhatti, R., Khan, A.: An exploration of how fake news is taking over social media and putting public health at risk. Health Inf. Libr. J. https://doi.org/10.1111/hir.12320

11. Iran: Over 700 dead after drinking alcohol to cure coronavirus. https://www.aljazeera.com/news/2020/4/27/iran-over-700-dead-after-drinking-alcohol-to-cure-coronavirus

12. A syndemic of COVID-19 and methanol poisoning in Iran: time for Iran to consider alcohol use as a public health challenge? https://www.ncbi.nlm.nih.gov/pmc/articles/PMC7272173/

13. Tee, W.J., Murugesan, R.K.: Trust network, blockchain and evolution in social media to build trust and prevent fake news. In: 2018 Fourth International Conference on Advances in Computing, Communication Automation (ICACCA), pp. 1–6 (2018). https://doi.org/10.1109/ICACCAF.2018.8776822

14. Tee, W.J., Murugesan, R.K.: A theoretical framework to build trust and prevent fake news in social media using blockchain. In: Saeed, F., Gazem, N., Mohammed, F., Busalim, A. (eds.) IRICT 2018. AISC, vol. 843, pp. 955–962. Springer, Cham (2019). https://doi.org/10.1007/978-3-319-99007-1_88

15. Qayyum, A., Qadir, J., Janjua, M., Vira, F.S.: Using blockchain to rein in the new post-truth world and check the spread of fake news. IT Prof. **21**, 16–24 (2019). https://doi.org/10.1109/MITP.2019.2910503. LNCS

16. Ochoa, I.S., de Mello, G., Silva, L.A., Gomes, A.J.P., Fernandes, A.M.R., Leithardt, V.R.Q.: FakeChain: a blockchain architecture to ensure trust in social media networks. In: Piattini, M., Rupino da Cunha, P., García Rodríguez de Guzmán, I., Pérez-Castillo, R. (eds.) QUATIC 2019. CCIS, vol. 1010, pp. 105–118. Springer, Cham (2019). https://doi.org/10.1007/978-3-030-29238-6_8

17. Paul, S., Joy, J., Sarker, S., Shakib, A., Ahmed, S., Das, A.: Fake news detection in social media using blockchain. In: 2019 7th International Conference on Smart Computing Communications (ICSCC), pp. 1–5 (2019). https://doi.org/10.1109/ICSCC.2019.8843597

18. Al Omar, A., et al.: Towards a transparent and privacy-preserving healthcare platform with blockchain for smart cities. In: 2020 IEEE 19th International Conference on Trust, Security and Privacy in Computing and Communications (TrustCom). IEEE (2020)

19. Vedova, M.L.D., Tacchini, E., Moret, S., Ballarin, G., DiPierro, M., Alfaro, L.D.: Automatic online fake news detection combining content and social signals. In: 2018 22nd Conference of Open Innovations Association (FRUCT), pp. 272–279 (2018). https://doi.org/10.23919/FRUCT.2018.8468301

20. Granik, M., Mesyura, V.: Fake news detection using naive Bayes classifier. In: 2017 IEEE First Ukraine Conference on Electrical and Computer Engineering (UKRCON), pp. 900–903 (2017). https://doi.org/10.1109/UKRCON.2017.8100379

21. Reis, J.C.S., Correia, A., Murai, F., Veloso, A., Benevenuto, F.: Supervised learning for fake news detection. IEEE Intell. Syst. **34**(2), 76–81 (2019). https://doi.org/10.1109/MIS.2019.2899143

22. Al Omar, A., et al.: A transparent and privacy-preserving healthcare platform with novel smart contract for smart cities. IEEE Access **9**, 90738–90749 (2021)

23. Bosri, R., Rahman, M.S., et al.: Integrating blockchain with artificial intelligence for privacy-preserving recommender systems. IEEE Trans. Netw. Sci. Eng. **8**(2), 1009–1018 (2020). https://doi.org/10.1109/TNSE.2020.3031179

24. Omar, A.A., Bosri, R., Rahman, M.S., Begum, N., Bhuiyan, M.Z.A.: Towards privacy-preserving recommender system with blockchains. In: Wang, G., Bhuiyan, M.Z.A., De Capitani di Vimercati, S., Ren, Y. (eds.) DependSys 2019. CCIS, vol. 1123, pp. 106–118. Springer, Singapore (2019). https://doi.org/10.1007/978-981-15-1304-6_9
25. Bosri, R., Uzzal, A.R., et al.: HIDEchain: a user-centric secure edge computing architecture for healthcare IoT devices. In: IEEE INFOCOM 2020 - IEEE Conference on Computer Communications Workshops (INFOCOM WKSHPS) (2020). https://doi.org/10.1109/INFOCOMWKSHPS50562.2020.9162729
26. Bosri, R., Uzzal, A.R., et al.: Towards a privacy-preserving voting system through blockchain technologies. In: 2019 IEEE International Conference on Dependable, Autonomic and Secure Computing, International Conference on Pervasive Intelligence and Computing, International Conference on Cloud and Big Data Computing, International Conference on Cyber Science and Technology Congress (DASC/PiCom/CBDCom/CyberSciTech), pp. 602–608. IEEE (2019). https://doi.org/10.1109/DASC/PiCom/CBDCom/CyberSciTech.2019.00116

Using Streaming Data Algorithm for Intrusion Detection on the Vehicular Controller Area Network

Shaila Sharmin$^{(\boxtimes)}$ ⓘ, Hafizah Mansor ⓘ, Andi Fitriah Abdul Kadir,
and Normaziah A. Aziz

Department of Computer Science, Kulliyyah of Information and Communication
Technology, International Islamic University Malaysia, 53100 Kuala Lumpur,
Selangor, Malaysia
`shailasharmin@protonmail.com`, {`hafizahmansor,andifitriah,naa`}`@iium.edu.my`

Abstract. The Controller Area Network (CAN), which is a protocol
for the in-vehicle network, is lacking in security features, making the
CAN bus vulnerable to a range of cyberattacks such as message injec-
tions, replay attacks, and denial of service attacks. This has prompted
researchers to develop statistical and machine learning based intrusion
detection systems for the CAN bus that use various features such as
message timing and frequency to detect attacks. In this paper, the
adapted streaming data Isolation Forest (iForestASD) algorithm has
been applied to CAN intrusion detection. While the Isolation Forest
(iForest) anomaly detection algorithm has a linear time complexity and
low memory requirement, iForestASD adapts iForest by employing a sliding window that introduces the ability to handle concept drift, which is
often characteristic of streaming data such as CAN bus traffic. The detection model is trained with only message timing information, making it
applicable to all vehicles regardless of make and model. Results of experiments that compare the attack detection performance of iForestASD and
iForest show that CAN traffic stream demonstrates insignificant concept
drift and the detection model does not benefit from being retrained with
a sliding window of latest CAN traffic, as in iForestASD. The size of the
training sample is, however, found to be an important consideration - a
model trained with only 30 s of CAN traffic always yields better detection performance than a model trained with a larger window of CAN
traffic.

Keywords: Controller Area Network · Intrusion detection · Isolation
forest · Message insertion · Automotive

1 Introduction

The various subsystems of a vehicle, such as body control, engine control, power
transmission, etc. are controlled by microcontrollers called Electronic Control
Units (ECUs) that are connected together in the internal vehicular network.

G. Wang et al. (Eds.): UbiSec 2021, CCIS 1557, pp. 131–144, 2022.
https://doi.org/10.1007/978-981-19-0468-4_10

Modern vehicles may have as many as 100 such ECUs, with some high-end vehicles equipped with 150 or more [4]. ECUs are networked using various technologies and protocols such as Local Interconnect Network (LIN), Controller Area Network (CAN), FlexRay, and Media Oriented Systems Transport (MOST) [14], of which CAN is the most commonly used protocol. Lacking in security features such as encryption and authentication, the CAN bus is susceptible to message injection, replay attack, denial of service (DoS), and other such cyberattacks that can interfere with the normal operations of a vehicle and cause dangerous, even fatal, accidents [11]. Vehicles are also increasingly being equipped with wired and wireless interfaces like Bluetooth that allow interaction with the external environment and expand the attack surface of modern vehicle electronic systems [5, 17].

Nodes on a CAN bus communicate by broadcasting messages at fairly fixed intervals [19]. As such, anomaly detection techniques, including machine learning algorithms, may be applied to detect intrusions in the form of deviations from normal CAN traffic patterns. However, since CAN bus traffic is generated rapidly and in large volume, it is akin to streaming data that can be subject to concept drift, whereby the statistical properties of the data stream shifts over time. This has the potential to make detection models less representative of the data stream and decrease detection performance over time.

Therefore, this work models CAN intrusion detection as a streaming data anomaly detection problem and uses the adapted streaming data Isolation Forest (iForestASD) algorithm [7]. The iForestASD algorithm is based on the Isolation Forest (iForest) anomaly detection algorithm [13], which has linear time complexity, low memory requirement, and the ability to build a model with only a small amount of data. This paper builds on a previous work that applied iForest to intrusion detection for the CAN bus with promising results [23]. The contribution of this work is that it applies to the same problem the iForestASD algorithm, which adapts iForest for streaming data by using a sliding window. This sliding window is used to retrain and update the model when it detects concept drift in the data stream to maintain the model's accuracy.

Our approach uses only the timing of messages to detect intrusions, which makes it applicable to all vehicles regardless of make and model. It does not require prior knowledge of the meaning and semantics of CAN messages, which may vary among vehicles of different manufacturers and is, in fact, often kept confidential as a "security through obscurity" measure [16]. This intrusion detection approach should therefore be able to detect any attack that affects the observed timing of messages on the CAN bus, such as message insertion attacks which is the most common type of attack on the CAN bus and include message injection, replay, and DoS attacks [31].

The remainder of this paper has been organized in the following manner. Section 2 provides an overview of the CAN protocol as well as the iForest and iForestASD algorithms. Section 3 discusses related works in the literature. Our experiments are described in Sect. 4 with the results reported in Sect. 5. Finally, Sect. 6 concludes this paper.

2   Background

2.1   Controller Area Network

CAN is the most widely used protocol for internal vehicular networks, finding application in powertrain and chassis subsystems that are critical to the operation of a vehicle and include power steering, engine control, braking, and suspension control [28]. It is a message-based protocol in which the nodes (i.e. the ECUs) communicate with each other by broadcasting messages on the network.

A CAN message mainly consists of an identifier (CAN ID) as well as data fields, along with some additional bits for control and error checking. A CAN message contains no identification of the sending or receiving nodes - only the CAN identifier (CAN ID) of messages is used by nodes to determine if a received message is to be acted upon or ignored. It is also only the CAN ID that is used to resolve contention on the CAN bus - messages with lower CAN ID values are broadcast first, while the others are queued to be broadcast later [6].

Vulnerabilities and Threats. The same simplistic nature of the CAN protocol that makes it suitable for the real-time environment of vehicular systems also makes it vulnerable to a host of cyber attacks. Both [3] and [2] identify the following three vulnerabilities of CAN and the attacks they facilitate: (1) lack of message authentication, allowing message insertion and replay attacks; (2) protocol misuse, allowing DoS attacks; (3) lack of encryption, which allows eavesdropping.

CAN was originally designed at a time when vehicles had only few microcontrollers and the internal network was not accessible from the external environment. However, modern vehicles are increasingly being provided with a range of wired and wireless interfaces, such as the On-Board Diagnostic (OBD-II) port, Bluetooth, and cellular connection, that enable diagnostics, infotainment, and other services. These interfaces allow external access to the CAN bus and expand the attack surface. The authors of [11] were the first to show that it was possible to infiltrate and gain control of virtually any ECU on a vehicular CAN bus. Attacks via both short- and long-range wireless channels, such as Bluetooth [5] and Wi-Fi [18], have also been demonstrated, requiring no prior access to the vehicle.

Intrusion Detection for the CAN Bus. Intrusion Detection Systems (IDS) that have been developed for computer networks are not fully applicable to the in-vehicle network due to the low processing power of ECUs, requirement for quick responses [26], lack of source and destination identification in CAN messages, etc. This has necessitated the development of intrusion detection methods for the CAN bus that take into account the specific features and constraints of CAN.

A CAN IDS must, most importantly, have low false negative rates due to the safety-critical nature of vehicular systems, and low false positive rates, due to the large volume of CAN message broadcasts. Such an IDS should also be able to detect attacks in real time and raise an alarm immediately, without affecting the broadcast of legitimate CAN traffic. The design of a CAN IDS is further limited by the computational power, multitasking capacity, and storage capacity of ECUs in vehicles.

Machine learning (ML) based methods of intrusion detection also raise concerns on how frequently a model would need to be updated, as well as considerations of implementation. It may not always be possible to retrain ML models on vehicle ECUs, due to computational and storage limitations [26], which may necessitate alternate update methods.

2.2   Isolation Forest for Intrusion Detection

Isolation Forest (iForest). Isolation Forest [13] is a machine learning algorithm for anomaly detection that takes advantage of two characteristics of anomalies: (1) anomalous data points are few and far in between, and (2) they differ from normal data points in their characteristics. Anomalous data points are therefore easily separable or isolated from other normal data points, which is the main idea behind the iForest algorithm. As such, iForest differs from other algorithms in that, instead of creating a profile of normal data, it explicitly isolates anomalous data points. Data points are isolated by randomly and recursively splitting the dataset until each partition contains only a single data point or multiple equal data points. The more anomalous a data point is, the fewer partitions it would take to isolate it from the rest of the data.

The random recursive partitioning used to isolate data points can be represented by a binary tree in which the number of splits required to isolate a data point is equivalent to the length of the path from the root of the tree to a leaf node. An anomalous data point would hence have a smaller path length compared to a normal data point. The Isolation Forest algorithm is an ensemble algorithm in which a forest of such binary trees, or Isolation Trees (iTrees), are constructed and the average path length for a particular data point over all the iTrees used as a measure of how anomalous the data point is.

The number of nodes in an iTree grows linearly with the number of data points, which results in a linear time and memory complexity. Furthermore, iForest does not require a large amount of data to build an accurate model - too many data points can, in fact, cause swamping and masking. These characteristics make iForest suitable for scenarios constrained with limited computation power and storage capacity such as the vehicular electronic system.

Isolation Forest for Streaming Data (iForestASD). The iForestASD algorithm presented in [7] is an adaptation of the iForest algorithm for anomaly detection in streaming data. Streaming data is generally generated very quickly and in large volumes, so it cannot be stored and processed all together. They also consist of large amounts of normal data points and very few anomalous data points, making for considerably unbalanced datasets. These characteristics make it difficult to use streaming data to train an anomaly detector. Furthermore, the statistical properties of streaming data may gradually shift with time, in a phenomenon known as concept drift. Concept drift can make a trained model less representative of the streaming data over time, resulting in degraded anomaly detection performance. iForestASD addresses these issues by retraining the iForest intrusion detection model with latest streaming data if concept drift is detected to have occurred.

The general framework for anomaly detection using iForestASD is represented in Fig. 1. The streaming dataset is divided into blocks or windows of data that are of the same size. An initial iForest anomaly detection model is first trained with few blocks of streaming data. Then, for each block of data, all the data points in the block are scored using the iForest model. After the data points of a window has been scored, the anomaly rate of the window is compared against a predefined threshold, u. If the anomaly rate exceeds u, then it is assumed that concept drift has occurred, and the anomaly detection model is retrained with the latest data window. This ensures that the anomaly detection method remains updated and representative of the streaming data.

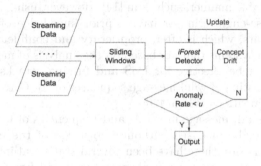

Fig. 1. Framework for anomaly detection using iForestASD. Reproduced from [7]

An important parameter is the size of the data blocks, or the sliding window. If the sliding window is too large, the model may not be an accurate representation of the current data stream, but if it is too small, then there may be insufficient data to build an accurate model.

Intrusion Detection Approach. Earlier works such as [9,19,20,24] have shown the efficacy of using message timing information in detecting intrusions on the CAN bus. Such an approach capitalizes on the fact that messages of a particular CAN ID are always broadcast at relatively regular intervals [19,25]. This means that the time interval between consecutive messages of the same CAN ID would remain almost constant, except in the situation of dropped messages due to contention with a higher priority CAN message. For an attacker to inject messages and successfully override normal traffic on the CAN bus, the frequency of the injected messages would need to be at least the same as, if not more than, the frequency of the normal messages. Miller and Valasek [17] report that while the rate of messages should be double in the event of an attack, in reality it is found to be 20–100 times higher, from which it follows that the message intervals would decrease by that much. Such a change can be detected using an anomaly detection model trained using an algorithm like iForest. Therefore, as described in later sections, we have trained an iForest model with samples of normal CAN traffic and used it to detect attacks as anomalies in attack datasets. In the case of the iForest detector, the trained model remains static. But in the iForestASD detector, the model is updated by retraining with data from the sliding window when concept drift is considered to have occurred, thereby ensuring that the model remains representative of current CAN traffic.

3   Related Works

CAN traffic has several features such as message timing, frequencies, sequences, and message contents that may be used to detect attacks on the CAN bus. Message contents can not only be used for detecting attacks, but they can also be useful for accident reconstruction provided that they are collected and analysed in a secure and reliable manner, such as in [14]. However, using message contents may require reverse-engineering or having prior knowledge of the meaning of the message contents, which is often proprietary and confidential information. Intrusion detection systems that are based on the analysis of message sequences, such as in [15], can be effective for DoS and fuzzing attacks, but not so for replay attacks consisting of valid message sequences or for CAN buses where the number of valid transitions is high [26].

On the other hand, message intervals and frequencies of CAN messages are predictable and can be analysed without knowledge of the meaning of CAN messages [19]. Therefore, there have been several statistical intrusion detection methods in the literature that use message interval and frequencies to positive results. These include [9,19,24], where the dropping of the time interval of a CAN message to below a certain threshold is considered to be indicative of an attack. Not only are these statistical methods lightweight in terms of computational power and memory requirements, but they do not require specific knowledge of the meaning of CAN messages and have been found to be very effective in quickly and accurately detecting various types of attacks, especially message insertion attacks. However, in these approaches, the statistical model is static and cannot be updated in the event of concept drift. A relatively recently work [20] models CAN intrusion detection as a change point detection problem and applies an adaptive cumulative sum algorithm, yielding better detection performance for fuzzy attacks than for spoofing.

Apart from statistical methods for intrusion detection, there have been works that study the application of machine learning to the same problem, such as One-Class Support Vector Machine (OCSVM) [1,25], clustering algorithms [27], neural networks, and Markov chains. Although the Compound Classifier method in [27] lends itself to visualization as well as generalization allowing fast classification, it performed poorly with a high rate of misclassification in fuzzing attack experiments. However, OCSVM was found to be better than t-tests at intrusion detection in [25], where it was also found that message timing could be used to the exclusion of other features for effective intrusion detection. Although iForest was found to be better than simple OCSVM in [1], the proposed OCSVM classifier optimized with a modified bat algorithm outperformed them both. Finally, a hybrid IDS that combines ML and specification-based methods is presented in [29] that uses Lightweight Online Detector of Anomalies (LODA) over Half-Space Trees (HS-Trees) and iForest. Despite iForest and LODA outperforming other one-class anomaly detection algorithms, LODA was ultimately selected since it does not require manual optimization of parameters, does not require data to be normalized, and outperforms HS-Trees in terms of speed.

This paper differs from other works in the literature in that it applies an ML algorithm which can update the intrusion detection model in the event of concept drift, making for a more robust IDS. For this, iForest and iForestASD algorithms have been used. The iForest algorithm is a lightweight algorithm with linear time complexity and low memory requirment, which allows fast training of the detection model, even with limited computing resources. Furthermore, iForestASD provides a way to retrain the model using a sliding window so that the detection performance does not decline even with concept drift. An iForestASD model may therefore be retrained faster than models trained with algorithms of higher order complexities such as OCSVM.

4 Experiment

4.1 Data

Data Collection. In order to develop and test the intrusion detection system based on the iForest and iForestASD algorithms, datasets published online as well as collected from a live vehicle have been used. The published datasets that have been used are the CAN datasets published in [22] and [8]. The former consists of normal and attack CAN datasets collected from a Hyundai YF Sonata (henceforth referred to as Sonata), while the latter consists of CAN traffic traces collected from an Opel Astra car (henceforth referred to as Astra). The data has been collected via the OBD-II port of the respective vehicles while the vehicles were operated normally. The Sonata datasets contain 30–40 min of CAN bus traffic, while the Astra contains approximately 23 min of CAN bus traffic.

In addition to these, CAN traffic traces were also collected from a 2015 Toyota Yaris Verso (henceforth refered to as Yaris) to further test the intrusion detection systems. An Arduino Uno fitted with a Sparkfun CAN-Bus shield (Fig. 2a) was used to collect a CAN traffic sample via the OBD-II port (Fig. 2b) as the vehicle was driven around in an urban environment for approximately 1 h and 10 min. The Arduino sketch used for data collection was based on [10]. The complete setup for data collection from the 2015 Toyota Yaris Verso is shown in Fig. 2c. The CAN data collected was also modified to create attack datasets which would be used to test the intrusion detection models developed later.

Fig. 2. CAN traffic data collection from a 2015 Toyota Verso, using (a) Arduino Uno with Sparkfun CAN-Bus shield attached and connected to (b) OBD-II port of the vehicle. Complete hardware setup shown in (c).

Data Pre-processing. Each message in a CAN traffic trace has a timestamp, CAN ID, Data Length Code (DLC), and a maximum of 8 data fields. Since we are concerned with only message timing information, all the datasets were processed to retain only the timestamp and CAN ID of each message. Furthermore, the time interval for each CAN message was calculated, which is the period of time between the arrival of the message and that of the previous message with the same CAN identifier.

Feature Extraction. Since the timing of CAN messages is being used for intrusion detection, the message interval for the messages of each CAN ID is the main feature that has been used to train and test the intrusion detection model. We chose to train the detection model using the average message intervals observed in each second of CAN traffic instead of the message intervals of each individual message because of the large number of CAN messages that are broadcast on the network every second (approximately 1900 in the attack-free Sonata dataset). Hence, the input features are the average time interval for the messages of each CAN ID observed during a particular second of traffic. This would be used by the detection model to score each second of CAN traffic as to the likelihood of it being anomalous.

4.2   Experiment with iForest and iForestASD

The pre-processed benign CAN traffic dataset from each of the three sources were used to train an iForest detector and an initial iForestASD model, each with 100 trees. These trained models were then tested with various attack datasets to compare their respective performances.

Experiments were conducted with different sizes of the sliding training window (M in [7]) - 30 s, 60 s, 120 s, 240 s, and 480 s - which are multiples of 30 increasing exponentially, in a manner to similar to [7]. For the iForest model, the size of the training window describes how much of the normal CAN traffic trace was used to train the model - if the training window size is M, the first M seconds of CAN traffic was used for training. In the case of the iForestASD model, the training window size also describes the size of the sliding window which is used to retrain the model if the anomaly rate exceeds the anomaly threshold (u in [7]). The threshold u, which is supposed to be a value obtained via statistical analysis, was set at 0.75, the upper quartile anomaly scores obtained with the attack-free Sonata dataset. In both the iForest and iForestASD detectors, the model was used to classify each second of traffic as to its likelihood of being anomalous, as described in the previous subsection. The Python scikit-learn [21] implementation of Isolation Forest has been used for these experiments.

Attacks that involve message insertion or deletion, which result in alteration of observed message timing, were used to test the iForest and iForestASD detection models. The attack types that have been tested are described below:

- Spoof/replay: In a spoofing or replay attack, messages of a particular legitimate CAN ID are inserted into the CAN traffic stream to spoof or override messages of a particular ECU.
- Suspension: A suspension attack occurs when a particular ECU is incapacitated and does not broadcast messages, which is observed as the messages of a particular CAN ID being missing in the message stream. The ECU may be suspended because it has been compromised or it may be the result of another attack.
- DoS: A denial of service or DoS attack can be carried out by flooding the CAN bus with messages of a high priority CAN ID to prevent the broadcast of other CAN messages on the network.
- Fuzzy: A fuzzy attack is carried out by injecting messages with random CAN ID and data to cause the vehicle to malfunction.
- Diagnostic: A diagnostic attack, as described in [30], involves inserting diagnostic messages into the CAN message stream to control ECUs.

The datasets from [22] includes two spoof attack datasets where CAN messages relating to gear and revolutions per minute (RPM) are inserted at 1 ms intervals. They also provide a DoS attack dataset, where messages of highest priority CAN ID are inserted every 0.3 ms, and a fuzzy attack dataset, where messages with random CAN ID and data are inserted every 0.5 ms. The attack datasets from [8] have been manually created by editing CAN traffic traces collected from an Astra, and include replay, suspension, diagnostic, DoS, and fuzzy attack datasets. Finally, the CAN traffic trace collected from the Toyota Yaris was also modified to create four replay attack datasets to observe differences in detection performance when the attack parameters are changed. The Yaris attack datasets have been created by selecting two CAN IDs at random and inserting each of them at 2 times and 10 times their usual respective frequencies.

5   Results and Discussion

To estimate the performance of the iForest and iForestASD intrusion detection models, experiments with each attack dataset and training window size were repeated five times. The Area Under Curve (AUC) measures obtained from

Table 1. Average AUC measures obtained in iForest intrusion detection experiments

Dataset source	Attack dataset	Training window size (in seconds)				
		30	60	120	240	480
Hyundai YF Sonata	Gear spoof	0.8516	0.8542	0.8489	0.8391	0.5629
	RPM spoof	0.8779	0.8769	0.8817	0.8782	0.5462
	DoS	0.0930	0.1073	0.0867	0.0589	0.0549
	Fuzzy	0.7175	0.7182	0.7134	0.7069	0.4131
Opel Astra	Replay	0.1254	0.1336	0.1260	0.1372	0.1145
	Suspension	0.4616	0.4337	0.3702	0.2950	0.2261
	Diagnostic	0.3082	0.2890	0.2520	0.2542	0.2601
	DoS	0.0007	0.0008	0.0003	0.0001	0.0001
	Fuzzy	0.5466	0.5042	0.5140	0.5111	0.4784
Toyota Yaris	Replay CAN ID 1 - 2x	0.6462	0.6328	0.5824	0.5626	0.4134
	Replay CAN ID 1 - 10x	0.7246	0.7121	0.6528	0.6218	0.4897
	Replay CAN ID 2 - 2x	0.5821	0.5095	0.4803	0.4729	0.4350
	Replay CAN ID 2 - 10x	0.6569	0.6008	0.5714	0.5656	0.4826

Table 2. Average AUC measures obtained in iForestASD intrusion detection experiments

Dataset source	Attack dataset	Training window size (in seconds)				
		30	60	120	240	480
Hyundai YF Sonata	Gear spoof	0.8506	0.8555	0.8481	0.8394	0.5629
	RPM spoof	0.8790	0.8784	0.8822	0.8784	0.5460
	DoS	0.0935	0.1285	0.0855	0.0611	0.0549
	Fuzzy	0.7208	0.7255	0.7140	0.7080	0.4131
Opel Astra	Replay	0.1262	0.2064	0.1662	0.1039	0.0729
	Suspension	0.4618	0.4195	0.3482	0.1799	0.1267
	Diagnostic	0.3412	0.2930	0.2086	0.1684	0.1362
	DoS	0.0006	0.0003	0.0005	0.0002	0.0001
	Fuzzy	0.5452	0.5716	0.5114	0.4407	0.3518
Toyota Yaris	Replay CAN ID 1 - 2x	0.5501	0.4666	0.3363	0.4827	0.5241
	Replay CAN ID 1 - 10x	0.5477	0.4983	0.3033	0.5346	0.5958
	Replay CAN ID 2 - 2x	0.4203	0.3612	0.3318	0.4804	0.4891
	Replay CAN ID 2 - 10x	0.4758	0.4116	0.3433	0.5032	0.5821

the Receiver Operator Characteristic (ROC) curve have been averaged for each experiment and reported in Table 1 and Table 2. Data from these tables have also been plotted in Fig. 3 for comparison.

Results of the experiments with the Sonata attack datasets (Fig. 3a) show no difference was observed in the performances of the iForest and iForestASD detection models. Performance remained steady across all training window sizes, except for the largest window size. With the Astra attack datasets (Fig. 3b), the

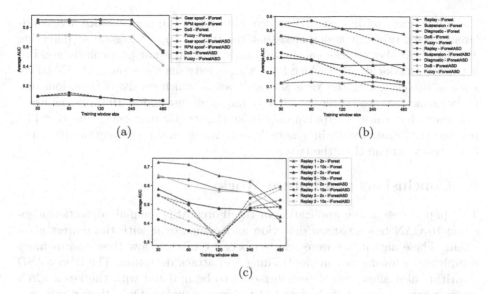

Fig. 3. Comparison of AUC values obtained for different training window sizes with (a) Hyundai YF Sonata, (b) Opel Astra, and (c) Toyota Yaris attack datasets.

iForest models were consistent in detecting attacks across all training window sizes, with the exception of the suspension attack where a declining trend is observed as the training window size becomes larger. This same declining trend is also seen with the iForestASD models. Finally, the experiments with the Yaris attack datasets (Fig. 3c) clearly show that the iForest detector is superior to the iForestASD detector across all window sizes except for the largest. The iForest detection performance declined when the training window size was increased. In all cases, the models were not equally good at detecting all types of attacks.

When we compare the iForest and iForestASD detection models, iForestASD yields little to no improvement over iForest. While the performance remains comparable in the Sonata experiments and with smaller window sizes in the Astra experiments, the iForest detector is better at detection than the corresponding iForestASD detectors in the Yaris experiments. Therefore, retraining the model, as in iForestASD, does not result in better detection performance. This indicates that there is no significant concept drift in CAN traffic stream, at least over time periods of 30–70 min.

The size of the training window appears to have an effect on the detection performance of both models. In almost all experiments, smaller training window sizes resulted in higher AUCs than larger training window sizes. This is because the large training sample causes swamping and masking [7], thereby diminishing the model's ability to separate the anomalous data points. As such, an iForest model benefits from being trained with only a small training sample, which in this case can be as small as a 30 s window of CAN traffic.

The iForest and iForestASD models also differed in performance across different attack types. It is observed that the iForest model is good at detecting attacks like replay attacks and fuzzy attacks, but it is not particularly good at detecting attacks like DoS which have a more extreme effect on the CAN traffic stream. However, with the Yaris attack datasets, which consist of variations of a replay attack, we see better detection of messages inserted at 10 times the usual frequency than those inserted at only twice the regular frequency. This could be because the former results in a more drastic change in the message timing in the CAN traffic stream than the latter.

6   Conclusions and Future Work

This paper presents an application of the iForestASD anomaly detection algorithm to CAN bus intrusion detection and compares it with the iForest algorithm. These algorithms were selected because of their low time and memory complexity, allowing fast model training and attack detection. The iForestASD algorithm also allows the detection model to be updated with the latest CAN traffic when concept drift is detected to have occurred. Only timing information was used in this intrusion detection method since this would make the IDS applicable to all vehicles regardless of make or model. Since most ECUs on a CAN bus broadcast messages at relatively regular intervals, an attack would produce observable changes in the CAN data stream that may be detected by an anomaly detection method.

Results of experiments indicated that the effect of concept drift is not significant enough to require retraining of the detection model with latest CAN traffic data. The size of the CAN traffic sample used for training the model was found to be an important consideration, since smaller training window sizes consistently yielded better performance from the detection models. Finally, while the models were relatively better at detecting replay and fuzzy attacks, they were not so good at detecting attacks like DoS attacks which have a more extreme effect on the CAN traffic stream. While it must be acknowledged that the detection performance is not good enough for application in safety-critical systems like automotive vehicles, the most important finding of this work is that the CAN traffic stream is not significantly impacted by concept drift. However, it is possible that the effect of concept drift becomes more apparent over a longer period of time.

This intrusion detection method relies on the regular nature of CAN message broadcasts and does not take into consideration CAN message broadcasts that are irregular and non-periodic, as is the case with other such methods in the literature that exploit properties like message frequency [12]. This method used average time interval per second, which yielded a feature for each CAN ID and are easily derived. But this feature set can also be expanded to include additional features like the CAN IDs themselves or data fields, which can be the subject of further study. Finally, experiments such as these would benefit from real attack datasets, such as the Sonata attack datasets, as opposed to the Astra and Yaris datasets where attack messages are manually inserted.

References

1. Avatefipour, O., et al.: An intelligent secured framework for cyberattack detection in electric vehicles' CAN bus using machine learning. IEEE Access **7**, 127580–127592 (2019). https://doi.org/10.1109/ACCESS.2019.2937576
2. Avatefipour, O., Malik, H.: State-of-the-art survey on in-vehicle network communication (CAN-Bus) security and vulnerabilities. Int. J. Comput. Sci. Netw. **6**(6), 720–727 (2017)
3. Bozdal, M., Samie, M., Jennions, I.: A survey on CAN bus protocol: attacks, challenges, and potential solutions. In: 2018 International Conference on Computing, Electronics & Communications Engineering (iCCECE), pp. 201–205 (2018). https://doi.org/10.1109/iCCECOME.2018.8658720
4. Charette, R.N.: How software is eating the car. IEEE Spectrum, June 2021. https://spectrum.ieee.org/cars-that-think/transportation/advanced-cars/ software-eating-car
5. Checkoway, S., et al.: Comprehensive experimental analyses of automotive attack surfaces. In: Proceedings of the 20th USENIX Conference on Security, SEC 2011, p. 6. USENIX Association (2011)
6. Corrigan, S.: Introduction to the controller area network (CAN). Application report, Texas Instruments (2016)
7. Ding, Z., Fei, M.: An anomaly detection approach based on isolation forest algorithm for streaming data using sliding window. IFAC Proc. Vol. **46**(20), 12–17 (2013). https://doi.org/10.3182/20130902-3-CN-3020.00044. https://www. sciencedirect.com/science/article/pii/S1474667016314999
8. Dupont, G., Lekidis, A., den Hartog, J.J., Etalle, S.S.: Automotive controller area network (CAN) bus intrusion dataset v2, November 2019. https://doi.org/10.4121/ uuid:b74b4928-c377-4585-9432-2004dfa20a5d
9. Gmiden, M., Gmiden, M.H., Trabelsi, H.: An intrusion detection method for securing in-vehicle CAN bus. In: 2016 17th International Conference on Sciences and Techniques of Automatic Control and Computer Engineering (STA), pp. 176–180 (2016). https://doi.org/10.1109/STA.2016.7952095
10. Klopfenstein, T., Kravets, I., Francis, C.M.: SparkFun CAN-bus Arduino library (2017). https://github.com/sparkfun/SparkFun_CAN-Bus_Arduino_Library
11. Koscher, K., et al.: Experimental security analysis of a modern automobile. In: 2010 IEEE Symposium on Security and Privacy, pp. 447–462 (2010). https://doi. org/10.1109/SP.2010.34
12. Le, V.H., den Hartog, J., Zannone, N.: Security and privacy for innovative automotive applications: a survey. Comput. Commun. **132**, 17–41 (2018)
13. Liu, F.T., Ting, K.M., Zhou, Z.H.: Isolation forest. In: 2008 Eighth IEEE International Conference on Data Mining, pp. 413–422 (2008). https://doi.org/10.1109/ ICDM.2008.17
14. Mansor, H., Markantonakis, K., Akram, R.N., Mayes, K., Gurulian, I.: Log your car: the non-invasive vehicle forensics. In: 2016 IEEE Trustcom/BigDataSE/ISPA, pp. 974–982 (2016). https://doi.org/10.1109/TrustCom.2016.0164
15. Marchetti, M., Stabili, D.: Anomaly detection of CAN bus messages through analysis of ID sequences. In: 2017 IEEE Intelligent Vehicles Symposium (IV), pp. 1577–1583 (2017). https://doi.org/10.1109/IVS.2017.7995934
16. Marchetti, M., Stabili, D.: READ: Reverse engineering of automotive data frames. IEEE Trans. Inf. Forensics Secur. **14**(4), 1083–1097 (2019). https://doi.org/10. 1109/TIFS.2018.2870826

17. Miller, C., Valasek, C.: A survey of remote automotive attack surfaces. Black Hat, USA (2014)
18. Miller, C., Valasek, C.: Remote exploitation of an unaltered passenger vehicle. Black Hat, USA (2015)
19. Moore, M.R., Bridges, R.A., Combs, F.L., Starr, M.S., Prowell, S.J.: Modeling inter-signal arrival times for accurate detection of CAN bus signal injection attacks: a data-driven approach to in-vehicle intrusion detection. In: Proceedings of the 12th Annual Conference on Cyber and Information Security Research, CISRC 2017. Association for Computing Machinery, New York (2017). https://doi.org/10.1145/3064814.3064816
20. Olufowobi, H., et al.: Anomaly detection approach using adaptive cumulative sum algorithm for controller area network. In: Proceedings of the ACM Workshop on Automotive Cybersecurity, AutoSec 2019, pp. 25–30. Association for Computing Machinery, New York (2019). https://doi.org/10.1145/3309171.3309178
21. Pedregosa, F., et al.: Scikit-learn: machine learning in Python. J. Mach. Learn. Res. 12(85), 2825–2830 (2011). http://jmlr.org/papers/v12/pedregosa11a.html
22. Seo, E., Song, H.M., Kim, H.K.: GIDS: GAN based intrusion detection system for in-vehicle network. In: 2018 16th Annual Conference on Privacy, Security and Trust (PST), pp. 1–6 (2018). https://doi.org/10.1109/PST.2018.8514157
23. Sharmin, S., Mansor, H.: Intrusion detection on the in-vehicle network using machine learning. In: 2021 3rd International Cyber Resilience Conference (CRC), pp. 1–6 (2021). https://doi.org/10.1109/CRC50527.2021.9392627
24. Song, H.M., Kim, H.R., Kim, H.K.: Intrusion detection system based on the analysis of time intervals of CAN messages for in-vehicle network. In: 2016 International Conference on Information Networking (ICOIN), pp. 63–68 (2016). https://doi.org/10.1109/ICOIN.2016.7427089
25. Taylor, A., Japkowicz, N., Leblanc, S.: Frequency-based anomaly detection for the automotive CAN bus. In: 2015 World Congress on Industrial Control Systems Security (WCICSS), pp. 45–49 (2015). https://doi.org/10.1109/WCICSS.2015.7420322
26. Tomlinson, A.J., Bryans, J., Shaikh, S.: Towards viable intrusion detection methods for the automotive controller area network. In: 2nd Computer Science in Cars Symposium - Future Challenges in Artificial Intelligence Security for Autonomous Vehicles (CSCS 2018). Association for Computing Machinery, September 2018
27. Tomlinson, A., Bryans, J., Shaikh, S.: Using a one-class compound classifier to detect in-vehicle network attacks. In: Proceedings of the Genetic and Evolutionary Computation Conference Companion, pp. 1926–1929. Association for Computing Machinery, July 2018. https://doi.org/10.1145/3205651.3208223
28. Umair, A., Khan, M.G.: Communication technologies and network protocols of automotive systems. Adv. Netw. 6(1), 48–65 (2018). https://doi.org/10.11648/j.net.20180601.15
29. Weber, M., Klug, S., Sax, E., Zimmer, B.: Embedded hybrid anomaly detection for automotive CAN communication. In: 9th European Congress on Embedded Real Time Software and Systems (ERTS 2018), January 2018
30. Woo, S., Jo, H.J., Lee, D.H.: A practical wireless attack on the connected car and security protocol for in-vehicle CAN. IEEE Trans. Intell. Transp. Syst. 16(2), 993–1006 (2015). https://doi.org/10.1109/TITS.2014.2351612
31. Young, C., Zambreno, J., Olufowobi, H., Bloom, G.: Survey of automotive controller area network intrusion detection systems. IEEE Des. Test 36(6), 48–55 (2019). https://doi.org/10.1109/MDAT.2019.2899062

Privacy-Enhanced Mean-Variance Scheme Against Malicious Signature Attacks in Smart Grids

Yuzhu Wang, Peiheng Zhang, Haitao Zhan, and Mingwu Zhang[✉]

Computer Science and Information Security, Guilin University of Electronic Technology, Guilin 541004, China

Abstract. Secure multidimensional data aggregation (SMDA) has been widely investigated to meet the requirement of protecting individual users' real-time electricity consumption data privacy in smart grid. However, most previous proposals require decryption of encrypted data to obtain the mean and variance, which leads to the inefficient and insecure in the protocols. This article presents an efficient and privacy-enhanced mean-variance scheme (namely PMVS) to provide the privacy-preserving, in which the Paillier cryptosystem is adopted in a fog-based architecture. To achieve efficient authentication functionality, batch verification technology is applied in our scheme. Our scheme provides two new features: Firstly, Electricity Service Provider (ESP) can directly obtain the mean and variance by decrypting the received ciphertext. Secondly, the PMVS can also resist malicious signature attacks. By identifying invalid signatures, the verified signatures can be aggregated, effectively preventing malicious signature attacks from causing batch verification to fail all the time and failing to enter the secure computing stage. The security analysis shows that the proposed scheme is secure and can preserve the meters' privacy.

Keywords: Smart grids · Privacy preserving · Invalid signature identification · Malicious signature attacks · Mean-variance

1 Introduction

As the next-generation power grid, the smart grid utilizes modern information and communication technologies to realize two-way communication between customers and service providers [1,2]. To support various network functions, many intelligent electronic devices, such as intelligent terminals and smart meters, have been deployed and used in smart grid systems [3]. With smart meters, ESP can count the sum, mean [4], and variance of consumption data of all users [5,6]. However, most of the schemes [7–13] are the mean value of one-dimensional data on the ciphertext, but the smart meter data is multi-dimensional, and in addition to the mean value, the variance of each dimension is also of practical significance. Therefore, it is essential to propose a safe multi-dimensional mean

G. Wang et al. (Eds.): UbiSec 2021, CCIS 1557, pp. 145–158, 2022.
https://doi.org/10.1007/978-981-19-0468-4_11

and variance calculation scheme. In addition, to ensure data integrity, digital signature technology [14, 15] can be used to sign the transmitted data. Meanwhile, many schemes use batch verification [8, 16–19] to improve efficiency. However, If an attacker maliciously forges or modifies the signature, causing batch verification to fail, the next stage cannot be entered. Therefore, it is urgent to present an against malicious signature attacks scheme in smart grids.

1.1 Related Work

The smart grid has become a research interest after the massive deployment of smart meters. Privacy is one of these research interests. Introduced in [7], protecting the user's privacy via data aggregation has recently become one of the most attractive research topics. Lu et al. [8] proposed an efficient and privacy-preserving multidimensional aggregation scheme, in which they used the Paillier cryptosystem and employed a super-increasing sequence to structure multidimensional data. Chen et al. [5] proposed a privacy-preserving multifunctional data aggregation scheme: MuDA. Their scheme is based on the BonehGoh-Nissim cryptosystem, and the utility supplier can get the average, variance, and one-way analysis of variance of the reporting data. Ge et al. [20] proposed a privacy-preserving Fine-grained data analysis scheme: FGDA. Their scheme allows the control center to compute the average, variance, skewness of users' electricity usage data in a privacy-preserving form. Zhao et al. [6] proposed a privacy-preserving data aggregation for fog-based smart grids that achieves multifunctional statistics (sum, inner product, one-way ANOVA, max, and min, etc.). Their scheme employs somewhat homomorphic encryption (SHE) to preserve the user's privacy. Chen et al. [18] proposed multiple data aggregation schemes for smart grids. However, all the above schemes' proposal incurs high overheads in terms of communication and computation.

1.2 Our Contribution

We propose PMVS, a privacy-enhanced mean-variance scheme against malicious signature attacks in smart grids. The main contributions of this article can be summarized as follows.

1) Our scheme supports the privacy protection of users' real-time data. No one can access the user's real-time data, including ESP and FN.
2) Our solution supports safe calculation of multi-dimensional mean and variance. Specifically, ESP can only obtain the mean and variance of all users in each dimension and cannot obtain real-time data of a single user.
3) Our scheme can resist malicious signature attacks. By identifying invalid signatures, the verified signatures can be aggregated first, effectively preventing malicious signature attacks from causing batch verification to fail all the time and failing to enter the aggregation stage.

1.3 Paper Organization

The remainder of this paper is organized as follows. Section 2 presents the system models and design goals. Section 3 introduces some technologies that are used in the paper. Section 4 provides our concrete PMVS scheme. Section 5 discusses security analysis. Finally, Sects. 6 and 7 give the performance evaluation and conclusion.

2 System model and Design goal

In this section, we formalize the system model and identify our design goals.

2.1 System Model

A PMVS system in the smart grid network consists of four types of entities. They are Trusted Authority (TA), Electricity Service Provider (ESP), Fog Node (FN), and Smart Meter (SM or User), respectively, which are shown in Fig. 1.

There is only one TA, one ESP, and one FN in the system. For simplicity, we assume that the fog node covers n SMs, and each user's electricity consumption data is l-dimensional. TA is considered fully trusted. It will go off-line after booting the whole system. ESP and FN follow the honest-but-curious model. They follow the protocol correctly but are curious about the real-time data contained in the reports. Users are honest but curious. They do not spitefully drop or distort any source value or intermediate result and keep the system running smoothly. However, they do try to infer other users' electricity usage. Specifically, FN aggregates all user data on the ciphertext. ESP is responsible for decrypting the received report and obtaining the mean and variance of each dimension data.

2.2 Design Goal

Our design goal is to propose a resist malicious signature attacks, efficient, and privacy-enhanced mean-variance scheme for FSG such that the ESP can obtain multiple real-time data from one single aggregated data. Specifically, the following goals should be satisfied.

1) The proposed scheme should support the user's private data will not be compromised by $\mathcal{A}$. The ESP is the only entity that can read the multidimensional statistical data in PMVS, and no one can have access to the real-time data of user, including the ESP and FN.
2) The proposed scheme should support secure multifunctional statistics. Specifically, ESP can obtain the mean and variance of users in each dimension by decrypting the received ciphertext.
3) The proposed scheme should support ESP and FN to verify the authenticity of the received report. They should also detect if a report has been modified during the transmission and comes really from the legal entity. In addition, if the signature is modified, it should identify which user's signature is invalid.

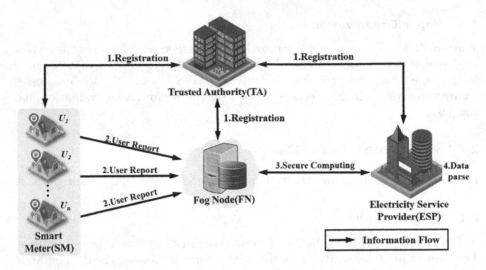

Fig. 1. The system model of our fog-based smart grid.

4) The proposed scheme should achieve efficiency. Specifically, the computation cost of cryptographic operations performed at SM, FN, and ESP should be efficient. Moreover, the multidimensional data should be encrypted into one single ciphertext to reduce the cost of communication.

3   Preliminaries

In this section, we briefly introduce the techniques used in our scheme, such as the Paillier homomorphic cryptosystem and Elliptic Curve Digital Signature Algorithm.

3.1   Paillier Cryptosystem

Homomorphic encryption allows certain computations to be carried out on ciphertexts to generate an encrypted result which matches the result of operations performed on the plaintext after being decrypted. In particular, we adopt the Paillier cryptosystem which is additively homomorphic in our construction [21].

In the Paillier cryptosystem, the public key is $pk_p = (N = p_1q_1, g)$, where $g \in \mathbb{Z}_{N^2}^*$, and p_1 and p_2 are two large prime numbers (of equivalent length) chosen randomly and independently. The private key is $sk_p = (\varphi(N), \varphi(N)^{-1})$. Given a message a, we write the encryption of a as $[\![a]\!]_{pk}$, or simply $[\![a]\!]$, where pk is the public key. The encryption of a message $M \in Z_N$ is $[\![M]\!] = g^M \cdot r^N \bmod N^2$, for some random $r \in \mathbb{Z}_N^*$. The decryption of the ciphertext is $M = L([\![M]\!]^{\varphi(N)} \bmod N^2) \cdot \varphi^{-1}(N) \bmod N$, where $L(u) = (u-1)/N$. The homomorphic property of the Paillier cryptosystem is given by $[\![M_1]\!] \cdot [\![M_2]\!] = (g^{M_1} \cdot r_1^N) \cdot (g^{M_2} \cdot r_2^N) = g^{M_1+M_2} \cdot (r_1r_2)^N \bmod N^2 = [\![M_1 + M_2]\!]$.

3.2 ECDSA∗

The elliptic curve digital signature algorithm (ECDSA) [14] is a widely standardized variant of the original ElGamal signature scheme. ECDSA∗ [22] is a modified version of ECDSA algorithm. It has been provided 40% more efficiency in the verification time compared with ECDSA signatures. The key generation, signature generation, and signature verification operate as follows.

1) *Key Generation*: Let $\mathbb{G}$ be a cyclic group of prime order p with generator $\mathbf{G}$. Select the secure cryptographic hash function $H : \{0,1\}^* \to \mathbf{G}$. The private key is $d_i \in Z_p^+$, and the public key is $\mathbf{Q}_i = d_i\mathbf{G}$.
2) *Signature Generation* $(\mathbf{R}_i, s_i)$: The signer chooses a random $k_i \in Z_p^+$, and computes $\mathbf{R}_i = k_i\mathbf{G} = (x(\mathbf{R}_i), y(\mathbf{R}_i))$. Let $x_i = x(\mathbf{R}_i)\ mod\ p$, and computes $s_i = k_i^{-1}(H(m_i) + d_ix_i)\ mod\ p$.
3) *Signature Verification*: The verifier calculates $x_i = x(\mathbf{R}_i)$, computes $\mathbf{R}_i = s_i^{-1}H(m_i)\mathbf{G} + s_i^{-1}x_i\mathbf{Q}_i$, and accept the signature if and only if $x(\mathbf{R}_i) = x_i\ mod\ p$.

4 Proposed PMVS Scheme

In this section, we present PMVS for FSG. It mainly consists of four main parts: system initialization, user report generation, secure computing, and data parsing. A list of acronyms and symbols used in this article along with their meaning is shown in Table 1.

4.1 System Initialization

The system initialization process consists of two tasks. The first is to generate the system parameter, and the second is to register the system entities.

1) Generation of System Parameters.
   - Let $\mathbb{G}$ be a cyclic group of prime order p with generator G. Let $H : \{0,1\}^* \to Z_p$ be a cryptographic hash function.
   - TA chooses security parameters τ, and calculates $pk = (N = p_1q_1, g)$ and $sk = (\varphi(N), \varphi^{-1}(N))$ of the Paillier cryptosystem.
2) System Entities' Registration.
   - The ESP first chooses an identity ID_{ESP}. Then, TA transmits sk to ESP by secure channels.
   - The FN first chooses an identity ID_{FN}. Then, TA randomly chooses a number $d_{FN} \in \mathbb{Z}_p^+$ and computes $Q_{FN} = d_{FN}\mathbf{G}$. Finally, the TA securely delivers d_{FN} to FN.
   - The SM_i (for all $i \in \{1, 2, \cdots, n\}$) first chooses an identity ID_i. Then, TA randomly chooses a number $d_i \in \mathbb{Z}_p^+$ and computes $Q_i = d_i\mathbf{G}$, and securely delivers d_i to SM_i.

At the end of this phase, TA publishes the system parameters as $\{N, g, \mathbf{G}, \mathbf{Q}_{FN}, \mathbf{Q}_i, H\}$.

Table 1. Notations

Notation	Definition
MDA	Multidimensional data aggregation
ESP	Electricity service provider
FN	Fog node
SM	Smart meter
(N, g)	The public key for the Paillier cryptosystem
(λ, μ)	ESP's private key for Paillier cryptosystem
(d_i, Q_i)	The public-private key pair of User U_i
(d_{FN}, Q_{FN})	The public-private key pair of FN
$\mathbb{G}$	A cyclic group of prime order p
H	A secure hash function, $H : \{0,1\}^* \to \mathbb{G}$
m	The number of SM covered by the FN
l	The number of data types
m_{ij}	The data type j of SM_i
M_{ij}	Converted integer form of m_{ij}
$\overline{M_{ij}}$	The encoded form of M_{ij}
$\overline{M_{ij}}'$	The encoded form of M_{ij}^2
2^z	The maximum value of M_{ij}
$\parallel$	String connection

4.2   User Report Generation

As the client's consumption information is periodically reported to FN, e.g., every quarter-hour, to protect consumer privacy from exposure, an SM needs to encrypt such private information. Thus, each SM_i measures and generates its l types of data $(m_{i1}, m_{i2}, \cdots, m_{il})$. We assume that the value of each dimensional item is less than a constant D_{max}, where $D_{max} < t^z$. The following specific steps are performed.

1) Generation of ciphertext.
   - Let $(m_{i1}, m_{i2}, \cdots, m_{il})$ and $(m_{i1}^2, m_{i2}^2, \cdots, m_{il}^2)$ are encoded as $(M_{i1}, M_{i2}, \cdots, M_{il})$ and $(M_{i1}', M_{i2}', \cdots, M_{il}')$. Let $M_{ij} = (m_{ij})_2 \parallel 0^{\theta_1}$ and $M_{ij}' = (m_{ij}^2)_2 \parallel 0^{\theta_2}$, where $j = 1, 2, \cdots, l$, $\theta_1 = (\lceil \log_2 n \rceil + z) \cdot (j-1)$ and $\theta_2 = (\lceil \log_2 n \rceil + 2z) \cdot (j-1)$. Let $M_i = M_{i1} + M_{i2} + \cdots + M_{il}$, $M_i' = M_{i1}' + M_{i2}' + \cdots + M_{il}'$.
   - SM_i chooses two random numbers $r_{i,1}, r_{i,2} \in Z_N^*$, and calculates the ciphertext:

$$[\![M_i]\!] = g^{M_i} r_{i,1}^N \ mod \ N^2 \tag{1}$$

$$[\![M_i']\!] = g^{M_i'} r_{i,2}^N \ mod \ N^2 \tag{2}$$

2) Generation of signature.
   - U_i selects a random integer k_i such that $1 < k < p$, and computes $R_i = k_i \mathbf{G} = (x(R_i), y(R_i))$.

- Let $x_i = x(R_i) \bmod p$. Then U_i generate signature s_i as $s_i = k_i^{-1}(H(m_i) + d_i \cdot x_i) \bmod p$, where $H(m_i) = H([\![M_i]\!] \parallel [\![M_i']\!] \parallel ID_i \parallel ID_{FN} \parallel T)$, T is the current time.

Finally, compute $D_i = [\![M_i]\!] \parallel [\![M_i']\!] \parallel ID_i \parallel ID_{FN} \parallel T \parallel (R_i, s_i)$, user U_i sends D_i to FN.

4.3 Secure Computing

This part consists of three stages. First, FN verifies the signatures of n user data in batches. If the verification fails, it will identify invalid signatures. Secondly, secure aggregation of the verified data. Finally, a signature is generated for the ciphertext data of the secure aggregation.

1) Identify invalid signatures in batch verification.
   - FN verifies whether these received signatures are from legal users. To improve processing efficiency, we use a batch verification method. It randomly divides $Set = (R_1, s_1), (R_2, s_2), \cdots, (R_n, s_n)$ into two subsets, $S_1(|S_1| = \lfloor n/2 \rfloor)$ and $S_2(|S_2| = \lceil n/2 \rceil)$. FN verifies the following equations,

$$\beta_{0,1} = \sum_{i \in S_1} s_i^{-1} H(m_i)) \mathbf{G} + \sum_{i \in S_1} s_i^{-1} x_i \mathbf{Q}_i - \sum_{i \in S_1} R_i \tag{3}$$

$$\beta_{0,2} = \sum_{i \in S_2} s_i^{-1} H(m_i)) \mathbf{G} + \sum_{i \in S_2} s_i^{-1} x_i \mathbf{Q}_i - \sum_{i \in S_2} R_i \tag{4}$$

If $\beta_{0,1}, \beta_{0,2}$ are equal to 0, then n metering data are all valid. Otherwise, identify invalid signatures.
   - If the batch verification of Set_1 (Set_2 is the same) fails, FN will execute the algorithm for identifying invalid signatures and find all invalid signatures in the Set_1. Algorithm 1 shows our algorithm for identifying invalid signatures, where the definition of elementary symmetric polynomials p_t is in [23].
2) Secure aggregation of legitimate data.
   - FN aggregates the verified ciphertexts $\overline{Set} = Set/Set_{inv}$ as

$$[\![\sum_{i \in \overline{Set}} M_i]\!] = \prod_{i \in \overline{Set}} [\![M_i]\!] \bmod N^2 \tag{5}$$

$$[\![\sum_{i \in \overline{Set}} M_i']\!] = \prod_{i \in \overline{Set}} [\![M_i']\!] \bmod N^2 \tag{6}$$

3) Generation signature of legitimate data.
   - FN uses its private key d_{FN} and selects a random integer k_{FN}' such that $1 < k_{FN}' < n$, and computes

$$R_{FN}' = k_{FN}' \mathbf{G} = (x(R_{FN}'), y(R_{FN}')) \tag{7}$$

Algorithm 1. Invalid Signature Identification Algorithm

Input: A bad batch of $\lfloor m/2 \rfloor$ signature pairs S_1 to be verified, along with the identities of each signer.

Output: A list of the invalid signature Set_{inv}, along with the identities of each signer.

1: **for** $\eta = 1$ to l **do**

2:    $\beta_j = \sum_{i \in S_1} i^j \cdot (s_i^{-1} H(M_i)) \mathbf{G} + s_i^{-1} x_i \mathbf{Q}_i - R_i)$

3:    **if** $\beta_j = \sum_{t=1}^{j} (-1)^{t-1} \cdot p_t \beta_{(j-t)}$ **then**

4:        **return** $(\varepsilon_1, \varepsilon_2, \cdots, \varepsilon_t)$

5:    **else**

6:        $j = j + 1$

7:    **end if**

8: **end for**

9: **return** S_1

Let $r'_{FN} = x(R'_{FN}) \bmod n$. Then FN generate signature s'_{FN} as

$$s'_{FN} = k'^{-1}_{FN}(H(M'_{FN}) + d_{FN} \cdot x'_{FN}) \bmod n \tag{8}$$

where $H(M'_{FN}) = [\![\sum_{i \in \overline{Set}} M_i]\!] \parallel [\![\sum_{i \in \overline{Set}} M'_i]\!] \parallel ID_{FN} \parallel ID_{ESP} \parallel T)$, T is the current time.

Finally, the FN send $\{[\![\sum_{i \in \overline{Set}} M_i]\!], [\![\sum_{i \in \overline{Set}} M'_i]\!], ID_{FN}, ID_{ESP}, T, (R'_{FN}, s'_{FN}), \overline{Set}\}$ to ESP.

4.4 Data Parsing

After receiving the data, the ESP first verifies the validity of the signature. After the verification is passed, the received ciphertext is decrypted. Finally, the mean and variance of each dimension data are solved.

1) Verification signature.
   - Upon receiving the all inclusive report from FN, ESP first verifies the signature according to the following equation:

$$R'_{FN} = s'^{-1}_{FN}(H(M_{FN})\mathbf{G} + x_{FN}Q_{FN}) \tag{9}$$

   If the equation does hold, it means the signatures are valid.
2) Decryption of data.
   - After checking the validity, ESP decrypts the aggregated ciphertexts $[\![\sum_{i \in \overline{Set}} M_i]\!]$.

$$[\![\sum_{i \in \overline{Set}} M_i]\!] = C_j = g^{\sum_{i \in \overline{Set}} M_{i,j}} \cdot \prod_{i \in \overline{Set}} r_{i,j}^{N} \bmod N^2 \tag{10}$$

Let $M'_j = \sum_{i \in \overline{Set}} M_{i,1} \bmod N$, $R'_j = \prod_{i \in \overline{Set}} r_{i,1}$, where $j = 1, 2, \cdots, k$. The report $g^{M'_j} \Delta R'_j \bmod N^2$ is still a ciphertext of the Paillier Cryptosystem. Thus, ESP uses the tuple $(\varphi(N), \varphi^{-1}(N))$ to recover $\sum_{i \in \overline{Set}} M_i$. Similarly, the ciphertext $[\![\sum_{i \in \overline{Set}} M'_i]\!]$ can be restored to obtain $\sum_{i \in \overline{Set}} M'_i$.

3) Parsing of data.
 - ESP performs bitwise segmentation on $\sum_{i \in \overline{Set}} M_i$ and $\sum_{i \in \overline{Set}} M'_i$, and finally obtains ($\sum_{i \in \overline{Set}} m_{i1}$, $\cdots$, $\sum_{i \in \overline{Set}} m_{il}$, $\sum_{i \in \overline{Set}} m_{i1}^2$, $\cdots$, $\sum_{i \in \overline{Set}} m_{il}^2$).
 - ESP gets the mean and variance of the j-th dimension meters' data in the following way:

$$E(m_{ij}) = \frac{1}{m'} \sum_{i \in \overline{Set}} m_{ij} \tag{11}$$

$$Var(m_{ij}) = E'(m_{ij}^2) - (E'(m_{ij}))^2 = \frac{1}{m'} \sum_{i \in \overline{Set}} m_{ij}^2 - \frac{1}{m'^2} (\sum_{i \in \overline{Set}} m_{ij})^2 \tag{12}$$

where m' is the number of $\overline{Set}$.

5 Security Analysis

Theorem 1. *The user's report is privacy preserving in the proposed scheme.*

Proof. In our scheme, U_i's ($i = 1, 2, \cdots, m$) electricity usage data $m_i = (m_{i,1}, \cdots, m_{i,l})$ is formed and encrypted by Eq. (1).

The ciphertext $[\![\sum_{i \in \overline{Set}} M_i]\!]$ is a valid and normative ciphertext of Paillier cryptosystem. Since Paillier cryptosystem is semantic secure against the chosen plaintext attack, U_i's data $m_i = (m_{i1}, m_{i2}, \cdots, m_{il})$ in $M_{i,j}$ also semantic secure and privacy preserving. Since r_{ij} is not a fixed random number, the same data $M_{i,j}$ is encrypted to different ciphertexts with different values of r_{ij}, resulting in the resistibility to dictionary attacks. If several users collude, they can share their information, including area Number, random number (for encryption), electricity consumption data, and the corresponding ciphertext. From this information in conjunction with the system's public information, they still cannot infer private information of other users.

Having received all the verified ciphertexts, FN performs the aggregation operation as in Eq. (5). Since these calculations are based on ciphertexts, Fn cannot infer users' electricity usage by analyzing intermediate results and information routed through them. In case of collusion, some users, the Fn attempt to obtain other users' electricity usage by sharing and analyzing their own information, which consists of ciphertext and public information. Since Paillier cryptosystem is semantic secure and its private keys are secretly protected, these collaborators cannot infer other users' electricity usage.

Moreover, even if an external adversary intrudes into FN's databases, he/she cannot obtain any individual user data. After receiving the aggregated cipher-text, the ESP recovers data as $(\sum_{i=1}^{m} m_{i1}, \cdots, \sum_{i=1}^{m} m_{il}, \sum_{i=1}^{m} m_{i1}^2, \cdots, \sum_{i=1}^{m} m_{il}^2)$, $E(m_{ij})$ and $Var(m_{ij})$. Even if the adversary steals these data, he/she will not be able to acquire any individual user data.

Theorem 2. *The authentication and data integrity of the user's report and the aggregated report are guaranteed in the proposed scheme.*

Proof. In our scheme, the ECDSA∗ signature [22] is adopted to sign the user's private data and the aggregated data. For the message $\{[\![M_i]\!], [\![M_i']\!], T, ID_{FN}, ID_{ESP}\}$ sent by U_i, the FN first checks ID_i and T and then verifies the message's integrity by checking if Eq. (3) holds. We can see that each element of the message is involved in verification, and any manipulation of the message will cause inequality. Therefore, the message's integrity sent by U_i can be verified by FN. Similarly, when receiving the message $([\![\sum_{i \in \overline{Set}} M_i]\!], [\![\sum_{i \in \overline{Set}} M_i']\!], T, ID_{FN}, ID_{ESP})$ sent by FN, ESP first checks ID_{FN} and T and then verifies the message's integrity by checking if Eq. (9) holds. From the equation, each element of the message is involved in verification, and any manipulation of the message will cause inequality. Therefore, the message's integrity sent by FN can be verified by ESP.

The signature (R_i, s_i) of U_i is generated with the corresponding private key d_i, and the signature (R_{FN}, s_{FN}) of FN is generated with the corresponding private key d_{FN}. Since the adversary does not know the private keys d_i and d_{FN}, it cannot produce the correct messages. Therefore, our scheme can guarantee that all users and their private data are legitimate.

Data integrity and authentication are then provided since the ECDSA∗ signature is provably secure [22]. Consequently, $\mathcal{A}$ cannot launch active attacks without being detected. The T included in the packet can prevent replay attacks. Any data modification or false data injection can be detected when the recipient fails to check the signature validity.

6 Performance Evaluation

In this section, we mainly compare our scheme with previous work to calculate cost and functionality.

6.1 Functionality Comparison

In this section, we make detailed functionality comparison between our scheme and existing ones [5,17,18]. Chen et al. [5] provided the first smart grid multi-functional data aggregation solution that supports mean, variance, ANOVA. Notice that data integrity was not considered in [5], which implies that the sensitive information at smart meter side may suffer from integrity attacks. Since the public/private key pairs of users are generated by themselves without being authenticated, they could be easily deduced and replaced by any attackers maliciously. Once an attacker successfully intercepted the ciphertext sent from some smart meters to the FN, it is possible to inject the polluted data into ciphertext, in a way to pass the batch verification by aggregator.

To address such issue, Chen et al. [18] provided an improved data aggregation scheme, which meets the security requirements of integrity and privacy, and the verification process is accelerated. Note that the two schemes [5,18] have the same statistical functions (mean, variance, and ANOVA). Although scheme [18] supports the processing of multi-dimensional data statistics, it uses super-increasing sequences to process multi-dimensional data.

Therefore, our scheme and scheme [17] achieve the efficient processing of multi-dimensional data compression. However, our scheme achieves efficient processing of large-scale dimensions. Table 2 compares the functionalities of our proposal with other three schemes [5,17,18].

Table 2. Functionality comparison

Comparison	Chen [5]	Chen [18]	Boudia [17]	Our scheme
Multidimensional data	✗	✓	✓	✓
Dimensional limit	✗	✗	✗	✓
Signature	✗	✓	✓	✓
Identify invalid signatures	✗	✗	✗	✓

6.2 Theoretical Analysis

We continue to make theoretical performance comparison between [5,17,18], and our scheme. We focus on the efficiency of the encryption, verification, and decryption. Particularly, we consider the processes of encryption, verification, batch verification, and decryption process at ESP side, respectively. In comparison, only the time-consuming operations are considered, including the bilinear pairing operation denoted as B and exponentiation operation denoted as E.

For encryption on one data, both our scheme and scheme [18] take two exponentiation operations on Z^2, while Chen et al.'s scheme involves two exponentiation on $\mathbb{G}$, Merad-Boudia et al.'s [17] take $l + 1$ exponentiation operation on Z^2.

For encryption on one data, both our scheme and scheme take two exponentiation operations on Z^2. In contrast, Chen et al.'s scheme [5] involves two exponentiation on $\mathbb{G}$, Merad-Boudia et al.'s take 2 exponentiation operation on Z. There are no bilinear pairing operations in our signing phase, but the scheme all need one pairing operation.

For the verification process, our construction executes $m + 2$ exponentiation operations on $\mathbb{G}$ without requiring bilinear pairings to verify the authenticity of a signature, whereas Chen et al.'s scheme [18] has to execute m bilinear pairing operations, however, Merad et al.'s [17] scheme needs to take one more bilinear pairing operations than [18]. Thus, the computation complexity of our scheme in the signing and verification process are less than [17,18].

For the decryption phase, our scheme and scheme [17,18] require equal operations, which contains two bilinear pairing operations. However, Chen et.'s scheme [5] contains one exponentiation operation on $\mathbb{G}$ and one bilinear pairing operation.

The comparison between our scheme and [5,17,18] are summarized in Table 3. It can be seen that our solution reduces the computational overhead at smart meter side and ESP side in comparison with [5,17,18]. Besides, Chen et al.'s scheme [5] cannot offer integrity protection for user-side data, which is addressed in our proposal. Thus, our scheme enhances the security protection on metering data compared with [5].

Table 3. Theoretical analysis

Comparison	Chen [5]	Chen [18]	Boudia [17]	Our scheme
Encryption	$2E_{\mathbf{G}}$	$2E_Z$	$(1+l)E_Z$	$2E_Z$
Signature	–	$1E_{\mathbf{G}}$	$1H$	$1E_{\mathbf{G}}$
Verification	–	mdB	$(m+1)B$	$(m+2)E_{\mathbf{G}}$
Decryption	$1E_{\mathbf{G}}+1B$	$2E_{N^2}$	$2E_{N^2}$	$2E_{N^2}$

6.3   Experimental Analysis

We conduct experimental performance analysis between our scheme and [5,17, 18]. The experiments are carried out on a 64-bit Windows 10 operating system with Inter Core i5-9500 CPU (3.0 GHz), and 8 GB of memory. The experimental code is compiled using the Java Pairing-based Cryptography Library (JPBC).

We compare the efficiency of our scheme with [5,17,18] on each procedure, that is, Encryption, Verification, and Decryption, which are summarized in Table 4. The experimental results show that our scheme is not less efficient than other schemes [5,17,18] while resisting malicious signature attacks.

Table 4. Experimental comparison (ms)

Comparison	Chen [5]	Chen [18]	Boudia [17]	Our scheme
Encryption	25.70	4.21	25.56	4.21
Verification	–	18.92	12.11	16.21
Decryption	27.94	9.22	9.22	9.22

7   Conclusion

In this article, we proposed an PMVS scheme, an efficient Privacy-Enhanced Mean-Variance Scheme Against Malicious Signature Attacks for smart grids, which can encrypt the multidimensional data into a single Paillier ciphertext. Thanks to the encoding function employed, which also gives the ability to the ESP to recover the aggregated data for every dimension efficiently and securely. The security analysis shows that the privacy, confidentiality, integrity, and authentication of the data are provided. The signature scheme in this study is more secure compared to related works, and the message encrypt or decrypt process at smart meter side and at the ESP side are accelerated. This experiment result shows that our solution achieves the safe calculation of the mean-variance of multi-dimensional data, and it is not lower than the operating efficiency of other schemes.

Acknowledgements. This work is partially supported by the National Natural Science Foundation of China under grants 62072134 and U2001205, and the Key projects of Guangxi Natural Science Foundation under grant 2019JJD170020.

References

1. Moslehi, K., Kumar, R.: A reliability perspective of the smart grid. IEEE Trans. Smart Grid **1**(1), 57–64 (2010)
2. Desai, S., Alhadad, R., Chilamkurti, N., Mahmood, A.: A survey of privacy preserving schemes in IoE enabled smart grid advanced metering infrastructure. Clust. Comput. **22**(1), 43–69 (2019). https://doi.org/10.1007/s10586-018-2820-9
3. Meng, W., Ma, R., Chen, H.-H.: Smart grid neighborhood area networks: a survey. IEEE Netw. **28**(1), 24–32 (2014)
4. Wei, Yu., An, D., Griffith, D., Yang, Q., Guobin, X.: Towards statistical modeling and machine learning based energy usage forecasting in smart grid. ACM SIGAPP Appl. Comput. Rev. **15**(1), 6–16 (2015)
5. Chen, L., Rongxing, L., Cao, Z., AlHarbi, K., Lin, X.: MuDA: multifunctional data aggregation in privacy-preserving smart grid communications. Peer-to-Peer Netw. Appl. **8**(5), 777–792 (2015). https://doi.org/10.1007/s12083-014-0292-0
6. Zhao, S., et al.: Smart and practical privacy-preserving data aggregation for fog-based smart grids. IEEE Trans. Inf. Forensics Secur. **16**, 521–536 (2020)
7. Li, F., Luo, B., Liu, P.: Secure information aggregation for smart grids using homomorphic encryption. In: 2010 First IEEE International Conference on Smart Grid Communications, pp. 327–332. IEEE (2010)
8. Rongxing, L., Xiaohui Liang, X., Li, X.L., Shen, X.: EPPA: an efficient and privacy-preserving aggregation scheme for secure smart grid communications. IEEE Trans. Parallel Distrib. Syst. **23**(9), 1621–1631 (2012)
9. Liu, Y., Guo, W., Fan, C.-I., Chang, L., Cheng, C.: A practical privacy-preserving data aggregation (3PDA) scheme for smart grid. IEEE Trans. Ind. Inform. **15**(3), 1767–1774 (2018)
10. Karampour, A., Ashouri-Talouki, M., Ladani, B.T.: An efficient privacy-preserving data aggregation scheme in smart grid. In: 2019 27th Iranian Conference on Electrical Engineering (ICEE), pp. 1967–1971. IEEE (2019)

11. Shen, H., Liu, Y., Xia, Z., Zhang, M.: An efficient aggregation scheme resisting on malicious data mining attacks for smart grid. Inf. Sci. **526**, 289–300 (2020)
12. Guo, C., Jiang, X., Choo, K.-K.R., Tang, X., Zhang, J.: Lightweight privacy preserving data aggregation with batch verification for smart grid. Future Gener. Comput. Syst. **112**, 512–523 (2020)
13. Zuo, X., Li, L., Peng, H., Luo, S., Yang, Y.: Privacy-preserving multidimensional data aggregation scheme without trusted authority in smart grid. IEEE Syst. J. **15**(1), 395–406 (2021)
14. Johnson, D., Menezes, A., Vanstone, S.: The elliptic curve digital signature algorithm (ECDSA). Int. J. Inf. Secur. **1**(1), 36–63 (2001). https://doi.org/10.1007/s102070100002
15. Boneh, D., Lynn, B., Shacham, H.: Short signatures from the Weil pairing. In: Boyd, C. (ed.) ASIACRYPT 2001. LNCS, vol. 2248, pp. 514–532. Springer, Heidelberg (2001). https://doi.org/10.1007/3-540-45682-1_30
16. Shen, H., Zhang, M., Shen, J.: Efficient privacy-preserving cube-data aggregation scheme for smart grids. IEEE Trans. Inf. Forensics Secur. **12**(6), 1369–1381 (2017)
17. Merad-Boudia, O.R., Senouci, S.M.: An efficient and secure multidimensional data aggregation for fog computing-based smart grid. IEEE Internet Things J. **8**(8), 6143–6153 (2020)
18. Chen, Y., Martínez-Ortega, J.-F., Castillejo, P., López, L.: A homomorphic-based multiple data aggregation scheme for smart grid. IEEE Sens. J. **19**(10), 3921–3929 (2019)
19. Ding, Y., Wang, B., Wang, Y., Zhang, K., Wang, H.: Secure metering data aggregation with batch verification in industrial smart grid. IEEE Trans. Ind. Inform. **16**(10), 6607–6616 (2020)
20. Ge, S., Zeng, P., Lu, R., Choo, K.-K.R.: FGDA: fine-grained data analysis in privacy-preserving smart grid communications. Peer-to-Peer Netw. Appl. **11**(5), 966–978 (2018). https://doi.org/10.1007/s12083-017-0618-9
21. Paillier, P.: Public-key cryptosystems based on composite degree residuosity classes. In: Stern, J. (ed.) EUROCRYPT 1999. LNCS, vol. 1592, pp. 223–238. Springer, Heidelberg (1999). https://doi.org/10.1007/3-540-48910-X_16
22. Antipa, A., Brown, D., Gallant, R., Lambert, R., Struik, R., Vanstone, S.: Accelerated verification of ECDSA signatures. In: Preneel, B., Tavares, S. (eds.) SAC 2005. LNCS, vol. 3897, pp. 307–318. Springer, Heidelberg (2006). https://doi.org/10.1007/11693383_21
23. Macdonald, I.G.: Symmetric Functions and Hall Polynomials. Oxford University Press, Oxford (1998)

Privacy-Preserving Cluster Validity

Peng Yang[iD], Shaohong Zhang[✉][iD], and Liu Yang

School of Computer Science and Cyber Engineering, Guangzhou University,
Guangzhou 510006, China

Abstract. In this paper, we proposed a new privacy-preserving clustering framework. We proposed two different types of data transformation
methods on clustering solution vectors and clustering ensemble consensus matrix in a unified way. The first one is encryption, which includes
cryptography-based methods and hashing functions. The other one is
the perturbation, which includes data swapping, spatial transformation,
and randomized perturbation. The related transformed clustering pairs
or the consensus matrix pairs are evaluated them using 19 popular pair-
counting similarity measures. The original evaluation results and those of
privacy-preserving methods are discussed according to different privacy-
preserving methods and different pair-counting similarity measures. We
found that 1) for clustering similarity, the information loss of clustering
similarity in cryptography-based methods and hashing functions is generally large and not applicable to the clustering ensemble case, while the
information loss of data swapping, spatial transformation, and randomized perturbation are small and applicable to a wide range. 2) Through
experimental validation, we found that different privacy-preserving methods and different pair-counting similarity measures show certain adapt-
ability, where five pair-counting similarity measures are stable for all types
of privacy protection methods. 3) Cryptography and hashing functions
have high security and too much complexity, while data swapping, spatial transformation, and randomized perturbation have low complexity
but low security. The above work can be used as an original investigation
in this field and as a reference for subsequent related future work.

Keywords: Privacy-preserving · Data mining · Cryptography · Data
perturbation · Clustering similarity

1 Introduction

As a powerful data analysis tool, data mining aims to extract potential knowledge
from data, which is prone to privacy leakage when mining useful information
from data. Therefore, the research of data mining under privacy protection is
significant.

The concept of secure two-party computation [22] was first introduced by
A.C. Yao in 1986, and later O. Goldreich extended the approach to multi-party
[8]. Secure multi-party computation has become the main means of privacy-
preserving techniques, mainly applied in distributed data mining. In 2000,

G. Wang et al. (Eds.): UbiSec 2021, CCIS 1557, pp. 159–170, 2022.
https://doi.org/10.1007/978-981-19-0468-4_12

Agrawal and Srikant [1] and Lindell and Pinkas [6] first proposed the concept of privacy-preserving data mining PPDM and proposed data scrambling techniques, which hide sensitive information by adding noise to the original data. Subsequently, Zhiqiang Yang and Sheng Zhong [21] proposed adding cryptographic techniques to data mining to protect privacy. In 2005, Liu and Kargupta [7] proposed a privacy-preserving data mining algorithm implemented based on random mapping theory.

Cluster analysis is an important research field of data mining. Many privacy-preserving clustering methods have been proposed. J. Vaidya and C. Clifton proposed a K-means clustering protocol built in a vertically distributed data environment in 2003 [19]. Later, O.R. Zaïane and S.R.M. Oliveiragave proposed a new spatial data transformation method (RBT) [11,12]. G. Jagannathan and R.N. Wright proposed an efficient security protocol based on K-means in an arbitrary distribution model of data in 2005 [5]. In 2013 a differential privacy preserving K-means clustering method [20] was proposed in 2013.

However, these approaches all protect data prior to clustering. First, the diversity of the data and the complexity of the computing environment pose significant challenges to privacy protection. Second, privacy-preserving techniques may lead to reduced data utility in clustering. Therefore, the balance between data utility and privacy protection is the focus of research.

In view of their problems above. We proposed a new privacy-preserving clustering framework. The privacy protections of the clustering solution vector and clustering ensemble consensus matrix can reduce the possibility of original sensitive data leakage and be more secure. We analyze the common privacy-preserving methods and use 19 pair-counting similarity measures [24] for privacy-preserving clustering solution evaluation.

The remainder of this paper is organized as follows. We introduce some preliminary information in Sect. 2, and in Sect. 3, we analyze the application of common privacy protection methods in clustering. Then, we use the UCI Machine Learning Datasets for experimental comparison and analyze the influence of various privacy protection methods on cluster similarity in Sect. 4. Finally, we conclude this paper and present future work in Sect. 5.

2   Preliminary

This section includes some preliminary introductions to clustering and clustering ensembles, and privacy-preserving clustering similarity. In this paper, the two terms "clustering solution" and "partition" are used interchangeably.

2.1   Clustering and Clustering Ensembles

The clustering algorithm divides data into different clusters according to a specific criterion (e.g., distance criterion). The data within the same cluster are as similar as possible, and the data in different clusters are as different as possible.

Let $X = \{x_1, x_2, \ldots, x_n\}$ be the set of n d-dimensional points to be clustered into a set of K clusters, $P = \{p_1, p_2, \ldots, p_n\}$ and $Q = \{q_1, q_2, \ldots, q_n\}$ be two partitions on a dataset X, p_i and $q_i, i = 1, \ldots, n$ be the corresponding class labels for the data point x_i in partitions P and Q respectively. Note that P and Q can be different clustering methods or the same clustering methods.

For P, an $N \times N$ co-association matrix M^P can be constructed as follows: the element M_{ij} in M^P indicates the similarity of x_i to x_j if their corresponding labels $P_i = P_j$, then $M_{ij} = 1$; otherwise $M_{ij} = 0$.

A Clustering ensemble is an algorithm that clusters the original dataset separately with multiple independent base clusters and then processes them using some integration method and obtains a final integrated result. It can be improved to improve the accuracy, stability, and robustness of the clustering solution [17].

We now introduce clustering ensembles based on the consensus matrix. Given a set of partitions $P_{l=1}^{L}$, the $N \times N$ consensus matrix can be computed as the average of their corresponding co-association matrices using

$$M = \frac{1}{L} \sum_{l=1}^{L} M^{(l)} \tag{1}$$

2.2 Clustering Similarity Under Privacy Protection

Clustering analysis is an essential tool in data mining, and it is a complex and challenging problem to evaluate the validity of the clustering results. Evaluating the performance of a clustering algorithm is not as trivial as counting the number of errors or the precision and recall of a supervised classification algorithm. In particular, any evaluation metric should not take the absolute values of the cluster labels into account. Instead, this clustering defines separations of the data similar to some ground truth set of classes or satisfying some assumption.

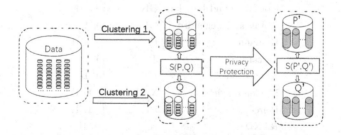

Fig. 1. Clustering similarity under privacy protection.

A good cluster validity evaluation index is indispensable to achieve the optimal number of clusters and optimal division selection. Cluster validity metrics have been proposed continuously and are mainly divided into three categories: internal validity metrics, external validity metrics, and relative validity metrics

[13]. Internally valid metrics are mainly based on the information of the set structure of the dataset to evaluate the clustering division in terms of tightness, separateness, connectivity, and overlap. Externally valid metrics are used to evaluate the performance of different clustering algorithms by comparing the matching of clustering divisions with external criteria when external information of the dataset is available. According to predefined evaluation criteria, relative evaluation metrics are tested against different parameter settings of the clustering algorithm, and the optimal parameter settings and clustering patterns are finally selected. We show the 19 bounded evaluation metrics [24] in Table 1, which includes their names, notation, and ranges.

The process of privacy preservation in clustering is illustrated in Fig. 1. We evaluate the privacy-preserving methods by comparing the similarity changes of P and Q before and after privacy preservation, the privacy-preserving methods are denoted as F, $F(P) = P'$, $F(Q) = Q'$. The clustering similarity is denoted by S. The difference between $S(P, Q)$ and $S(P', Q')$, $Gap = \left| S(P, Q) - S(P', Q') \right|$ using the common 19 clustering similarity evaluation metrics. At the same time, clustering evaluation metrics can be generalized to matrix-based comparisons [23] that can be used to evaluate clustering ensembles [24]. If the Gap under a privacy-preserving method is small, it means that it has less information on cluster similarity and better data utility.

Table 1. Pair-counting similarity measures.

Name	Notation	Range
Adjusted Rand Index	ARI	$(-1, 1]$
Baulieu	B	$[0, 1]$
Czekanowski	CZ	$[0, 1]$
Fowlkes-Mallows	FM	$[0, 1]$
Gamma(Γ)	G	$[-1, 1]$
Goodman and Kruskal	GK	$[-1, 1]$
Gower and Legendre	GL	$[0, 1]$
Hamann	H	$[-1, 1]$
Jaccard	J	$[0, 1]$
Kulczynski	K	$[0, 1]$
McConnaughey	MC	$[-1, 1]$
Peirce	PE	$[-1, 1]$
RAND	R	$(0, 1]$
Rogers and Tanimoto	RT	$[0, 1]$
Sokal and Sneath 1	SS1	$[0, 1]$
Sokal and Sneath 2	SS2	$[0, 1]$
Sokal and Sneath 3	SS3	$[0, 1]$
Wallance 1	W1	$[0, 1]$
Wallance 2	W2	$[0, 1]$

3   Privacy-Preserving Clustering

This section uses different privacy-preserving methods to protect the clustering solution. The commonly used privacy-preserving techniques mainly include cryptography and perturbation techniques.

3.1   Cryptographic Techniques

Privacy protection based on cryptography is mainly protected by encryption mechanisms that encrypt data into ciphertext, including symmetric and asymmetric encryption techniques. Symmetric encryption encrypts and decrypts information with the same key, also known as single-key encryption, mainly DES [16], TRIPLE DES [15], Blowfish [10] and AES [15]. Asymmetric encryption algorithm requires two keys for encryption and decryption, the public key and private key, respectively, with the public key for encryption and the private key for decryption. One of the most common asymmetric encryption algorithms is RSA [14].

To ensure the independence of each label in the clustering solution, we encrypt each label in the clustering solution separately and combine them to get the ciphertext.

3.2   Hashing Functions

Hashing functions are used to convert the target text into an irreversible hash string (or message digest) of the same length. Common functions include MD (Message Digest), SHA (Secure Hash Algorithm), and MAC (Message Authentication Code). Typical hashing functions include MD2, MD5 [2], SHA-1 [4], SHA-256 [4] and HMAC [3]. Since our study wants to maintain the same similarity between ciphertexts and plaintexts, the data can be encrypted here with a hashing function.

3.3   A New Privacy-Preserving Clustering Framework

Traditional encryption methods and hashing methods can encrypt the clustering solution vector of a single cluster. However, these encryption methods cause very high complexity and are not suitable for clustering ensembles.

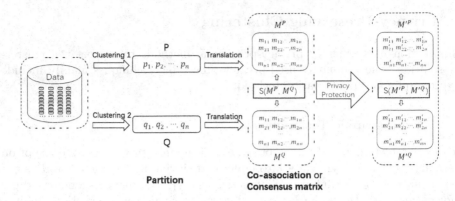

Fig. 2. A new privacy-preserving clustering framework.

Therefore, we propose a unified privacy-preserving clustering framework. As shown in Fig. 2, we use privacy-preserving techniques in the co-association matrix or consensus matrix to be widely applied to individual clustering solutions and clustering ensembles. The co-association matrices of P and Q are M^P and M^Q, respectively, and similarly, $F(M^P) = M'^P$, $F(M^Q) = M'^Q$. The difference between $S(P,Q)$ and $S(P',Q')$, $Gap = \left| S(M^P, M^Q) - S(M'^P, M'^Q) \right|$ using the 19 common clustering similarity evaluation metrics [24]. Note that the elements in M'^P and M'^Q must be between $[0, 1]$.

In the reference [24], metrics are given to evaluate the similarity of clusters through the co-association matrix or the consensus matrix, and we can evaluate the impact of privacy-preserving methods on the similarity of clusters through these metrics.

3.4   Data Swapping

Data swapping [18] is a method of data swapping that takes place at the same latitude of the data. In this way, the data information changes, and the marginal distribution characteristics of the variables are accurately retained [9], because data exchange does not modify the actual values of the data. At the macro level, the information on statistical characteristics remains unchanged. Exchange of adjacent records, or according to specific rules. In our work, we implement data swapping for the co-association matrix or consensus matrix to protect privacy. For matrix M, we use the simplest method of swapping adjacent rows of M.

3.5   Spatial Data Transformation

Rotation-Based Transformation (RBT) [11] is a geometric transformation technique that preserves data utility and privacy preservation. In this approach, rotation is used to confuse the data. This confusion is proposed to preserve the inherent clustering information of the data. Since the geometric transformations are equidistant, the transformed data retains its equidistant properties.

Although this technique involves modifying the data, it also maintains the inter-relationships between data elements in the dataset and across domains. Thus, the clustering availability of the data is well maintained.

The Rotation-Based Data Perturbation function F_r as a bijection of N-dimensional space into itself that transforms M into M' satisfying the following conditions [11]:

- Pairwise-Attribute Distortion: $\forall i, j$, such that $1 \leq i, j \leq n$ and $i \neq j$, the vector $V = (A_i, A_j)$ is transformed into $V' = (A_i', A_j')$ using the matrix representation $V' = R \times V$, where $A_i, A_j \in M$, $A_i', A_j' \in M'$, and R is the transformation matrix for rotation [11].

$$R = \begin{bmatrix} cos\theta & sin\theta \\ -sin\theta & cos\theta \end{bmatrix} \qquad (2)$$

- Pairwise-Security Threshold: The transformation of V into V' is performed based on the Pairwise-Security Threshold $PST(\rho1, \rho2)$, such that the constraints must hold: Variance$(A_i - A_i') \leq \rho1$ and Variance$(A_j - A_j') \leq \rho2$, with $\rho1 > 0$ and $\rho2 > 0$ [11].

We use one of its most straightforward ways, forming a pair of every two adjacent rows of M, setting the same rotation angle θ for each pair, and rotating each row space by the formula $V' = R \times V$ to finally obtain M' to achieve privacy protection.

3.6 Randomized Perturbation

The privacy protection of randomized perturbation is based on adding a noise vector to the original data so that the specific information content becomes insensitive [1]. Data randomization mainly operates on a subset of database tables, fields, and records and aims to preserve the statistical properties of the database. Random noise is generated by specific methods and then combined with the original data. Depending on the perturbation method, it is further divided into additive perturbation and multiplicative perturbation. Compared with the original data, these random noises change the original data relatively minor and do not seriously affect the main features of the data at the macro level.

We use randomly generated laplace noise to add perturbations to matrix M. First, a randomly generated laplace noise matrix Z with the same shape as M is generated. Parameter μ sets the position of the noise, the parameter b sets the size of the noise, and then the noise Z is combined with the raw data M to obtain the perturbed data M'.

4   Experiment

In this section, we perform an experimental analysis of various privacy-preserving methods with experimental data from well-known public datasets in the UCI

Machine Learning Repository[1], including UCI-Breast-Cancer-Wisconsin, and UCI-Iris.

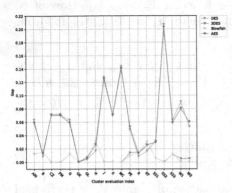

Fig. 3. Symmetric encryption.

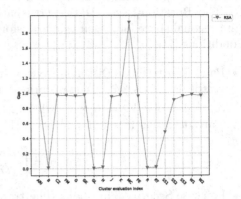

Fig. 4. Asymmetric encryption.

Figure 3 shows the experimental results of the symmetric encryption algorithm, in which 3DES and Blowfish have better results, and the similarity difference values of 19 evaluation metrics are less than 4%. Moreover, the similarity *Gap* between the DES and AES has 3 metrics over 10%. In symmetric encryption, the similarity change of evaluation metrics such as B, GK, GL, R, SS1 before and after encryption is small, which is compatible with symmetric encryption method. From Fig. 4, it can be seen that the RSA similarity difference *Gap* of the asymmetric encryption algorithm is very large, and the clustering similarity of the original data cannot be maintained after encryption.

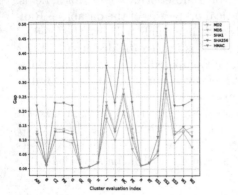

Fig. 5. Hashing functions.

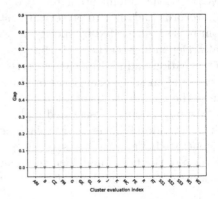

Fig. 6. Data swapping.

---

[1] http://archive.ics.uci.edu/ml/datasets.html.

In Fig. 5, it can be seen that the information loss of MD2 is the smallest among the hash algorithm methods. However, the similarity *Gap* of each evaluation index also reaches between 10% and 30%, which is not effective. With the hash algorithm encryption, the similarity of the seven evaluation metrics, B, GK, GL, H, R, RT, SS1 before and after encryption is close, matching the encryption method of the hash function.

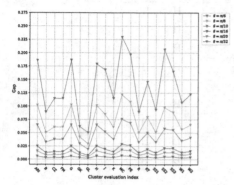
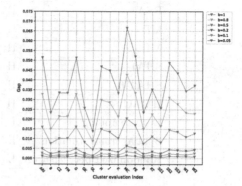

Fig. 7. Spatial transformation.   **Fig. 8.** Randomized perturbation.

From Fig. 6, it can be seen that the clustering similarity before and after privacy protection of the data swapping side has no loss and performs the best. Figure 7 shows that the similarity difference *Gap* of the RBT method is closely related to the rotation angle, and the smaller the rotation angle, the smaller the loss. The similarity evaluation metrics B, FM, GK, GL, K, R, SS1, and W1 match the RBT method and the similarity *Gap* is small before and after encryption. Figure 8 shows that the size of the scrambled method with added noise is closely related to the similarity loss, and the smaller the scrambling, the smaller the information loss. The similarity evaluation metrics B, GL, R, SS1, and W1 match the methods.

We compared the privacy-preserving methods from various aspects, including the computational complexity due to the encryption process, the similarity gap before and after encryption, and the scalability of the methods. H (High), M (Medium), and L (Low) denote their performance, as shown in Table 2. Methods based on cryptography with hash functions have high computational complexity and significant differences in clustering similarity before and after encryption. In addition, such methods cannot be applied to clustering ensemble consensus matrix. Moreover, the computational complexity of data perturbation-based data swapping, spatial transformation, and random perturbation is low. Such methods have less similarity loss and have better scalability for individual clustering solutions and clustering ensembles.

Table 2. Comparison of privacy protection technologies.

Methods	Complexity	Gap	Scalability
DES	H	H	L
3DES	H	M	L
Blowfish	H	M	L
AES	H	H	L
RSA	H	H	L
MD2	H	H	L
MD5	H	H	L
SHA1	H	H	L
SHA256	H	H	L
HMAC	H	H	L
Data swapping	L	L	H
Spatial transformation	L	L	H
Randomized perturbation	L	L	H

5   Conclusion

In this paper, a new privacy-preserving clustering framework is proposed to defend against the threat of privacy leakage in clustering. The main advantage of this solution is that it dramatically reduces the leakage of sensitive information from raw data and can be applied uniformly for clustering and clustering ensembles. Subsequently, we applied privacy-preserving methods such as encryption, hashing functions, data swapping, spatial transformation, and randomized perturbation to clustering. We compared the clustering similarity changes before and after encryption of these methods by 19 commonly used pair-counting similarity measures. It is experimentally verified that the traditional encryption method with hashing algorithm leads to a significant loss of clustering similarity. In contrast, the data swapping, spatial transformation, and randomized perturbation method have a minor loss of clustering similarity and better data utility. In addition, different privacy-preserving methods show some coupling with different clustering evaluation metrics, where the five evaluation metrics B, GL, R, SS1, and W1 are stable in the above privacy-preserving methods.

In the future, we will work separately on privacy protection for different data distributions, including distributed and centralized data distribution environments. In addition, we will explore more privacy-preserving approaches for clustering-related tasks to find the balance between privacy preservation and data utility. Providing personalized privacy-preserving solutions will be our next research focus problem.

Acknowledgments. The work described in this paper was partially supported by grants from Guang-dong Natural Science Foundation of China No. 2018A030313922, the funding of Guangzhou education scientific research project No. 1201730714, and the National Natural Science Foundation of China under grant No. 61801133.

References

1. Agrawal, R., Srikant, R.: Privacy-preserving data mining. In: Proceedings of the 2000 ACM SIGMOD International Conference on Management of Data, pp. 439–450 (2000)
2. Bakhtiari, S., Safavi-Naini, R., Pieprzyk, J., et al.: Cryptographic hash functions: a survey. Eur. Trans. Telecommun. Relat. Technol. **5**(4), 431–448 (1995)
3. Bellare, M.: New proofs for NMAC and HMAC: security without collision-resistance. In: Dwork, C. (ed.) CRYPTO 2006. LNCS, vol. 4117, pp. 602–619. Springer, Heidelberg (2006). https://doi.org/10.1007/11818175_36
4. Gilbert, H., Handschuh, H.: Security analysis of SHA-256 and sisters. In: Matsui, M., Zuccherato, R.J. (eds.) SAC 2003. LNCS, vol. 3006, pp. 175–193. Springer, Heidelberg (2004). https://doi.org/10.1007/978-3-540-24654-1_13
5. Jagannathan, G., Wright, R.N.: Privacy-preserving distributed k-means clustering over arbitrarily partitioned data. In: Proceedings of the eleventh ACM SIGKDD International Conference on Knowledge Discovery in Data Mining, pp. 593–599 (2005)
6. Lindell, Y., Pinkas, B.: Privacy preserving data mining. In: Bellare, M. (ed.) CRYPTO 2000. LNCS, vol. 1880, pp. 36–54. Springer, Heidelberg (2000). https://doi.org/10.1007/3-540-44598-6_3
7. Liu, K., Kargupta, H., Ryan, J.: Random projection-based multiplicative data perturbation for privacy preserving distributed data mining. IEEE Trans. Knowl. Data Eng. **18**(1), 92–106 (2005)
8. Micali, S., Goldreich, O., Wigderson, A.: How to play any mental game. In: Proceedings of the Nineteenth ACM Symposium on Theory of Computing, STOC, pp. 218–229. ACM (1987)
9. Muralidhar, K., Sarathy, R.: A theoretical basis for perturbation methods. Stat. Comput. **13**(4), 329–335 (2003)
10. Nie, T., Zhang, T.: A study of des and blowfish encryption algorithm. In: Tencon 2009-2009 IEEE Region 10 Conference, pp. 1–4. IEEE (2009)
11. Oliveira, S.R.M., Zaïane, O.R.: Achieving privacy preservation when sharing data for clustering. In: Jonker, W., Petković, M. (eds.) SDM 2004. LNCS, vol. 3178, pp. 67–82. Springer, Heidelberg (2004). https://doi.org/10.1007/978-3-540-30073-1_6
12. Oliveira, S.R., Zaiane, O.R.: Privacy preserving clustering by data transformation. J. Inf. Data Manag. **1**(1), 37 (2010)
13. Pfitzner, D., Leibbrandt, R., Powers, D.: Characterization and evaluation of similarity measures for pairs of clusterings. Knowl. Inf. Syst. **19**(3), 361–394 (2009)
14. Rivest, R.L., Shamir, A., Adleman, L.: A method for obtaining digital signatures and public-key cryptosystems. Commun. ACM **21**(2), 120–126 (1978)
15. Singh, S.P., Maini, R.: Comparison of data encryption algorithms. Int. J. Comput. Sci. Commun. **2**(1), 125–127 (2011)
16. Smid, M.E., Branstad, D.K.: Data encryption standard: past and future. Proc. IEEE **76**(5), 550–559 (1988)

17. Topchy, A., Jain, A.K., Punch, W.: A mixture model for clustering ensembles. In: Proceedings of the 2004 SIAM International Conference on Data Mining, pp. 379–390. SIAM (2004)
18. Dalenius, T., Reiss, S.P.: Data-swapping: a technique for disclosure control. J. Stat. Plan. Infer. **6**(1), 73–85 (1982)
19. Vaidya, J., Clifton, C.: Privacy-preserving k-means clustering over vertically partitioned data. In: Proceedings of the Ninth ACM SIGKDD International Conference on Knowledge Discovery and Data Mining, pp. 206–215 (2003)
20. Yang, L.I.: Research on differential privacy preserving k-means clustering. Comput. Sci. **59**(1), 1–34 (2013)
21. Yang, Z., Zhong, S., Wright, R.N.: Privacy-preserving classification of customer data without loss of accuracy. In: Proceedings of the 2005 SIAM International Conference on Data Mining, pp. 92–102. SIAM (2005)
22. Yao, A.C.C.: How to generate and exchange secrets. In: 27th Annual Symposium on Foundations of Computer Science (SFCS 1986), pp. 162–167. IEEE (1986)
23. Zhang, S., Wong, H.S., Shen, Y.: Generalized adjusted rand indices for cluster ensembles. Pattern Recogn. **45**(6), 2214–2226 (2012)
24. Zhang, S., Yang, Z., Xing, X., Gao, Y., Xie, D., Wong, H.S.: Generalized pair-counting similarity measures for clustering and cluster ensembles. IEEE Access **5**, 16904–16918 (2017)

A Large-Scale Study on the Security Vulnerabilities of Cloud Deployments

Andrei-Cristian Iosif[1,2]($\boxtimes$) (ID), Tiago Espinha Gasiba[1,3] (ID), Tiange Zhao[1,3] (ID),
Ulrike Lechner[3] (ID), and Maria Pinto-Albuquerque[4] (ID)

[1] Technische Universität München, Munich, Germany
andrei.iosif@tum.de
[2] Siemens AG, Munich, Germany
andrei-cristian.iosif@siemens.com
[3] Universität der Bundeswehr München, Neubiberg, Germany
{tiago.gasiba,tiange.zhao}@siemens.com,
{tiago.gasiba,tiange.zhao,ulrike.lechner}@unibw.de
[4] ISTAR, Instituto Universitário de Lisboa (ISCTE-IUL), Lisbon, Portugal
maria.albuquerque@iscte-iul.pt

Abstract. As cloud deployments are becoming ubiquitous, the rapid adoption of this new paradigm may potentially bring additional cyber security issues. It is crucial that practitioners and researchers pose questions about the current state of cloud deployment security. By better understanding existing vulnerabilities, progress towards a more secure cloud can be accelerated. This is of paramount importance especially with more and more critical infrastructures moving to the cloud, where the consequences of a security incident can be significantly broader. This study presents a data-centric approach to security research – by using three static code analysis tools and scraping the internet for publicly available codebases, a footprint of the current state of open-source infrastructure-as-code repositories can be achieved. Out of the scraped 44485 repository links, the study is concentrated on 8256 repositories from the same cloud provider, across which 292538 security violations have been collected. Our contributions consist of: understanding on existing security vulnerabilities of cloud deployments, contributing a list of *Top Guidelines* for practitioners to follow to securely deploy systems in the cloud, and providing the raw data for further studies.

Keywords: Cloud · Security · Industry · Critical infrastructures · Awareness · Infrastructure as Code · Terraform · Secure coding

1 Introduction

Cloud computing, as per the National Institute for Standards and Technology (NIST) definition [14], is "a model for enabling ubiquitous, convenient, on-demand network access to a shared pool of configurable computing resources", with rapid provisioning and minimum management requirements. Industry needs

G. Wang et al. (Eds.): UbiSec 2021, CCIS 1557, pp. 171–188, 2022.
https://doi.org/10.1007/978-981-19-0468-4_13

and trends correlate well with the advantages of using cloud-based resources – on-demand availability, reliability, and a strong accent on flexibility of the cloud have all contributed to the accelerated adoption of the cloud paradigm.

Cloud computing can be seen as a combination of existing successful technologies (i.e. virtualization, distributed storage, etc.). Recent demands for more robust infrastructure, as well as the underlying paradigm shift to *Everything-as-Service* (XaaS) have only heightened the adoption rate of companies using cloud resources for software deployment, due to both economic and performance considerations [1,4].

All previous points convey that cloud deployment inherently resilient to Distributed Denial of Service (DDoS) attacks, natural disasters, and large-scale power cuts, making it an appropriate and viable implementation option for critical infrastructures. On this topic, The Cloud Security Alliance points out, notwithstanding all advantages, that cloud critical infrastructures need to account for *concentration of resources*, i.e. having many resources in the same data center rather than distributed [18]. This can be an issue since exploits in widely used software are awaiting to be discovered, and the impact of a cyber attack can therefore be devastating. Cloud adoption within critical infrastructure sectors accentuates the imperative for ensuring resilience and security of deployment practices.

On the other hand, ensuring the security of cloud resources is an emerging research field, offering ample space for fruitful research. Whereas software vulnerabilities would be intrinsically related with secure coding, secure cloud deployment is more amorphous and multifaceted by comparison. Recent developments in terms of cloud practices have given birth to *Infrastructure as Code* (IaC), which allows to capture the architecture and configuration details of the deployment infrastructure with code (e.g. type and number of required resources). IaC as a practice thus enables version control and automation of operations.

Codebases, in the traditional sense of programming, can be developed and compared against a set of Secure Coding Guidelines (SCGs). SCGs are principles and practices for developers to follow for ensuring proper, verifiable, security [9]. Deployment code, on the other hand, namely IaC, has yet to currently mature enough to encompass similar directionality in its own ecosystem. *DevSecOps* [19] is a first step in constructing a similar set of principles, serving as a security-centric production lifecycle paradigm. The cornerstone of *DevSecOps* is that all development stages keep best practices into consideration and share responsibility, which consequentially leads to a smaller bridge to gap between development and operations teams.

Past cloud security incidents point to a consistent pattern, in which even a small misconfiguration can incur catastrophic consequences. Incidents focusing on Amazon Web Services (AWS) Scalable Storage Solution (S3) buckets have offered various news stories in the past, as the data breaches usually impress in size and negativity of outcome [15], usually due to improper access control policies. Moreover, searching publicly accessible S3 buckets is trivial [10]. As a notable example, the U.S. Department of Defense unintentionally disclosed login credentials and government intelligence data [21].

To the best of our knowledge, no study looks at real-world problems of Infrastructure as Code. Namely, the question of which most prominent problems exist in cloud deployments is seldom explored systematically across broader codebase collections. The current work addresses this question – our work focuses on Terraform as an IaC solution, and explores publicly available repositories with the help of three static code analysis tools to understand existing problems. *Real-world problems* in this context refer to security findings collected across all open-source projects hosted on GitHub – these serve as a vulnerability snapshot for the current state of cloud deployment security awareness. A total of 8256 repositories have been analysed, all of which contain Terraform deployment code and use AWS as a cloud provider. In total, no less than 292538 security violations were detected.

The main contributions of our study are the following:

- Providing an understanding of the most prominent security vulnerabilities for cloud environments.
- Deriving a list of *Top IaC Guidelines for Security* for Terraform projects
- Publishing the data gathered from all repositories, for further studies of similar nature.

This paper is organized as follows: Sect. 2 will introduce related work pertaining to standards and guidelines related to cloud security. Section 3 provides an overview of the experimental methodology employed for completing this study. Section 4 follows by presenting the technical details behind the methodology. The results are showcased and examined in Sect. 5. Based on these results, the section also includes a discussion centered around recommendations given the currently available security toolkits. Finally, Sect. 6 epitomizes through our work and presents further tangent research directions based on our findings.

2 Related Work

Although security services are the same between traditional and cloud deployments (Integrity, Confidentiality, Availability, Accountability, Authenticity, Privacy), ensuring these aspects can differ due to the underlying distributed implementation of the cloud. Furthermore, the convenience and deployment speed gained through the inherent abstraction provided by IaC may lead to *quick bugs* and vulnerabilities [17].

Tabrizchi et al. [20] elaborated a generalized taxonomy of cloud security issues, in which threats, attacks and solutions are discussed. While this security classification can serve as a consistent introductory reading to cloud architectures and potential issues surrounding them, it does not address the real-world occurrence probability of cloud security incidents. Another study conducted by Rahman et al. provides an onlook of open-source software (OSS) repository security and outlines the top 8 malpractices for IaC. Nonetheless, the authors' study is limited to the OSS repositories of solely one organization, and thus paints an incomplete picture of the *overall* security of OSS projects [17], whereas our study spans across the entirety of GitHub-hosted Terraform code.

There is a number of ongoing standardisation efforts to refine the issue of cloud security into a practical, applicable formula. For example, The Cloud Controls Matrix (CCM) is a cybersecurity control framework for cloud computing, based on best practices recommended by the Cloud Security Alliance, that is considered "the de-facto standard for cloud security and privacy" [2]. The CCM is constantly updated to reflect the newest developments and threats in the Cloud ecosystem. Government agency branches too are developing usage and security guidelines alongside these efforts – one such example is the BSI (German Federal Office for Information Security), which released two documents in 2021, pertaining to the secure usage of cloud services [7,8]. Similarly to the Cloud Security Alliance, the BSI Whitepaper on Cloud Security draws a stark warning about *concentration of resources* [6], with respect to critical infrastructures deployed in the cloud.

Other industry branches also employ their own set of security guidelines: IEC 62443 [12] is a set of standards, developed starting in 2009, focusing around Industrial Automation and Control Systems (IACS) security. However, the standard does not currently cover cloud security explicitly, which poses a severe risk: as more critical infrastructures and Industrial IoT systems begin relying on cloud resources, their certification will be only on par with an outdated standard.

On the issue of assessing the robustness of IaC deployment scripts, there are no standardized coding guidelines and best practices yet. According to industry practitioners surveyed by Guerriero et al. [11], lack of testability is quoted as the leading drawback of IaC solutions. The IaC ecosystem provides, however, a set of static code analysis (SAST) tools, which serve as a (semi-)automated way to ensure that a given piece of code does not present vulnerabilities. The practice of augmenting development pipelines with such SAST tools in the early stages is referred to as the *shift-left* security paradigm, as it offsets potential threats earlier before the code gets deployed.

All SAST tools accounted for in this study (`tfsec`, `terrascan`, `checkov`) share the following common information in the output format for a security violation: the tool would provide an error ID, a short description, a documentation link with secure and insecure code examples pertaining to the detected vulnerability, and a vendor-specific severity rating. All aforementioned tools are under constant development, with rapidly evolving security policy indexes, reflecting the underlying emergence of cloud technologies. The integration of the SAST tools into the methodology pipeline shall be presented in the following section.

3   Method

To assess real-world security of IaC implementations, we decided to focus on open-source repositories. The rationale behind this decision relies on the fact that openly available projects are very often used as either starting points, or directly as a *paste-in-place* solution. By analysing open-source repositories, we can estimate a vulnerability footprint of IaC, based on the security assessment results collected from each repository subjected to SAST testing. The collated results shall thus serve as a security snapshot of the open-source IaC ecosystem.

Figure 1 introduces an overview of the employed methodology, which we will describe in the following. The methodology can be divided into 3 phases, as shown in the same figure.

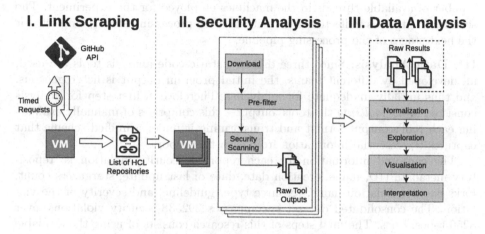

Fig. 1. Research design

I. Link Scraping: A list of GitHub repositories containing Terraform code was constructed by querying the website's API. The underlying syntax of Terraform itself is Hashicorp Configuration Language (HCL). The paper shall refer to HCL code as Terraform code, as the latter term provides a more transparent understanding. GitHub's API documentation provides useful options for searching within a given timespan and filtering for the HCL language. In terms of limitations, each query is limited to 10 pages of 100 results each, totalling a possible maximum of 1000 results. The constructed query for collecting the links, with string-interpolated query parameters, is:

```
api.github.com/search/repositories?q=language:HCL
+pushed:{start}..{end}&per_page=100&page={page}
```

The GitHub repository database was explored and the results were collected in one-month increments. The outcome of this stage of the methodology is a collated list of 44485 repository links (labeled by GitHub as Terraform code), and their associated metadata.

II. Security Analysis: Starting from the aforementioned list, the next step centers on static code analysis. Each repository is downloaded, then subjected to a number of sanity checks and filters. First, we assess whether the repository contains Terraform code or not, as one discovery consisted in uncovering that GitHub's labeling mechanism is prone to a small number of false positives (i.e. non-Terraform and empty repositories were initially included in the scraping results set). Next, the repository is evaluated by three security evaluation tools: `tfsec`, `terrascan` and `checkov`. Particular tools timed out on various repositories, which led to the need of pruning such cases out of the evaluation loop. The process was parallelized across 4 machines, by splitting the list of repositories in 4. Each quarter-list was further split across multiple processes to maximize the number of available threads in the machines employed for the experiment. The scanners' output is collected *as-is*, with further processing steps being left for the next stages of the processing pipeline.

III. Data Analysis: Since three different static code analysis tools are used, all developed by different teams, the initial program output is heterogeneous, and thus initially inadequate for analyzing. Therefore, a first step for analysis consisted of *normalizing* the tools' output – this comprises of manually evaluating each tool's output format and transforming it under a unified scheme that captures the essential information from each tool report.

The captured information for each reported security violation is: repository metadata (ID, name, creation date, date of last update, stargazers count, forks count), violation name, resource type, guideline, and severity of the violation. The consolidated dataset encompasses 292538 security violations, over 8256 repositories. The final steps of this research consists of using the available data to formulate conclusions, which shall be presented in Sect. 5. Data exploration, analysis, and visualization was performed in both R (v4.1.1) and Python (v3.8.10), with some intermediary data transformations being obtained through bash scripting and `jq`.

4   Experiment

This section will describe the technical details behind the first two stages of the implementation effort of the present study, in order to present a complete and transparent outlook on the resource and time requirements of the experiment.

The execution time of the webscraper for collecting links was approximately 3 h. This step resulted in the construction a dataset consisting of 44485 repository links, along with their relevant metadata: date created, date of last update, number of stars, number of forks, etc. The links were collected on July 15 2021, and their 'last pushed date' ranges from 07-2015 to 06-2021. After pruning for AWS-only providers and non-Terraform downloads, this list was narrowed down to 13627 repository links. A total of 70 repositories were rejected for not containing any Terraform code, and less than 10 repositories from the list of collected links had either turned private or been deleted in the timeframe between link acquisition and repository cloning. As the operation of querying the API is not resource-intensive, the machine running the script was sized accordingly – a `t3.small` AWS instance was used, with 2 GB RAM and two 3.1 GHz CPUs.

The second stage, constituting of scanning individual repositories for potential security malpractices, was parallelized across 4 machines. Each of the 4 machines ran 16 parallel threads, thus reducing the overall time of this operation 64-fold. The execution time was approximately 36 h. The employed resources for running the static code analysis tools and collecting results were AWS t3.2xlarge instances with eight 3.1 GHz CPUs, 2 threads per core and 16 GB RAM. The software versions of the employed security scanning tools were: tfsec v0.48.7, terrascan v1.4.0, and checkov v2.0.46. Various tools timed out while scanning specific repositories – any repository that could not be scanned by all three tools was discarded from the study. This resulted in the number of repositories being reduced to 8256.

5 Results and Discussions

The consolidated dataset has been analyzed to determine the distribution of resource types, which widespread security malpractices reside in the most widely used resources, and to establish underlying security trends in IaC repositories.

5.1 Cloud Vulnerability Trends

A first perspective on the data can be used to showcase yearly trends. Figure 2 shows how the number of Terraform repositories has increased over time, indicating the rise in popularity of the IaC paradigm. Furthermore, the number of security malpractices is seen to rise alongside the number of repositories. Not only does the number of total security violations rise, but so does the average count of observed violations per repository.

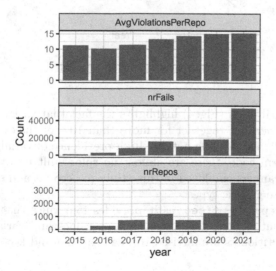

Fig. 2. Yearly evolution - Repositories, violations

Despite the sharp increase in repository numbers from 2020 to mid-2021, it appears that the number of average violations for a given public repository has stabilised around a value of 15. We find this result to be alarming, since it can imply that security awareness for IaC is stagnating.

As more and more Terraform repositories are created every year, the increase in IaC adoption does not automatically translate to better security practices being employed. This trend can be reflected from the lack of overall decline in the yearly count of average vulnerabilities per repository.

The three static code analysis tools employed for this study offer subjective *severity* ratings. The occurrence of security violation findings, grouped by severity, can be observed in Fig. 3. The ranking between the severity ratings does not change over the past recent years. Security findings ranked as high-severity are the most prevalent, and critical-severity ones being the least prevalent.

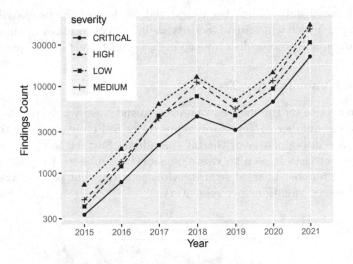

Fig. 3. Yearly evolution - Severity

Resource distribution (Fig. 4) highlights the fact that variables (6.32%) and outputs (5.03%) account together for more than 10% of the overall used types in Terraform code. Despite the notably high prevalence of variable and resource usage in Terraform code, there are almost no rules built into the policy index of the security scanners employed in this study to account and spot for security violations in these generic types.

The only exception is `tfsec`, as it provides four rules that scan for secret values stored in attributes, templates, default values and variables. Based on this finding, practitioners are advised to heed caution and keep this blind spot in mind.

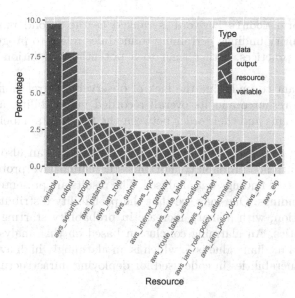

Fig. 4. Top 15 used types

Accounting only for resource subtypes, Fig. 5 highlights the top 10 most vulnerable AWS resources, based on the count of total associated observed security violations from the three SAST tools.

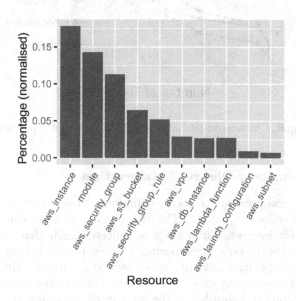

Fig. 5. Top 10 vulnerable resources

The Terraform `module` keyword is ranked as the second most vulnerable "resource". Security findings pertaining to modules relate to programming patterns and best practices, rather than to a potentially violation of a security policy.

It is important to underline the lack of observable correlation between the prevalence of a resource and its overall recorded vulnerability, as seen in the discrepancy of items and their order between the two charts' labels from Figs. 4 and 5.

The security of a given public Terraform repository can also be discussed in terms of occurrence probability. For this, the cumulative probability of the number of total tool findings was analysed. The results are presented in Fig. 6 for up to 15 tool findings. One may see that the probability distribution resembles a sigmoid function, with a sharp increase in probability starting at the count of 3 vulnerabilities. An alarming conclusion based on this analysis is that the average rounded median value is **5**, which is an alarmingly high average number of potential vulnerabilities in code used for deploying infrastructure.

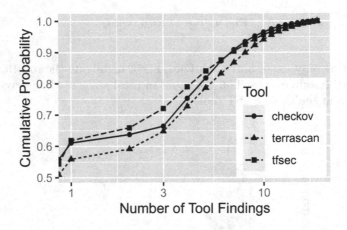

Fig. 6. Cumulative probability - SAST security violations

5.2 Most Commonly Observed Malpractices

We present the most prevalent security findings from the three SAST tools, ranked by occurrence, in Table 1. The last column clusters the results across different areas for interest. The data was collected such that each violation's rule ID is only collected once per repository. The rationale is that this approach allows for conveying the security of a given repository, irrespective of the size of its codebase – if two repositories of vastly different size and complexity trigger the same rule violation, regardless of the number of observations from the SAST tools, they are considered equally insecure.

Table 1. Most observed security violations across SAST tools

Ranking	Rule	Tool	Category
1	AWS079	tfsec	Hardening
2	AWS009	tfsec	Insecure defaults
3	CKV_AWS_8	checkov	Encryption
4	AC-AWS-NS-IN-M-1172	terrascan	Hardening
5	AWS.AI.LM.HIGH.0070	terrascan	Logging
6	AWS.CloudTrail.Logging.Medium.008	terrascan	Best practices
7	AWS008	tfsec	Insecure defaults
8	CKV_AWS_79	checkov	Insecure defaults
9	AWS.VPC.Logging.Medium.0470	terrascan	Logging
10	AWS018	tfsec	Code Documentation
11	CKV_AWS_135	checkov	Best practices
12	CKV_AWS_126	checkov	Logging
13	AWS002	tfsec	Logging
14	AWS098	tfsec	Hardening
15	AWS005	tfsec	Access control
16	AWS.S3Bucket.LM.MEDIUM.0078	terrascan	Logging
17	AWS017	tfsec	Encryption
18	AWS099	tfsec	Access control
19	AWS077	tfsec	Logging
20	AC_AWS_0228	terrascan	Access control (AC)
21	AC_AWS_0227	terrascan	AC & Insecure defaults
22	AWS.S3Bucket.EKM.High.0405	terrascan	Encryption
23	CKV_AWS_24	checkov	Logging
24	AWS.S3Bucket.IAM.High.0370	terrascan	Logging
25	AC-AW-IS-IN-M-0144	terrascan	Insecure defaults
26	AWS014	tfsec	Encryption
27	AC-AW-CA-LC-H-0439	terrascan	Insecure defaults
28	AWS012	tfsec	Access control
29	CKV_AWS_144	checkov	Hardening
30	CKV_AWS_52	checkov	N/A (deprecated)
31	AC_AWS_0276	terrascan	Access control
32	CKV_AWS_18	checkov	Logging

Grouping the most observed malpractices into categories revealed seven areas of blindsidedness in IaC scripts. Overall, our findings about the nature of the most frequently occurring security violations correlate well with the ones from Rahman et al. [17]. The results between the studies converge to show similar malpractices, both at a general level for open-source repositories, as well as in specific cases (as in the case of [17]).

Our most frequently observed vulnerability categories are listed below, from what we consider most to least severe, based on industry experience:

1. **Encryption**: The implications of not using encryption can be ample – a data breach on an unencrypted database can have consequences ranging from downtime to identity theft and privacy violations. Unencrypted resources deserve a category of their own, separate from *insecure defaults*, to further heighten the awareness regarding imperative use of encryption.
2. **Access control**: Misconfigured access control consequences range from simple data breaches, loss and corruption, to intellectual property implications and ransomware. This topic is refered to as CWE-200 [3] and results in exposing sensitive information to an actor that is not explicitly authorized to have access to that information. The OWASP project has rated Broken Access Control as the first-ranking web vulnerability in their 2021 Top 10 ranking of vulnerability classes [16].
3. **Insecure defaults**: Some resources come with very relaxed default security options, such as public access and no login gatekeeping. These defaults must be overridden before any other configuration options are accounted for.
4. **Enabling readily available hardening**: As the cloud providers' APIs need to account for more and more usecases, the configuration options are evolving to include more and more security hardening options. Some of these options are not enabled by default, and their addition is not always brought to the forefront of the providers' update notes. Therefore, the duty of routinely investigating into the addition of such options and enabling them in already deployed infrastructure lies with the practitioner.
5. **Logging**: As resources are no longer *in-house*, quantitative logging gains greater importance within the cloud paradigm.
6. **Best practices - enabling readily available options**: Similar to enabling security options, cloud providers offer out-of-the box customizations which can result in great performance boosts
7. **Best practices - documented code**: Due to the inherent complexity of large infrastructure, having a well-documented codebase related to the deployed architecture can ease security auditing and prevent unintended misconfigurations along the time.

5.3   SAST Tools Comparison

In the following, we provide a comparison between the static code analysis tools, based on the gathered results and experience, that focuses on their performance and clarity of delivering results. In terms of scanning duration, measuring the time between the three tools revealed that `tfsec` is two orders of magnitude faster than the other two SAST tools (avg 0.01 s/scan), with the latter being comparable in this regard (avg. 1 s/scan).

Documentation-wise, both `tfsec` and `terrascan` offer built-in, proprietary *severity* ratings, whereas `checkov` only does so on the website of its parent company. Each severity rating of a `checkov` rule had to be manually collected from the webpage of every rule, since the link and rule nomenclature lacked homogeneity.

Furthermore, a deeper look into the tools' ruleset documentation revealed that `terrascan` exhibits duplicate rules, listed under different rule ID's (i.e. `AWS.S3Bucket.IAM.High.[0378|0379|0381]`). Similarly, `checkov` exhibits mislabeled rules (i.e. `CKV_AWS_21`, labeled as an S3 bucket rule, states that *"all IAM users should be members of at least one IAM group"*, which refers to an unrelated resource). Another, less concerning finding about documentation is that rules which get deprecated are no longer included in the documentation in the case of `checkov` (i.e. `CKV_AWS_52`). Further metrics which the discussion about the SAST tools will rely on are presented in the tables below.

Table 2 highlight the detection overlap between the tools: in 34.77% of cases the tools agree that there is at least one security malpractice being detected, and similarly, in 44.02% of cases, all three tools agree that there is no detection of security violations. In the remaining 21.21% of cases, there is at least one tool that does not detect any error while the others do so. This leads us conclude that the tools' coverage focus varies – some SAST tools may offer security policy rules for resources which other tools either do not cover or simply have less rules to account for.

Table 2. Tools - Detection overlap

Tool	Number of tools finding at least one error			
	0	1	2	3
tfsec	44.02%	1.65%	19.56%	34.77%
terrascan		3.10%	18.11%	
checkov		2.04%	19.17%	

Table 3 further underlines the differences between the tools by highlighting a severely varying average count of vulnerabilities between the SAST tools. It is interesting to note as well that, accounting for the number of available rules for each tool, `tfsec` offers the most aggressive scans, displaying the highest number of average violations and lowest percentage of repositories with no violations, while having the smallest ruleset out of the three tools.

Table 3. Tools - Violation metrics

Metric	tfsec	terrascan	checkov
Zero violations	50.8%	51.22%	58.05%
Avg. violation #	6.66	4.87	3.14
# total rules	90	296	118

We observe that the distribution of available rules for each resource type varies between all three tools – some tools offer good coverage for certain resource types, while others do not. Due to this fact, we conclude that, from the tools we have analyzed, none offers can promise better *overall* coverage than the others. Tables 2 and 3 comprise of notable metrics between the tools and point to a similar conclusion – there is a great discrepancy between the available number of rules of each tool, and Table 2 further cements the intuitive conclusion that the tools have no unclear overlap between their coverage.

Having these points considered, our recommendation is that any IaC security pipeline should include all three. A security scan shall thus rather report duplicate violations from multiple tools, or include false positives, rather than the incident-prone alternative of having a false negative scan from a smaller number of SAST tools.

5.4   Discussion

Improving the current situation in terms of cyber security of cloud environments can be addressed through raising awareness surrounding the security of cloud deployments. This can be done through campaigns, either informative or structured as hands-on trainings [5, 22].

Furthermore, increasing the popularity of the already-existing SAST tools for IaC can not only boost the security of codebases, but also enforce pressure on the development teams to improve the tools' coverage and better tackle false positives/negatives.

Considering the rapid, constant evolution of cloud solutions, security practitioners and researchers alike must always stay informed about the latest changes to resource deployment methodologies, reasons behind the deprecation of security options and the introduction of updates. Ideally, cloud providers and SAST tool development teams should congregate to provide up-to-date, holistic changelogs that always reflect the current conditions.

Based on the interpretation of the data and our industry experience, we elaborate the following findings to augment our discussion:

1. As the number of Terraform repositories is increasing, so does the number of vulnerabilities. Whereas the first trend conveys an increase in adoption of IaC, we must argue about the latter trend observed in security malpractices is a problem for cloud deployments, especially in the case of critical infrastructures.
2. As the number of Terraform repositories is increasing over time, while the average count of vulnerabilities stays constant (flattening out at 15), we can conclude that security awareness is lacking for cloud deployment using IaC.
3. An unexpected result from analysing the data came in the form of the discrepancy between the most vulnerable observed resources, when compared to news outlets – the S3 bucket was not the highest finding, being ranked fourth in our assessment. The top 3 vulnerable resources are `instance`, `module` and `security group`. As these resources are more widely used than the S3 bucket, the security impact of malpractices concerning them can be higher.

4. Another unexpected conclusion is the high vulnerability ranking of the `module` Terraform type. However, malpractices concerning this type are firstly violations in terms of *best practices* and *DevOps*, rather than introducing problems in the deployed infrastructure.
5. We observed two classes of problems:
   (a) Before-deployment, related to best practices (i.e. logging of variables)
   (b) After-deployment, succeeding the application of a Terraform configuration, and resulting in potentially misconfigured and/or vulnerable resources (i.e. unencrypted S3 bucket)
6. We observe that `tfsec` outputs more finding than the other tools, followed by `checkov` and `terrascan`. This is an unanticipated finding, as `tfsec` employs the least amount of rules in its policy index, yet results in the highest amount of findings, cf. Table 2. Overall, this indicates that either the quality of the employed SAST tools can differ significantly, or that `tfsec`'s rules are more targeted.
7. Our experience has shown that tools are constantly evolving and changing. According to our experience, such ever-changing requirements can be seen as a *wicked problem* for software developers, in which practitioners struggle to always be up to date.

Based on the present work, as well as experience in the field of cyber security, we thus recommend practitioners to take the following guidelines into consideration:

1. Relying on a single SAST tool can be perilous, as our results indicate that findings between them are disperse and the overlap in coverage varies.
2. *Paste-in-place* solutions should be heeded cautiously, as our study revealed a multitude of problems in open source repositories, and drastically variable quality between repositories. Code should be analysed for potential vulnerabilities before being inserted into a deployable architecture.
3. Practitioners may use Table 1 to guide their decisions on tool selection.
4. In practical deployments, we recommend the use of a baseline of tools, in order to avoid introducing unstable requirements due to rule deprecation and/or creation.
5. Implementing awareness campaigns in an industrial setting with the goal of trying to raise awareness of secure cloud deployment problems can have a benefic impact. In a non-corporate setting, employing SAST tools can provide the same exposure to security malpractices and enhance one's code quality.

5.5 Threats to Validity

In terms of threats to validity, the study cannot account for false positives and negatives – the data spans across too many repositories to properly quantify and asses such metrics. The closest Figures are presented in Table 2, where coarse detection overlap is highlighted between the three employed SAST tools. Furthermore, the data is specialised, in the sense that only repositories that have AWS as a provider have been considered, as there is no one-to-one mapping between cloud providers. Nonetheless, we believe that our work can extend to other cloud providers, with different results between them. Another underlying feature of the data consists in the fact that some repositories are "collections of snippets" (i.e. book examples), which might be incomplete, thus unintentionally increasing the number of findings. This latter point is easily refutable, since published snippets should include security measures nonetheless.

6   Conclusions and Further Work

As trends in information technology are all congregating towards cloud computing, distributed infrastructures and off-site deployment become more and more ubiquitous. The industry is exerting sufficient pressure in this direction for cloud solutions to become more widely adopted, due to their inherent attractiveness in terms of lower, variable, costs and significantly shortened operations lifecycle. In terms of security, the deployment of infrastructure is currently ongoing a discovery phase before a unified body of security standards emerges.

Since deploying architectures is faster and more straightforward through the use programming languages for Infrastructure as Code, the pre-existing security problems of cloud deployment can potentially be amplified. Furthermore, due to the multitude of openly available, ready-to-use IaC repositories for any general use-case, the issue of propagating security malpractices thus gains fundamental importance.

In this work we look at the most prominent security vulnerabilities in cloud deployments. The study focuses on Terraform as an IaC solution, and AWS as a cloud provider. By using three tools for static code analysis, we conducted a security analysis on 8256 public repositories, over which 292538 security violations were detected.

Analysing the collected data, we conclude on a list of the most wide-spread vulnerable cloud resources. We grouped the most prevalent categories of vulnerabilities across seven categories, and on their basis propose a security guidelines list, acting as a security snapshot for the current state of cloud deployment security across publicly available Terraform code.

We intend that the proposed list of seven cloud security guidelines may act as a valuable source of information for industry practitioners, such that the security of their own deployments may improve, along with the overall security awareness in the cloud deployment landscape.

In a further work, the authors would like to explore mechanisms on how to raise the awareness of security vulnerabilities in IaC using Terraform. Additionally, the conclusions of the study can be adapted for cloud service providers apart from AWS, to explore whether the observed vulnerability trends are universally applicable or vendor-specific. Furthermore, as development concerning the static code analysis progresses, and as the number of newly created Terraform repositories is on the rise, this study provides a high degree of repeatability, in terms of assessing a time evolution of the security of open-source projects relying on Terraform.

Acknowledgments. Maria Pinto-Albuqueque thanks the Instituto Universitário de Lisboa and ISTAR for their support. Ulrike Lechner acknowledges partial funding of this work in project LIONS by dtec.bw.

Supporting Research Data

The consolidated dataset, which is the cornerstone of this work, is publicly available for inspection and further research on the Zenodo Platform [13]. The data is provided in Comma Separated Values (CSV) format, and comprises 292538 security violations collected across 8256 Terraform repositories (AWS-only provider).

References

1. Achilleos, A.P., Georgiou, K., Markides, C., Konstantinidis, A., Papadopoulos, G.A.: Adaptive runtime middleware: everything as a service. In: Nguyen, N.T., Papadopoulos, G.A., Trawiński, B., Vossen, G. (eds.) ICCCI 2017. LNCS (LNAI), vol. 10448, pp. 484–494. Springer, Cham (2017). https://doi.org/10.1007/978-3-319-67074-4_47
2. Cloud Security Alliance: Cloud Controls Matrix (2021). https://cloudsecurity alliance.org/artifacts/cloud-controls-matrix-v4/
3. Common Weakness Enumeration: Exposure of Sensitive Information to an Unauthorized Actor (2021). https://cwe.mitre.org/data/definitions/200.html
4. Duan, Y., Fu, G., Zhou, N., Sun, X., Narendra, N.C., Hu, B.: Everything as a service (XaaS) on the cloud: origins, current and future trends. In: 2015 IEEE 8th International Conference on Cloud Computing, pp. 621–628 (2015). https://doi.org/10.1109/CLOUD.2015.88
5. Espinha Gasiba, T., Andrei-Cristian, I., Lechner, U., Pinto-Albuquerque, M.: Raising security awareness of cloud deployments using infrastructure as code through CyberSecurity challenges. In: The 16th International Conference on Availability, Reliability and Security, pp. 1–8 (2021)
6. Federal Office for Information Security: Security Recommendations for Cloud Computing Providers - Minimum information security requirements. White Paper (2011). https://www.bsi.bund.de/SharedDocs/Downloads/EN/BSI/Publications/CloudComputing/SecurityRecommendationsCloudComputingProviders.html
7. Federal Office for Information Security: OPS.2: Cloud-Nutzung. White Paper (2021). https://www.bsi.bund.de/SharedDocs/Downloads/DE/BSI/Grundschutz/Kompendium_Einzel_PDFs_2021/04_OPS_Betrieb/OPS_2_2_Cloud-Nutzung_Editi on_2021.pdf?__blob=publicationFile&v=2
8. Federal Office for Information Security: Sichere Nutzung von Cloud-Diensten. White Paper (2021). https://www.bsi.bund.de/SharedDocs/Downloads/DE/BSI/Publikationen/Broschueren/Sichere_Nutzung_Cloud_Dienste.pdf?__blob=publicati onFile&v=1
9. Gasiba, T., Lechner, U., Cuellar, J., Zouitni, A.: Ranking secure coding guidelines for software developer awareness training in the industry. In: First International Computer Programming Education Conference (ICPEC 2020). OpenAccess Series in Informatics (OASIcs), vol. 81, pp. 11:1–11:11. Schloss Dagstuhl-Leibniz-Zentrum für Informatik, Dagstuhl, Germany (2020). https://doi.org/10.4230/OASIcs.ICPEC.2020.11, https://drops.dagstuhl.de/opus/volltexte/2020/12298
10. Greyhat Warfare: Public S3 Buckets (2021). https://buckets.grayhatwarfare.com/

11. Guerriero, M., Garriga, M., Tamburri, D.A., Palomba, F.: Adoption, support, and challenges of infrastructure-as-code: insights from industry. In: 2019 IEEE International Conference on Software Maintenance and Evolution (ICSME), pp. 580–589. IEEE, Cleveland (2019)
12. International Standard Organization: Industrial communication networks - Network and system security. Standard, International Electrical Commission (2009–2021)
13. Iosif, A.C.: Open-Source Terraform Repositories - SAST (tfsec, terrascan, checkov) vulnerability snapshot, December 2021. https://doi.org/10.5281/zenodo.5760482
14. Mell, P., Grance, T.: The NIST Definition of Cloud Computing, 28 Sept 2011. https://doi.org/10.6028/NIST.SP.800-145
15. Nag Media: List of AWS S3 Leaks (2021). https://github.com/nagwww/s3-leaks
16. Open Web Application Security Project: OWASP Top 10 (2017). https://owasp.org/Top10/A01_2021-Broken_Access_Control/
17. Rahman, A., Parnin, C., Williams, L.: The seven sins: security smells in infrastructure as code scripts. In: 2019 IEEE/ACM 41st International Conference on Software Engineering (ICSE), pp. 164–175. ACM, Montreal (2019). https://doi.org/10.1109/ICSE.2019.00033
18. Samani, R.: Critical Infrastructure and the Cloud (2013). https://cloudsecurityalliance.org/blog/2013/02/01/critical-infrastructure-and-the-cloud/
19. Sánchez-Gordón, M., Colomo-Palacios, R.: Security as culture: a systematic literature review of DevSecOps. In: Proceedings of the IEEE/ACM 42nd International Conference on Software Engineering Workshops, pp. 266–269. IEEE, Seoul Republic of Korea (2020)
20. Tabrizchi, H., Rafsanjani, M.K.: A survey on security challenges in cloud computing: issues, threats, and solutions. J. Supercomputing **76**(12), 9493–9532 (2020). https://doi.org/10.1007/s11227-020-03213-1
21. UpGuard Team: Black Box, Red Disk: How Top Secret NSA and Army Data Leaked Online (2017). https://www.upguard.com/breaches/cloud-leak-inscom
22. Zhao, T., Gasiba, T.E., Lechner, U., Pinto-Albuquerque, M.: Exploring a board game to improve cloud security training in industry. In: Henriques, P.R., Portela, F., Queirós, R., Simões, A. (eds.) Second International Computer Programming Education Conference (ICPEC 2021). Open Access Series in Informatics (OASIcs), vol. 91, pp. 11:1–11:8. Schloss Dagstuhl - Leibniz-Zentrum für Informatik, Dagstuhl, Germany (2021). https://doi.org/10.4230/OASIcs.ICPEC.2021.11, https://drops.dagstuhl.de/opus/volltexte/2021/14227

Design and Architecture of Progger 3: A Low-Overhead, Tamper-Proof Provenance System

Tristan Corrick and Vimal Kumar[✉]

School of Computing and Mathematical Sciences, University of Waikato,
Hamilton 3200, New Zealand
tristan@corrick.kiwi, vkumar@waikato.ac.nz

Abstract. This paper presents Progger 3, the latest version of the provenance collection tool, Progger. We outline the design goals for Progger 3 and describe in detail how the architecture achieves those goals. In contrast to previous versions of Progger, this version can observe any system call, guarantee tamper-proof provenance collection as long as the kernel on the client is not compromised, and transfer the provenance to other systems with confidentiality and integrity, all with a relatively low performance overhead.

Keywords: Data provenance · Accountability · Tamper-proof provenance · Security · Secure provenance

1 Introduction

For a set of data, its provenance is the metadata that is required to answer certain questions about the history of that set of data [1]. These questions may include: "Where did this set of data originate?", "What transformations has this set of data undergone over time?", "Who has used this set of data?", etc. [1].

Provenance is a powerful tool that has the potential to solve many problems. For example, in an experiment it can provide a link between final results and initial parameters, even when the data passes through many complex stages [1], aiding in scientific reproducibility. Furthermore, if one separates results into expected and unexpected, comparing the differences in provenance between the two groups can be used to help identify the cause of the unexpected results [1]. This is especially useful for software debugging, and also allows retroactive debugging. To give a final example: provenance can assist with system intrusion detection, by monitoring for abnormalities in the provenance generated.

There are multiple approaches to collecting provenance. One might choose to trace C library calls an application makes, for example, or instead choose to trace system calls. The latter approach was taken by Ko et al. in Progger 1 [3] and Progger 2. In this paper, we present the latest version of Progger, that we call Progger 3. Like its predecessors, Progger 3 also traces Linux system calls

© The Author(s), under exclusive license to Springer Nature Singapore Pte Ltd. 2022
G. Wang et al. (Eds.): UbiSec 2021, CCIS 1557, pp. 189–202, 2022.
https://doi.org/10.1007/978-981-19-0468-4_14

in order to collect provenance. It addresses certain security and performance issues in Progger 1 and Progger 2. Progger 3 is designed to be truly kernel-only. The kernel-only mode is combined with a Trusted Platform Module (TPM), which allows it to extend the tamper-proof property to the provenance as it is sent over the network to a remote server. This means that the provenance can be transferred over the network, encrypted, providing confidentiality and integrity. Also, as user space can never access the cryptographic keys, it cannot generate false provenance records. Progger 3 was also designed with efficiency as a primary objective, and as such is realistically usable with many workloads without causing an unacceptable drop in performance. It also has the ability to trace any system call, greatly enriching the provenance that can be collected.

2   Design Goals

Progger 3 was designed with the following goals in mind. It is very important to understand that a strong motivation behind Progger 3's design is to prevent an untrusted user space from being able to maliciously impact Progger 3's operation.

A. The provenance system is kernel-*only*, meaning that user space cannot alter the provenance system client's code, configuration, or any data generated by the provenance system client, both at rest and at runtime.
B. User space is never able to generate false provenance that would go undetected when received by the server.
C. The provenance has confidentiality in transit.
D. The provenance has integrity in transit.
E. Collecting and transferring the provenance has a minimal performance impact.
F. Any system call can be traced.
G. Provenance collection can begin before user space starts.
H. The provenance system cannot be unloaded once loaded.
 I. The provenance system is stable; that is, crashes are rare.
J. Existing APIs are used to trace system calls.

3   The Architecture of Progger 3

Progger 3 is designed as a Linux kernel module that collects data provenance through monitoring system calls. It uses tracepoints[1], an API of Linux allowing code to execute on entry and exit of certain functions, in order to log information about system calls. Progger 3 can be configured easily through Linux's `kbuild` system, by running `make menuconfig` or any other configuration interface, an experience that will be familiar to many who have compiled Linux before.

It should be kept in mind that values such as the system calls to trace and destination IP address have to be set at compile time, and cannot be changed during run time. This is because Progger 3 is designed so that user space cannot maliciously impact the operation of Progger 3, say by setting the list of traced

---

[1] This achieves design goal J.

system calls to be empty, or sending the (encrypted) provenance records to a different destination. This partially achieves design goal A.

Every time a system call that Progger 3 has been instructed to trace occurs, a provenance record is generated. There is currently no configuration to generate records for only a subset of the system calls that have been selected to be traced. For example, it is not possible to trace system calls made by only a specific process. This is because configuration must be made at compile time, not run time, and it is highly impractical to predetermine the PID of a particular process, except the init process. Of course, process filtering can be done later by a program that processes the data collected by Progger 3.

While this causes some limitations with flexibility, as just described, these limitations do exist for security purposes. In determining whether to use Progger 3, one should assess whether Progger 3's security advantages are beneficial under their threat model, and weigh those advantages against Progger 3's more limited flexibility compared to other provenance systems.

When it comes to transferring the collected provenance, Progger 3 sends the data it collects over TCP to a server, which runs in user space. The server can run on the same host as the Progger 3 client (for testing and debugging), or on a physically separate host that is reachable over the network. The remote server, collecting provenance from potentially multiple Progger 3 clients, is assumed to have a trusted user space. The implementation of the server can vary, but we have created an implementation that takes the data it receives and prints it as JSON. The next sections will define the record format Progger 3 uses to send data over the network, and then show the server's JSON output.

4   Record Format

Each message Progger 3 sends across the network contains a set of *records* that are encrypted and authenticated by XChaCha20-Poly1305 [8]. A record is composed of two parts: a header and a body. The header allows for multiple record types in the future, but currently there is only one: `RECORD_SYSCALL_X86_64` .

4.1   Header Format

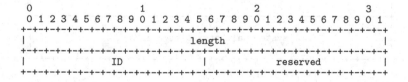

Fig. 1. The record header format

The record header format as set out in Fig. 1 has the following fields:

- length—The length in bytes of the whole record with header. A 4-octet field.
- ID—The ID of the record. A 2-octet field.
- reserved—A reserved value to ensure the data following the header has a 4-octet alignment for performance. A 2-octet field.

4.2 Body Format

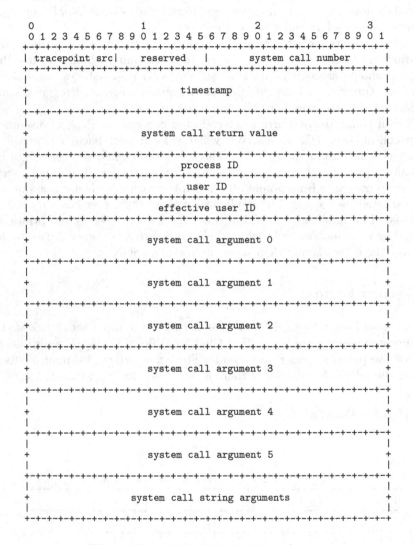

Fig. 2. The RECORD_SYSCALL_X86_64 format

With the record header just described, record types other than an x86-64 system call record can be easily added in the future. However, currently that is the only record that exists. Its record ID is `RECORD_SYSCALL_X86_64`. The format is described in Fig. 2. Each record represents one system call occurrence. Its fields have the following meanings:

- tracepoint src—The tracepoint that is the source of the data. MUST be either `TP_SRC_SYS_ENTER` (2) or `TP_SRC_SYS_EXIT` (4). These values respectively refer to the `sys_enter` and `sys_exit` tracepoints. A 1-octet field.
- reserved—A reserved value so that successive fields have a 4-octet alignment. A 1-octet field.
- system call number—The system call number from Linux. A 2-octet field.
- timestamp—A timestamp representing the number of nanoseconds since the system booted.
- system call return value—The return value of the system call, if the tracepoint source is `TP_SRC_SYS_EXIT`. 0 otherwise. A 4-octet field.
- process ID—The process ID of the process that made the system call, as seen from the initial PID namespace. A 4-octet field.
- user ID—The real user ID of the process that made the system call, as seen from the initial user namespace. A 4-octet field.
- effective user ID—The effective user ID of the process that made the system call, as seen from the initial user namespace. A 4-octet field.
- system call argument 0..5—The arguments to the system call. If, for some n, the system call doesn't use argument n, the system call argument n field is undefined and should be ignored. Each is a 4-octet field.
- system call string arguments—If a system call takes a C-string for an argument, its value will appear here. The strings are concatenated from arguments 0 to 5.

This record notably does not contain the contents pointed to by pointer arguments, other than C-strings. The approach taken by Progger 3, where only integer arguments and C-strings are copied, seeks to minimise complexity and maximise efficiency while still providing the most useful information for many use cases. Pointer arguments can point to complex `struct`s, which would require a lot of care to serialise and deserialise, increasing the risk for error. Errors are crucial to avoid in kernel code, as an error can lead to a system crash, or compromise at a very high privilege level.

4.3 Server JSON Output

Listing 1.1 provides a sample of the output of our Progger 3 server implementation when the system calls `openat`, and `setresuid` are being monitored.

Listing 1.1. Progger 3 server output

```
1  { "id": "openat", "tp_src": "sys_exit", "ts": 8901772142832, "ret":
       6, "pid": 12300, "uid": 0, "euid": 0, "args": [ 4294967196,
       140735053210000, 591872, 0, 140735053211440, 32 ], "strings": [
       "\/etc\/gss\/mech.d" ] }
2  { "id": "setresuid", "tp_src": "sys_exit", "ts": 8901772503698,
       "ret": 0, "pid": 12300, "uid": 105, "euid": 105, "args": [ 105,
       105, 105, 7, 94176267341920, 94176267341824 ], "strings": [ ] }
```

5   Kernel-Only Operation

The Progger 3 client operates in kernel-only mode, which means that there are no user space components in the client, and that user space cannot alter the code of the client or any data produced by the client. Additionally, operating entirely in kernel mode means that data doesn't have to be copied between user space and kernel space, leading to efficiency gains. The rest of this section describes how Progger 3 achieves its kernel-only mode of operation, i.e. design goal A.

5.1   Trusted Kernels

Having the Progger 3 client run entirely as a kernel module is necessary for a kernel-only mode of operation, but it is not sufficient. To ensure kernel-only operation, the user must verify that the kernel itself cannot be tampered with; that is, the kernel can be trusted. Since Progger 3 has a secret key in kernel memory, the user must boot with the kernel argument `lockdown=confidentiality`. This will ensure that, the kernel has dominion over user space, and user space is no longer able to modify the trusted kernel, assuming no bugs compromise this separation. Without `lockdown` set any root user would be able to insert arbitrary kernel modules. Thus being able to probe for Progger 3's secret key, or even stopping the tasks Progger 3 runs. A root user could also use `kexec` to load a new kernel with an altered or absent Progger 3. Furthermore, if the `/dev/kmem` interface is available, one might have a chance of recovering Progger 3's secret key by reading from that interface. These attacks are all negated by booting with `lockdown=confidentiality`.

Using a trusted kernel, however, can be a hindrance to the operation of some systems. For example, a user may be an administrator of their own personal computing device and may want to be able to easily modify the kernel. For this user, the traditional trust boundary between regular users and root users may provide sufficient security. Progger 3 can still be used in this case, without any modification, so it not a requirement that users implement a trusted kernel if they decide it is unnecessary for their threat model. Of course, the tamper-resistance is lower in that case, as a compromised user space could, potentially, read kernel memory to find the private key, and then produce false records.

In contrast, some example deployments where these trusted-kernel requirements may be easier to satisfy are virtual machine deployments, and organisations issuing many devices to its members through an IT department. So, while the use of Progger 3's kernel-only mode with a trusted kernel is not feasible in every system, there are certainly significant areas where it can be used.

5.2   Kernel-Only Implementation in Progger 3

The Progger 3 client has no user space components. It can be compiled as a standalone kernel module, or built-in to the kernel. The standalone module is intended for development and debugging, as it must be loaded by user space.

Being loaded by user space, there will be a duration before the module is loaded where provenance is not collected, which may render the installation untrustworthy in some threat models. Being built-in to the kernel, which is a new feature in Progger 3, means that every system call made can be logged, achieving design goal G. Furthermore, the built-in approach means that there is no risk that user space might be able to remove Progger 3 at run time achieving design goal H.

6 Cryptography

This Progger 3 logs include information such as the file names on a system, the time of each file access, as well as the programs being executed etc. Access to this level of detailed information can reveal to an adversary, in real-time or retroactively, what activities are, or might be taking place, on the system. Progger 3, therefore, uses strong cryptography to ensure that the collected provenance is confidential and cannot be tampered with in-flight, and to allow the receiver to verify the provenance truly came from the expected provenance client.

6.1 Cryptography Approach in Progger 3

In Progger 3, both confidentiality and integrity can be assured. In kernel mode, a complete TLS implementation is not available[2]. Such an implementation would be a serious undertaking, and likely add significant complexity and attack surface to the kernel [7]. Instead, Progger 3 uses a simpler approach based on XChaCha20-Poly1305 [8].

When a message is to be sent over the network, it is encrypted and authenticated with XChaCha20-Poly1305. This process also binds some plaintext, known as the associated data, to the cipher text. When decryption takes place, the message and the associated data must both be un-tampered for verification to succeed. The format of this message, can be seen in Fig. 3.

For security purposes, Progger 3 does not have its own implementation of any cryptographic algorithm instead relying on the Linux kernel's crypto library. XChaCha20-Poly1305 was chosen over ChaCha20-Poly1305 due to its 192-bit nonce as opposed to a 96-bit nonce in ChaCha20-Poly1305 [8]. Given that the keys used on each system running the Progger 3 client are static, as is explained later, a simple counter nonce is unsuitable, as that would lead to reuse of $\{key, nonce\}$ when the system reboots. Such reuse is to be avoided at all costs, as it reveals the XOR of the plaintexts [6]. Use of a random nonce for each message is also unsuitable, due to the overhead of repeatedly generating a random nonce. Progger 3 opts to construct the nonce by concatenating a random value R, generated once when Progger 3 starts, with a counter n that increments once with each message. 96 bits is not enough to allow for a large enough R and n, but 192 bits is. Progger 3 uses R for the first 128 bits of the nonce, and n for

---

[2] There is a feature of Linux called "kernel TLS", but that deals with data encryption only; the more complicated handshake is left to user space [5].

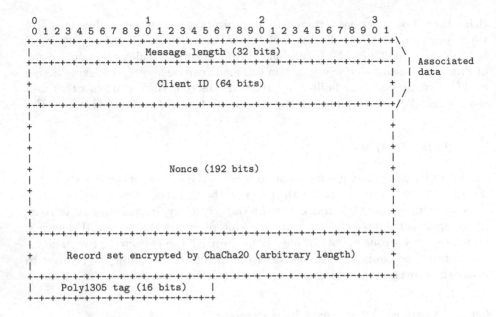

Fig. 3. Format of messages sent over the network by Progger 3

the final 64 bits. This construction is not security-affecting compared to using an entirely random nonce, or an entirely counter-based nonce [8]. With 128 bits for R, it would take $2^{128/2} = 2^{64} \approx 1.84 \times 10^{19}$ reloads of Progger 3 for there to be a 50% chance of reuse of R. Further, Progger 3 would have to send 2^{64} messages without the system rebooting before the counter cycles, which, at an absurd rate of 1,000,000 messages per second would take over 500,000 years. So, nonce reuse will not occur with this construction.

The associated data used in Progger 3 is simple: a 32-bit unsigned integer indicating the length of the message, so the server receiving the message knows when it has a complete message, and a 64-bit unsigned integer to act as a unique client ID, as seen in Fig. 3. Progger 3, ideally, should not reveal the client ID, yet, it seems to be the best approach, given that each client should have its own unique key used for encryption, and the server needs to be able to determine which key to use to decrypt each message it receives.

The message length placed in the associated data, unfortunately, needs to be used by the server before the message is authenticated, as the whole message must be received before it can be authenticated. If a malicious actor changed this value, it could cause Progger 3 to read too much or too little data. Upon receipt of the incorrect amount of data, the message would not authenticate, so it could be determined that the message was tampered with, but there would be no way of knowing what length of data is out of sync. So, Progger 3 would have to reinitiate the connection, losing some data in the process. However, this requires a network carrier to perform the attack, and they could simply drop part or all of the traffic anyway. So, effectively, there is no difference in security due to the fact that Progger 3 uses the length value in the associated data before it can authenticate it. That is, as long as Progger 3 sanitises repeated extremely large values that might cause memory exhaustion.

It is also vital to avoid replay attacks and detect dropped messages. This could be accomplished by adding a message sequence number to the authenticated data. However, a message sequence number already exists: it's the counter in the nonce. So, if the server successfully decrypts a message, it knows that the nonce is correct, and it can use the embedded sequence number to check if the message has been replayed, or potentially determine if a message has been lost in transmission. When considering confidentiality, one should also consider how the message length might reveal information about its contents. For example, if an attacker knows that the messages being sent are records generated by Progger 3 for the `openat` system call, the message length could reveal the length of the path of the file opened, assuming the message contains only a single `openat` record, and no padding is added to the message. To avoid this information leak, Progger 3 pads its messages to a multiple of 16 bytes. This assures that messages transferred by Progger 3 are done so with confidentiality and integrity and means that design goals C and D have been met.

6.2   Private Key Storage

In order to utilise XChaCha20-Poly1305, Progger 3 requires a symmetric key that both the client and receiving server know, but which is kept secret from user space. If user space could access the key, it could forge messages. These forged messages could potentially arrive at the receiving server before the real messages, causing the real messages to be discarded in favour of the forged messages. This would mean that design goal B would not be met.

To prevent this from happening, Progger 3 uses the Trusted Platform Module (TPM) to seal the key when the system is provisioned. A TPM policy is used so that the key can only be unsealed when a chosen Platform Configuration Register (PCR) is in a specific state. When Progger 3 has unsealed the key, before user space has had an opportunity to execute, the chosen PCR is extended so that the key can never be unsealed again until the system's power is cycled.

The key would also be stored on the receiving server. However, it is assumed that user space is trusted on the receiving server, so the key can be stored without precautions such as the use of a TPM. As long as the disk the key is stored on is encrypted, and the key is only readable by the appropriate user space processes, the key on the receiving server can be considered secure.

Another approach that might, at first, seem a reasonable solution, is to use an ephemeral Diffie–Hellman key exchange. But it is essential that the receiving server can verify that it is communicating with the kernel client of a particular system, and the ephemeral Diffie–Hellman key exchange does not, on its own, achieve that. In order for the kernel client to authenticate itself to the receiving server, it needs a private key that must, again, be kept secret from user space. This ends up back at the original problem of requiring a method to keep a persistent secret hidden from user space. Further, one could also seal the private key for client authentication using a TPM and use the Diffie–Hellman key exchange to generate the XChaCha20-Poly1305 key. While this would provide some security advantages, it would increase complexity and a large amount of computation would need to be done in the kernel.

As the disadvantages were deemed to outweigh the advantages, it was not considered appropriate to utilise an ephemeral Diffie–Hellman key exchange.

7   Trusted Platform Module

As previously described, Progger 3 makes use of a TPM to store the secret key used for XChaCha20-Poly1305. The following sections explore how Progger 3 utilises a TPM and what requirements exist. A proof of correctness of Progger 3's TPM operations can be later found in [2].

7.1   TPM Provisioning

When a system is provisioned with Progger 3, a unique symmetric key must be generated and then sealed with the TPM of the system. Progger 3 requires that the TPM support version 2.0 of the TPM specification [9].

When a TPM seals data, the final product is an object, split into a public and encrypted private part, that can be used in combination with the TPM to recover the data. This object is known as a *sealed data object* [9]. The data itself isn't persistently stored in the TPM, nor are the parts of the sealed data object. To unseal the data, the sealed data object parts must be reloaded into the TPM, and then the TPM must be instructed to perform the unsealing.

Reprovisioning is possible by using the owner authorisation value, but care should be taken to ensure there is no malware on the system that might be able to intercept the authorisation or new symmetric key and use it later maliciously.

7.2   TPM Unsealing

Once the TPM has been provisioned, the public and private part of the sealed data object, as well as the chosen PCR, can be provided to Progger 3 during compilation. Then, whenever Progger 3 starts, it takes the following steps.

1. Load the sealed data object into the TPM
2. Use the TPM to unseal the symmetric key
3. Extend the PCR allocated to Progger 3
4. Flush the loaded objects from the TPM

If Progger 3 fails at any point, meaning that the PCR cannot be extended, which would leave the key potentially available to user space, a kernel panic is induced. Any TPM object loaded by Progger 3 is also flushed in the error paths, so that the TPM does not reach its limit of loaded objects.

7.3   TPM Benefits

Combining the use of a TPM with Progger 3's kernel-only mode means that a cryptographic key is available to Progger 3 and user space can never access it. This makes it impossible for user space to create forged provenance records that would verify when decrypted by the remote server. Thus, the tamper-proof property extends to cover sending provenance over the network while in the presence of a malicious user space. This achieves design goal B.

8   Traceability

While Progger 1 was only able to trace 32 system calls [3], and Progger 2 only supported 23, Progger 3 is able to trace any Linux system call, of which there are over 300 on x86-64 [4] (the exact number depends on the kernel configuration). This is because Progger 3 uses a single, simple function for handling every system call, while Progger 1 and Progger 2 both used a separate function for each system call that they support (although sometimes one function is used for multiple similar system calls).

The design of Progger 1, where system calls were wrapped by replacing the address of the system call functions, naturally led to writing a new function for each supported system call. Meanwhile, with tracepoints, which Progger 2 and Progger 3 use, one callback function is executed upon each system call entry and another upon each system call exit. Details about the executing system call can be collected from inside the callback. Progger 3 provides a single function as the callback to both the system call entry and exit tracepoints, and as such can trace any system call with a single function. It is to be noted that the callback function used in Progger 2 for the system call entry tracepoint still ended up calling individual functions for different system calls.

A lot of the information can be collected in the same way across different system calls. For example, the system call number, the system call return value, process and user IDs of the currently executing task. But there is some variation in, for example, the system call arguments needing to be collected. Progger 3 tries to keep the management of these differences simple by using a single code path for each system call. It does this by keeping a table with a small amount of metadata about each system call. Most of this metadata is concerned with which of the arguments are C-strings and, in fact, most system calls do not need any metadata added to this table. This metadata doesn't need to include the number of arguments to the system call. Copying the maximum of six arguments each time ensures that each system call will always have all its arguments copied, and is probably even faster than trying to copy exactly only the number required, as that increases the size of the metadata table that has to be loaded into cache. Any excess arguments can be ignored when the data is processed later by other programs. Thus, a single code path can deal with tracing any system call.

It is worth pointing out that Progger 3's `syscall_tp` function, which deals with tracing each system call, is not very long or complex. In fact, it is only 45 lines, excluding whitespace. So, in addition to the extra usability of being able to trace any system call, the single code path massively reduces code complexity and increases maintainability. Naturally, design goal F is met.

9   Stability and Maintainability

During the development of Progger 3, extensive care was taken to ensure that it can be run for extended periods of time without crashing or harming the system. No system instability has been observed with Progger 3 thus far. Further, no warnings or errors from any kernel subsystem were printed to the kernel log[3] (as read with `dmesg`), even when running on a kernel with many of the debug options enabled under the "kernel hacking" configuration section.

We estimate that Progger 3 has been run for at least two hundred hours during testing, with the longest single run being eight hours. Progger 3 is likely to be able to run for much longer than eight hours, however; perhaps months or years. In addition to the runtime testing, we carefully checked the code itself for correctness. Hence, design goal I is met.

Progger 3 was developed against Linux 5.8.y. It very slightly modifies two files already present in Linux 5.8.y: `Kconfig`, and `drivers/net/Makefile`, adding just three lines of code to each. Then, it rewrites the `README` file to give information on Progger 3. The rest of the added code is self-contained. So, rebasing against later versions of Linux should be straightforward. The patch implementing Progger 3 adds 2465 source lines of code, 130 lines of comments, and 655 blank lines. This includes the kernel client, the server, and the TPM provisioning scripts. As such, with a small amount of code, maintenance should be relatively easy. Also, since Progger 3 uses a single code path to process system calls, it is straightforward to make changes to data that is gathered for each system call.

10   Performance Improvements

Progger 3 has significant performance improvements over Progger 1 and Progger 2. In this paper we focus on the steps taken to achieve the performance increase. Some benchmark results on the performance can be found in [2].

The primary reason that a provenance system that monitors system calls would reduce system performance is that extra code is run each time a system call executes. This code does not run in parallel with the system call; instead, it runs as a step in the system call's execution, increasing the total execution time of the system call. With system calls being a common operation, this can significantly slow down many workloads. Progger 3 minimises this overhead in order to achieve performance improvements over its predecessors. Progger 3 makes use of a ring

---

[3] The only exceptions to this were that Progger 3 warned when running without using the TPM—which is benign when done intentionally during testing—and that some ring buffer overflows occurred, as sometimes the test server didn't receive the data sent by Progger 3 fast enough, due to data reception and processing being on the same thread in the server.

buffer and writes information to it when a system call executes. Any further processing, such as encryption and transferring the data over TCP, is done by a separate kernel task. These separate kernel tasks run in parallel with other tasks on the system, so they do not directly add to system call execution time. As long as one ensures that these tasks do not use excessive CPU time, the overall reduction in system performance is not too severe. We have ensured that the ring buffer implementation at the code level is efficient. One ring buffer is created for each CPU, to reduce contention, which naturally improves efficiency. Having to support elements of variable length means that the ring buffer is not entirely lockless, but care has been taken to ensure that the locks are held only very briefly. As a result, adding data to the ring buffer is a relatively quick operation.

Thus, Progger 3 achieves efficiency by separating system call data collection from data processing and having code that works in an efficient manner. Progger 3 can be reasonably used in a wide range of workloads without reducing system performance to an unacceptable level. Therefore, design goal E is achieved. Below, we present our initial experiment of comparing Progger 3 with other tracer tools namely, Sysdig, SystemTap and bpftTrace. We compiled Linux 5.8.3 and observed the overhead caused by various system tracers. As can be seen in Fig. 4, Progger 3 incurs the least overhead when system calls are being traced while only being behind SystemTap when no system call tracing occurs.

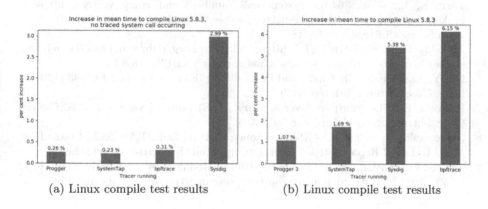

(a) Linux compile test results   (b) Linux compile test results

Fig. 4. Comparison of overhead with system tracers running

11 Conclusion

Progger 3 has an architecture with many parts, but still retains simplicity due to careful and purposeful architectural decisions. By ensuring kernel-only operation, along with the use of strong cryptography and a TPM, Progger 3 can provide tamper-proof logging of provenance both on the system running the Progger 3 client, and while the provenance is in transit to another system. Progger 3's message format allows for future expansion. If desired, additional sources of provenance could be implemented, or existing sources could have more detail collected from them. All this can be done while allowing the servers receiving the provenance to maintain compatibility with older versions of the client. Furthermore, an efficiency-focused design means that Progger 3 can realistically be used under many workloads. The focus on simplicity results in increased usability that allows one to trace any system call with continuous, error-free operation.

Acknowledgments. This work was supported by funding from STRATUS (https://stratus.org.nz), a science investment project funded by the New Zealand Ministry of Business, Innovation and Employment (MBIE). The authors would also like to acknowledge support from Prof. Ryan Ko and the team at Firstwatch for providing access to Progger 1 and 2.

References

1. Carata, L., et al.: A primer on provenance. Commun. ACM **57**(5), 52–60 (2014). https://doi.org/10.1145/2596628
2. Corrick, T.: Progger 3: A low-overhead, tamper-proof provenance system. Master's thesis, The University of Waikato (2021). https://hdl.handle.net/10289/14280
3. Ko, R.K.L., Will, M.A.: Progger: an efficient, tamper-evident kernel-space logger for cloud data provenance tracking. In: IEEE 7th International Conference on Cloud Computing, pp. 881–889 (2014). https://doi.org/10.1109/CLOUD.2014.121
4. Torvalds, L., et al.: 64-bit system call numbers and entry vectors. https://git.kernel.org/pub/scm/linux/kernel/git/stable/linux.git/tree/arch/x86/entry/syscalls/syscall_64.tbl?h=v5.8.18
5. Torvalds, L., et al.: Kernel TLS. https://git.kernel.org/pub/scm/linux/kernel/git/stable/linux.git/tree/Documentation/networking/tls.rst?h=v5.8.18
6. Nir, Y., Langley, A.: ChaCha20 and Poly1305 for IETF protocols. RFC 8439 (2018). https://tools.ietf.org/html/rfc8439
7. Rescorla, E.: The transport layer security (TLS) protocol version 1.3. RFC 8446 (2018). https://tools.ietf.org/html/rfc8446
8. Arciszewski, S.: XChaCha: eXtended-nonce ChaCha and AEAD_XChaCha20_Poly 1305. Technical Report. https://tools.ietf.org/html/draft-irtf-cfrg-xchacha-03
9. Trusted Computing Group: Trusted Platform Module Library, Family "2.0", Rev. 01.59. https://trustedcomputinggroup.org/resource/tpm-library-specification/

Skill Reward for Safe Deep Reinforcement Learning

Jiangchang Cheng[1] , Fumin Yu[1] , Hongliang Zhang[1] ,
and Yinglong Dai[2,3](✉)

[1] College of Information Science and Engineering, Hunan Normal University,
Changsha 410081, China
[2] College of Liberal Arts and Sciences, National University of Defense Technology,
Changsha 410073, China
[3] Hunan Provincial Key Laboratory of Intelligent Computing and Language
Information Processing, Changsha 410081, China
daiyl@hunnu.edu.cn

Abstract. Reinforcement learning technology enables an agent to interact with the environment and learn from experience to maximize the
cumulative reward of specific tasks, and get a powerful agent to solve
decision optimization problems. This process is highly similar to our
human learning process, that is, learning from the interaction with the
environment. As we know, the behavior of an agent based on deep reinforcement learning is often unpredictable, and the agent will produce
some weird and unsafe behavior sometimes. To make the behavior and
the decision process of the agent explainable and controllable, this paper
proposed the skill reward method that the agent can be constrained to
learn some controllable and safe behaviors. When an agent finishes specific skills in the process of interaction with the environment, we can
design the rewards obtained by the agent during the exploration process based on prior knowledge to make the learning process converge
quickly. The skill reward can be embedded into the existing reinforcement learning algorithms. In this work, we embed the skill reward into
the asynchronous advantage actor-critic (A3C) algorithm, and test the
method in an Atari 2600 environment (Breakout-v4). The experiments
demonstrate the effectiveness of the skill reward embedding method.

Keywords: Reinforcement learning · Deep reinforcement learning ·
Reward shaping · Skill reward · Safe agent

1 Introduction

Deep reinforcement learning becomes more and more popular in many research
areas of decision-making tasks, such as games [18,24], robotics [8,26], finance
[12,14], healthcare [3,25], and transportation [6,11,15]. As we know, the models
based on deep learning can achieve excellent performance, but they are lacking of
interpretability. The intermediate computational processes of the deep learning

© The Author(s), under exclusive license to Springer Nature Singapore Pte Ltd. 2022
G. Wang et al. (Eds.): UbiSec 2021, CCIS 1557, pp. 203–213, 2022.
https://doi.org/10.1007/978-981-19-0468-4_15

models are usually uncontrollable. However, the decision-making tasks require more reliable performance and higher safety than the recognition tasks based on deep learning. The mistakes on the decision-making tasks may cause severe consequences. And we might not accept the decision-making model if we could not understand the reasoning process of the model so as to control the behavior of the agent.

Recently, various deep reinforcement learning algorithms are proposed to improve the reliability or sample efficiency, which make agent train faster and achieve higher accumulative reward. The family of on-policy algorithms trades off sample efficiency in favor of stability, and we can see the progression of techniques working to make up the deficit on sample efficiency from vanilla policy gradient methods (VPG) [16] to trust region policy optimization (TRPO) [19] to proximal policy optimization (PPO) [20]. The off-policy algorithms such as deep deterministic policy gradient (DDPG) [20], Q-Learning [17], which are able to reuse old data very efficiently, but there are no guarantees that doing a good job of satisfying Bellmans equations leads to having great policy performance. Twin delayed deep deterministic policy gradient (TD3) [7] and soft actor-critic (SAC) [9] are descendants of DDPG which make use of a variety of insights to mitigate these issues.

In addition to the improvement of deep reinforcement learning algorithm, we can also embed human understandable knowledge into deep reinforcement learning model to improve the performance of the model. More importantly, the behavior of an agent based on deep reinforcement learning can become controllable and safe by introducing the human understandable knowledge. In order to achieve this, we propose skill reward, as an additional reward besides the task reward obtained by the agent when completing a specific skill task. By maximizing the sum of task reward and skill reward, the agent can learn specific skills in the process of interacting with the environment, so as to obtain task reward more effectively. This method can be applied to existing reinforcement learning algorithms including on-policy and off-policy algorithms.

We choose an Atari game, i.e. Breakout-v4, as the experimental environment to demonstrate the effectiveness of the proposed method. The experimental results show that by embedding skill reward into the reinforcement learning framework, the agent can learn the skills that human can understand, greatly accelerate the speed of agent training, and reach a higher cumulative task reward upper limit. Besides, embedding human understandable knowledge into deep reinforcement learning model through skill reward can improve the interpretability of deep reinforcement learning model. Because of the improvement of model interpretability, the behavior of an agent will become controllable and easy to be debugged. This kind of improvement will be of great help to the deployment and application of the model.

In the following, we briefly introduce the related work in Sect. 2. Then, we introduce the method of skill reward embedding technique and provide the objective function of the A3C algorithm with skill reward in Sect. 3. In Sect. 4, we demonstrate the experiments in the Breakout-v4 environment to validate the skill reward method. We have some discussion in Sect. 5. Finally, we conclude this paper in Sect. 6.

2 Related Work

In order to make the behavior of an agent controllable, some researchers proposed the hierarchical strategy for reinforcement learning. For example, Dayan and Hinton [4] proposed feudal reinforcement learning that make an agent form a hierarchical decision process. To construct hierarchical architecture for deep reinforcement learning method, Vezhnevets et al. [23] proposed Feudal Networks based on feudal reinforcement learning. Bacon et al. [2] proposed an option-critic architecture based on option framework [21]. However, it is hard to design complex hierarchical architectures for specific tasks.

This work can be classified into the research area termed reward shaping. Reward shaping in reinforcement learning is a natural extension of the concept of operating conditions from psychology to computation-oriented machine learning. Reward shaping attempts to shape the behavior of learning agents by adding additional localized rewards that encourage behavior consistent with some prior knowledge. As long as the expected behavior is consistent with good performance, the learning process leads to correct decisions. And providing localized suggestions because of shaping rewards can significantly reduce the amount of training time that it takes to learn the designated behavior [5].

The real reward signal R is enhanced by the additional shaping reward F provided by the designer. When environmental rewards are sparse or uninformative, shaping rewards are designed to guide agents to speed up learning. In its most general form [10]:

$$R_1 = R + F.$$

Similar to our work, Torabi et al. [22] proposed learning policies using behavior cloning method based on observations only. They introduced the prior knowledge contained in the observation to clone the experts' behavior. Although it maybe effective, the trained agent would lose the exploration ability. Kimura et al. [13] proposed a reinforcement learning method that uses an internal model based on expert-demonstrated state trajectories to predict rewards. Their method can work in some environments. However it is not enough for the environments where there is no change in the definition of reward. Aotani et al. [1] proposed the bottom-up multi-agent reinforcement learning method, using reward shaping algorithms to represent group behavior. Their method can be useful to a certain extent. However, there are still some unresolved problems, such as state-dependent interests, learning convergence, and model stability. By contrast, in our work, we explicitly introduce the prior knowledge in the reward that would be more flexible to adjust the training process.

3 Method

In this section, we firstly provide a brief introduction to the concept of reinforcement learning and explain the elements of the five tuples of the Markov decision-making process. Then, we introduce the cumulative reward process in the interaction process of reinforcement learning agent. After that, we propose the skill reward method. Our skill reward method can optimize the learning of one or more skills. The skill reward value can be regarded as a hyperparameter, which will vary according to the importance of skills. At the same time, the form of the problem is still an MDP after introducing our method, and we can still guarantee the theoretical convergence of the Bellman equation. Finally, we use the skill reward technique for the A3C algorithm to prove the effectiveness of the proposed method.

3.1   Reinforcement Learning

Reinforcement learning is the process of constantly interacting with the environment, obtaining an observation and a reward from the environment, and then the agent makes the next action according to the observation and reward. Generally speaking, it is the process of the agent constantly trying to make mistakes, and updating his actions according to the reward value of the environment feedback, so as to obtain the maximum reward.

Reinforcement learning can be described as a discounted MDP defined by a 5-tuple $(\mathcal{S}, \mathcal{A}, \mathcal{P}, \mathcal{R}, \gamma)$. $\mathcal{S}$ represents the current state of the environment feedback to the agent, $\mathcal{A}$ represents the action to be taken by the agent, $\mathcal{P}$ represents the state transition probability, $\mathcal{R}$ represents the reward obtained by the agent taking action $\mathcal{A}$ in state $\mathcal{S}$, and γ represents the discount factor representing the value of agent in the current state is the value of all possible reward discounted to this moment in the future.

At each time step t, Agent receives a state s_t in state space $\mathcal{S}$, then take an action a_t from action space $\mathcal{A}$ according to a stationary policy π, then the state s_t is transformed into s_{t+1} according to transition probability kernel $\mathcal{P}$ and get the corresponding reward r_t in reward space $\mathcal{R}$. The return is cumulative reward from time step t with discount factor $\gamma \in (0, 1]$, which can be formulated as $R_t = \sum_{k=0}^{a} \gamma^k r_{t+k}$. The final goal of the agent is to maximize the expected return for each state s_t.

3.2   Skill Reward

Based on the reinforcement learning framework, we propose the skill reward method that can introduce prior knowledge. We set the reward that an agent gets from the environment in time step t as

$$r_t = r_t^{task} + r_t^{skill} \tag{1}$$

s.t.

$$r_t^{skill} = \begin{cases} \beta \text{ if agent finish the skill task} \\ 0 \text{ otherwise} \end{cases} \tag{2}$$

where r^{task} is task reward that agent get from environment and r^{skill} is the skill reward for agent when it finish the specific skill task. β is a hyperparameter that can measure the importance of the skill for achieving higher task reward.

More generally, we can set up multiple skill tasks for agent to make it learn multiple skills, when we set up n skill tasks, the corresponding skill rewards are $\{r^{skill-1}, r^{skill-2}, \ldots, r^{skill-n}\}$, and we set hyperparameters $\{\beta_1, \beta_2, \ldots, \beta_n\}$, then the reward that agent get in time step t will be

$$r_t = r_t^{task} + \sum_{i=1}^{n} r_t^{skill-i} \tag{3}$$

s.t.

$$r_t^{skill} = \begin{cases} \beta_i \text{ if agent finish the skill task } i \\ 0 \text{ otherwise} \end{cases} \tag{4}$$

When we set up multiple skill task, the return of following policy π will be

$$G^{\pi} = \sum_{t=1}^{T} \gamma^{t-1} (R_t^{task} + \sum_{i=1}^{n} R_t^{skill-i}) \tag{5}$$

In this process, we only change the way that an agent gets rewards from interaction with environment, the optimization objective of the agent does not change, that is to maximize the expectation of return $\mathbb{E}[G^{\pi}]$, and the introduction of skill reward allows the agent to implement the skills that are conducive to getting task reward as much as possible. At the same time, the form of the problem is still a MDP, we can still guarantee the theoretical convergence of the Bellman equation.

3.3   Skill Reward Embedding in Reinforcement Learning Algorithm

The skill reward method can be embedded in the existing reinforcement learning algorithms.

In this work, we choose to use A3C (Asynchronous Advantage Actor-Critic) to verify the effectiveness of our proposed skill reward, which is a sample-efficient deep reinforcement learning algorithm. In actor-critic reinforcement learning methods, state value function $V^{\pi}(s)$ represents the cumulative reward expects to be obtained after seeing state s. When we take N-step sampling to accelerate the convergence, the state advantage function introduced skill reward will be

$$A(S, t) = \sum_{t=1}^{N} \gamma^{t-1} (R_t^{task} + \sum_{i=1}^{n} R_t^{skill-i}) + \gamma^N V(S') - V(S). \tag{6}$$

The optimization objective function is

$$J(\theta) = \alpha log \pi_\theta(s_t, a_t) A(S, t) + c H(\pi(S_t, \theta)), \tag{7}$$

where c is the entropy coefficient, and α is the learning rate. $H(\pi(S_t, \theta))$ is the entropy term for policy π.

As shown in Eqs. (6) and (7), the skill reward can be embedded into the existing reinforcement learning algorithms easily. And the training process is almost the same with the original algorithm that has not added much extra training cost.

4   Experiments

In this section, we adopt an Atari game, i.e. Breakout-v4, as our experimental environment to verify the proposed method. In order to introduce the skill reward, we need to analyze the environment and the observation space of the agent. We test an agent's performance with respect to three observational spaces, including original observation, masked observation and pad-ball only observation. After that, we embed the skill reward into the A3C algorithm to validate the effectiveness of the method.

4.1   Environment Setup

Breakout-v4: Breakout-v4 is an environment in gym provided by Open AI. Gym is a toolkit for developing and comparing reinforcement learning algorithms. Breakout is a classic 2D game released in 1976 running on Atari 2600, which requires players to control a pad to rebound the ball, so as to destroy all bricks, but not let the ball reach the bottom of the screen, and the game will be finished when the player destroys all the bricks or failed to catch the ball more than a certain number of times.

The state space, action space and reward space when agent interacts with the environment Breakout-v4 are as follows:

$\mathcal{S}$: The agent receives the RGB image with the height of 210 and the width of 160 as input at each time step, thus $\mathcal{S} \in \mathbb{R}^{210 \times 160 \times 3}$.
$\mathcal{A}$: The agent can choose to leave the pad motionless, right or left, which can be represented as the value of action $1, 2, 3$, thus $\mathcal{A} = \{1, 2, 3\}$.
$\mathcal{R}$: If the agent makes the ball hit a brick, it will get 1 score, otherwise it get no score, thus $\mathcal{R} = \{0, 1\}$.

4.2   Environment Analysis

When we play Breakout as human beings, it's easy for us to conceive that as long as we can control the pad to catch the ball that bounces back every time, we will definitely get high scores. Therefore, we consider that catch the ball will be the significant skill to play this game. However, it is impossible for agent to think of these in the training process. The only thing it can do is to constantly update the parameters to maximize the cumulative task reward.

On the other side, we need to determine whether the skill is helpful for the agent to get higher final task reward. Therefore, we use feature engineering to let agent only observe the position information of the ball and the pad, so it can only focus on controlling the pad to catch the ball to ensure a higher score, which is intuitive. We designed three input observation spaces for agent as follows.

Original observation s_1: The original image observed from the environment.
Masked observation s_2: The original image observed from the environment, but the part containing the brick is cropped out.
Pad-ball only observation s_3: Only the coordinates of the ball and pad in the image are retained, which is a 4-dimensional vector $(x_{pad}, y_{pad}, x_{ball}, y_{ball})$.

Figure 1 illustrates the three observation spaces.

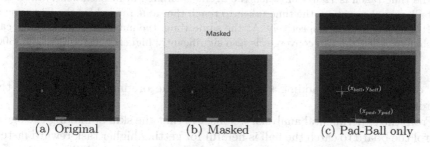

(a) Original   (b) Masked   (c) Pad-Ball only

Fig. 1. Three observation spaces for agent. Figure (a) shows the original observation that the original image observed from the environment. Figure (b) shows the masked observation that the original image observed from the environment, but the part containing the brick is cropped out. Figure (c) shows the pad-ball only observation that only the coordinates of the ball and pad in the image are retained.

We let the agent interact with the environment under the above three observation spaces, and record the mean episode reward in the training process. The results are shown in Fig. 2. Training results show that the agent receives masked observation and pad ball only observation, it takes less time to achieve the same training effect compared with receiving original observation, and the agent can achieve higher mean episode reward.

In the game environment of Breakout-v4, we can draw two obvious conclusions from the experimental results of the three observation spaces of the original observation, masked observation, and pad-ball only observation. First, when the agents reach the same score, the two observation spaces of masked observation and pad-ball only observation take less time than the original observation. Secondly, in the mask observation and pad-ball only observation, the agent's mean episode reward can achieve higher scores. The improvement of the above two aspects is mainly caused by the skill of letting the agent control the pad to catch the ball. Therefore, we conduct a comparative experiment in the original observation by adding skill rewards to let the agent learn the skill of catching the ball on the controlled pad. As a result, we can make the agent achieve the effect similar to the two observation spaces of mask observation and pad-ball

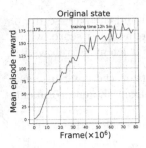
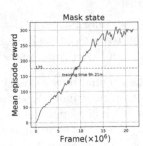
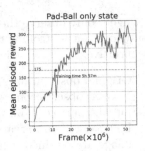

Fig. 2. Mean episode reward in training process. When the agent is trained in the original observation, it converges when the mean episode reward reaches about 175 and the time taken is 12 h 5 m. when the agent is trained in masked observation and pad ball only observation, the time taken to reach the same reward for the first time is 9 h 21 m and 5 h 57 m respectively. At the same time, the maximum reward that can be achieved when the two converges is also significantly higher, which all close to 300.

only observation after adding skill rewards in the original observation of the environment.

From the experimental analysis, we observe that the skill of making the agent control the board to catch the ball is helpful for getting higher task reward faster. In the following, we will let the agent learn this skill through skill reward, so as to achieve a similar effect.

4.3 Skill Reward Embedding

From the experiment in the previous section, we know that we need to train the agent's ability to catch the ball. Therefore, in the next part of the experiment, we compare the value of mean episode reward with or without skill reward in the original observation. The skill reward mainly trains the agent's ability to catch the ball, so every time the agent successfully catches the ball, it will get the corresponding skill reward β, and if the ball successfully hits the brick at the same time, it will also get the corresponding task reward. In this way, in the original observation, compared with the case of no skill reward, the skill reward can make the agent strengthen the skill of catching the ball. In this experiment, in the original observation, we set the skill reward $\beta = 1$ for each board catching the ball. We compared the agents in the training process who only got the task reward and both the task reward and the skill reward. The results are shown in Fig. 3.

The experimental results show that the agent can learn the skills that can contribute to the task through skill reward, which can greatly improve the speed of agent training and the upper limit of task reward from the environment. Based on this, we can also set more skill tasks that are helpful to the task, and make the agent learn them through skill reward, so as to improve the performance of agent in a human understandable way.

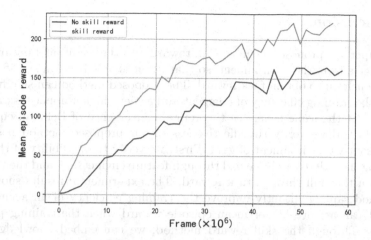

Fig. 3. Mean episode reward in training process. This is a comparison chart of whether the agent has skill rewards in its original state. First of all, under the same number of training frames, a skill reward will get a higher score than no skill reward. Secondly, with the same average reward, the number of training frames with skill rewards will be less than without skill rewards. Third, with skill rewards, you will eventually get a larger average reward.

5   Discussion

By adding extra skill rewards, the agent can learn the skills that are helpful to the task implementation, which can embed human understandable knowledge into the reinforcement learning model and improve the performance and inter-pretability of the model. However, sometimes we may not be able to ensure that the skill task that we set can be helpful to improve the final task. And it is difficult to accurately evaluate the value of skill reward, which may require a lot of experiments to determine the appropriate value of skill reward. Another diffi-culty is that we may sometimes adopt skill rewards that may not converge well, because it may depend on several skills, and we need to keep trying to explore various key skills. Moreover, under some complicated conditions, we can't be sure whether the poor results are caused by inappropriate optimized skill settings, so this is also an urgent problem to be solved in skill reward.

We believe that skill rewards enable agents to learn knowledge that human beings can understand, which will effectively promote the deployment and appli-cation of deep reinforcement learning model, and also make deep reinforcement learning more interpretable, which will greatly promote the rapid combination of reinforcement learning and practical application, and make it better used in real life. In the future work, we will conduct more experiments to explore the feasibility of skill reward in more complicated situations, and promote the combi-nation of skill reward and deep reinforcement learning model to more realistically deploy the practical application of life.

6   Conclusion

In this paper, we propose to embed skill reward into the traditional reward that an agent gets from the environment, so that agent is able to learn specific skills which are helpful to obtain task reward. The proposed method can significantly improve the training efficiency of an agent and achieve higher upper task reward boundary. At the same time, the theoretical convergence of Bellman equation is assured. And we verify the effectiveness of our proposed method based on the Breakout-v4 environment of gym. First, we verify the feasibility of the skill controlling the ball to catch the pad through feature engineering, and then let the agent learn the skill through task reward. The experimental results show that our method can significantly improve the training efficiency of an agent. And the agent can achieve higher mean episode reward when the training process converges. Through the skill reward method, we can embed knowledge that human can understand into reinforcement learning model in the training process, so as to achieve a leap in performance and make the model more interpretable and safe.

Acknowledgments. This work is partly supported by Hunan Provincial Natural Science Foundation under Grant Number 2020JJ5367, Project of Hunan Social Science Achievement Appraisal Committee in 2020 (No. XSP20YBZ043), Key Project of Teaching Reform in Colleges and Universities of Hunan Province under Grant Number HNJG-2021-0251, Scientific Research Fund of Hunan Provincial Education Department under Grant Number 21A0599, and Scientific Research Innovation Project of Xiangjiang College of Artificial Intelligence, Hunan Normal University.

References

1. Aotani, T., Kobayashi, T., Sugimoto, K.: Bottom-up multi-agent reinforcement learning by reward shaping for cooperative-competitive tasks. Appl. Intell. **51**(7), 4434–4452 (2021). https://doi.org/10.1007/s10489-020-02034-2
2. Bacon, P.L., Harb, J., Precup, D.: The option-critic architecture. In: Proceedings of the Thirty-First AAAI Conference on Artificial Intelligence, AAAI 2017, p. 1726C1734. AAAI Press (2017)
3. Dai, Y., Wang, G., Muhammad, K., Liu, S.: A closed-loop healthcare processing approach based on deep reinforcement learning. Multimedia Tools Appl. 1–23 (2020). https://doi.org/10.1007/s11042-020-08896-5
4. Dayan, P., Hinton, G.E.: Feudal reinforcement learning. In: Advances in Neural Information Processing Systems, vol. 5, (NIPS Conference), p. 271C278. Morgan Kaufmann Publishers Inc., San Francisco (1992)
5. Dong, Y., Tang, X., Yuan, Y.: Principled reward shaping for reinforcement learning via Lyapunov stability theory. Neurocomputing **393**, 83–90 (2020)
6. Farazi, N.P., Zou, B., Ahamed, T., Barua, L.: Deep reinforcement learning in transportation research: a review. Transp. Res. Interdisc. Perspect. **11**, 100425 (2021)
7. Fujimoto, S., Hoof, H., Meger, D.: Addressing function approximation error in actor-critic methods. In: International Conference on Machine Learning, pp. 1587–1596. PMLR (2018)

8. Gu, S., Holly, E., Lillicrap, T., Levine, S.: Deep reinforcement learning for robotic manipulation with asynchronous off-policy updates. In: 2017 IEEE International Conference on Robotics and Automation (ICRA), pp. 3389–3396. IEEE (2017)
9. Haarnoja, T., Zhou, A., Abbeel, P., Levine, S.: Soft actor-critic: off-policy maximum entropy deep reinforcement learning with a stochastic actor. In: International Conference on Machine Learning, pp. 1861–1870. PMLR (2018)
10. Harutyunyan, A., Brys, T., Vrancx, P., Nowé, A.: Off-policy reward shaping with ensembles. arXiv preprint arXiv:1502.03248 (2015)
11. Haydari, A., Yilmaz, Y.: Deep reinforcement learning for intelligent transportation systems: a survey. IEEE Trans. Intell. Transp. Syst. **23**(1), 11–32 (2022). https://doi.org/10.1109/TITS.2020.3008612
12. Hu, Y.J., Lin, S.J.: Deep reinforcement learning for optimizing finance portfolio management. In: 2019 Amity International Conference on Artificial Intelligence (AICAI), pp. 14–20. IEEE (2019)
13. Kimura, D., Chaudhury, S., Tachibana, R., Dasgupta, S.: Internal model from observations for reward shaping. arXiv preprint arXiv:1806.01267 (2018)
14. Liu, X.Y., et al.: FinRL: A deep reinforcement learning library for automated stock trading in quantitative finance. arXiv preprint arXiv:2011.09607 (2020)
15. Manchella, K., Umrawal, A.K., Aggarwal, V.: FlexPool: a distributed model-free deep reinforcement learning algorithm for joint passengers and goods transportation. IEEE Trans. Intell. Transp. Syst. **22**(4), 2035–2047 (2021)
16. Mnih, V., et al.: Asynchronous methods for deep reinforcement learning. In: International Conference on Machine Learning, pp. 1928–1937. PMLR (2016)
17. Mnih, V., et al.: Human-level control through deep reinforcement learning. Nature **518**(7540), 529–533 (2015)
18. Pang, Z.J., Liu, R.Z., Meng, Z.Y., Zhang, Y., Yu, Y., Lu, T.: On reinforcement learning for full-length game of starcraft. In: Proceedings of the AAAI Conference on Artificial Intelligence, vol. 33, pp. 4691–4698 (2019)
19. Schulman, J., Levine, S., Abbeel, P., Jordan, M., Moritz, P.: Trust region policy optimization. In: International Conference on Machine Learning, pp. 1889–1897. PMLR (2015)
20. Schulman, J., Wolski, F., Dhariwal, P., Radford, A., Klimov, O.: Proximal policy optimization algorithms. arXiv preprint arXiv:1707.06347 (2017)
21. Sutton, R.S., Precup, D., Singh, S.: Between MDPs and semi-MDPs: a framework for temporal abstraction in reinforcement learning. Artif. Intell. **112**(1C2), 181–211 (1999)
22. Torabi, F., Warnell, G., Stone, P.: Behavioral cloning from observation. In: Proceedings of the 27th International Joint Conference on Artificial Intelligence, pp. 4950–4957 (2018)
23. Vezhnevets, A.S., et al.: FeUdal networks for hierarchical reinforcement learning. In: Precup, D., Teh, Y.W. (eds.) Proceedings of the 34th International Conference on Machine Learning. Proceedings of Machine Learning Research, vol. 70, pp. 3540–3549. PMLR, International Convention Centre, Sydney, Australia, 06–11 August 2017
24. Vinyals, O., Babuschkin, I., Czarnecki, W.M., Mathieu, M., Silver, D.: Grandmaster level in StarCraft II using multi-agent reinforcement learning. Nature **575**(7782), 350–354 (2019)
25. Yu, C., Liu, J., Nemati, S., Yin, G.: Reinforcement learning in healthcare: a survey. ACM Comput. Surv. (CSUR) **55**(1), 1–36 (2021)
26. Zhao, W., Queralta, J.P., Westerlund, T.: Sim-to-real transfer in deep reinforcement learning for robotics: a survey. In: 2020 IEEE Symposium Series on Computational Intelligence (SSCI), pp. 737–744. IEEE (2020)

Generalizing Supervised Learning for Intrusion Detection in IoT Mesh Networks

Hossein Keipour[1(✉)], Saptarshi Hazra[3], Niclas Finne[3], and Thiemo Voigt[2,3]

[1] Blekinge Institute of Technology, 37179 Karlskrona, Sweden
hoke19@student.bth.se
[2] Uppsala University, 75105 Uppsala, Sweden
[3] Research Institutes of Sweden (RISE), 16440 Stockholm, Sweden
{saptarshi.hazra,niclas.finne,thiemo.voigt}@ri.se

Abstract. IoT mesh networks typically consist of resource-constrained devices that communicate wirelessly. Since such networks are exposed to numerous attacks, designing intrusion detection systems is an important task and has attracted a lot of attention from the research community. Most existing work, however, has only considered a few network topologies, often also assuming a fixed number of nodes. In this paper, we generate a new large attack dataset, using Multi-Trace, a tool that we recently devised to generate traces to train machine learning algorithms. We show that using more and more diverse training data, the resulting intrusion detection models generalize better compared to those trained with less and less diverse training data. They even generalize well for larger topologies with more IoT devices. We also show that when we train different machine learning methods on our dataset, the resulting intrusion detection systems achieve very high performance.

Keywords: Internet of Things · 6LoWPAN · RPL · Intrusion detection system · Blackhole · Machine learning · Deep learning · Dataset

1 Introduction

The IoT [4] internetworks everyday objects equipped with sensing, computation, and communication capabilities. The number of connected IoT devices is expected to increase to 38.6 billion by 2025 and an estimated 50 billion by 2030 [12]. IoT is playing a vital role with applications in a variety of areas, such as health care, industrial systems, smart homes, transportation networks, energy management, smart cities, and the energy industry [15].

Recently, we have been witnessing a tremendous increase in attacks on Internet infrastructures. For instance, IoT devices were hacked and used in a DDoS attack by the Mirai botnet in October 2016. This example shows that IoT

G. Wang et al. (Eds.): UbiSec 2021, CCIS 1557, pp. 214–228, 2022.
https://doi.org/10.1007/978-981-19-0468-4_16

security is a major concern since it does not only affect the IoT networks themselves but can have a strong negative impact on the Internet.

To prevent such attacks, IoT networks typically employ three main components [6]: First, there are components that aim at *preventing* attacks. Second, there are components that are tasked to *detect* attacks and finally, there are components that should *mitigate* attacks. Once the first line of defense, i.e., the attack prevention component, has been crossed, the second line of defense's task is to detect any suspicious behaviour. The latter is done via intrusion detection systems (IDS). Due to the resource constraints of low-power embedded platforms, designing efficient intrusion detection systems is extremely challenging [6].

Recent research has designed a number of IDS for IoT networks. Most of them, however, are trained on small datasets or datasets not specifically collected for resource-constrained IoT networks [3,10,23,25]. Others do not consider the computational constraints of low-power IoT networks [13,22].

In this study, we design an ML-based IDS for 6LoWPAN. To train our IDS models, we implement various IoT network scenarios with and without attacks in the Cooja simulator [17] and use our Multi-Trace extensions to generate the dataset [11]. We depart from previous work in that we generate and use a new dataset that covers many different IoT mesh network topologies.

We use this new dataset to train a variety of ML algorithms. Using DNN and SVM-RBF learning algorithms, we achieve a high accuracy (97%) and precision of (95%) and (96%) respectively. RFC also achieves 98% accuracy and 96% precision. RFC models have less complexity and are able to run on resource-constrained low-power IoT mesh networks. Meanwhile, DNN and SVM-RBF need to be implemented in collaboration with the cloud. We train the machine learning algorithms using our dataset. Our results show that with more and more diverse scenarios, i.e., different topologies with different attackers, the machine learning algorithms generalize better, i.e., they achieve better results on the test data.

We also expect our dataset and dataset generation approach to be useful for researchers in the field of security for low-power wireless multi-hop networks and help them to evaluate their machine learning models on this larger dataset.

Contributions. We make the following contributions in this paper:

- We generate a new attack dataset for IoT multi-hop networks that is larger and has more distinct network topologies than previous datasets.
- We show that using more and more diverse training data, the resulting models generalize better compared to those trained with less and less diverse training data. Our models even generalize well when the test set consists of larger topologies with more nodes than the training set.
- We also show that when we train different machine learning methods on our dataset, the resulting intrusion detection systems achieve very high performance.

Outline. After presenting some background, we outline our methodology in Sect. 3. Section 4 discusses how we generate our attack traces and the following section presents the IDS design. Section 6 is concerned with the ML algorithms. While Sect. 7 presents our experimental results, Sect. 8 concludes the paper.

2   Background

2.1   IoT Mesh Networks and RPL Routing

Low-power and lossy networks (LLNs) are a type of IoT network whose nodes collaboratively interact and perform various tasks autonomously. As they are often resource-constrained and battery-powered it is important to keep the energy consumption, in particular for communication, low. Due to the limited IPv4 address space, IoT networks typically use IPv6 to connect directly to the Internet using open standards.

In multi-hop wireless networks, not all nodes are able to reach the gateway with their wireless transmissions. Hence, nodes need to forward packets on behalf of other nodes towards the gateway. The latter is often called sink or root node.

RPL is a widely used routing protocol for LLNs. Usually, one root node is connected to the Internet via an IPv6 Border Router (6BR). Nodes in RPL use a Destination Oriented Directed Acyclic Graph (DODAG) to create and maintain the network topology. The distance from the root is calculated by a scalar value called rank that determines nodes' position in the network. A node's rank value increases with the distance from the root.

2.2   Attacks on RPL

LLNs face two main security challenges. The first challenge is node removal or attacks on nodes' hardware [20]. Second, there are a large number of attacks at the network layer that include Denial of Service (DoS) attacks, sinkhole, blackhole, hello flooding, clone ID, local repair, sybil, and selective forwarding attacks [21,28]. We categorize attacks on RPL into three classes: (i) attacks that affect traffic, (ii) attacks that disrupt the network topology, and (iii) attacks that aim to affect network resources [2]. Figure 1 shows attacks on RPL and the related categories [21].

2.3   Blackhole Attack

In a blackhole attack the malicious node drops all packets it is supposed to forward to the root node. Malicious nodes accomplish this in two steps. First, the attacker node advertises a fake low-rank value to attract neighbors to select it as their parent (sinkhole attack). Second, it could drop some of the packets based on predefined rules (selective forwarding attack), or drop all packets originated from other nodes (blackhole attack, see Algorithm 1). Blackhole attacks affect network performance. Sharma et al. demonstrate a 26% performance reduction caused by a blackhole attack [24]. Pasikhani et al. [18] compare different attacks on RPL and evaluate their impact. They show that blackhole attacks have a high impact on packet delivery rate and delay and medium impact on control packet overhead and battery drain.

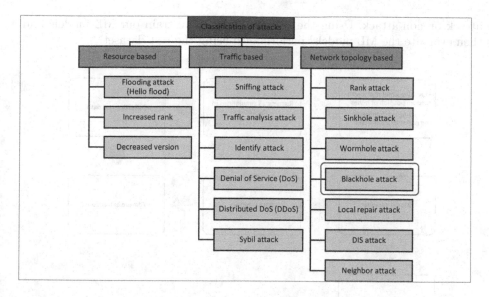

Fig. 1. RPL attacks classification

Algorithm 1. Attack Scenario: Blackhole Attack
___
Require: Attacker Node-ID
  if Node-ID *Matches* Attacker Node-id **then**
    Decrease the rank value
    Keep parents with higher rank
    Drop all packets originated from other nodes except parent
  else
    Keep defined rank calculations
  end if

---

3 Methodology

In this study, we use a simulator to design, run and collect network data from different scenarios. We have earlier devised Multi-Trace [11] an extension to Cooja that collects simulation logs at multiple levels at the same time. We use Contiki's network simulator Cooja to run our experiments and Multi-Trace to generate our dataset. Figure 2 shows the steps from the generation of the dataset to training and evaluating the ML models.

We first create initial simulations with different number of nodes. Then using Multi-trace, we create simulations with random positions of the nodes and a random attacker node in each simulation. Then we run all simulations using Cooja's non-GUI mode for fast performance. In the next step, we collect the raw data from the simulations' output. We then normalize the raw data and extract the features. In the data labeling step, we label each node's traces as attack or non-attack. Using the training dataset we train our ML models and then evaluate the ML models' performance using the test dataset.

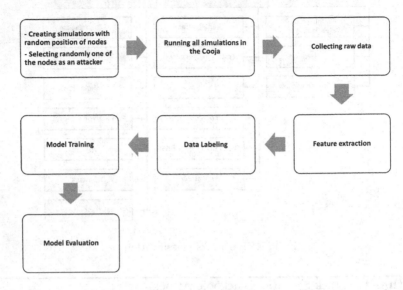

Fig. 2. Approach to design our intrusion detection system. The major novelty is that we use simulations to create a large dataset with varying number of nodes.

4   Attack Trace Generation

4.1   Simulation Setup Tool

We use Contiki's network simulator Cooja [17] to simulate embedded devices running the Contiki OS [9]. Using Cooja's Multi-Trace extension [11], we create our own IDS dataset. With this dataset, we test and evaluate our proposed ML models.

The advantage of our dataset compared to previous efforts is that it contains much more variability in terms of the number of nodes and their positions. To achieve that, we simulate several multi-hop IoT networks with a different number of nodes, random node positions, and we select the attacker node randomly.

4.2   Data Collection

To collect network data, we conduct simulations using the Cooja simulator. We call each network topology a scenario. Each scenario has several nodes positioned randomly and one attacker node selected randomly from the nodes as shown in Fig. 3.

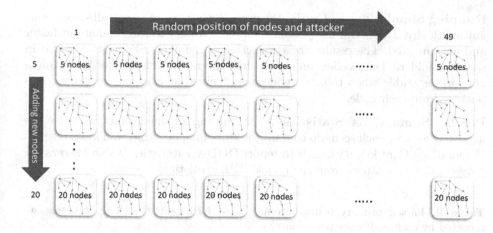

Fig. 3. Different scenarios used for data collection

We collect simulations data from 735 attack scenarios (blackhole attack) and 661 non-attack scenarios (overall 1396 scenarios). Table 1 shows the Cooja simulation setup for the experiments.

Table 1. Cooja simulation setup

Parameters	Values
Node operating system	ContikiNG
Routing protocol	RPL
Radio medium model	Unit Disk Graph Medium (UDGM) Distance Loss
Communication range	50 m, Interference: 100 m
Number of nodes	5 to 20 (root is excluded)
Distance between neighbors	Random <50 m
Number of root nodes	1
Number of attacker nodes	1
MAC driver	CSMA/CA
Network layer	ContikiRPL
Network driver	Sicslowpan
Transport layer	UDP
Traffic model	Constant bit rate
Attack start time	30 min after start of simulation
Simulations duration	60 min

Placing Nodes Randomly. To place the nodes in random positions in each scenario, we use a Python script that receives an initial scenario as input and then creates a specific number of new topologies with random nodes' placement. We put some limitations on the nodes' positions to keep the nodes in the radio range of at least one node to avoid that the network partitions.

Running Simulations in Cooja. We use a Python script to run all simulations automatically. This script uses Cooja's non-GUI ability to run simulations faster and automatized. The results are a collection of simulations statistics stored in separate folders. Data collection starts after the network is stable. We define a network as stable when the root node has received at least one message (data packet) from each node.

Parsing Simulations' Statistics. After running all simulations, we parse the logs. The logs for each scenario contain the run-time, pcap file, and mote output. We modified Contiki's RPL code to report DODAG statistics. Table 2 shows the parsed primary features from the nodes' RPL statistics.

Table 2. Parsed primary features from nodes' RPL statistics. The statistics are reported by each node once per minute.

Time	Time stamp of events in the simulation
Mote	Nodes' ID (number)
Seq	Sequence number of the statistics report from the node
Rank	Rank value of the node
Version	DODAG version
DIS-R	Number of DIS messages received last minute
DIS-S	Number of DIS messages sent last minute
DIO-R	Number of DIO messages received last minute
DIO-S	Number of DIO messages sent last minute
DAO-R	Number of DAO messages received last minute

5   Design of the Intrusion Detection System

5.1   Data Pre-processing

After collecting the data, we normalize it. Using normalization makes the ML model training faster and achieves better generalization accuracy [27]. In this study we use "scaling to a range" normalization method to map our data for each feature to the range of $[-1, +1]$ using Eq. 1.

$$x' = 2 * \frac{x - x_{min}}{x_{max} + 1} - 1 \tag{1}$$

5.2   Chunking

After normalizing the collected data, we split our data traces into intervals (chunks) of equal duration to analyse the selected features' changes between these intervals. We select three different chunk sizes that lead to different number of chunks (three, six, and ten). For example, to get ten chunks, we divide the data traces into ten time intervals, each with a duration of six minutes. The attack will starts after 30 min of simulation time.

To ensure that the network is stable we do not consider data trace values for following the intervals: the first interval when have three chunks, the first two intervals when we have six chunks, and the first three intervals when we have 10 chunks. Then we average the features' values in the remaining time intervals and store them in a vector. We form a feature matrix that consists of the vectors of each node in each scenario. Figure 4 shows the process of using chunks and removing the initial ones (t1 and t2 when using six chunks).

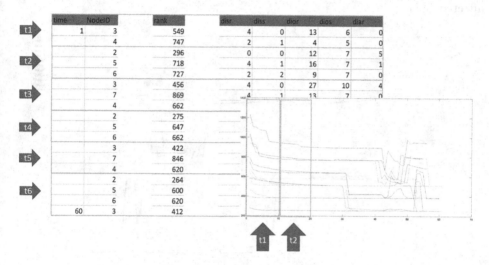

Fig. 4. Process of using chunks (e.g., six chunks)

5.3 Feature Engineering

Feature engineering categorizes the collected data to improve classification performance. Towards this end, we implement the two steps of feature extraction and feature selection. We perform feature extraction using the chunking method described above.

Then we use Principal Component Analysis (PCA) to reduce the feature dimension. The dimension reduction compresses the data and reduces the required storage space. It also helps to decrease the computational complexity of the ML model and running the ML model faster.

5.4 Data Labelling

After having cleaned the data, we label it. We label the nodes affected by the attacker as under attack nodes and the nodes that are not affected by the attacker in attack scenarios and normal scenarios as non-attack nodes.

We use the variance in the node's rank between pre-defined intervals (chunks) as a metric to understand whether a node is affected by an attack or not.

The blackhole attack first uses the Rank attack to attract neighbor nodes to select the intruder node as a parent. So the vulnerable nodes' rank decreases after the attack has started. Figure 5 shows how the blackhole attack changes the rank value of the intruder's neighbors. It is also visible that after starting the attack (30 min in the simulation), some nodes are not affected by the attack and hence their rank value does not change (nodes presented by dashed line) and some nodes experience a dramatic change in their rank value (nodes presented by solid line). When a node is affected by the attack, its children will also be affected.

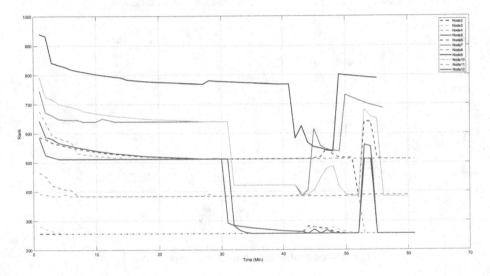

Fig. 5. Rank changes after the starting of an attack

6 Machine Learning Models

After preparing the feature matrix, we use ML methods to perform the classification task. We use this feature matrix to train our predictive model. The model then maps the input data to one of the attack or non-attack classes.

There are several ML classifiers used by researchers to train the ML models for IDS: According to [8,14,16,26] both supervised (e.g., SVM, DNN, RFC) and unsupervised (e.g., K-means, K-Dimensional Tree.) ML algorithms can be used for IDSs.

In this study, we use DNN, RFC, and SVM to detect an attack in the network because of their success in binary classification (two-class) problems.

We use the Keras library to create the ML models in Python. Keras is an open-source Python library for developing and evaluating ML models [7]. We also use the sklearn library to evaluate our ML models' performance since it is a simple and efficient tool for predictive data analysis [19].

6.1   Deep Neural Networks

A Deep Neural Network (DNN) is an Artificial Neural Network (ANN) that consists of multiple hidden layers between the input and output layers [5]. Our proposed DNN model has one input layer, three hidden layers, and one output layer. The input layer has four nodes to handle the feature matrix, the first, second, and third hidden layer have 50, 50, and 20 nodes respectively and finally one node forms the output layer. We select these model parameters empirically.

We use a *ReLU* (Rectified Linear Unit) activation function in the hidden layers for better performance. Using the *ReLU* function, all the neurons are not active at the same time. The output layer uses a *Sigmoid* activation function to ensure the model output is in the range (0,1) and later map to one of two classes (attack or non-attack) with a default threshold of 0.5.

We train our DNN model with the following parameters: The number of epochs is 150. We use *binary_crossentropy* as our loss function. It is a cross entropy loss function defined in Keras which is used for binary classification problems. We also use *adam* as our model optimizer. This optimizer is an efficient stochastic gradient descent algorithm. It is a self-tuned version of gradient descent. All these parameters are selected based on our experimental results.

6.2   Support Vector Machines

Support vector machines are one of the supervised learning methods used for classification. SVM aims to find a hyper-plane in vector space (or a line in 2D space) to classify data points into two binary classes [1]. It produces significant accuracy with low computation power which is a good match for IoT networks.

To separate data into two classes, several hyper-planes could be selected. Our aim is to find the one that maximizes the margin between the two classes. SVM uses closer data points to the hyper-plane named support vectors, to find the shape and position of the hyper-plane. These support vectors help to maximize the margin of the classifier.

SVM uses a technique called kernel-trick to transform the data points and create an optimal decision boundary between the classes. In this study we use the two main kernels, i.e., Radial Basis Function (RBF) and Polynomial Function. RBF is one of the most preferred and used kernel functions in SVM. It works well for non-linear data. It also helps to properly classify the points when there is no prior knowledge of data.

6.3   Random Forest Classifiers

We also use RFC, an ensemble learning method using Decision Trees. Random forest algorithms have been popular in embedded devices because of their simple nature, performance, low memory requirements, and since they are less susceptible to over-fitting [1, 26].

6.4   Training Set

After data labeling, we split our data into train, validation and test sets. The train set is used for training the ML models. We use the validation set to tune the model's parameters. Finally, the test set is used to evaluate the performance of ML models with an unseen dataset. We split the labeled dataset into three sets of train (60%), validation (20%), and test (20%). The ratio is widely used in ML problems and works well when we have enough labeled data.

7   Evaluation

7.1   Metrics

We measure the ML models' performance using the test data set which includes unseen data. The two main metrics we use are prediction accuracy and precision.

Prediction Accuracy. Prediction accuracy is the number of correct predictions made by the model divided by all the predictions made (Eq. 2).

$$Accuracy = \frac{TP + TN}{TP + TN + FP + FN} \qquad (2)$$

Precision. Precision is a measure that defines what proportion of nodes that we diagnosed as under attack, actually was under attack. The predicted positives (nodes that are predicted as under attack are TP and FP) and the nodes that are under attack are TP (Eq. 3). Precision gives us information about the model's performance with respect to false positives. In other words, it shows that how successful is an ML model to catch the attacks.

$$Precision = \frac{TP}{TP + FP} \qquad (3)$$

7.2   Basic Model Performance

Table 3 compares the accuracy and precision of the DNN, RFC, and SVM-RBF models. The table shows that DNN and SVM with RFB kernel have almost identical accuracy (97%) and precision of (95%) and (96%) respectively. The highest accuracy is achieved by the RFC model with 98% accuracy and 96% precision. The proposed ML models have different complexity. DNN and SVM need more resources for the training part, so we need train our ML model on the edge or the cloud. On the other hand, RFC models have less complexity to run on resource constraint low-power IoT mesh networks.

7.3   Number of Chunks

Figure 6 shows the accuracy difference between using different numbers of chunks (see Sect. 5.3).

The experimental results show that for DNN and RFC, six chunks perform better than three and 10 chunks.

Table 3. Performance of machine learning models using six chunks

Model type	Accuracy (%)	Precision (%)
DNN	97	95
RFC	98	96
SVM-RBF	97	96

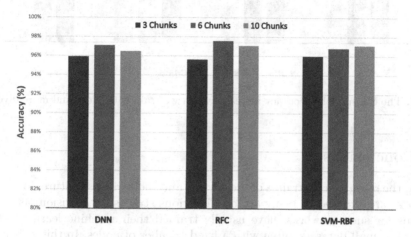

Fig. 6. The number of chunks and its effect on the detection accuracy

7.4   Generalization

To understand how well our models generalize, we compare the ML models performance using different training sets. For this, we train our models with datasets that include more and diverse data, i.e., the extended data trace includes new topologies with different number of nodes. We use six chunks in these experiments since this leads to good performance. Our test set consisting of topologies with five to 20 nodes (10 different topologies for each number of nodes). Figure 7 demonstrates that by adding new data traces from new scenarios, the accuracy of the ML models increases. For example, the accuracy of SVM-RBF increases from about 92% when trained with scenarios consisting of five nodes to more than 96% when training with scenarios consisting of five to 20 nodes.

We also conduct an experiment in which we train our ML models with scenarios consisting of 5 to 20 nodes and then test with an unseen dataset of scenarios of 30 nodes, i.e., the size of the networks in the test set is larger than in the train set. Even in this scenario, DNN and RFC, SVM-RBF achieve an accuracy of 95% confirming that our models generalize well to unseen topologies.

Overall, these experiments show that our approach to extend the dataset with new topologies with a different number of nodes leads to ML models that detect attacks with higher accuracy.

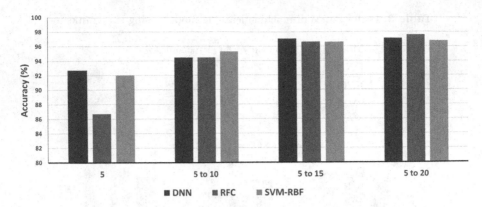

Fig. 7. The ML models' accuracy increases when we train with more and more diverse data.

8   Conclusions

Due to the resource-constraints of the devices and their wireless nature, IoT mesh networks are exposed to many attacks. Previous studies on intrusion detection systems for such networks, have usually trained their machine learning algorithms on small datasets, often with a fixed number of nodes. In this paper, we have shown that using larger training datasets that are also more diverse, has a positive affect on model accuracy. Our results using the blackhole attack on the RPL routing protocol have shown that we achieve high accuracy on unseen test data even when the size of the networks is larger in the test than in the training set.

The generated new attack dataset for IoT multi-hop networks can be found at the following repository at Github: (https://github.com/STACK-ITEA-Project/multi-trace-data/raw/master/data/data_attack_blackhole.zip).

Acknowledgments. This work was supported by the ITEA 3 project STACK funded by the Swedish Innovation Agency VINNOVA.

References

1. Ahmad, I., Basheri, M., Iqbal, M.J., Rahim, A.: Performance comparison of support vector machine, random forest, and extreme learning machine for intrusion detection. IEEE Access **6**, 33789–33795 (2018)
2. Alabsi, B.A., Anbar, M.: A comprehensive review on security attacks in dynamic wireless sensor networks based on RPL protocol. Int. J. Pure Appl. Math. **119**(12), 12481–12495 (2018)
3. Ambili, K., Jose, J.: TN-IDS for network layer attacks in RPL based IoT systems. IACR Cryptol. ePrint Arch. **2020**, 1094 (2020)
4. Ashton, K., et al.: That 'internet of things' thing. RFID J. **22**(7), 97–114 (2009)
5. Bengio, Y.: Learning deep architectures for AI. Found. Trends® Mach. Learn. **2**(1), 1–127 (2009). https://doi.org/10.1561/2200000006. ISSN 1935-8237

6. Butun, I., Morgera, S.D., Sankar, R.: A survey of intrusion detection systems in wireless sensor networks. IEEE Commun. Surv. Tutor. **16**(1), 266–282 (2013)

7. Chollet, F., et al.: Keras (2015). https://github.com/fchollet/keras

8. Diro, A.A., Chilamkurti, N.: Distributed attack detection scheme using deep learning approach for internet of things. Future Gener. Comput. Syst. **82**, 761–768 (2018)

9. Dunkels, A., Grönvall, B., Voigt, T.: Contiki - a lightweight and flexible operating system for tiny networked sensors. In: Proceedings of the IEEE Workshop on Embedded Networked Sensor Systems (IEEE EmNetS), Tampa, Florida, USA, November 2004

10. Essop, I., Ribeiro, J.C., Papaioannou, M., Zachos, G., Mantas, G., Rodriguez, J.: Generating datasets for anomaly-based intrusion detection systems in IoT and industrial IoT networks. Sensors **21**(4), 1528 (2021)

11. Finne, N., et al.: Multi-trace: multi-level data trace generation with the Cooja simulator. In: Workshop on Machine Learning for Smart Wireless Networks (2021)

12. Karie, N.M., Sahri, N.M., Haskell-Dowland, P.: IoT threat detection advances, challenges and future directions, pp. 22–29 (2020)

13. Liang, C., et al.: Intrusion detection system for the internet of things based on blockchain and multi-agent systems. Electronics **9**(7), 1120 (2020)

14. Moustafa, N., Hu, J., Slay, J.: A holistic review of network anomaly detection systems: a comprehensive survey. J. Netw. Comput. Appl. **128**, 33–55 (2019)

15. Nikoukar, A., Raza, S., Poole, A., Güneş, M., Dezfouli, B.: Low-power wireless for the internet of things: standards and applications. IEEE Access **6**, 67893–67926 (2018)

16. Nobakht, M., Sivaraman, V., Boreli, R.: A host-based intrusion detection and mitigation framework for smart home IoT using OpenFlow. In: 2016 11th International conference on availability, reliability and security (ARES), pp. 147–156. IEEE

17. Österlind, F., Dunkels, A., Eriksson, J., Finne, N., Voigt, T.: Cross-level sensor network simulation with Cooja. In: Proceedings of the First IEEE International Workshop on Practical Issues in Building Sensor Network Applications (SenseApp 2006), Tampa, Florida, USA, November 2006

18. Pasikhani, A.M., Clark, J.A., Gope, P., Alshahrani, A.: Intrusion detection systems in RPL-based 6LoWPAN: a systematic literature review. IEEE Sens. J. **21**(11), 12940–12968 (2021). https://doi.org/10.1109/JSEN.2021.3068240

19. Pedregosa, F., et al.: Scikit-learn: machine learning in Python. J. Mach. Learn. Res. **12**, 2825–2830 (2011)

20. Phukan, J., Li, K.F., Gebali, F.: Hardware covert attacks and countermeasures. In: 2016 IEEE 30th International Conference on Advanced Information Networking and Applications (AINA), pp. 1051–1054. IEEE (2016)

21. Pongle, P., Chavan, G.: A survey: Attacks on RPL and 6lowpan in IoT. In: 2015 International Conference on Pervasive Computing (ICPC), pp. 1–6. IEEE (2015)

22. Samaila, M.G., Neto, M., Fernandes, D.A., Freire, M.M., Inácio, P.R.: Challenges of securing internet of things devices: a survey. Secur. Priv. **1**(2), e20 (2018)

23. Sharma, M., Elmiligi, H., Gebali, F., Verma, A.: Simulating attacks for RPL and generating multi-class dataset for supervised machine learning. In: 2019 IEEE 10th Annual Information Technology, Electronics and Mobile Communication Conference (IEMCON), pp. 0020–0026. IEEE (2019)

24. Sharma, S., Gupta, R.: Simulation study of blackhole attack in the mobile ad hoc networks. J. Eng. Sci. Technol. **4**(2), 243–250 (2009)

25. Verma, A., Ranga, V.: Evaluation of network intrusion detection systems for RPL based 6lowpan networks in IoT. Wirel. Pers. Commun. **108**(3), 1571–1594 (2019). https://doi.org/10.1007/s11277-019-06485-w
26. Wang, H., Barriga, L., Vahidi, A., Raza, S.: Machine learning for security at the IoT edge-a feasibility study. In: 2019 IEEE 16th International Conference on Mobile Ad Hoc and Sensor Systems Workshops (MASSW), pp. 7–12. IEEE (2019)
27. Xu, J., Sun, X., Zhang, Z., Zhao, G., Lin, J.: Understanding and improving layer normalization. arXiv preprint arXiv:1911.07013 (2019)
28. Zarpelão, B.B., Miani, R.S., Kawakani, C.T., de Alvarenga, S.C.: A survey of intrusion detection in internet of things. J. Netw. Comput. Appl. **84**, 25–37 (2017)

Reliable and Controllable Data Sharing Based on Blockchain

Yipeng Zou, Tao Peng$^{(\boxtimes)}$, Wentao Zhong, Kejian Guan,
and Guojun Wang

School of Computer Science and Cyber Engineering, Guangzhou University,
Guangzhou 510006, China

Abstract. Nowadays, cloud-based data sharing becomes a notably fascinating service provided by the cloud platform due to its convenience and economy. Ciphertext-policy attribute-based encryption (CP-ABE) system is one of the best candidates for cloud-data sharing solutions because it can provide data encryption and fine-grained access control means for cloud storage systems. However, existing centralized schemes inevitably suffer from the limitations of a single point of failure, low reliability, and poor scalability. In addition, the management and maintenance of attributes in CP-ABE solutions often require higher costs. In this paper, we propose a reliable and controllable data sharing scheme based on blockchain, mapping the attributes in the CP-ABE scheme to attribute tokens. Users with the corresponding attribute token are granted access and decryption rights for encrypted data after paying the attribute token. The scheme is implemented based on the permissioned blockchain architecture Hyperledger Fabric, and a multi-channel Fabric deployment architecture and smart contracts are designed for data management and access control. By combining CP-ABE with blockchain, a common solution for data sharing that supports fine-grained data access control is realized, which is suitable for access control management of data sharing in a distributed environment. We further implemented a smart contract prototype on Fabric, and the experimental results show that our scheme is feasible.

Keywords: Blockchain · Attribute-based encryption · Data sharing · Attribute token · Access control

1 Introduction

With the rapid development of big data, cloud computing, mobile internet, and other emerging information technology, the secure storage and controlled sharing of massive data has become an urgent problem. Data sharing is the best way to fully maximize the value of data. Since most organizations exist in isolation from each other, storing and maintaining data individually, forming data silos. This not only hinders the development of the industry but also results in wasted storage space and redundancy of data resources. The sharing of healthcare data

G. Wang et al. (Eds.): UbiSec 2021, CCIS 1557, pp. 229–240, 2022.
https://doi.org/10.1007/978-981-19-0468-4_17

is one of the most typical examples. In order to maximize the value of data, the trend of sharing data among different organizations and their related entities is inevitable. However, in the process of storing and sharing data, the systems have long been facing a single point of failure, the risk of data malicious tampering and data leakage, and imperfect access control mechanism [5,6,11,12], Therefore, finding a way to achieve reliable and controllable data sharing is essential.

With the rise of digital cryptocurrencies, blockchain is receiving more and more attention and research as important information technology. The powerful potential of blockchain is being gradually explored. Through peer-to-peer network, cryptography, and consensus mechanisms that guarantee the integrity of data on the chain without trusted third-party organization. This provides a new way to establish secure data sharing. Some researches have already proposed the security features of blockchain-based [9] in data communication [3] and sharing [1,4,7] in the innovative application. Blockchain technology combined with access control and data sharing mechanisms can eliminate the problems in traditional schemes to some extent. By utilizing the decentralized storage and data tamper-proof [2,14] and data traceability features of blockchain, it can achieve credible storage of data and avoid risks, such as single point of failure and data tampering of centralized data storage. Ciphertext-policy attribute-based encryption (CP-ABE) is considered as one of the most suitable solutions to provide secure data access control in public cloud storage [15]. The data control authority is put into the hands of data owners through CP-ABE technology, and data owners customize the access control policy to decide with which users to share the data. Thus, combining blockchain technology with CP-ABE technology can lead to a more secure, trusted, and flexible data sharing mechanism.

In this paper, we propose a data sharing scheme based on blockchain and CP-ABE with multi-chain architecture. The multi-chain architecture design improves the data storage capacity and efficiency of the blockchain to a certain extent. By mapping attributes in the CP-ABE scheme to attribute tokens on the blockchain, each attribute is mapped to a kind of attribute token. Utilizing blockchain's ledger capabilities to securely and efficiently manage attributes. The scheme grants full access control permissions to the data owner, and it is entirely up to the data owner to control sharing data and decide with which users to share the data. It enables secure data sharing in an efficient, fine-grained, transparent, and auditable manner. Specifically, we adopt the CP-ABE algorithm to encrypt the data and the blockchain to verify the hash value of data, which ensures data confidentiality and integrity to realize secure data sharing. Reliable data sharing is accomplished by completing transactions of attribute tokens on the blockchain to trigger smart contracts.

The scheme is designed to provide a reliable and controllable data sharing solution for users who are concerned about confidentiality and data management, build a valuable chain for data sharing based on Hyperledger Fabric blockchain. The main contributions of our work are as follows:

- We propose a multi-channel Fabric deployment architecture and four smart contracts to realize a reliable and controllable data sharing scheme.

The scheme achieves fine-grained access control of data in a distributed storage system and overcomes the challenges of centralized architecture.
- An attribute-token-based data sharing mechanism is designed on blockchain that supports real-time and fine-grained attribute revocation, which enables lightweight, secure, and trusted management of user attributes in the CP-ABE technology through the blockchain.
- We implement a smart contract prototype to evaluate the feasibility and performance of the scheme. The experiments show that our proposed scheme is feasible and that the scheme can effectively solve the problem of data access authorization and revocation in a distributed environment.

Paper Organization. The paper is organized as follows. In Sect. 2, we describe some related technologies involved in the system. Section 3 describes the system construction. Section 4 is the experiment and performance analysis, Finally a conclusion and our future work are drawn in Sect. 5.

2 Preliminaries

2.1 Hyperledger Fabric Blockchain and Smart Contract

Hyperledger Fabric blockchain is a permissioned blockchain (or called consortium blockchain) system, which allows only identified nodes to participate in the network. In addition, Fabric provides the ability to create channels. A channel-specific ledger is shared across the peers in the channel, and transacting parties must be properly authenticated to a channel to interact with it. This feature becomes particularly important when some participants in the network are competitors. The multi-channel structure ensures the privacy of data between different channels and stimulates the willingness of users to share data to some extent.

Smart contract was first introduced in 1995 by Nick Szabo [10] as a computer protocol designed to disseminate, validate or enforce contracts. A smart contract deployed on the blockchain is not only a computer program that can be executed automatically, but also a participant of the blockchain system, which automatically executes according to the program written when the execution conditions are met, responds to the received information, and transfers and stores the smart assets in the system without any possibility of third-party intervention. The smart contract is called chaincode in the Hyperledger Fabric blockchain.

2.2 Attribute-Based Encryption (ABE)

The ABE notion could be traced back to 2005, when Sahai, Waters et al. [8] extended IBE and proposed ABE. In ABE, the identity of a user can be represented by a set of attributes. According to whether the access policy is key-related or ciphertext-related, attribute-based encryption is divided into key-policy attribute-based encryption (KP-ABE) and ciphertext-policy attribute-based encryption (CP-ABE). In the CP-ABE [13] scheme, the attributes are related to the key, while the access policy is related to the ciphertext. In this paper, we will adopt the CP-ABE scheme.

In the CP-ABE scheme, the access structure is described by the policy As and the user's key is related to its own set of attribute values U, and the user can decrypt the corresponding ciphertext only when the set of user attributes U satisfies the policy of the access structure As. In a basic CP-ABE scheme, four algorithms are acting as main ingredients:

1. $Setup(\lambda) \rightarrow \{PK, MSK\}$: This algorithm is called the system setup algorithm, and it will run at the beginning. After inputting a security parameter λ, the algorithm returns system public keys PK and master keys MSK.
2. $KeyGen(PK, MSK, U) \rightarrow SK$: It is called the attribute key generation algorithm. It takes PK, MSK, and U as inputs, where U is an attribute list, and returns SK as the attribute secret key corresponding to U.
3. $Encrypt(PK, As, M) \rightarrow CT$: This algorithm is called the encryption algorithm, which will be performed by the data owner (DO). The DO first chooses an access policy As for the target message M, and then takes as inputs PK, M, and As. The algorithm outputs a ciphertext CT of M associated with As, which will be stored on the cloud service provider (CSP).
4. $Decrypt(PK, CT, SK) \rightarrow M$: This algorithm is called the decryption algorithm, which will be run by the data user (DU). After inputting PK, a ciphertext CT of M with As, and an attribute secret key SK corresponding to U, the algorithm returns M if U matches As.

3   System Construction

3.1   System Model

The system model is shown in Fig. 1, which mainly consists of six entities: certification authority, attribute authority, cloud service provider, data owner, data user, and a blockchain network.

Certification Authority (CA): CA provides services such as initialization parameters issuance, key generation, user management, etc. We usually consider CA as trusted. Only CA can authorize AA to issue attribute tokens.

Attribute Authority (AA): AA is responsible for managing and issuing attribute tokens. Usually, it is a government agency/medical institution/research institute, etc. AA, as the party that issues the attribute token, can revoke the user's attribute by freezing the user's attribute token to achieve the revocation of the corresponding access rights. In our proposed multi-channel architecture, each channel corresponds to at least an AA.

Cloud Service Provider (CSP): CSP is mainly used to provide storage services for ciphertext data to reduce the burden of local storage for users. The DOs store the ciphertext into the CSP. This model assumes that the cloud is untrusted, which relaxes the general assumption that the cloud is semi-trusted.

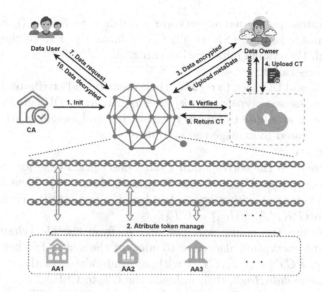

Fig. 1. The system model of proposed scheme

Data Owner (DO): DO performs symmetric encryption and stores the ciphertext in the cloud. Then, the symmetric key is encrypted by CP-ABE encryption algorithm. DO uploads the ciphertext to CSP and then generates metadata to be uploaded to the blockchain via smart contract.

Data User (DU): After the DU is registered in CA, AA will assign the corresponding attribute token to the DU. So the DU will use these attribute tokens to pay to AA when requesting data. After completing the transaction with AA, CSP will return the ciphertext to DU. The attribute tokens owned by DU represent the user's ability to access data.

Blockchain: Blockchain is a decentralized system that provides an open and transparent trust platform to guarantee the integrity and authenticity of data. The metadata is stored on the blockchain.

3.2 System Implementation

The proposed system process consists of the following five main interaction processes: system initialization, data encryption, data access, data decryption, and user attribute revocation.

1. System initialization and user registration:
   (a) Setup(λ) → (PK, MSK):
      The setup algorithm is run by CA. It takes security parameter λ as input. Let $\mathbb{G}$ and $\mathbb{G}_T$ be two multiplicative cyclic groups of prime order p, and g be a generator of $\mathbb{G}$. And $e : \mathbb{G} \times \mathbb{G} \to \mathbb{G}_T$ is a bilinear map. Define a hash function $H(0,1)^* \to \mathbb{G}$. Then the algorithm randomly chooses $\alpha, \beta \in \mathbb{Z}_p$.

The system public parameters are published as $PK = (g, e(g, g)^\alpha, g^\beta)$. The master key is $MSK = g^\alpha$. CA uploads the PK to the blockchain through the system initialization contract.

(b) UserRegistration:
AA, DU and DO need to register their identity and attributes in CA. Each entity possesses keypair (pk, sk) after registration. DU gets the initialized amount of attribute token after registering and assigning attributes, and AA is allowed to manage the attribute token.

2. Data Encryption:
   (a) DO generates the corresponding data description $desc$ for sharing data, and $desc = \{dataVersion, dataSummary, dataSize\}$. Then the DO performs encryption with a symmetric key K_A and gets the ciphertext CT_1.
   (b) Encrypt$(PK, (A, \rho), K_A) = CT_A$:
   DO obtains the public parameters PK from the blockchain, then DO performs encryption algorithm to encrypt the symmetric key K_A.
   (c) DO signs $CT = (CT_1, CT_A)$ with sk and calculates the corresponding hash value $dataHash$, then uploads the CT to CSP.
   (d) CSP is responsible for storing the encrypted data CT, generating the corresponding encrypted data index $dataIndex$, and returning the data index $dataIndex$ to DO.
   (e) DO generates $metaData = (dataIndex, dataHash, desc)$ and publishes to the blockchain.

3. Data Access:
   (a) DU searches for the data on blockchain and sends access requests.
   (b) According to the policy attributes in the access policy As, the attribute token transaction between DU and AA will be completed. Then DU will download the corresponding ciphertext from CSP after successfully paying the corresponding attribute tokens.
   (c) After the CSP verifies that the corresponding attribute token transaction of the requesting user is successful, the $dataIndex$ is decrypted to return the corresponding ciphertext data $CT = (CT_1, CT_A)$ to DU.

4. Data Decryption:
   (a) DU verifies the signature of CT, calculates its hash value and verifies whether it is consistent with the $dataHash$ in the $metaData$ to ensure data integrity and authenticity.
   (b) KeyGen$(PK, MSK, U) \rightarrow SK$:
   U is the set of user attributes, CA runs decryption algorithm, and generates the attribute secret key SK. Then CA generates the shared key USK through Diffle-Hellman key exchange protocol, encrypts SK to get the key ciphertext CT_{SK}, which is sent to DU through a secure channel.
   (c) Decrypt$(PK, CT_A, SK) \rightarrow M$:
   DU decrypts CT_{SK} with USK to get attribute key SK, then runs decryption algorithm to get K_A. Finally, DU decrypts CT_1 with K_A to get plaintext data.

5. User Attribute Revocation:

   Our scheme proposes an attribute-token-based attribute revocation mechanism that supports real-time and fine-grained attribute revocation, which can achieve revoking single or several attributes of a user without affecting the normal use of other legitimate attributes of the user. Attribute revocation mainly performs the following operations.

   (a) AA first freezes the user's corresponding attribute token to ensure the ciphertext data is controlled, which means the user has lost access to the data, realizing real-time attribute-level user revocation.

   (b) CA updates the corresponding attribute of DU's attribute certificate. Then AA will destroy this part of the frozen attribute token.

3.3 Design of Smart Contract

This section introduces the smart contract related interfaces in the proposed scheme. There are four smart contracts are designed in the system as follows: system initialization contract, user management contract, attribute token management contract and data sharing contract.

Protocol 1: System Initialization

---

    procedure *pubParam()*:
        PK← Read PK in CA;
        excute upload PK;
    procedure *getParam(uid)*:
        if *user's identity is legal* **then**
            return *PK*
    end

Protocol 2: User Management

---

    procedure *register(newUser)*:
        Register(newUser,attribute [ ]) in CA;
        true ← authorizeUsers(newUser);
        trigger transferToken algorithm to distribute attribute tokens;
    procedure *degister(uid,attribute[ ])*:
        for *each attribute in attributes set* **do**
            update user's attribute in CA
    end

---

1. System Initialization Contract (SIC):
   The contract is responsible for uploading the system initialization parameters to the blockchain and providing them to the DO as input parameters for the CP-ABE algorithm. As shown in protocol 1, the contract mainly contains two interface functions, *pubParam* and *getPubParam*. CA initiates a transaction through SIC contract to upload the public parameters to blockchain. DO obtains the public parameters PK through the contract.

2. User Management Contract (UMC):
   The UMC contract is responsible for user registration, authentication and management functions, and only the CA can invoke UMC contract to provide the service. As shown in protocol 2, the contract includes two interface functions, *register* and *deregister*. AA, DO and DU need to register legal identity and attributes in the system through the function *register* in the contract, and AA distributes the attribute token with the initialized amount to the user after the user completes the registration of identity and attributes. When the user's attribute tokens are frozen, the *deregister* function will be triggered to update the user's attributes.

Protocol 3: Attribute Token Management

---

procedure *mint(aid,tokenID,amount)*:
    if *true* ← *checkAuthorization(aid)* **then**
        excute tokenInit(token,totalSupply)
    end
procedure *transferToken(from,to,tokenID,amount)*:
    if *!frozen* ← *checkTokenStatus(tokenID)* **then**
        if *identity_fromAccount != identity_toAccount* **then**
            excute transferToken algorithm
        end
    end
procedure *renewToken(uid,attribute[ ])*:
    for *each attribute in attribute set* **do**
        if *true* ←*(checkAttribute(uid) && balanceOf(tokenID) ≤ 0)* **then**
            excute transferToken algorithm
        end
    end
procedure *lockToken(account,aid,tokenID)*:
    if *majority of AA set lock* **then**
        setLock(true,tokenID)
    end
procedure *burnToken(aid,uid,tokenID,amount)*:
    if *true* ←*(checkAdmin(aid) && tokenLocked(tokenID))* **then**
        excute burn uid.BalanceOf(tokenID)
    end

---

3. Attribute Token Management Contract (ATMC):

The contract mainly contains five interface functions, *mint, transferToken, renewToken, lockToken* and *burnToken*. Protocol 3 illustrates the management of attribute token. The *mint* function is called by AA to issue the attribute tokens after checking AA's identity or permission. The *transferToken* function will be called automatically after the user's identity and attribute registration are successful, and the distribution of attribute tokens will be transacted by AA. After the user's attribute token is spent, the *renewToken* function is responsible for re-verification of the user's attributes and redistribution of attribute tokens. In the attribute revocation phase, AA calls the *lockToken* function to freeze the corresponding attribute tokens of the user, so that the attribute tokens of the user will not be available, and the user will not get the ciphertext, thus achieving real-time attribute-level user permission revocation. After the freeze timeout, AA will destroy the frozen attribute tokens of the user by the *burnToken* function. This completes the fine-grained and flexible approach to attribute revocation. The ATMC contract is responsible for the management and maintenance of attribute tokens in the system.

4. Data Sharing Contract (DSC):

Protocol 4: Data Sharing

---

procedure *uploadMetaData(metaData,uid)*:
    if *metaData is validated* **then**
        upload metaData
    end
procedure *searchMeta(Key Word)*:
    get Meta ID by Key Word;
    metaData ← getMetaData(Meta ID);
procedure *getCT(uid,dataIndex)*:
    if *true* ← *payment_status* **then**
        CSP return ciphertext to DO
    end
    calculating hash value of ciphertext;
    comparing with metaData;
procedure *setAttributeKey(uid,encrypted key)*:
    if *true* ← *checkIdentity(uid)* && *checkAttribute(uid)* **then**
        generate D-H shared key;
        encrypted key ← Encrypt(key, shared key);
        send encrypted key to user
    end

The DSC contract consists of four interface functions, *uploadMetaData, searchMeta, getCT* and *setAttributeKey*. The specific process is shown in protocol 4. The DO uploads the *metaData* to the blockchain. The DU searches the data through the *searchMeta* function, then the DU sends an access request through the *getCT* function, and after verifying the legitimate identity of the DU and the corresponding attribute token transaction, the CSP returns the corresponding ciphertext data to the DU. CA generates the attribute secret key SK off the chain. Then CA and DU generate the shared key USK through Diffle-Hellman key exchange protocol to encrypt the attribute secret key SK with the shared key. CA call the function $setAttributeKey$ to send the key ciphertext CT_{SK} to DU through a secure channel, then DU decrypts with the shared key USK to get the attribute key SK. The interactions of the data sharing process are performed by this contract.

4   Experiment and Performance Analysis

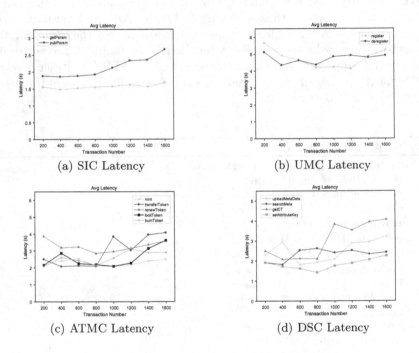

(a) SIC Latency   (b) UMC Latency

(c) ATMC Latency   (d) DSC Latency

Fig. 2. Average latency of smart contracts

We implemented a prototype to analyze the feasibility and performance of the solution. The specific configuration of the experimental platform and environment is intel core i7-7700@3.60 GHz processor, 8 GB RAM, and ubuntu 20.04 LTS. A Fabric blockchain network environment with multiple nodes is deployed on a machine using docker container technology to validate the effectiveness of smart contracts. Since the consensus mechanism is out of the scope of this paper, the experiment uses the solo consensus algorithm. To measure the performance of smart contracts, we used a benchmark tool called Caliper. It is a blockchain performance testing tool that supports performance analysis of transaction latency, transaction throughput,and other performance analysis.

Figure 2 shows the average latency of function calls in the four smart contracts. We can see that the average latency of the UMC contract increases significantly compared to the other contracts because the CA needs to verify or update the certificate when registering or deregistering user's corresponding attributes, and the certificate update is a larger overhead. We conducted tests with the number of concurrent transactions is in the range of 200 to 1600, and the overall trend shows that the response latency increases linearly with the growth of transaction number.

5 Conclusion

In this paper, we propose a secure data sharing scheme based on CP-ABE and multi-chain-structured blockchain. It can address the problems of confidentiality, ownership and fine-grained access control during data sharing. Smart contracts can be invoked to enable on-chain and off-chain interactions. The attribute-token-based revocation mechanism that supports real-time and fine-grained attribute revocation. The solution overcomes the challenges of centralized architecture and provides a decentralized and universal platform for secure data sharing. Besides, we evaluated our approach on Fabric through sufficient experiments.

In the future, the extension of our work aims at incentive mechanism to promote users' willingness to share their data. In addition, as far as we know, most of the current blockchain-based access control mechanisms do not propose a standardized data lifecycle management. The data lifecycle management in the data sharing framework will help us to control the data and reduce the risk of data leakage. We will explore this topic more, and integrate these processes into data sharing to fully implement a secure data sharing framework.

Acknowledgement. This work was supported in part by the National Natural Science Foundation of China under Grant 61802076, 61632009 and 61872097, in part by the National Key Research and Development Program of China (2020YFB1005804).

References

1. Chen, Z., Xu, W., Wang, B., Yu, H.: A blockchain-based preserving and sharing system for medical data privacy. Future Gener. Comput. Syst. **124**, 338–350 (2021)
2. Danzi, P., Kalor, A.E., Stefanovic, C., Popovski, P.: Analysis of the communication traffic for blockchain synchronization of IoT devices. In: 2018 IEEE International Conference on Communications (ICC), pp. 1–7 (2018)
3. Ge, C., Ma, X., Liu, Z.: A semi-autonomous distributed blockchain-based framework for UAVs system. J. Syst. Archit. **107**, 101728 (2020)
4. Guo, Yu., Wang, S., Huang, J.: A blockchain-assisted framework for secure and reliable data sharing in distributed systems. EURASIP J. Wirel. Commun. Netw. **2021**(1), 1–19 (2021). https://doi.org/10.1186/s13638-021-02041-y
5. Li, M., Sun, Y., Lu, H., Maharjan, S., Tian, Z.: Deep reinforcement learning for partially observable data poisoning attack in crowdsensing systems. IEEE IoT J. **7**(7), 6266–6278 (2020)

6. Lu, H., et al.: Research on intelligent detection of command level stack pollution for binary program analysis. Mob. Netw. Appl. 1–10 (2020)

7. Lyu, Q., Qi, Y., Zhang, X., Liu, H., Wang, Q., Zheng, N.: SBAC: a secure blockchain-based access control framework for information-centric networking. J. Netw. Comput. Appl. **149**, 102444 (2020)

8. Sahai, A., Waters, B.: Fuzzy identity-based encryption. In: Cramer, R. (ed.) EURO-CRYPT 2005. LNCS, vol. 3494, pp. 457–473. Springer, Heidelberg (2005). https://doi.org/10.1007/11426639_27

9. Salman, T., Zolanvari, M., Erbad, A., Jain, R., Samaka, M.: Security services using blockchains: a state of the art survey. IEEE Commun. Surv. Tutor. **21**(1), 858–880 (2018)

10. Szabo, N.: The idea of smart contracts. Nick Szabo's Pap. Concise Tutor. **6**(1), 199 (1997)

11. Tan, Q., Gao, Y., Shi, J., Wang, X., Fang, B., Tian, Z.: Toward a comprehensive insight into the eclipse attacks of tor hidden services. IEEE IoT J. **6**(2), 1584–1593 (2018)

12. Tian, Z., Luo, C., Qiu, J., Du, X., Guizani, M.: A distributed deep learning system for web attack detection on edge devices. IEEE Trans. Indust. Inf. **16**(3), 1963–1971 (2019)

13. Waters, B.: Ciphertext-policy attribute-based encryption: an expressive, efficient, and provably secure realization. In: Catalano, D., Fazio, N., Gennaro, R., Nicolosi, A. (eds.) PKC 2011. LNCS, vol. 6571, pp. 53–70. Springer, Heidelberg (2011). https://doi.org/10.1007/978-3-642-19379-8_4

14. Xu, C., et al.: Making big data open in edges: a resource-efficient blockchain-based approach. IEEE Trans. Parallel Distrib. Syst. **30**, 870–882 (2018)

15. Xue, Y., Xue, K., Gai, N., Hong, J., Wei, D.S., Hong, P.: An attribute-based controlled collaborative access control scheme for public cloud storage. IEEE Trans. Inf. Forensics Secur. **14**(11), 2927–2942 (2019)

A Network Forensics Investigating Method Based on Weak Consistency for Distributed SDN

Xuehua Liu[1,2,3], Liping Ding[1,4(✉)], Tao Zheng[5], Fang Yu[4], Zhen Jia[3], and Wang Xiao[6,7]

[1] Laboratory of Parallel Software and Computational Science, Institute of Software, Chinese Academy of Sciences, Beijing 100190, China
[2] School of Computer Science and Technology, University of Chinese Academy of Sciences, Beijing 100049, China
[3] Cloud Computing and Big Data Research Institute, China Academy of Information and Communications Technology, Beijing 100191, China
[4] Digital Forensics Laboratory, Institute of Software Application Technology, Guangzhou and Chinese Academy of Sciences (GZIS), Guangzhou 511458, China
[5] China Unicom VSENS Communications Co. Ltd., Beijing 100005, China
[6] Laboratory of Information Security, Institute of Information Engineering, Chinese Academy of Sciences, Beijing 100093, China
[7] School of Cyber Security, University of Chinese Academy of Sciences, Beijing 100149, China

Abstract. The difficulty of network forensics investigation has occurred for a long time since the authentication of packet source was not supported by TCP/IP protocol. Software defined network (i.e., SDN) is good at monitoring and managing the behaviors and states of the network with SDN controller, which brings great convenience for network forensics investigation. However, the most of existing network forensics investigating methods for SDN are just extensions of old ones designed for traditional network framework. Their performance and availability still need improvements. To solve these problems, a network forensics investigating method based on weak consistency for distributed SDN is proposed. A distributed lightweight flow table is given to implement full record of flow information to avoid failures. The weak consistency mechanism is used to reduce synchronization overhead of distributed SDN. What's more, this method assigns the workload to each distributed controller, as a result, the efficiency of network forensics investigation has significantly improved. Comparison experiments show that this method is applicable for distributed SDN, it has obvious advantages over other method in performance.

Keywords: Software Defined Network (SDN) · Network forensics investigation · Distributed SDN · Distributed lightweight flow table · Weak consistency

1 Introduction

In recent years, concealing techniques, such as IP spoofing and stepping stones, are used by network attackers to cover themselves in dark. Network forensics investigation therefore soonly becam e one of the most effective ways to defend network attacks. The main

G. Wang et al. (Eds.): UbiSec 2021, CCIS 1557, pp. 241–254, 2022.
https://doi.org/10.1007/978-981-19-0468-4_18

objective of network forensics investigation is to trace the sources of network attacks as well as reconstruct attack paths. However, the authentication of packet source is not supported by TCP/IP protocol. In order to carry out authentication of packet source, most of the existing network forensics investigating methods resorts to network equipment, putting forward stringent requirements such as computing capacity and storage capacity. Hence, they are unapplicable in most traditional network environments.

SDN [1] is a new network architecture form, the control plane and the data plane of SDN are separate. The SDN controller in the control plane is able to monitor and manage the behaviors and states of the whole network, that brings opportunities to network forensics. Distributed SDN uses multiple distributed controllers in the control layer to reduces the workload of each controller and improves the robustness and expansibility of the whole network. And there is still room for improvement in performance or accuracy of the existing network forensics investigating methods for SDN. To take full advantage of distributed SDN, this paper demonstrates a network forensics investigating method based on weak consistency for distributed SDN. A distributed lightweight flow table mechanism is given to implement full record of flow information, based on the network path that can be constructed to identify the cyber attack source. With the full record of flow information, failures caused by missing path information of packet marking algorithm are eliminated. This method assigns the workload to each distributed controller, as a result, the efficiency of network forensics investigation has significantly improved. What's more, this method takes the advantage of weak consistency mechanism, which is able to reduce synchronization overhead of distributed SDN. Comparison experiments show that this method is applicable for distributed SDN, and has obvious advantages over other method in performance.

Section 2 analyses the traditional network forensics investigating methods and existing SDN network forensics investigating methods. Section 3 elaborates the main idea of the proposed method. Section 4 designs several experiments to verify the algorithm based on correctness verification and performance comparison.

2 Related Work

Since the main objective of network forensics investigation is to trace the sources of network attacks as well as reconstruct attack paths. Related work can be classified as: probabilistic packet marking algorithm, determined packet marking algorithm, ICMP (Internet Control Message Protocol) marking algorithm, and packet record method, according to network devices capabilities [2].

When the routers can be accessed and modified by network forensics investigating tools, it is permissible to trace the attack source with probabilistic packet marking algorithm, determined packet marking algorithm, and ICMP marking algorithm. Probabilistic packet marking algorithm [3, 4] assumed that the routing frequency of malicious packets are much higher than normal quantity, and therefore we can propose an idea of marking each packet with a certain probability in IP packet header by every router and reconstructing the attack path from the victim host. In 2002, Peng T and Kim B proposed a range-based variable probability marking method in order to improve the marking probability of routers between longer distance [5, 6]. Paruchuri V and Liu J calculated the probability of marking packets based on TTL (time to live) value in network packet header in order to reduce the impact caused by forged marking information created by attackers [7, 8]. Dawn S and Kim H were using HMAC-SHA1 mechanism to ensure the integrity of router marking information from the perspective of network forensics [9–11]. Belenky A and Ansari N argued that the ultimate purposes of network attack traceback are locating attack sources and proposing a packet marking algorithm that stores the IP address of the edge router from which the packet comes by using two packets [12].

Through the previous analysis, the application network forensics investigating methods based on traditional network infrastructures are limited by the capabilities of network devices because most of the network attack traceback schemes requires large number of storage space and computing resources.

As a new network architecture, SDN makes up the defect of the traditional network in network forensics investigation [13]. Agarwal K, a routing tracking tool (i.e. SDN traceroute) was proposed under the condition that the network behavior is not changed [14]. A forwarding mechanism is used to track the forwarding paths of packets in the network. Inspired by GDB (GNU symbolic debugger), a network debugging prototype system NDB [15] was proposed, which mainly realized two functions: breakpoint debugging and packet backtracking. A global flow table algorithm [16] was proposed based on SDN, which periodically traversed all switches through the controller interface to obtain the flow table as well as maintained every flow in SDN. The global flow table improved the efficiency of security detection, analysis of users' online behavior and network forensics investigation. A network forensics investigating Method based on packet marking algorithm [17] was proposed for distributed SDN, which was able to lower error rate caused by packets making algorithm [3, 4], but cannot put an end to failures. In a word, there is still room for improvement in performance or accuracy of the existing network forensics investigating methods for SDN.

3 The Network Forensics Investigating Method Based on Weak Consistency for Distributed SDN

In order to make up for the shortcomings of the existing methods, we propose a network forensics investigating method based on weak consistency for distributed SDN (i.e., DLFT). The use of weak consistency mechanism is able to reduce synchronization overhead of distributed SDN. A distributed lightweight flow table mechanism is given to implement full record of flow information to avoid failures. What's more, this method assigns the workload to each distributed controller, as a result, the efficiency of network forensics investigation has significantly improved.

3.1 The Global Network View Based on Weak Consistency Mechanism

Distributed SDN contains several controllers, they divide the network into multiple subnets, and each controller manages its own subnet. Therefore, the network view is broken up into pieces. To maintain a consistent global network view among all the distributed controllers, DLFT maintains a global network topology through all the controllers based on an undirected graph. In order to resolve the conflict between consistency and performance and availability [18] of the global network view, the synchronization of this global network topology is implemented based on weak consistency mechanism.

The consistency of the global network topology is affected by network events in the control plane. That is, network events should be updated on each controller in time to maintain the consistency of the global network. Strong consistency leads to performance and availability degradation. The conflict between consistency and performance and availability has always been a problem for distributed controllers. Different applications have different consistency requirements. In order to measure the consistency of the global network topology among all the controllers and seek the best balance, the consistency is measured by network event variance [19]. The greater the network event variance is, the weaker the consistency will be. Since the operations of flow tables of controller can be reflect the changes of the whole network topology, a network event classification based on flow table operations is proposed by this paper. The normal flow table operation events are shown in Table 1.

Table 1. Flow table events and DLFT operations

No.	Openflow CMDs	Flow table operations	DLFT operations
1	ADD	Add a flow table entry	Add a new record
2	DELETE	Delete flow table entries	Delete a record
3	DELETE-STRICT	Delete a flow table entry	Delete a record
4	MODIFY	Modify flow table entries	Update record ID
5	MODIFY-STRICT	Modify a flow table entry	Update record ID

The Definition of Related Concepts

Definition 1. Global network topology. Global network topology is represented by an undirected graph G:

$$G = (V, E) \tag{1}$$

V is topology nodes, including switches, hosts and intermediaries. E is the set of links between two nodes.

$$V = (id, type, reg) \tag{2}$$

id is the ID of the devices, each ID represents a unique node, $type$ is the node type, and $type = \{vm, switch, middleware\}$, respectively representing virtual machine, switch, and intermediate devices. As the distributed SDN controller divides the network into multiple subnets, reg is the subnet that the node belongs.

$$E = (v_1, p_1, v_2, p_2) \tag{3}$$

It represents the link between port p_1 of node v_1 and port p_2 of node v_2.

Definition 2. Consistency. The consistency of the whole system is denoted by C [19]:

$$C = \sum_{i=1}^{n} c_i \tag{4}$$

$$c_i = \sum_{j=1}^{m} \lambda_j |\Delta E_{ij}| \tag{5}$$

c_i is the consistency of controller node i, which is calculated by the unsynced flow table operation events. Flow table opreation event is denoted by E_{ij}, which means there are j events happened on controller node i. $|\Delta E_{ij}|$ denotes the maximums for different events. λ_j denotes the consistency factors of different events. The bigger the c_i is and the more the controllers is, the weaker the consistency will be.

The performance can be expressed by the Minimum rate of communication overhead [19]. The definition of performance is as follow:

Definition 3. Performance. The performance of the whole system is denoted by V [19]:

$$V = \sum_{i=1}^{n} v_i \tag{6}$$

$$v_i = \frac{\rho(n-1) \sum_{j=1}^{m} \lambda_j g_{ij}}{c_i} \tag{7}$$

v_i denotes the minimum rate of communication of controller i, ρ is a constant determined by the consistency protocol. g_{ij} denotes the rate of emergence of event j in controller i. λ_j denotes the consistency factors of different events.

Definition 4. Availability. The availability of the whole system is denoted by Ava [19]:

$$Ava = \sum_{i=1}^{n} Ava_i \tag{8}$$

$$Ava_i = Min\{c_i, t_f \sum_{j=1}^{m} \lambda_j g_{ij}\} \tag{9}$$

Ava_i denotes the acceptable number of new events of controller i, c_i is the consistency of controller node i, t_f is the recovery time of the faulty node, g_{ij} denotes the rate of emergence of event j in controller i. λ_j denotes the consistency factors of different events.

Synchronization of Global Network Topology
Different network applications usually have different requirements for the consistency of the network state. The network path construction for the network forensics is a typical low frequency process since the network forensics is always triggered by specific events,

for example, cyber attack. Therefore, the network path construction requires low update rate of the global network topology, which makes network path construction a weak consistency application for distributed SDN. To minimize the computational overhead, the synchronization of global network topology adopts the consistency mechanism of Onix [20]. A clearly defined consistency window is used to quantify the consistency of network stats. The bigger the window is, the weaker the consistency is. To achieve weak consistency, relaxed mode strategy is adopted. That is, the weakest consistency is selected between nodes to achieve the maximum performance v_i under the premise of satisfying the global consistency constraint.

The calculation of weakest consistency of controller node i is as follows [19]:

$$c_i = Min\left\{Min\{b_i\}, \frac{C_b}{n}\right\} \tag{10}$$

C_b is the global consistency constraint, and b_i is the specific constraint of controller node i.

3.2   The Distributed Lightweight Flow Table Mechanism

Distributed lightweight flow table mechanism is designed for recording network flows information of the whole network at the control plane. Each controller maintains a lightweight flow table and records the information of every network flow in real-time in its subnet only. To reduce the computing and storage overhead of the controller, each lightweight flow table only records the switch nodes that the network flow goes through instead of recording the information of the complete flow paths.

DLFT calculates all the subpaths based on distributed lightweight flow table, then, it sorts all the subpaths to restore the full path according to the global network topology. The source of the full path is the cyber attach source, which is the main target of network forensics investigation.

The Definition of Related Concepts
Definition 5. A Link of a Switch. A link of a switch is denoted by s:

$$s = (id, port, reg) \tag{11}$$

id is the ID of the devices of the switch, which represents its unique switch. $port$ is the Port number corresponding to the switch. reg is the subnet to which the node belongs. A network flow path can be illustrated as a sequence of switch links.

Definition 6. Distributed lightweight flow table. The distributed lightweight flow table is represented by F:

$$F = \{f_1, f_2, ..., f_n\} \tag{12}$$

$f_i = (fid, S), f_i$ is a lightweight flow, fid represents the flow. $fid = \{h_1, h_2, ..., h_n\}, fid$ is a set of hash values which are calculated according to the flow table match field. Since the flow table match field may change during the forwarding process of the network flow, multiple hash values are required to represent this flow.

$S = \{s_1, s_2, ..., s_n\}$, S is the set of switches through which the network flow goes. s_i refers to a link of a specific switch as described in definition 5. In order to reduce the burden of the controller, the distributed lightweight flow table does not maintain the information of flow paths, that means switch links are not sorted.

Definition 7. Network flow path. A network flow path is denoted by f':

$$f' = (fid, path) \tag{13}$$

fid is the calculated hash value based on the flow table match field. It is used to uniquely represent the flow.

$$path = (src, S, dst) \tag{14}$$

path refers to the sequence of switch links through which the network flow goes. *src* and *dst* may be a VM or an edge switch of the cloud network. S is a sequence of switch links as described in definition 6.

Distributed Light Global Flow Table Generation and Synchronization
The distributed lightweight flow table is different from the flow table of an Openflow switch. The flow table of an Openflow switch is the basis for packet forwarding. After receiving the packet from the host, an Openflow switch will execute corresponding actions on the packet according to the flow table. By adding, deleting and modifying the items in the flow table of the switch, the controller have fine-grained control of the data packet processing operation of the switch. The distributed lightweight flow table is used to record the set of switches through which each network flow goes in the network.

Since the SDN controller manages the flow table of the Openflow switch through Packet_in and FLOW_MOD (a part of flow table management mechanism) messages, distributed lightweight flow table also manage their table entries according to Packet_in and FLOW_MOD messages.

There are 5 classes of Flow_mode message in OpenFlow protocol. The corresponding actions to distributed lightweight flow table entry are shown in Table 1.
Identify Subpaths of Network Flow
The subpaths are synchronously calculated by the distributed controllers of each subnet through which the network flow goes. There are three kinds of subpaths.1) network flow goes through the subnet. In this case, the endpoint switches in the subpath should be at the edge of the subnet. 2) network flow goes out of or into the subnet. In this case, at least one endpoint of the subpath is at the edge of the subnet. 3) the flow is in the subnet. In this case, neither of the two endpoints of the subpath should be at the edge of the subnet. To facilitate path calculation, choose either endpoint in case 1) or case 2), subpaths can be backtracked in the network topology graph from there. In case 3), traceback subpaths are in the network topology graph from destination switch. Since different controllers manage different subnets, the calculation of subpaths can be carried out synchronously, which could reduce the computing time and equalizes the computing overhead.
Identify Fullpath of Network Flow
Sorting subpaths is based on network topology graph and then connect them together. The main idea of the algorithm is listed as follows:

(1) the sorted path is initially empty, the subpath where the victim node belongs is inserted into the sorted path, and the source node of the subpath is set as the source node of the sorted path.
(2) extract source nodes and destination nodes one by one for each subpath.
(3) find the relationship of direct connection between the destination node and the source node of the sorted path in network topology graph. If they are directly connected, insert the subpath path into the sorted path, and set the source node of the subpath path as the source node of the sorted path.
(4) return to step (2) until all subpaths are sorted.

Locating the Network Attack Source

It is unnecessary to restore the full path for locating the network attack source. Only the subnet where the source node belongs needs to locate the network attack source. The main idea of the algorithm is listed as follows:

(1) If the network flow goes through only one subnet, calculate the subpath of this flow, the source node of the subpath path will be the network attack source.
(2) If the network flow goes through multiple subnets, find the edge nodes of each subnet.
(3) Beside the subnet where destination node is located, if one pair of edge nodes can be found in each switch set, then find their connection relations in the network topology. Except for destination nodes, the only node without connection relations is the network attack source.
(4) Beside the subnet where the dst node locates, if there is only one subnet with only one edge node, the attack source will be in the subnet, and the source node of the subpath will be the network attack source.

4 Evaluation

In order to verify the feasibility of DLFT method and evaluate its performance, we design two kinds of experiments, including correctness verification experiment and performance comparison experiments. A distributed SDN is constructed using Mininet and Floodlight.

4.1 Correctness Verification

In order to verify the correctness of DLFT. We locate the Ping Flood attack source using DLFT, we also cut off the attack network flow to test its validity. The experimental process is listed as follows:

(1) Simulate a network topology with Mininet as shown in Fig. 1. The network topology consists of 4 Openflow subnets, each one contains about 4–15 Openflow switches and 1 controller, 26 virtual hosts are connected to the network. The h1 is the attacker that locates at C2 subnet, h13 is the victim that locates at C4 subnet. At the same time, set the global consistency constraints C_b to 8 and b_i to random value between [1, 3].

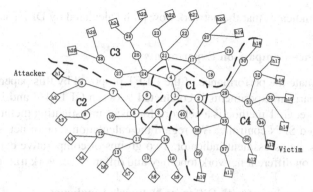

Fig. 1. Experimental network topology

(2) Start a web service on the h13 and launch Ping Flood attack from h1 to h13 through Mininet with disguised IP. The traffic from the s34 where the victim connected is shown in Fig. 2(a). The traffic increases sharply at about 15:44:00 and stays at a high level as the attack proceeds.

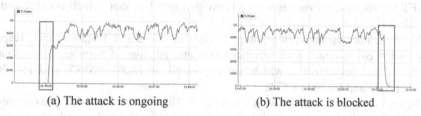

(a) The attack is ongoing   (b) The attack is blocked

Fig. 2. The flow graph of the switch where the victim is connected to

(3) Carry out network forensics investigation with DLFT. The network flow path of the attack is shown as follow:

(4) (1,9,2), (1,7,2), (1,5,2), (1,3,1), (3,1,1), (1,2,1), (4,29,4), (4,31,4), (1,34,4)

(5) Issue a flow table entry to drop SYN packets from s9, to which h1 is connected, as shown in Fig. 3.

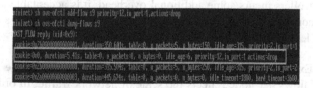

Fig. 3. Flow table entry with drop command

(6) The traffic of the switch where the victim is connected is shown in Fig. 2(b). The traffic of s34 dropped sharply around 15:51:00 when the network flow is blocked.

The output indicates that the network flow path calculated by DLFT is correct.

4.2 Performance Comparison Experiments

In order to evaluate the performance of the DLFT proposed by this paper, several performance comparison experiments is conducted between GFT [16] and DLFT. As we mentioned before, GFT method is a network forensics investigating method based on a single centralized SDN controller. We regard the calculation time of network forensics investigation as the assessment indicator. Two groups of comparative experiments are designed based on different network topology and different network traffic scale.

Comparative Experiment with Different Network Topologies
We simulate simple tree network topology with 10, 20, 40 and 60 nodes respectively. Take the network topology with 40 nodes for example, the network is divided into 1,2 and 4 subnets as shown in Fig. 4:

Experimental parameters are set as follows:

Consistency parameters: set C_b to 2,4,8, and b_i to a random value between [1, 3].

Attack parameters: The Hping3 tool was used to construct the SYN Flooding attack data of 100flows/s.

GFT parameters: network topology is divided into 1 subnet, which is expressed as GFT:1:PATH.

DLFT parameters: network topology is divided into 2 and 4 SDN subnets respectively, and network attack path reconstruction and location of network attack source are carried out respectively, which are expressed as DLFT:2:SRC, DLFT:4:SRC, DLFT:2:PATH and DLFT:4:PATH.

The result of the experiment is shown in Fig. 5. The abscissa represents the number of nodes, and the ordinate represents the calculating time of network flow path construction.

As can be seen from Fig. 5, with the increase of the number of switches in the network topology, the calculation time of both methods presents an upward trend. Due to the increase of the number of switches, the network topology becomes more complex and takes more time to carry out network forensics investigation. As a comparison, the increasing trend of calculation time of DLFT is obviously slower than that of GFT, and this advantage is more significant with the increase in the number of subnets. The main reason is that DLFT delegates the workload to each distributed controller, which greatly reduces the calculation time of each controller. Although the synchronization between distributed controllers incurs some additional overhead, it is acceptable because of the usage of weak consistency mechanism. What's more, the network attack source location of DLFT takes less time than network attack path reconstruct.

Comparative Experiment with Different Number of Flows Per Node
The number of flows per node reflects the scale of network traffic. In order to analyze the impact of network traffic on the performance of DLFT, a comparison experiment based on the number of flows per node is designed.

The network topology is set to the simple tree network with 20 nodes, which is the same as the previous experiment. Besides, GFT parameters, DLFT parameters and consistency parameters are the same as the previous experiment as well.

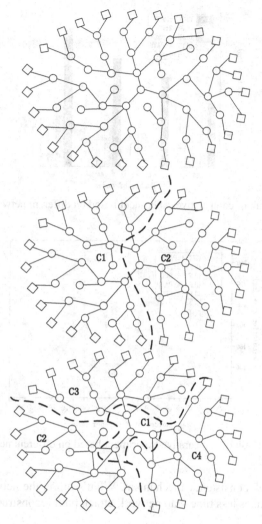

Fig. 4. The simple tree network topology with 1, 2 and 4 subnets

The result of the experiment is shown in Fig. 6. The abscissa represents the number of flows per node, and the ordinate represents the calculating time of network flow path construction.

As can be seen from Fig. 6, with the increase of flows per node, the calculation time of both methods presents an upward trend. Other than that, the calculation time of both methods are linearly related to the number of flows per node. As a comparison, the increasing trend of calculation time of DLFT is obviously slower than that of GFT. The main reason is that DLFT delegates the workload to each distributed controller, which greatly reduces the calculation time of each controller. Although the synchronization between distributed controllers incurs some additional overhead, it is acceptable because

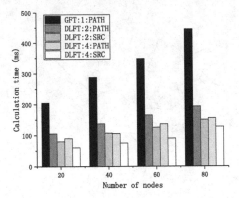

Fig. 5. The result of comparative experiment based on different network topologies

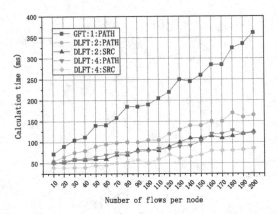

Fig. 6. The result of comparative experiment based on different network scale

of the usage of weak consistency mechanism. What's more, the network attack source location of DLFT takes less time than network attack path reconstruct.

5   Conclusion

This paper mainly studies the network forensics investigation problem in distributed SDN. A network forensics investigating method based on weak consistency for distributed SDN is proposed. It takes advantages of distributed lightweight flow table mechanism and weak consistency mechanism to improve performance and availability. Although the difficulties in device dependence and performance problem faced by network forensics investigation are greatly alleviated with SDN. Challenges still exist due to the design of Internet architecture. This brings some inspiration to the design of the next generation Internet architecture. Careful consideration about whether to support network forensics investigation or not is needed in the design of the next generation Internet architecture.

Acknowledgements. This work has been supported by the 2019 Artificial Intelligence Application Demonstration Project of Nansha District (No.2019SF01).

References

1. Feamster, N., Rexford, J., Zegura, E.: The road to SDN: an intellectual history of programmable networks. ACM SIGCOMM Comput. Commun. Rev. **44**(2), 87–98 (2014)
2. Jiang, J., et al.: On the survey of network attack source traceback. J. Cyber Secur. **3**(1), 111–131 (2018)
3. Doeppner, T.W., Klein, P.N. and Koyfman, A.: Using router stamping to identify the source of IP packets. In: Proceedings of the 7th ACM conference on Computer and Communications Security, pp.184–189. ACM, New York, NY (2000)
4. Savage, S., et al.: Network support for IP traceback. IEEE/ACM Trans. Netw. **9**(3), 226–237 (2001)
5. Peng, T., Leckie, C., Ramamohanarao, K.: Adjusted probabilistic packet marking for IP traceback. In: Gregori, E., Conti, M., Campbell, A.T., Omidyar, G., Zukerman, M. (eds.) NETWORKING 2002: Networking Technologies, Services, and Protocols; Performance of Computer and Communication Networks; Mobile and Wireless Communications. Lecture Notes in Computer Science, vol. 2345, pp. 697–708. Springer, Heidelberg (2002). https://doi.org/10.1007/3-540-47906-6_56
6. Kim, B.: Efficient technique for fast IP traceback. In: Luo, Y. (ed.) Cooperative Design, Visualization, and Engineering, pp. 211–218. Springer, Berlin (2006)
7. Paruchuri, V., Durresi, A., Chellappan, S.: TTL based packet marking for IP traceback. In: 2008 IEEE Global Telecommunications Conference, pp. 1–5. IEEE, Piscataway (2008)
8. Liu, J., Lee, Z.J., Chung, Y.C.: Dynamic probabilistic packet marking for efficient IP traceback. Comput. Netw. **51**(3), 866–882 (2007)
9. Dawn, S. and Perrig, A.: Advanced and authenticated marking schemes for IP traceback. In: Proceedings IEEE INFOCOM 2001. Conference on Computer Communications. Twentieth Annual Joint Conference of the IEEE Computer and Communications Society, Vol. 872, pp. 878–886. IEEE, Piscataway (2001)
10. Dean, D., Franklin, M., Stubblefield, A.: An algebraic approach to IP traceback. ACM Trans. Inf. Syst. Secur. **5**(2), 119–137 (2002). https://doi.org/10.1145/505586.505588
11. Kim, H., et al.: Network forensic evidence generation and verification scheme (NFEGVS). Telecommun. Syst. **60**(2), 261–273 (2015)
12. Belenky, A., Ansari, N.: IP traceback with deterministic packet marking. IEEE Commun. Lett. **7**(4), 162–164 (2003)
13. Liu, X.H., et al.: Analysis of cyber attack traceback techniques from the perspective of network forensics. Ruan Jian Xue Bao/J. Softw. **32**(1), 194–217 (2021)
14. Agarwal, K., et al.: SDN traceroute: tracing SDN forwarding without changing network behavior. In: Third Workshop on Hot Topics in Software Defined Networking, pp. 145–150. ACM, New York (2014)
15. Handigol, N., et al.: Where is the debugger for my software-defined network? In: First Workshop on Hot Topics in Software Defined Networks, pp. 55–60. ACM, New York (2012)
16. Ren, Q.Z., et al.: The global flow table based on the software-defined networking. In: 2015 IEEE International Conference on Communication Problem-Solving (ICCP), pp. 264–267. IEEE, Piscataway (2015)
17. Li, B., et al.: A distributed network tracing system and method based on SDN, CN112350948A. https://d.wanfangdata.com.cn/patent/ChJQYXRlbnROZXdTMjAyMTEwMjYSEENOMjAyMDExMTc0ODc1LjUaCHh4cXlucmV6. Accessed 15 Nov 2021

18. Peter Bailis, S.V., Franklin, M.J., Hellerstein, J.M., Stoica, I.: Probabilistically bounded staleness for practical partial quorums. Proc. VLDB Endow. **5**(8), 776–787 (2012)
19. Li, J.F., et al.: Quantitative approach of much-controller's consensus in SDN. J. Commun. **37**(6), 86–93 (2016)
20. Koponen, T., et al.: Onix: a distributed control platform for large-scale production networks. In: Proceedings of the 9th USENIX Conference on Operating Systems Design and Implementation, pp. 351–364. USENIX Association, Berkeley, CA (2010)

Intrusion Detection System Based on Deep Neural Network and Incremental Learning for In-Vehicle CAN Networks

Jiaying Lin[1], Yehua Wei[1(✉)], Wenjia Li[2], and Jing Long[1]

[1] College of Information Science and Engineering, Hunan Normal University, Changsha, China
jlong@hunnu.edu.cn
[2] Department of Computer Science, New York Institute of Technology, New York, NY, USA
wli20@nyit.edu

Abstract. With the application of information technology in automotive electronic system and the development of internet of vehicles, automobiles face increasing security threats. Controller area network (CAN) is the main bus system for communication between electronic control units (ECUs) in modern automobiles. CAN bus network easily suffers from cyberattacks because it lacks security protection mechanisms. Intrusion detection is an effective method to defend a network against attacks. However, the detection accuracy may be affected by the change in driving environment or driving behavior and the occurrence of unknown attacks. A two-stage intrusion detection method based on Deep Neural Network (DNN) and Incremental Learning (IL) is proposed to improve detection performance. In an offline training stage, DNN is applied to obtain basic classification model using marked actual CAN data. Then, in the online detection and updating stage, the model is updated with IL technology based on new unlabeled data, at the same time performing intrusion detection. Experimental results show that the proposed method has high detection accuracy and good generalization ability.

Keywords: In-vehicle network security · Intrusion detection · Incremental learning · Deep neural network · Controller area network

1 Introduction

With the maturity of IEEE 802.11p and C-V2X standards, the industrialization process of networked vehicles speeds up, and the intelligence and networking of vehicles can provide passengers with convenient and comfortable driving experience. Meanwhile, intelligent networked vehicles integrate multiple external communication interfaces, such as Bluetooth, 4G/5G, and OBD II, which can be utilized to launch attacks at automotive electronic system. Thus, the vehicle faces serious security threats.

In the current automotive electronic systems, CAN is still a mainstream bus network given its low wiring cost and safe and reliable communication. However, CAN lacks encryption and authentication protection mechanism. The transmitting messages can easily be stolen or tampered, and the CAN network is vulnerable to injection attacks, such as denial of service (DoS) and fuzzy attack [1]. If the message encryption and authentication technology is applied to CAN network, computing time and communication bandwidth increase, thereby affecting the real-time automotive electronic system and resulting in system function failure. Intrusion detection method has become an important research direction for the in-vehicle network security given its easy deployment and high timeliness.

Deep learning has been widely used in existing research works about intrusion detection for in-vehicle network. However, most intrusion detection models based on deep learning mainly adopt the fixed model obtained by off-line training. This approach is effective for known types of attack detection, not considering unknown types of attack and data change caused by changes in driving environment or driving behavior. Therefore, to improve the generalization ability of the learning model, a two-stage intrusion detection system combining incremental learning and deep neural network for in-vehicle network, referred to as IL-DNN, is proposed. The DNN is applied to obtain a basic classification model using marked real CAN data in the offline training stage. Then, the model is updated with incremental learning method based on new unlabeled data, at the same time performing intrusion detection in online detection and updating stage. The experimental results show that the proposed method can realize online incremental update of detection model by using only unlabeled new data. Therefore, the detection model can maintain high generalization ability and obtain detection ability of unknown types of attacks.

2 Related Works

Some related research works have been conducted given the advantages of intrusion detection for in-vehicle networks security [1, 2]. [3] proposed an in-vehicle network intrusion detection system based on remote frames; the work determined whether an intrusion has occurred on the bus by measuring the frame delay between the data frame and the remote frame. [4] considered the output voltage of ECU as a detection feature to identify the abnormal ECU. [5] used clock offset as a fingerprint to construct baseline of normal clock behavior of ECU based on active learning technology; the baseline is considered the threshold to detect intrusion. [6] using the voltage physical characteristics of CAN frame to identify legal ECU similarly, an on-board network intrusion detection scheme based on local outlier factor (LOF) is proposed. They verify the effectiveness of the proposed method through real vehicles experimental and the detection performance of attacks from external devices. However, the physical characteristics of ECU are limited by many factors, that is, it is easily affected by the environment, thereby influencing the detection accuracy. Therefore, the method based on deep learning has stronger stability than the vehicle network intrusion detection method based on physical characteristics.

[7] proposed an anomaly detection algorithm of vehicular CAN bus based on linear chain conditional random field, considering the correlation among multiple messages of CAN network. For the security of electric vehicles' CAN bus, [8] proposed a new effective anomaly detection model based on a modified one-class support vector machine in the CAN traffic. With the development of artificial intelligence, intrusion detection for in-vehicle network based on deep learning has been widely considered. [9] used

long- and short-memory networks to detect DoS attacks, fuzzy attacks, and spoofing attacks. [10] improved the ability of single GAN model to detect false counterexamples by designing a new loss function. [11] uused deep belief network to initialize model parameters, which could improve detection accuracy and reduce response time of DNN. [12] built a deep convolutional neural network based on ResNet model to identify malicious messages by learning the normal traffic pattern of CAN network. [13] develop an unsupervised learning approach to monitor the normal behavior within the CAN bus data and detect malicious traffic. And propose an algorithm based on hierarchical agglomerative clustering that considers multiple approaches for linkages and pairwise distances between observations. [14] designed a LeCun model based on deep transfer learning to improve detection accuracy of abnormal activities and enhance the real-time vehicle network intrusion detection. The works based on deep learning can usually achieve higher detection accuracy for the known types of attacks under a given sample set of in-vehicle network, but do not consider the unknown types of attacks and the change in driving behavior which may cause irregular changes in the in-network data.

As mentioned in [15], offline model based on deep neural network cannot be updated immediately when encountering unknown types of attacks. Updating the detection model in time can effectively ensure that the intrusion detection system has long-term generalization ability for in-vehicle networks. The updating of on-board detection model must satisfy the conditions of high efficiency and speed given the high real-time requirements of the automotive electronic system. Therefore, the traditional offline intrusion detection model based on DNN is improved, and the incremental learning method is used to realize the online update of vehicle network intrusion detection model.

3   CAN Network and Attack Models

Can bus was developed by BOSCH company in 1980s. It is a serial communication bus defined by International Organization for Standardization (ISO). After decades of development, CAN has become a standardized communication protocol widely used in automotive internal control system [16]. Because of its outstanding reliability and real-time, CAN bus greatly reduces the complexity and wiring cost of on-board network, so it is widely favored by automobile manufacturers. The electronic control unit (ECU) in automotive electronic system communicates with each other through standard CAN bus protocol, and transmits messages in the form of broadcast. As the carrier of information transmitted on CAN bus, CAN frame has a specific message format. It includes start of frame, arbitration field, control field, data field, check field, acknowledgement field, and end of frame. Among them, arbitration field consists of 11 bits as identifier (CAN ID) to denote which ECU transmitted message should be received. The data field consists of 64 bits, which refer to payload data (Fig. 1).

The safety problem was not considered at the beginning of CAN bus design. The message broadcasting mechanism, plaintext transmission mechanism and no authentication mechanism all make the CAN bus face serious information security problems in the era of automobile full networking. Attacks on in-vehicle CAN networks can be divided into passive and active attacks. The main purpose of passive attack is to steal the transmitted messages. Passive network attacks such as eavesdropping mainly destroy

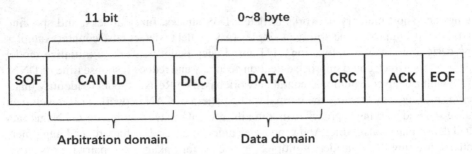

Fig. 1. Structure of the CAN frame

the confidentiality of the car system, resulting in privacy disclosure, such as access location information, session data, camera records and other private data. If an attacker obtains network traffic and knows the transmission mode and attributes of data packets of a specific node, he can simulate the node and launch an active attack. Active attacks mainly modify vehicle system messages or inject attack messages into network systems, such as DoS attacks, fuzzy attacks and replay attacks. When DoS attack occurs, the attacker sends a large number of interference messages with the highest priority, resulting in arbitration failure and network system paralysis. When a fuzzy attack occurs, the attacker randomly changes the content of the message, hoping to control the target ECU by exhaustive method. Active attacks on vehicle network can be monitored by intrusion detection system. When an active attack occurs, the abnormal frames show different data characteristics from the normal frames. They can be used to identify attack by analyzing real-time data on CAN bus. The detection of DoS attack and fuzzy attack is mainly studied.

4 Intrusion Detection System Based on IL-DNN

Aiming at the information security problem of vehicle CAN bus, a two-level intrusion detection system IL-DNN is proposed. The system breaks the traditional fixed detection model mode of deep learning and realizes the online update of vehicle intrusion detection model. IL-DNN can update the detection model online with unmarked real-time data to deal with possible irregular changes in CAN network data and unknown types of attacks. The flow chart of IL-DNN is shown in Fig. 2, including offline training stage and online detection and update stage.

In the off-line training stage, the real vehicle CAN network data set is preprocessed, mainly for feature extraction and missing value filling. Then the processed data set is used to train DNN to obtain the basic classification model. Finally, the online intrusion detection model is deployed according to the parameters of the basic classification model. In the online detection and update phase, the deployed detection model is used to forecast the unlabeled CAN messages collected online to judge whether they are abnormal. If they are abnormal data, the system will give a warning. While forecasting the unlabeled data, the incremental learning method is used to update the detection model online.

Offline training phase

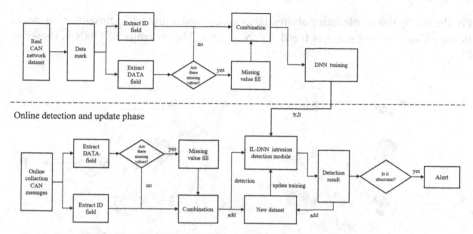

Fig. 2. Flowchart of IL-DNN

4.1 Data Preprocessing

The real CAN bus data set consists of normal data and attack data; the attack samples have been manually labeled. Data preprocessing usually includes feature selection, missing value filling, and label replacement in the off-line training stage. It includes feature selection, missing value filling, and label deletion in the online detection and updating stage. According to the structural characteristics of CAN data frame, for simplicity, the ID field of arbitration domain and all the bytes of the data field are selected as features. In addition, the missing values of the data field are filled. The label replacement refers to replacing normal data label with 0 and the attack data label with 1. The offline training samples T and online update samples T' are represented by formula 1 and formula 2, respectively.

$$
T = \begin{bmatrix} t_1 \\ t_2 \\ \vdots \\ t_m \end{bmatrix} = \begin{bmatrix} t_{11} & \ldots & t_{19} & y_1 \\ t_{21} & & t_{29} & y_2 \\ \vdots & & \vdots & \vdots \\ t_{m1} & \cdots & t_{m9} & y_m \end{bmatrix} \tag{1}
$$

$$
T' = \begin{bmatrix} t_1 \\ t_2 \\ \vdots \\ t_m \end{bmatrix} = \begin{bmatrix} t_{11} & \ldots & t_{18} & t_{19} \\ t_{21} & & t_{28} & t_{29} \\ \vdots & & \vdots & \vdots \\ t_{m1} & \cdots & t_{m8} & t_{m9} \end{bmatrix} \tag{2}
$$

where $t_i(i \in [1, m])$ is the *ith* training sample, t_{ij} is the *jth*($j \in [1, 9]$) eigenvalue of the *ith* training sample; yi is the label corresponding to the *ith* training sample. The value for normal data is 0; otherwise, the value is 1.

4.2 Offline Training of Model

For the strong transfer learning ability, DNN is selected as the basic classification model in the offline training stage of the IL-DNN system. The structure of DNN is shown in Fig. 3.

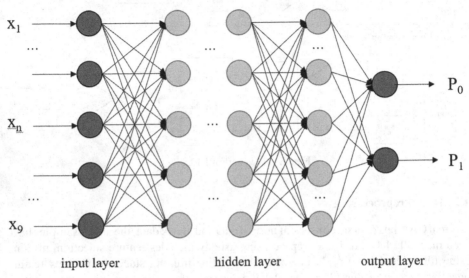

input layer   hidden layer   output layer

Fig. 3. Structure of DNN

The input layer has nine input nodes, which are responsible for processing the labeled training samples in batches. The samples are organized into input vectors $x = \{x1, x2, \cdots, x9\}$. The hidden layer is responsible for the learning data characteristics of the samples. It is the fundamental guarantee for the detection accuracy of IL-DNN. The calculation formula for the hidden layer is as follows:

$$\begin{cases} z^{[i]} = w^{[i]}a^{[i-1]} + b^{[i]} \\ \\ a^{[i]} = ReLu\left(z^{[i]}\right) \end{cases} \tag{3}$$

where, $w^{[i]}$, $b^{[i]}$, and $a^{[i]}$ are the weight matrix, bias vector, and output vector of the *ith* hidden layer, respectively. if $i = 1$, then it is the input vector x of the entire model. $z[i]$ is the intermediate vector for the *ith* hidden layer to perform linear operations on its input vector. $ReLU(f)$ is the activation function of the hidden layer used to realize nonlinear conversion of the input parameter f. $ReLU$ is obtained as follows:

$$ReLU(x) = max(0, x) \tag{4}$$

Compared with the commonly used *sigmoid* and *Tanh* function, ReLU has less computation cost, and can greatly shorten the calculation time of back propagation. Meanwhile,

ReLU can alleviate the overfitting of deep network and gradient disappearance. According to the output result of the last hidden layer, the corresponding value of the training sample, which belongs to the normal data or abnormal data, can be computed using formula 5, as follows:

$$P = w^{out} a^{[h]} + b^{[out]} \tag{5}$$

where $a^{[h]}$ is the output vector of the last hidden layer, $w^{[out]}$ is the weight matrix of the output layer, and $b^{[out]}$ is the bias vector of the output layer. $P = \{P_0, P_1\}$, where P_0 and P_1 are the corresponding probability values of normal and abnormal CAN bus data, respectively. The values are computed using *softmax* function, and the detection result is judged according to the probability values.

To obtain the optimal parameter sets and achieve high detection accuracy, cross-entropy loss function is used as the loss function of offline training, as follows:

$$L = -[y \log \hat{y} + (1 - y) \log(1 - \hat{y})] \tag{6}$$

From the formula 6, the average loss value of processing m samples can be calculated as follows:

$$L(w, b) = -\frac{1}{m} \sum_{i=1}^{m} [y_i \log(\hat{y}_i) + (1 - y_i) \log(\hat{y}_i)] \tag{7}$$

To minimize the average loss, the adaptive moment (Adam) estimation algorithm is used to update the weight matrix and bias vector in the back propagation process of model training.

4.3 Online Updating of Model

The basic classification model obtained from the offline training stage is deployed as an online detection model. The basic model is difficult to cope with the irregular change in network data and cannot effectively detect unknown types of attacks due to the limited number of offline training samples. Therefore, we design an online updating stage using incremental learning based on parameter importance.

Online updating of model adopts semi-supervised learning method. When the unlabeled new data are judged by the basic detection model, they are used to update training for detection model. To ensure the fitting degree of model for the new data, the parameters of each neuron should be adjusted. Once the neuron parameters, which are closely related to historical data, are covered, the fitting degree of the neural network to old data is greatly reduced. This condition becomes a catastrophic forgetting [17] problem of the neural network. For the problem, the incremental learning method based on parameter importance is used to update the intrusion detection model online.

The importance matrix F is obtained based on the gradient covariance of the probability distribution [18], which is used to measure the importance of each parameter in the neural network. Furthermore, the regularization term is added to the loss function based on F; it can limit the update range according to the importance of the parameters to ensure that the intrusion detection model can not only maintain memory ability to the characteristics of history data, but also has the transfer ability to the new data. The loss function used in online updating stage is as follows:

$$L = L_B + \sum_i \frac{\lambda}{2} F_i (\theta_i - \theta_{A,i})^2 \tag{8}$$

where L_B is the cross-entropy loss function for the new training sample set, λ is the hyperparameter, θ_i is the *ith* parameter during online updating training, and $\theta_{A,i}$ is the *ith* parameter prior to update training.

5 Experiments

5.1 Experimental Setup

The opensource data set of the information security laboratory of Korea University [19] is used in our experiments. The data set is obtained using Raspberry Pi device as an attack node to execute injection attack message in the CAN network of automotive electronic system and collect the data of CAN bus through OBD- II port. It includes five data subsets, namely, no attack, DoS attack, fuzzy attack, deceptive gear attack, and deceptive RPM attack. To verify the effect of online updating stage, fuzzy attack data set is used for offline training, online updating, and detection. Among them, 17% of samples are used for offline training of IL-DNN, and 83% of samples are used for online update training and detecting of IL-DNN. To evaluate the detection performance of IL-DNN to an unknown type of attack, fuzzy attack is considered a known type of attack, and the corresponding data set is used for offline training. DoS attack is considered an unknown type of attack. The hardware environment of the experiment is a laptop with 1.80 GHz, 8-core CPU, and 16 GB RAM.

5.2 Evaluation Indicator

The accuracy (ACC) and F1-Score are used as evaluation indicator to verify the effectiveness of IL-DNN. ACC denotes the proportion of the number of samples with accurate classification to total number of samples, F1-Score is the harmonic average of precision (P) and recall (R); its value is from 0 to 1. The higher value indicates better IDS performance.

$$Acc = \frac{TP + TN}{TP + FN + FP + TN} \tag{9}$$

$$\frac{1}{F1} = \frac{1}{2}\left(\frac{1}{P} + \frac{1}{R}\right) \tag{10}$$

$$P = \frac{TP}{TP + FP} \tag{11}$$

$$R = \frac{TP}{TP + FN} \tag{12}$$

Table 1. Confusion matrix of detection result

True label	Test results	
	normal	abnormal
normal	TP	FN
abnormal	FP	TN

TP, FN, FP, and TN in the confusion matrix of detection result (Table 1) are normal data with accurate classification, normal data with inaccurate classification, intrusion data with inaccurate classification, and intrusion data with accurate classification, respectively.

In addition, the updating time Tu and detection time Td are used to evaluate the time cost of intrusion detection system.

5.3 Analysis of Experimental Results

To compare the detection performance, the DNN without updating stage [10], incremental convolutional neural network (CNN), and incremental recurrent neural network (RNN) are used as the comparison models.

Detection Accuracy. To verify the impact of online updating on the detection performance, the number of updating is set from 0 to 50. The results of ACC and F1-Score are shown in Fig. 4. Figure 4(a) shows that, for the fuzzy attack dataset, the detection accuracy of DNN without updating is lower than that of IL-DNN, and the accuracy of the former decreases greatly. However, IL-DNN can maintain high detection accuracy for a long time. At the same time, the detection accuracy increases with the increase in updating times. This is because the proposed detection model learns the knowledge of new data in the process of updating, thereby improve the generalization ability. Figures 4(a) and (b) also shows that the detection accuracy and F1-Score of IL-DNN and incremental CNN are stably maintained at a high level. But the detection accuracy and F1-Score of incremental RNN fluctuate greatly. After ten updates, the accuracy decreases to about 85% and F1-Score decreases to about 0.9. This indicates that incremental RNN is not an ideal choice.

Updating and Detection Time. Figure 5 shows the time performance of IL-DNN, incremental RNN and incremental CNN, including updating time and detection time under different online update times. The detection time is the time required for anomaly detection of a single CAN message frame, and the updating time is the time required to update the model online with 50000 new samples. Figure 5(a) shows that the average detection time of IL-DNN for a single CAN message frame is 0.015 ms, but the average detection time of incremental RNN and incremental CNN for a single can message

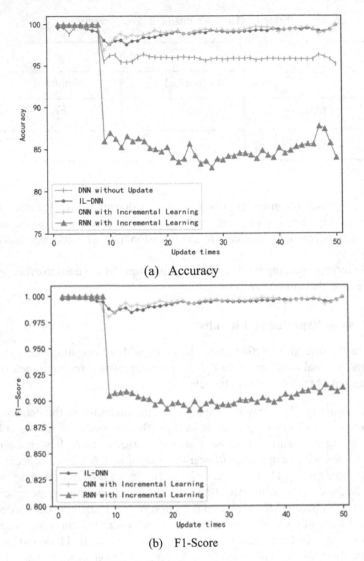

(a) Accuracy

(b) F1-Score

Fig. 4. Detection performance

frame is 0.019 ms and 0.03 ms respectively. Figure 5(b) shows that the average model update time of IL-DNN is 0.06 ms, while the model update time of incremental RNN and incremental CNN fluctuates greatly. Thus, among the three, IL-DNN has the best time performance and the strongest stability. The proposed IL-DNN is more suitable for in-vehicle network systems than the incremental RNN and incremental CNN given their real-time requirement.

Unknown Type Attacks Detection. In the detection experiment of unknown types of attacks, fuzzy attack is considered as a known type of attack, and DoS attack is considered

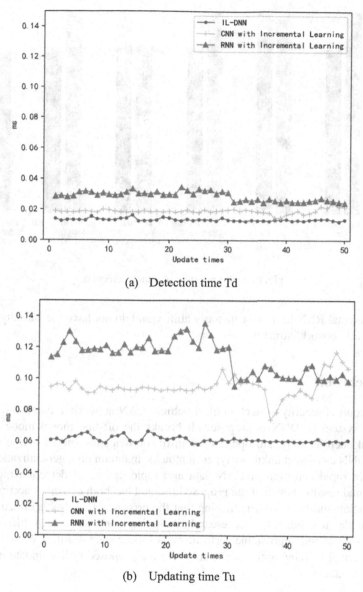

(a) Detection time Td

(b) Updating time Tu

Fig. 5. Time analysis

as an unknown type of attack. It can be seen from Fig. 6 that IL-DNN has high detection accuracy for fuzzy attacks before model update, and has high detection accuracy for fuzzy attacks and DOS attacks after model update. This proves the ability of IL-DNN to detect unknown types of attacks. Incremental CNN and incremental RNN have high detection accuracy for fuzzy attacks before model update, but the detection accuracy for fuzzy attacks is greatly reduced after model update. This shows that incremental CNN

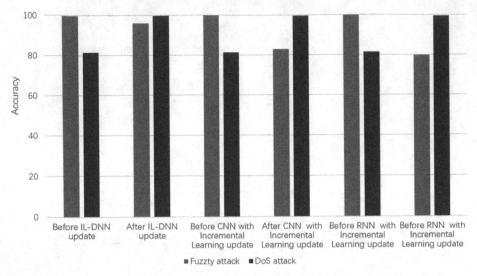

Fig. 6. Unknown type of attack detection

and incremental RNN have poor memory ability and do not have the stability required for on-board network intrusion detection.

6   Conclusion

For the required security protection of in-vehicle CAN network, a two-stage intrusion detection system IL-DNN is proposed. It breaks the off-line model mode based on traditional deep learning and updates the intrusion detection model online with new data. IL-DNN can detect unknown types of attacks, maintain high generalization ability, and realize rapid detection of CAN data and rapid update of detection model. The experimental results show that the proposed method has high detection accuracy, good generalization ability, thereby indicating that the proposed IL-DNN is effective. In the future, we plan to conduct further research, including using data sets of different attack types to evaluate and improve the performance of the system. Further, we will improve the incremental learning algorithm to improve the proposed online update method of detection model.

Acknowledgment. This work is supported by the Natural Science Foundation of Hunan Province of China (No. 2020JJ4058) and Guangxi Key Laboratory of Crytography and Information Security (No. GCIS201920) and is supported in part by the National Natural Science Foundation of China (No. 62072175).

References

1. Wu, F.: A survey of intrusion detection for in-vehicle networks. IEEE Trans. Intell. Transp. Syst. **21**(3), 919–933 (2020)

2. Lokman, S.-F.: Intrusion detection system for automotive Controller Area Network (CAN) bus system: a review. EURASIP J. Wirel. Commun. Netw. **2019**, 184 (2019)
3. Lee, H., Jeong, S.H., Kim, S.: OTIDS: a novel intrusion detection system for in-vehicle network by using remote frame. In: 2017 15th Annual Conference on Privacy, Security and Trust (PST), IEEE, Piscataway (2017)
4. Cho, K.-T., Shin, K.: Viden: Attacker identification on in-vehicle networks. In: 2017 ACM SIGSAC Conference on Computer and Communications Security, pp. 1109–1123. ACM, New York (2017)
5. Subir Halder, F., Mauro Conti, S.: COIDS: a clock offset based intrusion detection system for controller area networks. In: 21st International Conference on Distributed Computing and Networking (ICDCN 2020), pp. 1–10. ACM, New York (2020)
6. Ning, J., Liu, J.: An experimental study towards attacker identification in automotive networks. In: 2019 IEEE Global Communications Conference (GLOBECOM), pp. 1–6. IEEE, Piscataway (2019)
7. Kai, T., Zhongwei, L., Wenqi, J., Yadong, G., Weiming, T.: In-vehicle CAN bus anomaly detection algorithm based on linear chain condition random field. In: 2019 IEEE 19th International Conference on Communication Technology (ICCT), pp. 1153–1159. IEEE, Piscataway (2020)
8. Avatefipour, O., et al.: An intelligent secured framework for cyberattack detection in electric vehicles' can bus using machine learning. IEEE Access **7**, 127580–127592 (2019)
9. Hossain, M.D., Inoue, H., Ochiai, H., Fall, D., Kadobayashi, Y.: LSTM-based intrusion detection system for in-vehicle can bus communications. IEEE Access **8**, 185489–185502 (2020)
10. Yuanda Yang, F.: Intrusion detection for in-vehicle network by using single GAN in connected vehicles. J. Circ. Syst. Comput. **30**(1), 2150007 (2021)
11. Kang, M.-J., Kang, J.-W.: Intrusion detection system using deep neural network for in-vehicle network security. PLoS ONE **11**(6), e0155781 (2016)
12. Song, H.M., Woo, J., Kim, H.K.: In-vehicle network intrusion detection using deep convolutional neural network. Veh. Commun. **21**, 100198 (2020)
13. Leslie, N.: An unsupervised learning approach for in-vehicle network intrusion detection. In: 2021 55th Annual Conference on Information Sciences and Systems (CISS), pp. 1–4. IEEE, Piscataway (2021)
14. Mehedi, S.K., Anwar, A., Rahman, Z., AhmedMehedi, K.: Deep transfer learning based intrusion detection system for electric vehicular networks. Sensors **21**(14), 4736 (2021)
15. Qiang, H., Luo, F.: Review of secure communication approaches for in-vehicle network. Int. J. Autom. Technol. **19**, 879–894 (2018)
16. Young, C., Zambreno, J., Olufowobi, H., Bloom, G.: Survey of automotive controller area network intrusion detection systems. IEEE Design Test **36**(6), 48–55 (2019)
17. German. I.F.: Continual lifelong learning with neural networks: a review. Neural Netw. **113**, 54–71 (2019)
18. Kirkpatrick, J., et al.: Overcoming catastrophic forgetting in neural networks. Proc. Natl. Acad. Sci. USA **114**(13), 3521–3526 (2017)
19. CAR-HACKING DATASET Homepage. https://ocslab.hksecurity.net/Datasets/CAN-intrusion-dataset

Towards a Two-Tier Architecture for Privacy-Enabled Recommender Systems (PeRS)

Shakil[1], Muhammad Arif[2], Shahab Saquib Sohail[1], Mohammed Talha Alam[1], Syed Ubaid[1], Md Tabrez Nafis[1], and Guojun Wang[2(✉)] (iD)

[1] Department of Computer Science and Engineering, Jamia Hamdard, New Delhi 110062, India
{shahabssohail,tabrez.nafis}@jamiahamdard.ac.in
[2] School of Computer Science, Guangzhou University, Guangzhou 510006, Guangdong Province, People's Republic of China
csgjwang@gzhu.edu.cn

Abstract. The current surge in recommender systems research is impressive, but it has highlighted a number of concerns, including users' privacy and data security. Although various solutions to these privacy breaches have been proposed, the existing solutions fall short of directly addressing the real issues, and most of them continue to rely on third parties. Moreover, giving third parties access to users' personally identifiable information (PII) is a cause for concern. In this paper, we have suggested a two-tiered architecture. The identity of the users is anonymized in the first tier, in the next tier, homomorphic encryption is exploited for the purpose of randomization of the users' data. With the help of proposed solution, on one hand, third-party involvement can be eliminated. On the other hand, there can be improvement in the privacy mechanism by providing a two-tier architecture for user data security. The suggested framework is intended to serve as a baseline for safeguarding users' privacy and integrity when conducting online purchases and other associated activities.

Keywords: Privacy · Data encryption · Recommender system · Security

1 Introduction

The recommender systems (RS) are being used to filter large amounts of data based on user preferences, which helps in handling information overload issues. Prior to providing relevant and matched recommendations, it uses the user's personal data. Despite the fact that RS research isn't new, there is a significant increase in this area of research which has spread across several domains [1]. Providing relevant recommendations to users necessitates an understanding of their personal preferences, which includes sensitive data about the user, referred to as personally identifiable information (PII) [2]. User sensitive information includes purchase history, ratings, location, and demographic data (age, sex, and so on). The most prevalent threats to the exposure of these personal information include hacking, snooping, unsolicited marketing, government monitoring, selling data to third parties, and fake recommendations made by an intruder [3].

Due to such privacy risks, people are frequently hesitant to use the RS since they are bound to share their confidential data [4]. This has created a sense of privacy violation among users, and as a result, the issue has been a topic of discussion among researchers in the field. Therefore, it's clear how important it is to preserve users' privacy and integrity while still improving technology to provide reliable recommendations. The authors who first introduced the concept of PII indicated that users are not aware of how their personal information is exploited by merchants when it is used in recommendation technologies, hence, they must be intimated about its use, in addition to this, they should also be given authority to access users' rights. Furthermore, the authors have thoroughly examined the misuse of personal information and the potential calamity that this could cause [5, 6].

To that end, we described a two-tiered security strategy that can protect users' privacy. We used obfuscation to assist anonymize the user's identity in the first stage, and then we advised utilising homomorphic encryption to reinforce the privacy-preserving method and prevent the leakage of individual users' PII. There are two distinct advantages to the proposed system. On the one hand, it provides a secure mechanism for the recommendation engine, while on the other hand, it has no detrimental impact on the major merchandisers' commercial aims and does not decrease the quality of the recommendations.

The remaining of the article is organised as follows: the background is presented in in Sect. 2. In the Sect. 3, privacy implications of recommender systems as well as potential threats are described. The suggested framework is addressed in detail in Sect. 4. In Sect. 5, we have concluded our work and recommendations for the future is also suggested.

2 Materials and Methods

2.1 Background

In the mid-1990s, recommender systems research was introduced [17, 18]. The growing interest of researchers in related fields has resulted in a variety of developments and, as a result, has raised a number of issues. One of the key problems is the users' privacy. Users' personal information is regularly profiled and exploited to make suggestions, providing a risk to users' vulnerable identification and details, which can have an impact on their lives and behaviour [7, 23]. A large number of works have been written to address the issues. Arjan Jeckmans et al. investigated both intentional (snooping, hacking) and unintentional privacy vulnerabilities in the recommender systems (mismanagement, lingering data). They've also warned that there could be catastrophic consequences depending on how sensitive the material is [8]. Arik Friedman et al. noted how unauthorised access by staff, unwanted data collection, and data sharing with third parties could jeopardise consumers' privacy [9]. A. Jeckmans has indicated in his work about cryptography-based solutions that overcome these difficulties while simultaneously providing high-quality and accurate service [10].

We may categorise privacy enabled recommender systems into two categories based on the different solutions for privacy concerns in the recommendation: obfuscation and cryptography techniques.

2.2 Obfuscation

Obfuscation is referred to as perturbation technique where noises are infused on users while designing privacy-preserved recommender system. One component of obfuscation is anonymization, which removes the link between the user and the data for user profile obfuscation. In RS research, it is widely explored for privacy protection. Singular Value Decomposition and K-means clustering were two data regeneration methods demonstrated by Sheng Zhang et al. in their article [11]. With the use of randomised perturbation-based techniques, different singular value decompositions with privacy have been developed that maintain adequate accuracy for recommendation while simultaneously safeguarding the privacy of users.

K-anonymity shall continue to be in great demand [4, 19–21] as it introduces noise to provide guaranteed privacy as well as recommendation accuracy. The recommendation model is vulnerable to attacks that may allow the user to be re-identified. Pierangela Samarati et al. propose a solution using a k-anonymity-based method and a computational disclosure strategy to address these problems [12]. This strategy works well for resolving the re-identification problem. Perturbation techniques, in which sounds are implanted on the user's private data before it is transferred to the server for generating the recommendation, are used in some portions of obfuscation, although perturbation techniques may not be capable of fully securing the data [9].

2.3 Cryptography Techniques

Data encryption and decryption are the subjects of cryptography. It is a powerful tool that supports in protecting data confidentiality and integrity, even if it does not solve all information security challenges. For privacy-preserving recommendation techniques, cryptographic primitives such as homomorphic encryption and secure multi-party computing are among the most widely used cryptographic techniques. John Canny [13] proposed a collaborative filtering system based on homomorphic encryption, arguing that it is a privacy-preserving technique for more accurate and secure suggestion. It was created to protect personal information without jeopardising privacy. Badsha proposed an ElGamal homomorphic encryption method, which enhances recommendation precision and performance, but the issue of excessive dependency on third parties remained. As a result, we start using the secure multi-party calculation method.

Hoens et al. [14] presented a method that uses secure multi-party computing and homomorphic encryption to preserve the privacy of individual user ratings. Erkin et al. implemented homomorphic encryption and safe multi-party computing in a centralised protocol to ensure user privacy [15]. For a large number of people, however, this technique is unrealistic. The issue of extensive reliance on a third party has returned as a result of the latter solution being impractical for a large number of users.

The suggested framework is an upgraded version of decentralised privacy-preserving recommender systems based on homomorphic encryption. An anonymization strategy for a user profile has been implemented in first tier, in addition to anonymization, it also hides the user's personal information from third parties in second tier. As a result, it solves the problem in a realistic and effective manner.

3 Privacy Aspects in Recommender System

There are a variety of privacy-enabled recommender systems available [4], including perturbation, differential privacy, and homomorphic encryption, however homomorphic encryption-enabled recommender systems are the most popular [16, 30, 31]. Homomorphic encryption is a sort of cryptosystem that allows you to compute on the encrypted text without having to decrypt it. After computation, the result is also encrypted, which must be decrypted using the private key.

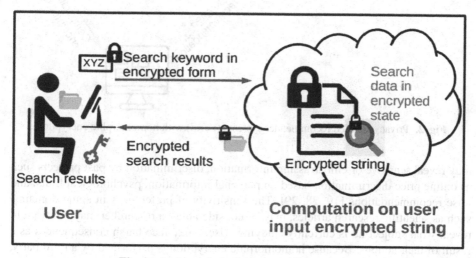

Fig. 1. An example for homomorphic encryption

When a user searches for something, the search keyword is converted to ciphertext before being sent on to the query, as seen in Fig. 1. The search query is encrypted by means of arithmetic operation which is applied on ciphertext and hence it is no more needed to decrypt it, resulting in an encrypted search result for the user. Using the private key, the user can now decrypt the search results. With homomorphic encryption, the service provider does not need a secret key to decode data because they may compute on it without decryption. This is by far the most important advantage of this encryption.

We present a block diagram in Fig. 2 for PeRS by exploiting homomorphic encryption. Random users' preferences are collected, and a trustworthy third party encrypts and sends the choices to the service provider for recommendation generating. The service provider generates the ciphertext and sends it together with the suggestion to the trusted third party. After it has been encrypted, it is sent to the user by a trusted third party. However, the existing privacy-enabled recommender systems (PeRS) places a large reliance on reliable and semi-reliable third parties.

Users should be wary of putting their trust in third parties when it comes to their privacy. The main issue with third-party is that it may sell user information such as ratings, preferences, and purchase history to "another party without owners". After being exposed to that, the user may experience issues such as targeted advertisements, which

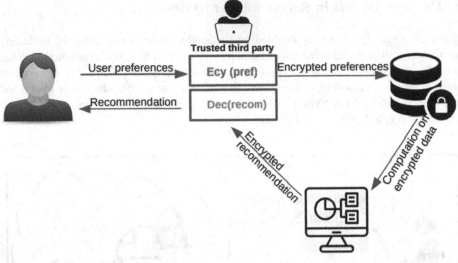

Fig. 2. Privacy enabled recommender systems (PeRS) with homomorphic encryption

may reveal sensitive or embarrassing information, discrimination by past projects such as online price discrimination based on personal information, psychological traits, and false recommendations [19, 28, 29]. The sensitivity of preferences in some domains, such as scientific research articles, may be considerable - a researcher may not want to reveal what subject he is currently studying. Users may face harsh consequences as a result of their actions. Because homomorphic encryption is performed by a third party, users may encounter these issues while using this privacy-enabled recommender system, which is necessary to protect user data while offering reliable recommendations [5, 9, 10, 28, 29].

4   Proposed Privacy Enabled Recommender System (PeRS)

4.1   Architecture of the Proposed PeRS

To address these critical issues, we propose an enhanced privacy enabled recommender system (PeRS) that employs appropriate privacy-conscious techniques to protect user privacy. To overcome the issue of placing a great deal of trust in a third party, we devised a framework that allows us to avoid relying on them. If we consider the privacy technique to be a privacy-enhanced lock, we've added two locks for user privacy rather than one. We utilise two locks: one for user identification and the other for user data, and it's clear that having two locks adds another degree of security to users' privacy.

In the first tier we perform anonymization, and the in the second tier, homomorphic encryption is applied. The addition of homomorphic encryption for anonymization is the icing on the cake. Anonymization obscures a user's profile by introducing noise to it using perturbation techniques. The quantity of noise added to the user profile should be governed by the privacy budget of the user, making it cost-effective. The amount of money invested is related to the level of profile security that is provided.

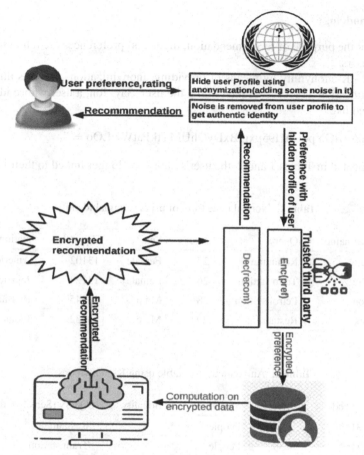

Fig. 3. Two-tier architecture for privacy enabled recommender systems (PeRS)

As a result, we may do computations on the user's encrypted data without having to divulge the plain text using homomorphic encryption. After merging the two and utilising anonymization, we no longer reveal the user's profile in front of a trustworthy third party. To calculate in the recommendation process, we just reveal the encrypted preferences without the secret key.

Figure 3 depicts the recommended strategy for improving privacy in the recommender system. Preferences are collected from random people who are looking for the best advice. The k-anonymity perturbation approach is then used to anonymize the user's identity. The anonymous profile including the user's choices is subsequently transferred to a trusted third party. This party encrypts the user's preferences and transmits user data to the service provider for suggestion generation without knowing the user's profile. On ciphertext, the service provider does computation. After the recommendations are generated, they are encrypted and sent to a trusted third party. The recommendations are then decrypted by that party. It is then sent to the user after the noise has been removed.

The following example explains the diagram and how it works.

4.2 Methodology

Step 1:- for the purpose of recommendation, the users' preferences are randomly taken from the users.

Step 2:- K-anonymity by means of providing anonymization, prevents third-party or re-identification attacks from identifying the user. Say, Jon, a user whose identity is anonymized like:

"oY3gjZqwiGYpqOh1I95pxgiBxDyQhUMTtkPatWzjLOo = ".

As indicated in Tables 1 and 2, the user's data is no longer linked to their identity.

Table 1. Normal table form of users' original identity

Id	User name	Query	Age	Sex	Zip code	Nationality
1	Noby	Restaurant	27	Female	13102	American
2	John	Train station	26	Female	13123	Japanese
3	Mon	Petrol station	28	Male	13145	Russian
4	Jack	Restaurant	29	Male	13132	Indian

Table 2. Anonymous user table using K-anonymous

Id	Zip code	Age	Sex	Nationality	Query (Sensitive data)
1	131**	<30	People	*	Restaurant
2	131**	<30	People	*	Train station
3	131**	<30	People	*	Petrol station
4	131**	<30	People	*	Restaurant

This is depicted in Fig. 4 which describes the re-identification attack scenario. It is not possible to obtain sensitive information about the user if someone already has some information about the user, such as "Noby and Zipcode," as shown in the below image.

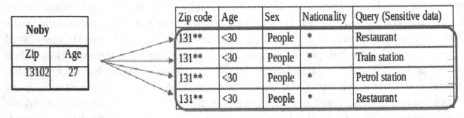

Fig. 4. User identity is protected from attack and no re-identification attacks are able to reveal.

Step 3:- in this step, Now the preferences are sent to the third party with an anonymized user profile.

Step 4:- The preferences are homomorphic encrypted by a third-party. It is then decrypted and turned into a character stream similar to the one below, which is subsequently submitted to be computed.

"QOPnfssd1FzUoDmsY/LUhrI0wQpTYPd12Z/ruq + skrHW7RdEkLou3tZt KzK2YSORLRX49okPMRzpB5KsXhX6xhfUBlJiM5tx/wthAr6LjS1UYpz VlevLj0KeD3zo/9xP".

Step 5:- In step5, we perform computation on ciphertext which, which in turn was obtained through the third party in the text above.

Step 6:- The recommendations are obtained. The user data has been considered for the purpose of recommendation as shown in the text.

"Kj8ThVosTQHhHNAslyc0Wdb52+tgDkDtsnxIbO398ulF5qjxkJDpj72KsT xwn4xb40znKYtCSGdAqwsaazAT1HKRV6zaJHu+4Oj97M3Lsnu4NtgXn ZSI6Og01/0ynjxvpgPMGoCozxb6Y+C8m39nMA6/vOXtx8MTjK2Lp2Z+ Wng=".

Step 7:- Figure 5 displays the user's recommendations after the anonymous table was compared to the original table to determine the user's identity.

For a user looking for a restaurant, generated recommendations include Rasoi Dhaba, Gulab Restaurant, and Subway, among others.

Zipcode	Age	Sex	Nationality	Query(Sensitive data)	Id		Id	User Name	Query	Age	Sex	Zipcode	Nationality
131**	<30	People	*	Restaurant	1.	→	1.	Noby	Restaurant	27	Female	13102	American
131**	<30	People	*	Train station	2.	→	2.	John	Train station	26	Female	13123	Japanese
131**	<30	People	*	Petrol station	3.	→	3.	Mon	Petrol station	28	Male	13145	Russian
131**	<30	People	*	Restaurant	4.	→	4.	Jack	Restaurant	29	Male	13132	Indian

Fig. 5. Illustration of how user profiling is done with the help of comparison of existing table with anonymous user table.

5 Discussion

We are aimed here to create a framework in such a way that user can have options to secure their privacy rights. Users were subjected to privacy threats such as third-party data sales and, as a result, threats such as targeted advertising, online price discrimination, physiological features, and deceptive recommendations [24, 24]. It is common knowledge that third-party data sales are at the root of these privacy concerns. By avoiding sharing data with third parties, we can reduce these privacy threats. User profiles are kept private in the proposed framework by being anonymized and not shared with third parties [27–29].

As a result, selling user data without knowing the user's identity is impossible for a third party. And the issue of over-reliance on a trustworthy or semi-trusted third party is no longer an issue. In some cases, hacking and spoofing may create some issues if it is intended by some pre-minded hackers, however it can be resolved as well. If hackers can obtain user data through compromising service provider data or from somewhere in the middle, decoding the data will be extremely difficult. They must do some high-level calculation to determine the user identification since they must first decrypt the data and then reconstruct it from the decrypted data. As a result, their task becomes more difficult, and their level of seclusion is increased.

6   Conclusion and Future Direction

The rapid growth of recommendation research has spawned a slew of new technologies that make online buying and other related activities easier for users. The users are lured to come and use a site where the personal data of the users are compromised, which leads to some serious privacy threats. While making any advice to them over the Internet, the current work has addressed how we can protect third parties to steal users' data or even how it can be controlled before granting it to any third party. Furthermore, illustrations are used to demonstrate how without jeopardizing, reliable recommendations are provided.

Here, we have proposed a theoretical framework aimed at addressing possible solutions to privacy issue in recommender systems. For future work, researchers can consider various approaches which have been discussed in the paper for exploring their potential to secure a recommendation model. In addition, it would also lay a platform for evaluation purpose of the privacy in recommendation.

Acknowledgment. This work is supported by the National Key Research and Development Program of China under Grant No. 2020YFB1005804, the Key Project of the National Natural Science Foundation of China under Grant No. 61632009, and the Key Project Initiative of the Guangdong Provincial Natural Science Foundation under Grant No. 2017A030308006.

References

1. Sohail, S.S., Siddiqui, J., Ali, R.: Feature-based opinion mining approach (FOMA) for improved book recommendation. Arab. J. Sci. Eng. **43**(12), 8029–8048 (2018). https://doi.org/10.1007/s13369-018-3282-3
2. Knijnenburg, B.P., Berkovsky, S.: Privacy for recommender systems: tutorial abstract. In: Proceedings of the Eleventh ACM Conference on Recommender Systems, pp. 394–395, 27 August 2017
3. Batmaz, Z., Kaleli, C.: Methods of privacy preserving in collaborative filtering. In: 2017 IEEE International Conference on Computer Science and Engineering (UBMK), pp. 261–266, 5 October 2017
4. Badsha, S., Yi, X., Khalil, I.: A practical privacy-preserving recommender system. Data Sci. Eng. **1**(3), 161–177 (2016)
5. Mohallick, I., Özgöbek, Ö.: Exploring privacy concerns in news recommender systems. In: Proceedings of the International Conference on Web Intelligence, pp. 1054–1061, 23 August 2017

6. Krishnamurthy, B., Wills, C.E.: On the leakage of personally identifiable information via online social networks. In: Proceedings of the 2nd ACM Workshop on Online Social Networks, pp. 7–12, 17 August 2009

7. Lu, J., Wu, D., Mao, M., Wang, W., Zhang, G.: Recommender system application developments: a survey. Decis. Support Syst. 1(74), 12–32 (2015)

8. Jeckmans, A.J.P., Beye, M., Erkin, Z., Hartel, P., Lagendijk, R.L., Tang, Q.: Privacy in recommender systems. In: Ramzan, N., van Zwol, R., Lee, J.S., Clüver, K., Hua, X.S. (eds.) Social Media Retrieval. CCN. Springer, London (2013). https://doi.org/10.1007/978-1-4471-4555-4_12

9. Friedman, A., Knijnenburg, B.P., Vanhecke, K., Martens, L., Berkovsky, S.: Privacy aspects of recommender systems. In: Ricci, F., Rokach, L., Shapira, B. (eds.) Recommender Systems Handbook. Springer, Boston (2015). https://doi.org/10.1007/978-1-4899-7637-6_19

10. Jeckmans, A.J.: Cryptographically-Enhanced Privacy for Recommender Systems. University of Twente, 15 February 2014

11. Zhang, S., Ford, J., Makedon, F.: Deriving private information from randomly perturbed ratings. In: Proceedings of the 2006 SIAM International Conference on Data Mining, pp. 59–69. Society for Industrial and Applied Mathematics, 20 April 2006

12. Rajendran, K., Jayabalan, M., Rana, M.E.: A study on k-anonymity, l-diversity, and t-closeness techniques. IJCSNS 17(12), 172 (2017)

13. Canny, J.: Collaborative filtering with privacy. In: Proceedings 2002 IEEE Symposium on Security and Privacy, pp. 45–57. IEEE, 12 May 2002

14. Hoens, T.R., Blanton, M., Chawla, N.V.: A private and reliable recommendation system for social networks. In: 2010 IEEE Second International Conference on Social Computing, pp. 816–825. IEEE, 20 August 2010

15. Erkin, Z., Beye, M., Veugen, T., Lagendijk, R.L.: Privacy enhanced recommender system. In: Thirty-First Symposium on Information Theory in the Benelux, pp. 35–42, 11 May 2010

16. Sun, X., Pan, Z., Bertino, E. (eds.): Cloud Computing and Security: 4th International Conference, ICCCS 2018, Haikou, China, 8–10 June 2018, Revised Selected Papers, Part III. Springer, Cham, 8 December 2021. https://doi.org/10.1007/978-3-030-00012-7

17. Shakil, U.S., et al.: The impact of randomized algorithm over recommender system. Procedia Comput. Sci. 194, 218–223 (2021)

18. Sohail, S.S., Siddiqui, J., Ali, R.: An OWA-based ranking approach for university books recommendation. Int. J. Intell. Syst. 33(2), 396–416 (2018)

19. Arif, M., Wang, G., Bhuiyan, M.Z.A., Wang, T., Chen, J.: A survey on security attacks in VANETs: communication, applications and challenges. Veh. Commun. 19, 100179 (2019)

20. Arif, M., Wang, G., Balas, V.E.: Secure VANETs: trusted communication scheme between vehicles and infrastructure based on fog computing. Stud. Inform. Control 27(2), 235–246 (2018)

21. Arif, M., Wang, G., Wang, T., Peng, T.: SDN-based secure VANETs communication with fog computing. In: Wang, G., Chen, J., Yang, L.T. (eds.) SpaCCS 2018. LNCS, vol. 11342, pp. 46–59. Springer, Cham (2018). https://doi.org/10.1007/978-3-030-05345-1_4

22. Shakil, U.S., Alam, M.T., Sohail, S.S.: Rising cyber crime in rural India: a review. Int. J. Adv. Res. Sci. Commun. Technol. [Internet] 6(1), 199–205 (2021). https://doi.org/10.48175/ijarsct-1372

23. Alam, M.T., Ubaid, S., Sohail, S.S., Alam, M.A.: A Neutrosophic cognitive map based approach to explore the health deterioration factors. Neutrosophic Sets Syst. 1, 41 (2021)

24. Alam, M.T., Ubaid, S., Sohail, S.S., Nadeem, M., Hussain, S., Siddiqui, J.: Comparative analysis of machine learning based filtering techniques using MovieLens dataset. Procedia Comput Sci. 1(194), 210–217 (2021)

25. Arif, M., et al.: SDN-based VANETs, security attacks, applications, and challenges. Appl. Sci. 10(9), 3217 (2020)

26. Arif, M., Wang, G., Chen, S.: Deep learning with non-parametric regression model for traffic flow prediction. In: 2018 IEEE 16th International Conference on Dependable, Autonomic and Secure Computing, 16th International Conference on Pervasive Intelligence and Computing, 4th International Conference on Big Data Intelligence and Computing and Cyber Science and Technology Congress (DASC/PiCom/DataCom/CyberSciTech), pp. 681–688. IEEE (2018)
27. Liu, X., Wang, G., Bhuiyan, M.Z.A.: Personalised context-aware re-ranking in recommender system. Connection Sci. 1–20 (2021). https://doi.org/10.1080/09540091.2021.1997915
28. Liu, X., Wang, G., Bhuiyan, M.Z.A.: Re-ranking with multiple objective optimization in recommender system. Trans. Emerg. Telecommun. Technol. **33**(1), e4398 (2022). https://doi.org/10.1002/ett.4398
29. Arif, M., Wang, G., Balas, V.E., Geman, O., Castiglione, A., Chen, J.: SDN based communications privacy-preserving architecture for VANETs using fog computing. Veh. Commun. **26**, 100265 (2020)
30. Arif, M., Wang, G., Peng, T., Balas, V.E., Geman, O., Chen, J.: Optimization of communication in VANETs using fuzzy logic and artificial Bee colony. J. Intell. Fuzzy Syst. **38**(5), 6145–6157 (2020)
31. Arif, M., Wang, G.: Cloud-based service oriented architecture for social vehicular ad hoc network communications. Int. J. Commun. Networks Distrib. Syst. **24**(2), 143–166 (2020)

A Supervised Rare Anomaly Detection Technique via Cooperative Co-evolution-Based Feature Selection Using Benchmark UNSW_NB15 Dataset

A. N. M. Bazlur Rashid[1]([⊠]), Mohiuddin Ahmed[1], and Sheikh Rabiul Islam[2]

[1] School of Science, Edith Cowan University, Joondalup, WA 6027, Australia
{a.rashid,mohiuddin.ahmed}@ecu.edu.au
[2] Department of Computing Sciences, University of Hartford,
West Hartford, CT 06117, USA
shislam@hartford.edu

Abstract. Anomaly detection is important in many domains, including cybersecurity. There are a number of rare anomalies in cybersecurity datasets, and detection of these rare anomalies is computationally expensive. Cybersecurity datasets consist of many features, mostly irrelevant, resulting in lower classification performance of many machine learning algorithms. Therefore, a feature selection approach to select only the relevant features from a dataset is an important preprocessing step in anomaly detection. Many feature selection approaches are available in the literature. However, to deal with Big Data, cooperative co-evolution, a meta-heuristic algorithm-based feature selection approach is more suitable for cybersecurity datasets for its preprocessing step. This paper has applied our previously proposed cooperative co-evolution-based feature selection with random grouping (CCFSRFG) approach to the UNSW_NB15 cybersecurity dataset as the preprocessing step. Then, the original dataset and the dataset with a reduced number of features are used to detect the rare anomalies. The experimental analysis was performed and evaluated using five widely used supervised classifiers. Hence, the proposed anomaly detection approach is called *Supervised Rare Anomaly Detection (SRAD)*. The experimental results were compared with and without feature selection in terms of true positive rate (TPR). The experimental analysis indicates that the naïve Bayes classifier increased the TPR by 25.55% for all rare anomaly detection. Furthermore, the k-NN classifier increased the TPR of Exploits anomaly detection by 58.91%.

Keywords: Rare anomaly detection · Supervised · Feature selection · Cooperative co-evolution · UNSW_NB15

1 Introduction

With the advancement of modern technologies, a massive amount of data is generated by devices, including sensors, Internet of Things (IoT), cybersecurity, and health [9,12,13]. The massive generation of data is termed as Big Data in the literature, with several V's indicate its characteristics, such as volume (the amount of data generation), variety (the different types of data), and velocity (the speed of data generation) [2,11]. Big Data open the door to the research community to discover new knowledge, for example, exploring the different types of cyberattacks in cybersecurity [10]. Anomaly detection is, therefore, very important in this domain. A number of different approaches have been studied to detect anomalous data from cybersecurity datasets [3]. There are several rare anomalies in the cybersecurity dataset, detection of which is required for the cybersafety issues. Rare anomaly detection from cybersecurity datasets is computationally expensive because of the Big Data characteristics [1,14]. Cybersecurity datasets consist of many features (attributes in dataset terminology). However, not all the features are important, and as such, some are irrelevant. Moreover, these irrelevant features may degrade the performance of *machine learning (ML)* classifiers [12]. *Feature selection (FS)* is a technique that selects a subset of relevant features and removes the irrelevant features. Hence, FS is an important preprocessing step for anomaly detection in the cybersecurity domain. Feature selection involves a search process to select a subset of features [11,12]. While *Evolutionary Algorithms (EAs)* are widely used search techniques in FS process, a variant of EA, called the *Cooperative Co-Evolution (CC)* has been a proven search technique for feature selection process, for example, a *Cooperative Co-Evolutionary Algorithm-Based Feature Selection (CCEAFS)* with a penalty-based wrapper objective function for Big Data [11] and Cooperative Co-Evolution-Based Feature Selection with Random Feature Grouping (CCFSRFG) [10].

In the literature, anomaly detection approaches have been studied based on feature selection, such as in [5,7,15]. This paper introduces a novel supervised rare anomaly detection approach, called *Supervised Rare Anomaly Detection (SRAD)*. The proposed approach has been evaluated using five widely used ML classifiers on UNSW_NB15 dataset collected from the UNSW Canberra Cyber Centre repository[1][8]. This paper aims at answering the following fundamental and associated subquestions:

– How can a feature selection process be applied to the UNSW_NB15 dataset that can select a suitable subset of features, which can improve the performance of the supervised rare anomaly detection techniques?
  • How can the supervised rare anomaly detection techniques be applied to the original dataset and the dataset with fewer features?
  • Can the rare anomaly detection techniques perform as well on a dataset with feature selection as on the original dataset?
  • Can the dataset with feature selection reduce the execution time of anomaly detection?

---

[1] https://www.unsw.adfa.edu.au/unsw-canberra-cyber/.

The contributions of the paper are:

- A supervised rare anomaly detection approach;
- Application of a new type of evolutionary algorithm-based feature selection approach;
- Performance improvement in terms of TPR increase;
- Reduced execution time for rare anomaly detection.

The rest of the paper is organized as follows. Section 2 presents a literature review on anomaly detection in cybersecurity datasets. Section 3 discusses the background techniques used in the paper. Section 4 illustrates the novel rare anomaly detection approach by feature selection using cooperative co-evolution. Section 5 contains experimental results and analysis based on UNSW_NB15 dataset. The conclusion and future work directions are included in Sect. 6.

2 Literature Review

Anomaly detection is associate with identifying interesting data patterns or rare items that deviate differently from expected behavior. Anomaly detection is also termed as outlier detection [3,16]. Anomaly detection is very common in several domains, such as cybersecurity, fraud detection, healthcare, and IoT. For example, a cyberattack is a malicious attack that can damage a computing system through unauthorized network access, code, or data injection. There can be three different types of anomaly: 1) *point/rare anomaly* (a specific data instance deviates from the normal pattern), 2) *contextual anomaly* (a data instance behaves anomalously in a specific context), and 3) *collective anomaly* (a collection of data instances behave anomalously) [1,4]. The major cyberattacks include: 1) *denial of service (DoS)* (interruption of normal computing and unavailability of services), 2) *probe* (attacking a targeted host or network for reconnaissance purpose), 3) *user to root (U2R)* (trying to get illegal access to an administrative account), and *remote to user (R2U)* (trying to get local access of a targeted system). In the literature, U2R and R2L are grouped into point/rare anomalies, DoS is grouped into collective anomalies, and the probe is grouped into contextual anomalies [1,2]. In the literature, cybersecurity attacks have been handled by three dominant approaches: supervised, semi-supervised, and unsupervised to learn, predict, detect, and classify data. The anomaly detection techniques that rely on labeled training are supervised. Supervised techniques require training data, which is usually expensive to generate, and these techniques face difficulties when it comes to detecting new types of attacks. Semi-supervised methods require a small amount of labeled data for building a model to detect anomalies. Unsupervised techniques do not need any training data and can detect previously unseen attacks [3,4]. Any type of information is very crucial for any business, including government, commercial, and defense. Therefore, cybersecurity data analysis is important to unveil security breaches and to take countermeasures. Feature selection plays an important preprocessing step in cybersecurity data analysis. Hence, a cybersecurity data analysis based on feature selection and supervised rare anomaly detection can be studied in this regard.

3 Background Techniques

3.1 Feature Selection

Feature selection (FS) is a technique to select a subset of relevant features. At the same time, remove the irrelevant features to improve the ML performance. Formally speaking, feature selection is a process of selecting s features from a dataset of n features and removing the irrelevant or unimportant features. This results in representing the dataset with a reduced number of relevant features. A search technique is required to discover a subset of features. The subset of features is then evaluated by different performance measures, including classification accuracy. A termination condition is required to terminate the FS process, and a validation method at the end may test the validity of the selected features [12]. A taxonomy of FS approaches can be found in [10,11].

3.2 Cooperative Co-evolution

In 1994, Potter and De Jong first introduced the cooperative co-evolution (CC) concept for solving large-scale and complex optimization problems. CC follows a divide-and-conquer strategy to divide a large problem into several subproblems. To build a complete solution to the problem, it evolves co-adapted subproblems on an iterative basis. Formally speaking, a CC technique decomposes an $n-$dimensional problem of search space $S = 1, 2, ..., n$ into m subproblems $S_1, S_2, ..., S_m$. Each subproblem with a maximum of n-dimensions represents a new search space $SP^{(i)}$ for a particular problem, while the rest of the dimensions n_j, with $j \neq S_i$ are kept fixed. Other subproblems follow this to decompose the entire search space with lower dimensions that can be evolved by any population-based evolutionary computation (EC) algorithm. The optimization of each subproblem can be performed independently of each other. Communication between the subproblems is required to build a complete solution to the problem using an objective or fitness function. A CC is, therefore, consists of three main phases: 1) problem decomposition (decomposing a large problem into several subproblems based on the problem structure), 2) subproblem evolution (optimization of each subproblem by a homogeneous or heterogeneous evolutionary optimizer), and 3) collaboration and evaluation (evaluating the objective or fitness function in collaboration with other subproblems to build a complete solution to the problem) [10,11,13].

4 A Novel Supervised Rare Anomaly Detection Approach

In this paper, a novel rare anomaly detection approach, SRAD, is introduced via a cooperative co-evolution-based feature selection (CCFSRFG) [10]. The proposed methodology has been discussed in Sect. 4.1 following a brief discussion on the related techniques.

4.1   Methodology

The proposed anomaly detection approach, supervised rare anomaly detection (SRAD), is illustrated in Fig. 1. The methodology for SRAD involves a pre-processing step of converting the dataset from comma-separated values (CSV) to Attribute-Relation File Format (ARFF) format to make it compatible with the experimental environment. Microsoft Excel and Waikato Environment for Knowledge Analysis (WEKA)[2] have been used for this purpose. Preprocessing step also includes partitioning the dataset into training and test set. The split ratio between the training and test datasets was 60% and 40%, respectively. The training dataset was used to train the model, while the test dataset was used to evaluate its performance. The rare anomaly detection performance was performed in terms of TPR using five widely used standard supervised ML clas-sifers, naïve Bayes (NB), support vector machine (SVM), J48, random forest (RF), and k-Nearest Neighbor.

First, the original UNSW_NB15 dataset has been used to detect rare anoma-lies and evaluated using standard five ML classifiers in terms of TPR. Next, the feature selection approach, CCFSRFG [10], has been applied to select a reduced subset of features that represent the dataset. Then, the dataset with a reduced number of features has been used for rare anomaly detection and evaluated using the same standard five ML classifiers in terms of TPR. Finally, the rare anomaly detection performance has been compared with and without feature selection in terms of TPR. A JAVA-based implementation of SRAD is available at GitHub.[3]

5   Results and Discussions

Experimental results are included in this section and analyzed with and without feature selection approaches. There are a number of databases publicly avail-able, such as NSL-KDD, KDD99, and UNSW_NB15 on intrusion detection. The UNSW_NB15 dataset is the most recent intrusion detection dataset, and the other two datasets are more than 10 years old. Therefore, the proposed SRAD approach's experimental analysis can be evaluated using only the UNSW_NB15 dataset.

5.1   Dataset Details

The UNSW_NB15[4] dataset used in the experiments is listed in Table 1 with nor-mal and rare anomaly data distribution. Table 2 lists the rare anomalies with data samples in the dataset with respect to the total samples and with respect to the anomalous samples, respectively. The UNSW_NB15 dataset [8] contains a hybrid of the real modern normal and the contemporary synthesised attacks

---

[2] https://www.cs.waikato.ac.nz/ml/weka/.

[3] https://github.com/bazlurrashid/cooperative-coevolution/tree/SRAD/.

[4] https://www.unsw.adfa.edu.au/unsw-canberra-cyber/cybersecurity/ADFA-NB15-Datasets/.

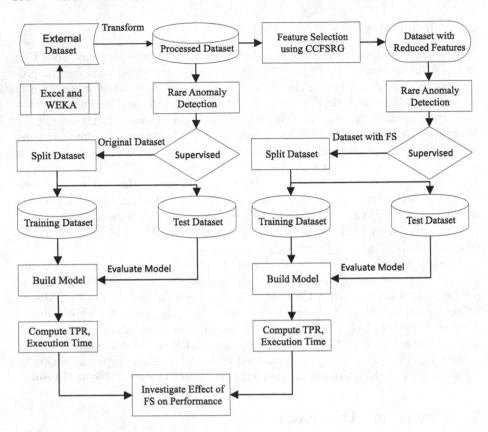

Fig. 1. Proposed CCFSRFG-based supervised rare anomaly detection (SRAD) approach.

of the network traffic. The dataset is comprised of 9 different attacks, including fuzzers, analysis, backdoor, DoS, exploits, generic, reconnaissance, shellcode, and worms. The dataset has been created to deal with the current network threat environment because the existing benchmark datasets, such as KDD98, KDD99, and NSL-KDD do not inclusively include network traffic and modern low footprint attacks [ref].

Table 1. Distribution of normal and anomalous data.

Dataset	Normal (%)	Anomalous (%)	No. of instances	No. of features
UNSW_NB15	44.94	55.06	82,332	42

Table 2. Distribution of rare anomalous data in UNSW_NB15 dataset.

Anomaly	Weight (%)	Anomalous (%)	No. of instances
Reconnaissance	04.25	07.71	3,496
Backdoor	00.71	01.29	583
DoS	04.97	09.02	4,089
Exploits	13.52	24.56	11,132
Analysis	00.82	01.49	677
Fuzzers	07.36	13.37	6,062
Worms	00.05	00.10	44
Shellcode	00.46	00.83	378
Generic	22.92	41.63	18,871

Note: "Weight" indicates the (%) of data samples with respect to the total samples in the dataset. "Anomalous" indicates the (%) of data samples with respect to the anomaly samples in the dataset.

5.2 Parameters and Evaluation Measures

The different parameters used in the experiments are as follows: A dynamic decomposition method, called random feature grouping (RFG), the genetic algorithm (GA) as subproblem optimizer, and random and best collaboration model with $1 + N$ have been used for the feature selection framework CCFSRFG. Subpopulation size: 30, number of subpopulations: 2, and number of features in each subpopulation are 21 and 20, respectively. GA parameters: binary representation, 100% crossover rate, 5% mutation rate, one elitism, and tournament selection. In the case of CCFSRFG termination, 100 successive generations with no improvement have been used. This paper aims to improve the rare anomaly detection performance by using a feature selection approach. Therefore, evaluation measures classification accuracy and true positive rates of the detection are appropriate in this study and other evaluation measures, such as $F1$ score, precision, and recall, may present some unnecessary experimental results for this study and can thus be avoided. Accordingly, classification accuracy and true positive rate (TRP) have been used as evaluation measures to analyse the experimental results.

5.3 Experimental Results and Analysis

The first phase of the proposed methodology is to apply the feature selection framework, CCFSRFG [10], to the UNSW_NB15 dataset and compare the classification accuracy with and without FS using naïve Bayes classifier. The FS process was evaluated using cross-validation. A summary of the performance results of CCFSRFG is listed in Table 3 in terms of classification accuracy, the number of features, and execution time (ET).

Table 3. Summary of results for UNSW_NB15 dataset with and without FS using a naïve Bayes classifier.

Dataset	Without FS		With FS		
	Accuracy (%)	No. of features	Accuracy (%)	No. of features	Execution time (hour)
UNSW_NB15	45.91	42	60.29	10	1.58
			72.78	3	9.72

From Table 3, it can be observed that CCFSRFG was able to select a suitable subset of features with a very low number of features (only 3) in the later case compared to the original dataset. On the other hand, the number of features was predefined to select 10 only in the former case. In both cases, while the original accuracy was 45.91, the FS accuracy was 60.29 and 72.78, respectively. Because the feature selection process is computationally expensive, it took 1.58 h to select 10 features. In contrast, it took 9.72 h to terminate the FS process for selecting 3 features.

The original dataset and the dataset with a reduced number of features (10 and 3 features, respectively) are used based on five supervised anomaly detection techniques for rare anomaly detection. The summary of the experimental results in terms of TPR is listed in Table 4. The values indicated in bold and color in this table represent the improvements in detecting rare anomalies with feature selection. The experimental results were compared with and without feature selection in terms of true positive rate (TPR). It can also be observed that J48 and k-NN classifiers increased the TPR of Exploits anomaly detection by 30.14% and 58.91%, respectively.

Figure 2 shows the improvement of TPR in detecting rare anomalies, including the normal data samples evaluated by different classifiers. It can be observed that with 10 features, there is at least one classifier that was able to improve the TPR for a few rare anomalies except for SVM. However, with 3 features, although other classifiers improved the TPR for three rare anomalies, RF could not improve TPR for anyone. It can be noted that J48 improved TPR for Backdoor and Fuzzers anomalies in the first case while Exploits anomaly in the second case. TPR of Reconnaissance, Exploits, and Fuzzers anomalies was improved by two classifiers, whereas TPR of Backdoor, DoS, Generic anomalies was improved by one classifier. In summary, there were six anomalies whose TPR was improved by at least one classifier. In contrast, any classifier did not improve TPR of Analysis, Worms, and Shellcode anomalies with feature selection.

Figure 3 displays the TPR of all anomalies together. It can be observed that the highest TPR for all rare anomaly detection was 69.19% by RF classifier using the original dataset. The lowest TPR achieved by SVM using the original dataset was 25.78%. When the CCFSRFG was applied to select a reduced number of features (10) from the dataset, the highest TPR was achieved by NB (46.63%), and the lowest TPR was by k-NN (15.40%). When the number of selected features

Table 4. Summary of performance of the individual supervised rare anomaly detection in terms of TPR (%) with and without FS for UNSW_NB15 dataset.

Rare anomaly	With or without FS	Classifier				
		NB	SVM	J48	RF	k-NN
Normal	Ori	54.37	53.28	94.92	96.12	66.39
	FS_{10}	54.30	61.27	44.39	66.16	64.97
	FS_3	**88.14**	**92.62**	42.51	85.09	45.76
Reconnaissance	Ori	16.67	39.17	72.01	70.73	47.01
	FS_{10}	72.22	21.65	29.13	41.10	12.18
	FS_3	00.00	00.00	00.00	00.00	00.00
Backdoor	Ori	82.35	00.00	00.84	00.84	04.62
	FS_{10}	00.00	00.00	01.26	00.00	00.42
	FS_3	00.00	00.00	00.00	00.00	00.00
DoS	Ori	01.86	40.51	53.49	11.19	38.78
	FS_{10}	00.31	00.12	24.30	02.97	06.43
	FS_3	**04.82**	19.05	00.25	00.12	22.88
Exploits	Ori	28.70	68.38	72.40	78.25	52.54
	FS_{10}	41.90	64.35	60.48	85.70	39.86
	FS_3	27.67	21.23	**94.22**	43.03	**83.49**
Analysis	Ori	01.17	00.00	00.00	00.39	00.39
	FS_{10}	00.00	00.00	00.00	00.00	00.00
	FS_3	00.00	00.00	00.00	00.00	00.00
Fuzzers	Ori	19.37	17.63	41.41	61.48	40.34
	FS_{10}	32.34	07.13	47.30	38.40	29.30
	FS_3	00.00	00.00	00.00	00.00	00.25
Worms	Ori	17.65	00.00	11.76	00.00	00.00
	FS_{10}	05.88	00.00	00.00	00.00	05.88
	FS_3	00.00	00.00	00.00	00.00	00.00
Shellcode	Ori	91.67	00.00	10.42	24.31	20.14
	FS_{10}	00.00	00.00	00.00	00.00	00.69
	FS_3	00.00	00.00	00.00	00.00	00.00
Generic	Ori	57.89	00.04	01.44	83.90	05.46
	FS_{10}	63.12	00.04	00.63	00.46	00.41
	FS_3	00.88	00.04	00.05	00.88	00.76

Note: "Ori" indicates TPR (%) without FS, "FS_{10}" indicates TPR (%) with FS consisting 10 features, and "FS_3" indicates TPR (%) with FS consisting 3 features.

was only 3, the highest and lowest TPR of all rare anomalies obtained were 23.14 (J48) and 6.92 (SVM), respectively. It can be observed that whether using the original dataset and dataset with feature selection, SVM returned lower TPR

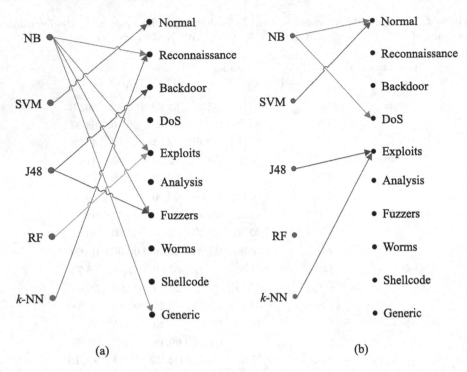

Fig. 2. Improvement of TPR for rare anomaly detection with FS, (a) with 10 features and (b) with 3 features.

compared to other classifiers. The experimental analysis indicates that the naïve Bayes classifier increased the TPR by 25.55% for all rare anomaly detection.

Figure 4 presents the ET of all anomalies together for all classifiers. As it was expected that rare anomaly detection from a dataset with a reduced number of features takes less computing time than the original dataset, the figure presented the same. It can be seen from the figure that SVM took higher computing time in all cases, whether using the orginal dataset or dataset with a reduced number of features to detect rare anomalies.

From the experimental analysis, it was observed that there were some misclassifications. Misclassifications can occur while classifying data or detecting an anomaly by the underlying machine learning algorithms. Misclassification can result from the inappropriate selection of classes or variables [6]. One example of dealing with misclassification issues for anomaly detection is using data summarization, such as in [1].

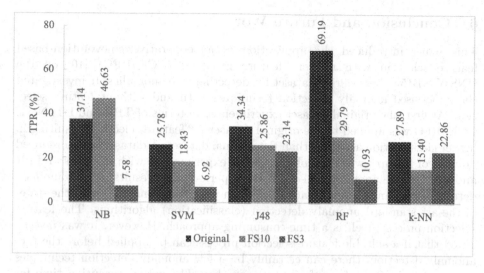

Fig. 3. TPR of all rare anomaly with and without FS.

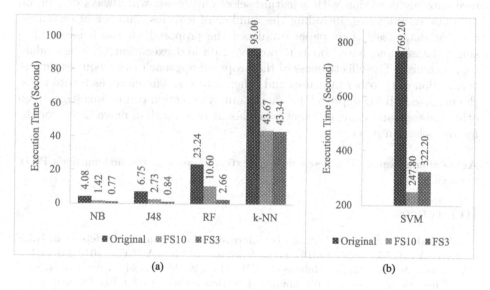

Fig. 4. Execution time of all rare anomaly with and without FS, (a) NB, J48, RF, and
k-NN and (b) SVM.

In the discussion summary, it can be observed that the proposed supervised
rare anomaly detection (SRAD) approach can detect rare anomalies with an
improved TPR for a few cases using different classifiers.

6   Conclusion and Future Work

This paper introduced the application of a cooperative co-evolution-based feature selection with random feature grouping (CCFSRFG) [10] on the UNSW_NB15 cybersecurity dataset for detecting rare anomalies. It investigated the supervised anomaly detection techniques with and without feature selection. At first, the original dataset experimented in terms of TPR and ET. Next, CCFSRFG was applied to the original dataset for feature selection, resulting in higher classification accuracy than the original dataset. A dataset with a reduced number of features was then obtained and experimented with in terms of TPR and ET for rare anomaly detection. Both performance results of rare anomaly detection with and without feature selection were then compared with the state-of-the-art standard anomaly detection (classification) algorithms. The feature selection process itself is a time-consuming approach. However, it was investigated that if a suitable feature selection process can be applied before the rare anomaly detection, there can certainly be a few anomaly detection techniques to improve the TPR for a few rare anomalies. The actual execution time for rare anomaly detection with a feature selection process will always depend on datasets' complexities, including the number of features, number of instances, and the data itself. This paper evaluated the proposed approach based on a single dataset and based on true positive rate and execution time as evaluation measures. The effectiveness of the proposed approach thus requires further verification using other measures and other datasets. Therefore, as future work, the proposed SRAD approach for rare anomaly detection can be investigated on other datasets and using different base classifiers other than naïve Bayes for the feature selection process.

Acknowledgments. This research is an extended work of the first author's Ph.D. research.

References

1. Ahmed, M.: Intelligent big data summarization for rare anomaly detection. IEEE Access **7**, 68669–68677 (2019). https://doi.org/10.1109/ACCESS.2019.2918364
2. Ahmed, M., Anwar, A., Mahmood, A.N., Shah, Z., Maher, M.J.: An investigation of performance analysis of anomaly detection techniques for Big Data in scada systems. EAI Endorsed Trans. Indust. Netw. Intell. Syst. **2**(3), e5 (2015). https://doi.org/10.4108/inis.2.3.e5
3. Ahmed, M., Mahmood, A.N., Hu, J.: A survey of network anomaly detection techniques. J. Netw. Comput. Appl. **60**, 19–31 (2016). https://doi.org/10.1016/j.jnca.2015.11.016
4. Ahmed, M., Mahmood, A.N., Islam, M.R.: A survey of anomaly detection techniques in financial domain. Fut. Gener. Comput. Syst. **55**, 278–288 (2016). https://doi.org/10.1016/j.future.2015.01.001
5. Alabi, R., Yurtkan, K.: Entropy-based feature selection for network anomaly detection. In: 2018 2nd International Symposium on Multidisciplinary Studies and Innovative Technologies (ISMSIT), pp. 1–7 (2018). https://doi.org/10.1109/ISMSIT.2018.8566694

6. Alruhaily, N., Bordbar, B., Chothia, T.: Towards an understanding of the misclassification rates of machine learning-based malware detection systems. In: Proceedings of the 3rd International Conference on Information Systems Security and Privacy - ICISSP, pp. 101–112. INSTICC, SciTePress (2017). https://doi.org/10.5220/0006174301010112

7. Arai, T., Nakano, K., Chakraborty, B.: Selection of effective features for BGP anomaly detection. In: 2019 IEEE 10th International Conference on Awareness Science and Technology (iCAST), pp. 1–6 (2019). https://doi.org/10.1109/ICAwST.2019.8923583

8. Moustafa, N., Slay, J.: UNSW-NB15: a comprehensive data set for network intrusion detection systems (UNSW-NB15 network data set). In: 2015 Military Communications and Information Systems Conference (MilCIS), pp. 1–6 (2015). https://doi.org/10.1109/MilCIS.2015.7348942

9. Rashid, A.N.M.B.: Access methods for Big Data: current status and future directions. EAI Endorsed Trans. Scalable Inf. Syst. 4(15) (2018). https://doi.org/10.4108/eai.28-12-2017.153520

10. Rashid, A.N.M.B., Ahmed, M., Sikos, L.F., Haskell-Dowland, P.: Cooperative co-evolution for feature selection in Big Data with random feature grouping. J. Big Data 7(1), 1–42 (2020). https://doi.org/10.1186/s40537-020-00381-y

11. Rashid, A.N.M.B., Ahmed, M., Sikos, L.F., Haskell-Dowland, P.: A novel penalty-based wrapper objective function for feature selection in Big Data using cooperative co-evolution. IEEE Access 8, 150113–150129 (2020). https://doi.org/10.1109/ACCESS.2020.3016679

12. Rashid, A.N.M.B., Choudhury, T.: Knowledge management overview of feature selection problem in high-dimensional financial data: cooperative co-evolution and MapReduce perspectives. Probl. Perspect. Manag. 17(4), 340 (2019). https://doi.org/10.21511/ppm.17(4).2019.28

13. Rashid, A.N.M.B., Choudhury, T.: Cooperative co-evolution and mapreduce: a review and new insights for large-scale optimization. Int. J. Inf. Technol. Proj. Manag. 12(1), 29–62 (2021). https://doi.org/10.4018/IJITPM.2021010102

14. Rashid, A.N.M.B., Ahmed, M., Pathan, A.S.K.: Infrequent pattern detection for reliable network traffic analysis using robust evolutionary computation. Sensors 21(9) (2021). https://doi.org/10.3390/s21093005

15. Teh, H.Y., Wang, K.I.K., Kempa-Liehr, A.W.: Expect the unexpected: unsupervised feature selection for automated sensor anomaly detection. IEEE Sens. J. 21(16), 18033–18046 (2021). https://doi.org/10.1109/JSEN.2021.3084970

16. Vinayakumar, R., Alazab, M., Soman, K.P., Poornachandran, P., Al-Nemrat, A., Venkatraman, S.: Deep learning approach for intelligent intrusion detection system. IEEE Access 7, 41525–41550 (2019). https://doi.org/10.1109/ACCESS.2019.2895334

Towards Evaluating the Effectiveness of Botnet Detection Techniques

Ashley Woodiss-Field[✉], Michael N. Johnstone, and Paul Haskell-Dowland

School of Science, Edith Cowan University, Joondalup 6027, Australia
{a.woodiss-field,m.johnstone,p.haskelldowland}@edu.edu.au

Abstract. Botnets are a group of compromised devices taken over and commanded by a malicious actor known as a botmaster. In recent years botnets have targeted Internet of Things (IoT) devices, significantly increasing their ability to cause disruption due to the scale of the IoT. One such IoT-based botnet was Mirai, which compromised over 140,000 devices in 2016 and was able to conduct attacks at speeds over 1 Tbps. The dynamic structure and protocols used in the IoT may potentially render conventional botnet detection techniques described in the literature incapable of exposing compromised devices. This paper discusses part of a larger project where traditional botnet detection techniques are evaluated to demonstrate their capabilities on IoT-based botnets. This paper describes an experiment involving the reconstruction of a traditional botnet detection technique, BotMiner. The experimental parameters were varied in an attempt to exploit potential weaknesses in Bot-Miner and to start to understand its potential performance against IoT-based botnets. The results indicated that BotMiner was able to detect IoT-based botnets surprisingly well in various small-scale scenarios, but produced false positives in more realistic, scaled-up scenarios involving IoT devices that generated traffic similar to botnet commands.

Keywords: Botnet · Internet of Things · Mirai · BotMiner · Detection

1 Introduction

A botnet is a collection of compromised devices used by a malicious actor to conduct various activities. A device taken over by a botnet is often referred to as a bot or a zombie. The controller of a botnet is known as a botmaster. The structure from which bots are coordinated, to conduct attacks or takeover more devices, is known as a command and control structure, often abbreviated as CnC, C&C or C2. Botnets pose a threat primarily through their ability to grant a single malicious actor the processing power of the bots under their control. Botnet threats commonly include large scale Distributed Denial of Service (DDoS) attacks, spamming, phishing, malware distribution, click fraud, and crypto-jacking [2,7,12,15].

Traditionally botnets would target workstations, personal computers, and server to propagate. Historically botnets would first utilise the IRC protocol to

G. Wang et al. (Eds.): UbiSec 2021, CCIS 1557, pp. 292–308, 2022.
https://doi.org/10.1007/978-981-19-0468-4_22

send commands to infected devices. Later botnets would utilise various peer to peer protocols and the HTTP protocol, the former allowing for complex decentralised botnets and the latter facilitating a pull-based CnC approach [7,8]. Most recently, the advent of botnets that utilise the Internet of Things (IoT) to propagate and perpetrate attacks presents new challenges in contrast with their traditional counterparts, both in terms of the threats posed and approaches towards detection [3]. The IoT has been instrumental in the advent of smart cities [4]. Their mixture of networks, protocols and devices has provided an ideal environment for botnets [4].

Various botnet detection techniques have been developed, most commonly based on honeypots and passive signature-based detection techniques but these techniques are incapable of detecting zero-day (or unknown/unpublished) threats. More advanced techniques that focus on particular botnet attributes such as deterministic command responses, netflow patterns among compromised networks, and infection lifecycles have been more effective for specific types of botnet. Many detection techniques were designed for traditional botnets as opposed to more recent IoT-based threats [9–11,20].

This paper describes a reconstruction of a botnet detection technique known as BotMiner, with the goal of understanding its capabilities towards detecting IoT-based bots. The reconstructed BotMiner is tested on several simulated networks which include both traditional and IoT infection targets, various kinds of botnets using known CnC protocols, and variable infection rates. The goals of the experiment are to both test hypotheses surrounding the strengths and weaknesses of the BotMiner detection technique, while also validating the reconstruction thereof by applying it to the traditional targets and environments for which it had originally been built.

BotMiner is a botnet detection technique that operates by clustering alerts and netflows, and the performing cross-clustering analysis on the results. Utilising alert categories, X-Means clustering on flow features, and an established threshold, selected hosts on a given network are evaluated with a results that breaches the threshold indicating that it is a bot. BotMiner is designed to find common flow and alert patterns which are typical for devices that have become part of a single botnet. However, potential weaknesses in BotMiners detection approach may include over reliance on alert signatures and reliance on a botnet taking over entire target networks. Alert signatures that are triggered by benign or non-bot related activities may produce false positives. Bots that operate alone on a given host network may better evade detection. The conditions that allow IoT-based botnets to thrive may facilitate these circumstances, rendering BotMiner as an either inadequate or weakened solution to current botnet detection needs [9].

This paper seeks to address the potential weaknesses of BotMiner on IoT-based botnets, particularly in the context of non-standard CnC protocols, the potential for false positives, and lone bots among host networks. A particular case, that of the infamous Mirai botnet, forms the basis by which one the IoT-based botnets are simulated. Mirai is known to have used a non-standard bitstream-based CnC protocol which, unlike IRC, would likely evade detection by an Intrusion Detection System (IDS) on its own. Mirai's propagation approach, similar to other IoT botnets such as Aidra, Linix/IRCTelnet, and Bashlite, did not target entire networks. The large number of available insecure IoT devices accommodates such an approach where a botmaster does not need to produce a greater infection footprint than what is necessary.

2   Botnets

The experiment undertaken for this paper involves testing the recreated botnet detection technique on traditionally structured botnets. Three broad categories of traditional botnets exist, two of which were simulated for the experiment. The two botnets simulated include an HTTP-based Pull Botnet and an IRC-based Push Botnet. The third type of traditional botnet is the Peer-to-Peer (P2P) botnet. The latter is typically more complex than its centralised counterparts and requires expert knowledge to set up [7,18]. HTTP-based botnets use a centralised CnC structure where each bot routinely queries an HTTP server to receive commands [16,18]. IRC-based botnets also use a centralised CnC structure where all bots listen on an IRC server for commands from the botmaster [16,18] . Many IoT-based botnets also continue to use the IRC protocol, with the original 2016 Mirai being a prominent exception [3].

IoT-based botnets are a more recent threat compared to traditional botnet structures. IoT-based botnets have an advantage over other botnets due to the attributes of the devices they target. IoT devices are exceptionally numerous by design, with approximately 9 billion devices distributed worldwide in 2016 [3] and was predicted to have reached over 20 billion devices by the end of 2020 [17], which allows for IoT-based botnets to not only propagate faster but also to be selective in which devices they compromise. IoT devices are often insecure, either due to poor deployment practices such as not changing default credentials or software and firmware exploits [3,13]. IoT devices are typically always switched on (although, not always active), whereas workstations and home computers are often shut down when not in use. Being always on means that IoT bots are always available to their botmaster [18]. A particularly notable IoT-based botnet was Mirai, which was able to infect over 140,000 devices and conduct attacks at speeds over 1 Tbps [6]. Other IoT-based botnets include Linux/IRCTelnet, Aidra, Bashlite, The Moon, and Linux/Hydra. Among other IoT-based botnets Bashlite; Mirai's predecessor, Aidra, and Linux/IRCTelnet would follow similar propagation approaches, performing dictionary attacks in order to compromise poorly secured devices over Telnet [5].

3   BotMiner

BotMiner was developed over a decade ago by Gu, Perdisci, and Lee [9]. An analysis and reconstruction of BotMiner with respect to its potential for detecting IoT botnets was discussed in [19]. BotMiner operates on the premise that bots on the same network will operate in patterns distinguishable from ordinary traffic but similar to other bots. Under this assumption, bots can be grouped by their netflow activity and the alerts that they trigger. BotMiner operates in several stages that involve collecting and clustering netflow and alert data. The clusters found are then put through a cross-clustering process, which is used to establish a bot score for each examined host. The components responsible for this functionality were labelled as the A-Plane Monitor, C-Plane Monitor, A-Plane Clustering, C-Plane Clustering, and Cross-Plane Correlation respectively by both the original work and this reconstruction [9].

The technique, using the A-Plane components, collects alerts and clusters them based on certain categorisations. The original technique used its own categorisation based on bot activity. However, the categorisation was modified in this current work due to its arbitrary nature, as noted in [19]. Bot activities can be dynamic, so any approaches based on a fixed taxonomy will fail over time. The examples provided include scan activity, spam activity, and binary downloads, which may be inadequate or ill-defined for certain attacks. DDoS attacks and click fraud for example can be loosely defined as spam activity, but that does not properly describe them. Botnet crypto-jacking cannot be categorised into any of the provided example categories. Both the original technique and this version use a Snort IDS ruleset to find alerts. The original technique also used a statistical scan anomaly detection engine for finding and categorising scan activities; however, this was deemed out of scope for the experimental setup. Instead, standard Snort categorisations were used to cluster alerts, which proved to be effective. The primary purpose of categorisation was to apply differential weightings to specific categories when determining the final bot score. Gu et al. [9] however did not utilise these. In order to remain true to the original published work, our reconstruction also does not utilise these weights. It is suggested, however, that if these weights can be applied in such a way that requires minimal curation, they may prove a valuable addition to the technique [9,19].

Alongside alert collection and clustering is netflow collection and clustering, the C-Plane components. The original technique used fcapture to collect netflow, whereas a custom collection program was developed for the reconstruction operating over the same features. Both the original and reconstruction collect TCP and UDP flows. Flow features include time, duration, source IP, source port, destination IP, destination port, and the bidirectional volume of bytes and packets. Once collected, flows were grouped together into C-Flows if they had the same properties, namely: source IP, source port, destination IP, destination port, and protocol. These C-flows were split over 13 intervals where sample distribution features for flows per hour (fph), packets per flow (ppf), average bytes per packets (bpp), and average bytes per second (bps) were collected. For each C-Flow, the collected sample distribution features over the 13 intervals produced a 52-feature dataset. The means and variances of the fph, ppf, bpp, and bps generated an 8-feature dataset, one for each C-Flow. This 8-feature dataset was put through X-means clustering, where X provided the best value of K.

The 52-feature dataset was then put through K-means clustering, using the best K value, to produce the netflow clusters [9,19].

Once the alert clusters and netflow clusters had been calculated, each host found within the clusters was put through a cross-clustering process, utilising the Cross-Plane Correlation component. Equation 1 is used to calculate a final bot likelihood score. The score is compared to a threshold to determine if it is a bot, which is 1 by default. Activity type weights are available but are not used by the original technique as presented in the original paper or the reconstruction created for this experiment.

$$s(h) = \sum_{\substack{i,j \\ j>i \\ t(A_i) \neq t(A_j)}} w(A_i)w(A_j)\frac{|A_i \cap A_j|}{|A_i \cup A_j|} + \sum_{i,k} w(A_i)\frac{|A_i \cap C_k|}{|A_i \cup C_k|} \qquad (1)$$

Equation 1: Where A is the sequence of hosts within alert clusters; C is the sequence of hosts within flow clusters; w are activity type weights.

Through analysis and reconstruction of BotMiner, it was determined that the technique has various strengths but also some potential flaws. It is, unlike BotProbe, protocol independent. However, based on the assumptions of the original work and some of the flaws found with alert weighting, it was determined that in botnets using only one device per network, such as Mirai, the technique is likely to fail. However, if the weights can be properly implemented, it would strengthen the ability for BotMiner to find alerts using generic signatures while preventing false positives [19]. The determinations made during the analysis and reconstruction of BotMiner form the basis of the hypotheses proposed in the next section.

4   Experiment

The purpose of the experiment undertaken was to determine the strengths of BotMiner when applied to hosts infected to become part of an IoT-based botnet. Another goal was to ensure that the BotMiner reconstruction could faithfully carry out its original functionality, by successfully detecting infected hosts on traditional networks particularly in instances where the number of bots is greater than one. To achieve those ends aberrantboth IoT-based and traditional networks were simulated. Each of the two networks had multiple kinds of botnets applied to them. To further test BotMiner's capabilities, some instances of the simulated networks would be assigned a device that would frequently emit aberrant behaviour that would purposefully trigger a false alert on a standard Snort IDS ruleset. This was done in order to test BotMiner's resistance to false positives, both on traditional and IoT-based networks.

Two traditional botnets were simulated for the experiment, one used HTTP as its communication protocol and the other used the IRC protocol. The HTTP botnet had its bots periodically access a command server from which commands would be issued. The IRC botnet would periodically send commands to its bots via an IRC server. Each time the bots would retrieve/receive their (attack) commands they would initiate an attack on a target host.

Both simulated botnets consisted of a fixed number of hosts, of which a certain proportion were infected as bots. All simulated hosts, including the infected hosts, produced conventional HTTP traffic to present a realistic environment for the experiment. The CnC of both botnets routinely commanded the infected hosts to send an ICMP attack to a target server external to the simulated network (a common Denial of Service attack achieved with botnets).

Traffic over the traditional networks would be recorded to include several variation. Variables included the total number of hosts, the number of infected hosts and the inclusion of an aberrant host. The variable number of hosts would allow for examination of any significant difference based on the total number of hosts, of which none was expected. However the total number of hosts was still relevant in relation to examining IoT-based networks due to their greater scale. The total number of infected hosts, however, was expected to make a significant difference due to BotMiner would operate. The aberrant host would test the technique's capabilities in the face of IDS false positives, triggering the IDS with internal ICMP communications, which should trigger the same category of alert as the bots themselves without generating the same flow patterns as the bots. The chosen experimental scenarios accommodate networks with 10 and 100 total devices, 1 and 3 infected devices, and 1 or no aberrant device. Each scenario, for both traditional botnet protocols, produce 16 variations-of which 5 generations were created.

Two IoT-based botnets were also simulated. One utilised a TCP-based bitstream communication protocol and heartbeat similar to the Mirai botnet. The other used the more common IRC communication protocol, still used among many IoT-based botnets. The use of the Mirai-based approach represents the use of non-standard communication protocols which may not trigger the same rates of detection from an IDS. As with the traditional network simulation, the IoT network simulated would include a variable number of devices, infection rates, and aberrant devices to trigger IDS false positives. Whereas the traditional network sizes were 10 and 100 devices, the IoT networks would also include 500 device scenarios to model the scale of IoT networks. The chosen experimental scenarios accommodate networks with 10, 100, and 500 total devices, 1 and 3 infected devices, and 1 or no aberrant device. Each scenario, for both IoT botnet protocols, produced 24 variations-of which 5 generations were created.

The approach of simulating the botnets allows to establish a generic baseline derived from the common attributes of IRC and HTTP botnets, instead of a specific known botnet that fall under either category. Experimentation on established botnet datasets can be conducted alongside the simulated botnets for further validation and will be undertaken in future work. The choice to base one of the simulated IoT-based botnet on Mirai was made due to the challenges it would present to BotMiner, among other techniques. Many common IoT-based botnets still utilise an IRC-based CnC, whereas Mirai uses a binary stream, an uncommon CnC protocol. Mirai also had the tendency to only infect one device per network due to its randomly directed method of propagation, whereas BotMiner is designed to detect bot activity by groups. Based on the original Mirai bot code, the heartbeat and attack commands would be sent out using a binary stream protocol. The bot would periodically send a heartbeat message to the CnC every 60 s, to which the CnC would respond with its own heartbeat. The format of the attack commands would include the attack duration, vector (attack type), targets (and number of them), and attack options (and the number of them) [14].

For the experiment, as with the HTTP and IRC botnets, commands would be periodically sent to initiate an ICMP attack against a single target server. The simulated hosts for the IoT-based botnet would operate differently to the host for the traditional botnets as they would simulate IoT traffic. Whereas the traditional networks would generate randomly distributed HTTP traffic, the IoT network would produce AMQP traffic that would operate over fixed periods. AMQP is an IoT protocol that sends messages through queue exchanges which are then consumed by subscribed workers [1]. This would act as realistic traffic for the simulated IoT network.

These different scenario combinations produced 40 enviroment variations, from which five hours were recorded each. The BotMiner detection technique was applied five times, one for each hour, producing a 200 row dataset. The results included the number of True Positives (Bots found), True Negatives (Non-Bot Hosts found), False Positives (Hosts incorrectly identified as Bots), and False Negatives (Bots not found). Also taken into consideration were the bot scores produced by the technique. If the bot score for a host exists and is greater than 1, that bot score will be indicative of a bot detection. In some instances the scores could also be used to determine the results reliability, where values closer to 1 may indicate a result subject to change under subtle condition changes or the adjustment of the threshold.

4.1 Hypotheses

Based on an examination of the original work and determinations made during the reconstruction process, the following hypotheses were constructed:

- H_1 The BotMiner detection technique shall successfully detect all bots on the simulated networks where the number of bots is greater than one.
- H_2 The BotMiner detection technique shall fail to detect all bots on the simulated networks where there is only one bot.
- H_3 The BotMiner detection technique shall generate false positives where an IDS has been triggered by non-bot aberrant activity on all simulated networks.

- H_4 The total number of hosts on all simulated networks shall have no observable effect on the number true positives or false positives generated by the BotMiner detection technique.

Each hypothesis was designed to operate over all datasets that would be produced from the experiment. H_1 tests the validity of the technique reconstruction. Under experimental conditions the reconstructed BotMiner should be able to detect the bots when more than one is present.

Based on the idea that IoT-based botnets are not constrained to infecting entire networks, as seen with those which randomly select propagation targets, H_2 asserts that singularly infected devices will not be detected. As with H_1 being applied to simulated IoT-based networks, H_2 is also applied to traditional networks. By applying H_1 and H_2 to their opposing targets the cause of detection failure, that BotMiner can only detect multiple bots, can be further validated if hypotheses are proven true.

H_3 tests BotMiner's resistance to false positives, which was observed during its reconstruction as potentially weak. The IDS alert triggered by the aberrant host would be the same category as that of the bot attack. This scenario would provide a realistic situation that would bypass the alert cluster weighting were it applied as the alerts would belong to the same cluster. The distinguishing feature of the traffic would be the flow patterns and the communication endpoints, which would not involve a victim host or CnC server unlike the bots themselves. If H_3 is shown to be true it could reveal a potential weakness of BotMiner regardless of the bots it is applied to, though the result may be different between traditional and IoT-based networks.

H_4 focusses on the total number of hosts to observe the potential differences between traditional networks and larger IoT networks. Though no observation has been made towards BotMiner's capabilities based on the scale of a given target network, the feature of scale with regards to common IoT deployments warrants observation. H_4, if proven true, will demonstrate that BotMiner is, or is not, capable of detection regardless of network scale.

5   Results

The results recorded through Tables 1, 2, 3, 4, 5, and 6 include those for both traditional and IoT-based botnet detections. Tables 1 and 2 contain the results for traditional HTTP and IRC botnets respectively, while Tables 3 4, 5, and 6 contain results for IoT-based botnets. Tables 3 and 4 contain results for the Bit-Stream botnet based on Mirai, the first table containing results for single bot infections and the latter for multiple bot infections. Tables 5 and 6 pertain to the IRC IoT-based botnet results, divided in the same as 3 and 4. Each hypothesis was addressed with the results found in the tables.

H_1 asserts that where more than a single bot would exist on a network, BotMiner would detect those bots with no false negatives. Such detection would be rendered regardless of protocol or network type, traditional or IoT-based. The primary purpose of this hypothesis would be to demonstrate that the technique reconstruction would be valid by its capabilities compared to the original work, as well demonstrating BotMiner's ability in its intended environment. H_1 was proven true, all bots were detected on the networks where more than a single infection has occurred.

In contrast to H_1, H_2 would assert that not all bots would be detect in such a case where only a single device would be infected. This hypothesis was designed to demonstrate BotMiner's potential failure in the face of certain IoT-based botnet initiatives that would not necessarily utilise entire networks. Despite assumptions made based on the original work and analysis, this hypothesis was actually proven false. Not only did BotMiner detect all bots where many existed, it also detected all bots where only one existed. This observation indicates that BotMiners strength in this respect was underestimated, and under the right circumstances in can be used to detect IoT-based botnets.

Despite the outcomes of H_1 and H_2 reflecting positively on BotMiner's performance, H_3 would bring insight to another predicted weakness of the detection technique. H_3 was designed to demonstrate that BotMiner, due to its approach towards alert detection and clustering, could be prone to false positives. This hypothesis appears to have been proven true, the majority of the results demonstrate false positives where aberrant device behaviour would trigger an alert. However, not all instances did trigger false positives by the established BotMiner threshold (1). In the majority instances where the IRC protocol had been employed by the botnet, false positives were either not produced or the scores thereof were significantly closer to the threshold that those for other devices detected. It appears that the IRC communications would produce their own alerts, where non-IRC communications would not. The additional alerts would produce a stronger basis for alert clustering among the infected devices, distinguishing them from the aberrant device.

H_4 pertains to the number of total hosts on the network, asserting that that would have no effect on the BotMiner results. Reviewing the results over all tables appears to indicate that H_4 is true, no significant differences in detection rates appears to be present between networks solely based on different total host numbers.

Table 1. Results for BotMiner applied to Traditional Networks with HTTP Botnet activity (False positive scores are marked with *)

Set #	Total devices	Infected	Aberrant	TP	FP	TN	FN	BotMiner scores
1	10	1	0	1	0	9	0	6.42
2	10	1	0	1	0	9	0	2.40
3	10	1	0	1	0	9	0	1.74
4	10	1	0	1	0	9	0	1.07
5	10	1	0	1	0	9	0	5.34
1	100	1	0	1	0	99	0	10.67
2	100	1	0	1	0	99	0	3.09
3	100	1	0	1	0	99	0	4.19
4	100	1	0	1	0	99	0	2.70
5	100	1	0	1	0	99	0	1.41
1	10	1	1	1	1	8	0	1.89,1.89*
2	10	1	1	1	1	8	0	2.46,2.79*
3	10	1	1	1	1	8	0	2.99,3.73*
4	10	1	1	1	1	8	0	1.62,1.95*
5	10	1	1	1	1	8	0	3.16, 3.56*
1	100	1	1	1	1	98	0	4.49,2.88*
2	100	1	1	1	1	98	0	4.17,3.51*
3	100	1	1	1	1	98	0	5.49,4.04*
4	100	1	1	1	1	98	0	6.78,6.24*
5	100	1	1	1	1	98	0	2.98,2.48*
1	10	3	0	3	0	7	0	6.8 (3)
2	10	3	0	3	0	7	0	4.44,3.44 (2)
3	10	3	0	3	0	7	0	4.43 (3)
4	10	3	0	3	0	7	0	2.98 (2),3.4
5	10	3	0	3	0	7	0	3.88,2.63(2)
1	10	3	1	3	1	6	0	4.01, 3.21,2.21,2.21*
2	10	3	1	3	1	6	0	4.04,2.67,3.24,4.04*
3	10	3	1	3	1	6	0	3.63,3.13,2.55,1.76*
4	10	3	1	3	1	6	0	3.9,4.73,5.15,3.24*
5	10	3	1	3	1	6	0	3.29,4.36(2),3.29*
1	100	3	0	3	0	97	0	13.99,13.66,13.23
2	100	3	0	3	0	97	0	10.77,10.27(2)
3	100	3	0	3	0	97	0	5.15,6.48(2)
4	100	3	0	3	0	97	0	6.69,7.54,7.27
5	100	3	0	3	0	97	0	4.47,5.22,5.72
1	100	3	1	3	1	96	0	7.74,6.33,6.9,4.93*
2	100	3	1	3	1	96	0	12.85,11.85,12.85,7.01*
3	100	3	1	3	1	96	0	8.67 (2),7.67,5.42*
4	100	3	1	3	1	96	0	6.81,8.99,7.75,5.88*
5	100	3	1	3	1	96	0	5.88(3),5.09*

Table 2. Results for BotMiner applied to Traditional Networks with IRC Botnet activity (False positive scores are marked with *)

Set #	Total devices	Infected	Aberrant	TP	FP	TN	FN	BotMiner scores
1	10	1	0	1	0	9	0	2.40
2	10	1	0	1	0	9	0	3.64
3	10	1	0	1	0	9	0	3.47
4	10	1	0	1	0	9	0	2.48
5	10	1	0	1	0	9	0	3.48
1	100	1	0	1	0	99	0	3.68
2	100	1	0	1	0	99	0	4.04
3	100	1	0	1	0	99	0	2.85
4	100	1	0	1	0	99	0	2.13
5	100	1	0	1	0	99	0	4.04
1	10	1	1	1	1	8	0	2.21,1.14*
2	10	1	1	1	0	9	0	2.15,0.77*
3	10	1	1	1	1	8	0	4.88,1.16*
4	10	1	1	1	0	9	0	2.75,0.81*
5	10	1	1	1	0	9	0	2.36,0.94*
1	100	1	1	1	0	99	0	1.85,0.9*
2	100	1	1	1	1	98	0	3.37,1.18*
3	100	1	1	1	0	99	0	3.83,0.93*
4	100	1	1	1	0	99	0	2.23,0.48*
5	100	1	1	1	1	98	0	5.69,2.22*
1	10	3	0	3	0	7	0	3.62 (2),2.95
2	10	3	0	3	0	7	0	4.67 (2),6.67
3	10	3	0	3	0	7	0	4.43 (3)
4	10	3	0	3	0	7	0	3.47 (2), 4.22
5	10	3	0	3	0	7	0	3.68 (2),4.08
1	10	3	1	3	1	6	0	3.45 (2),3.9,1.42*
2	10	3	1	3	0	7	0	3.18 (3),0.71*
3	10	3	1	3	1	6	0	4.47 (3),1.63*
4	10	3	1	3	0	7	0	3.38 (2),2.93,0.68*
5	10	3	1	3	1	6	0	4.04,4.35 (2),1.71*
1	100	3	0	3	0	7	0	1.89,2.56(2)
2	100	3	0	3	0	7	0	7.01 (2), 6.26
3	100	3	0	3	0	7	0	6.56,7.22,8.49
4	100	3	0	3	0	7	0	4.04 (2),4.44
5	100	3	0	3	0	7	0	6.33 (2),4.79
1	100	3	1	3	0	7	0	2.47 (2),2.95,0.98*
2	100	3	1	3	1	6	0	4.58 (2),5.03,1.31*
3	100	3	1	3	1	6	0	6.39 (2),5.51,2.39*
4	100	3	1	3	1	6	0	3.55 (3),1.2*
5	100	3	1	3	1	6	0	4.81,5.99 (2),2.33*

Table 3. Results for BotMiner applied to IoT networks with bit-stream Botnet activity with single device infections (False positive scores are marked with *)

Set #	Total devices	Infected	Aberrant	TP	FP	TN	FN	BotMiner scores
1	10	1	0	1	0	9	0	6.02
2	10	1	0	1	0	9	0	14.19
3	10	1	0	1	0	9	0	13.20
4	10	1	0	1	0	9	0	23.97
5	10	1	0	1	0	9	0	17.57
1	100	1	0	1	0	99	0	2.81
2	100	1	0	1	0	99	0	9.32
3	100	1	0	1	0	99	0	16.31
4	100	1	0	1	0	99	0	9.77
5	100	1	0	1	0	99	0	10.67
1	500	1	0	1	0	499	0	3.16
2	500	1	0	1	0	499	0	4.74
3	500	1	0	1	0	499	0	11.85
4	500	1	0	1	0	499	0	8.71
5	500	1	0	1	0	499	0	6.25
1	10	1	1	1	1	8	0	8.4,1*
2	10	1	1	1	1	8	0	9.42,1.67*
3	10	1	1	1	1	8	0	13.97,1*
4	10	1	1	1	1	8	0	14.37,1*
5	10	1	1	1	1	8	0	12.12,1.67*
1	100	1	1	1	1	98	0	3.32,1.1*
2	100	1	1	1	1	98	0	4.12,1.29*
3	100	1	1	1	1	98	0	9.12,1.13*
4	100	1	1	1	1	98	0	6.18,1*
5	100	1	1	1	1	98	0	5.35,1*
1	500	1	1	1	1	498	0	3.32,1.1*
2	500	1	1	1	1	498	0	4.19,1.29*
3	500	1	1	1	1	498	0	9.12,1.13*
4	500	1	1	1	1	498	0	6.18,1.1*
5	500	1	1	1	1	498	0	5.35,1*

Table 4. Results for BotMiner applied to IoT networks with bit-stream Botnet activity with mutliple device infections (False positive scores are marked with *)

Set #	Total devices	Infected	Aberrant	TP	FP	TN	FN	BotMiner scores
1	10	3	0	3	0	7	0	19.65(2), 22.05
2	10	3	0	3	0	7	0	23.76 (2),26.26
3	10	3	0	3	0	7	0	34.87 (2),36.87
4	10	3	0	3	0	7	0	31.52,28.02,30.52
5	10	3	0	3	0	7	0	22.71 (2),26.71
1	100	3	0	3	0	97	0	7.3,7.64,7.42
2	100	3	0	3	0	97	0	10.06,12.37,11.87
3	100	3	0	3	0	97	0	21.11,22.43,21.68
4	100	3	0	3	0	97	0	18.36,21.17,21.86
5	100	3	0	3	0	97	0	17.44,14.88,16.77
1	500	3	0	3	0	497	0	10.15(3)
2	500	3	0	3	0	497	0	11.28,12.89(2)
3	500	3	0	3	0	497	0	22.05,23.14,22.81
4	500	3	0	3	0	497	0	20.21,20.61,22.77
5	500	3	0	3	0	497	0	15.81,14.99 (2)
1	10	3	1	3	1	6	0	16.53,17.53(2),2.2*
2	10	3	1	3	1	6	0	19.25,24.45,21.25,1*
3	10	3	1	3	1	6	0	25.61,29.21,29.61,1.6*
4	10	3	1	3	1	6	0	22.57,21.11,23.37,1*
5	10	3	1	3	1	6	0	24.26,25.46,21.86,1*
1	100	3	1	3	1	96	0	7 (2),7.29,1.2*
2	100	3	1	3	1	96	0	9.69,11.63,10.12,1*
3	100	3	1	3	1	96	0	20.24,20.57,20.87,1.4*
4	100	3	1	3	1	96	0	18.25,18.77,19.27,1*
5	100	3	1	3	1	96	0	15.44,13.42,15.29,1.3*
1	500	3	1	3	1	496	0	7 (2),7.29,1.2*
2	500	3	1	3	1	496	0	9.69,11.63,10.12,1*
3	500	3	1	3	1	496	0	20.24,20.57,20.87,1.4*
4	500	3	1	3	1	496	0	18.25,18.77,19.27,1*
5	500	3	1	3	1	496	0	15.44,13.42,15.29,1.3*

Table 5. Results for BotMiner applied to IoT networks with IRC Botnet activity with single device infections (False positive scores are marked with *)

Set #	Total devices	Infected	Aberrant	TP	FP	TN	FN	BotMiner scores
1	10	1	0	1	0	9	0	3.75
2	10	1	0	1	0	9	0	3.00
3	10	1	0	1	0	9	0	5.25
4	10	1	0	1	0	9	0	5.50
5	10	1	0	1	0	9	0	6.00
1	100	1	0	1	0	99	0	3.38
2	100	1	0	1	0	99	0	4.68
3	100	1	0	1	0	99	0	4.06
4	100	1	0	1	0	99	0	3.88
5	100	1	0	1	0	99	0	4.92
1	500	1	0	1	0	499	0	3.15
2	500	1	0	1	0	499	0	3.97
3	500	1	0	1	0	499	0	4.38
4	500	1	0	1	0	499	0	3.50
5	500	1	0	1	0	499	0	3.26
1	10	1	1	1	0	9	0	2,0.5*
2	10	1	1	1	1	8	0	4.8,2*
3	10	1	1	1	0	9	0	2,0*
4	10	1	1	1	0	9	0	4.98,0*
5	10	1	1	1	0	9	0	3.92,0*
1	100	1	1	1	0	99	0	2.57,0.71*
2	100	1	1	1	0	99	0	2.32,0.5*
3	100	1	1	1	0	99	0	2.57,0*
4	100	1	1	1	0	99	0	2.68,0*
5	100	1	1	1	0	99	0	4.13,0.11*
1	500	1	1	1	0	499	0	2.28,0.5*
2	500	1	1	1	0	499	0	2.76,0.5*
3	500	1	1	1	0	499	0	3.57,0.11*
4	500	1	1	1	0	499	0	2.99,0*
5	500	1	1	1	0	499	0	2.3,0.01*

Table 6. Results for BotMiner applied to IoT networks with IRC Botnet activity with mutliple device infections (False positive scores are marked with *)

Set #	Total devices	Infected	Aberrant	TP	FP	TN	FN	BotMiner scores
1	10	3	0	3	0	7	0	7.2,6 (2)
2	10	3	0	3	0	7	0	4.8 (3)
3	10	3	0	3	0	7	0	6 (2),4.5
4	10	3	0	3	0	7	0	5 (2),3
5	10	3	0	3	0	7	0	3.75,4.95 (2)
1	100	3	0	3	0	97	0	3.9 (3)
2	100	3	0	3	0	97	0	6.3 (3)
3	100	3	0	3	0	97	0	6.36 (2),3.6
4	100	3	0	3	0	97	0	5.27 (2),3.92
5	100	3	0	3	0	97	0	5.88 (2),6.3
1	500	3	0	3	0	497	0	3.33 (3)
2	500	3	0	3	0	497	0	3.4 (2),3.69
3	500	3	0	3	0	497	0	6.4 (2),3.49
4	500	3	0	3	0	497	0	4.15,3.48,5.44
5	500	3	0	3	0	497	0	4.36 (2),4.04
1	10	3	1	3	0	7	0	5 (3), 0.75*
2	10	3	1	3	0	7	0	4.45 (3),0.75*
3	10	3	1	3	0	7	0	7 (2),5.6,0*
4	10	3	1	3	0	7	0	4.59(2),2.5,0*
5	10	3	1	3	0	7	0	4.6 (2),5.77,0*
1	100	3	1	3	1	96	0	3.29 (3), 1.29*
2	100	3	1	3	0	97	0	7.51 (3),0.75*
3	100	3	1	3	0	97	0	6.6 (2),4.38,0.09*
4	100	3	1	3	0	97	0	4.84 (2), 3.46, 0.25*
5	100	3	1	3	0	97	0	5.7,4.74 (2),0.3*
1	500	3	1	3	1	496	0	3.09 (3), 1.03*
2	500	3	1	3	0	497	0	4.39 (3),0.83*
3	500	3	1	3	0	497	0	5.18 (2),3.12,0.03*
4	500	3	1	3	0	497	0	4.32 (2),2.95,0*
5	500	3	1	3	0	497	0	3.98 (3),0.06*

6   Conclusion

The purpose of this work was to assess the capabilities of the traditional botnet detection technique BotMiner when applied on IoT-based botnets, while also validating a reconstruction thereof. The results indicate that the reconstruction of BotMiner operates as per the original work, it appears able to detect bots at a rate of 100% when more than a single bot exists on a network. BotMiner then went on to defy expectations and proceeded to detect bots on networks where only a single bot would be present. The single bot behaviour was meant to reflect the infection patterns of certain IoT-based botnets, including Mirai. BotMiner demonstrated that even when only a single bot exists on a given network, it is able to perform adequately when detecting said bots.

However, despite its strengths it was found that BotMiner still suffers from a notable weakness in that it can be prone to producing false positives. A device that would demonstrate aberrant behaviour that could trigger the alert detection component of BotMiner was planted in the network simulations for the experiment. In the majority of the results BotMiner would flag the device as a bot incorrectly. Exceptions that occurred appeared to have been produced due to the volume of alerts produced by the actuals bots. In such cases where bots do not use the IRC protocol, such as Mirai, or there are no actual bots on the network being analysed, then BotMiner may be prone to producing misleading results that could disrupt the environments it would have been intended to protect.

Overall it appears that BotMiner could be a tool potentially well designed enough to detect contemporary botnet threats, such as IoT-based threats. However it does appear to suffer from disadvantage that without proper tuning may render the technique inadequate in many circumstances due to the volume of false alerts.

Future work will include applying BotMiner to externally produced datasets in order to further validate the results produced by this paper. The same experimental approach will then be applied towards other traditional botnet detection techniques such as BotProbe and BotHunter. Finally, based on the strengths and weaknesses found from BotMiner and other technique, future work shall include initiatives toward creating a botnet detection technique that can leverage the abilities of existing work while ensuring their capabilities towards detecting IoT-based botnets.

References

1. Al-Fuqaha, A., Guizani, M., Mohammadi, M., Aledhari, M., Ayyash, M.: Internet of things: a survey on enabling technologies, protocols, and applications. IEEE Commun. Surv. Tutor. **17**(4), 2347–2376 (2015)
2. Alieyan, K., Almomani, A., Abdullah, R., Almutairi, B., Alauthman, M.: Botnet and internet of things (IoTs): a definition, taxonomy, challenges, and future directions. In: Research Anthology on Combating Denial-of-Service Attacks, pp. 138–150. IGI Global (2021)
3. Angrishi, K.: Turning internet of things (IoT) into internet of vulnerabilities (IoV): Iot botnets. arXiv preprint arXiv:1702.03681 (2017)
4. Baig, Z., et al.: Future challenges for smart cities: cyber-security and digital forensics. Digit. Investig. **22** (2017). https://doi.org/10.1016/j.diin.2017.06.015

5. Dange, S., Chatterjee, M.: IoT botnet: the largest threat to the IoT network. In: Jain, L.C., Tsihrintzis, G.A., Balas, V.E., Sharma, D.K. (eds.) Data Communication and Networks. AISC, vol. 1049, pp. 137–157. Springer, Singapore (2020). https://doi.org/10.1007/978-981-15-0132-6_10

6. Elzen, I., Heugten, J.: Techniques for detecting compromised IoT devices. Master's thesis, University of Amsterdam (2017). http://work.delaat.net/rp/2016-2017/p59/report.pdf

7. Eslahi, M., Salleh, R., Anuar, N.B.: Bots and botnets: an overview of characteristics, detection and challenges. In: 2012 IEEE International Conference on Control System, Computing and Engineering (ICCSCE), pp. 349–354. IEEE (2012)

8. Grizzard, J.B., Sharma, V., Nunnery, C., Kang, B.B., Dagon, D.: Peer-to-peer botnets: overview and case study. HotBots 7(2007) (2007)

9. Gu, G., Perdisci, R., Zhang, J., Lee, W., et al.: Botminer: clustering analysis of network traffic for protocol-and structure-independent botnet detection. In: USENIX Security Symposium, vol. 5, pp. 139–154 (2008)

10. Gu, G., Porras, P.A., Yegneswaran, V., Fong, M.W., Lee, W.: Bothunter: detecting malware infection through IDS-driven dialog correlation. In: Usenix Security, vol. 7, pp. 1–16 (2007)

11. Gu, G., Yegneswaran, V., Porras, P., Stoll, J., Lee, W.: Active botnet probing to identify obscure command and control channels. In: 2009 Annual, Computer Security Applications Conference, ACSAC 2009, pp. 241–253. IEEE (2009)

12. Jayasinghe, K., Poravi, G.: A survey of attack instances of cryptojacking targeting cloud infrastructure. In: Proceedings of the 2020 2nd Asia Pacific Information Technology Conference, pp. 100–107 (2020)

13. Kumar, A., Lim, T.J.: A secure contained testbed for analyzing IoT botnets. In: Gao, H., Yin, Y., Yang, X., Miao, H. (eds.) TridentCom 2018. LNICST, vol. 270, pp. 124–137. Springer, Cham (2019). https://doi.org/10.1007/978-3-030-12971-2_8

14. Lester, T.: How does mirai's c&c communicate with its bots? stack. Stack Exchange (2017). https://security.stackexchange.com/questions/151507/how-does-mirais-cc-communicate-with-its-bots

15. Liu, J., Xiao, Y., Ghaboosi, K., Deng, H., Zhang, J.: Botnet: classification, attacks, detection, tracing, and preventive measures. EURASIP I. Wirel. Commun. Netw. 2009, 1184–1187. IEEE Computer Society (2009)

16. Paganini, P.: Http-botnets: the dark side of a standard protocol! security affairs (2013). https://securityaffairs.co/wordpress/13747/cyber-crime/http-botnets.html

17. Ramson, S.J., Vishnu, S., Shanmugam, M.: Applications of internet of things (iot)-an overview. In: 2020 5th international conference on devices, circuits and systems (ICDCS). pp. 92–95. IEEE (2020)

18. Shanthi, K., Seenivasan, D.: Detection of botnet by analyzing network traffic flow characteristics using open source tools. In: 2015 IEEE 9th International Conference on Intelligent Systems and Control (ISCO), pp. 1–5. IEEE (2015)

19. Woodiss-Field, A., Johnstone, M.N.: Assessing the suitability of traditional botnet detection against contemporary threats. In: 2020 Workshop on Emerging Technologies for Security in IoT (ETSecIoT), pp. 18–21. IEEE (2020)

20. Zeidanloo, H.R., Shooshtari, M.J.Z., Amoli, P.V., Safari, M., Zamani, M.: A taxonomy of botnet detection techniques. In: 2010 3rd IEEE International Conference on Computer Science and Information Technology (ICCSIT), vol. 2, pp. 158–162. IEEE (2010)

A Robust Malware Detection Approach for Android System Based on Ensemble Learning

Wenjia Li[✉], Juecong Cai, Zi Wang, and Sihua Cheng

Department of Computer Science, New York Institute of Technology, New York, NY 10023, USA
wli20@nyit.edu

Abstract. As the number of mobile devices which is based on the Android system continues to grow rapidly, it becomes a primary target for security exploitation through undesirable malicious apps (malware) being unwittingly downloaded, which is often due to negligent user behavior patterns that grant unnecessary permissions to malicious apps or simply malware evolving to be sophisticated enough to bypass systematic detection. There have been numerous attempts to use machine learning to capture an application's malicious behavior focusing on features deemed to be germane to high security risks, but most of them typically focus only on a single algorithm, which is not representative of a huge family of ensemble techniques. In this paper, we develop an ensemble learning based malware detection approach for the Android system. To validate the performance of the proposed approach, we have conducted some experiments on the real world Android app dataset, which contains 3618 features that are initially obtained from the static, dynamic and ICC analyses. We then select 567 important features through feature selection. The overall detection accuracy is 97.73%, accompanied by a high 97.66% F-1 score that reflects a high relationship between precision (97.06%) and recall (98.28%). The experimental results clearly show that the ensemble learning based malware detection approach could effectively identify malware for the Android system.

Keywords: Android · Security · Malware · Machine learning · Ensemble learning

1 Introduction

In the second quarter of 2021, the Android operating system is reported to have 72.84% share of the mobile operating system market, which continues to dominate the mobile OS market throughout the world [1]. Given how common it is to find an Android device today, it is without doubt that its prevalence and open source nature easily opens up security vulnerabilities, where various security exploitations are used to gain unwanted access into Android phones. While Google Play provides some level of security protection, it is still inevitable that break-ins still occur [2].

© The Author(s), under exclusive license to Springer Nature Singapore Pte Ltd. 2022
G. Wang et al. (Eds.): UbiSec 2021, CCIS 1557, pp. 309–321, 2022.
https://doi.org/10.1007/978-981-19-0468-4_23

The Android platform is known to be a permission based system [11]. The apps are required to explicitly request for a corresponding permission from the user during the installation process to perform certain tasks on the Android devices, such as sending a SMS message or gaining access to the Internet. However, many users tend to arbitrarily grant permissions to unknown Android apps without even looking at what types of permissions they are requesting, therefore significantly weakening the protocols set in place for protection provided by the Android permission system [3, 5, 13].

Apart from user problems, malware themselves have become adept at circumventing standard detection protocols such as Google Bouncer and other standard anti-intrusion gateways that Google uses as deterrence. The Google Bouncer is capable of reducing the number of malicious apps by as much as 40% [3], but its predictability makes it easy to overcome. Google Bouncer uses the generic and open source QEMU as a machine emulator [4], and only performs dynamic analysis. In 2017, Google Bouncer became part of Google Play Protect, which is a system that regularly scans Android apps for potential security threats.

There are two broad methods of bypassing the security mechanism deployed at Google Play, which are namely Delayed Attack and Update Attack [3]. Delayed Attack involves meeting Bouncer's basic criteria, meaning an app with malicious payload (i.e. Trojan) does not misbehave during dynamic analysis and pretends to be "clean" until the five-minute scan has passed. The malicious code only starts to run after the app is downloaded onto the Android device. Update Attack is even harder to detect than Delayed Attack because the app does not even have to contain any malicious component at all. The basic app is downloaded as clean, but once on a device, it starts to "update" itself with malicious code or connect to a remote server to upload stolen personal data [3]. These malicious apps can make themselves behave like legit apps and are only flagged as malicious when they activate selected functions to perform their infiltration process. As such, it becomes more difficult to identify a malware because it can cleverly disguise itself from detection by either suppressing its malicious "tendencies" or simulate benign app behavior during the detection phase, until they gain access into a user's phone.

With so many varieties of Android malware, it is fair to hypothesize for the need to have an algorithm that is capable of detecting different types of malware. However, most of the prior research efforts typically focus only on using one single algorithm to detect malware, which may not work well on various types of Android malware. By applying the concept of ensemble learning, there could be many different ways in which one can effectively combine those algorithms together to achieve better detection results. Thus, it makes more sense to find the best algorithm that brings the most optimized results to solve the problem, preferring flexibility over proving the effectiveness of one single algorithm [12].

Ensemble learning is chosen because it has a proven track record in many fields [15], and more importantly, it is flexible and customizable, allowing many combinations. Using multiple learning algorithms tends to obtain better performance compared to any single learning algorithm, and most of the ensemble algorithms are fairly easy to implement, scale well to large datasets, and are quick to execute.

The main contributions of this paper are:

- We implement multiple ensemble algorithms at the same time for comprehensive in-depth comparison measured by different metrics such as accuracy, precision and recall. On top of that, this paper will also compare the performance of ensemble learning algorithms with those of individual machine learning algorithms to illustrate the effectiveness of the ensemble algorithms.
- We deploy multiple algorithms as a basket of models with diverse applications, and then combine the accuracy scores using an ensemble voting algorithm to boost results.
- We illustrate the feasibility and performance of the proposed malware detection approach using a real world Android app dataset. Experimental results show that the ensemble learning based malware detection approach can effectively identify malware with very high accuracy.

2   Related Work

2.1   Common Techniques Used in Malware Detection

A recent survey has been conducted by Liu et al. [8]. In this work, the authors first introduce the basics of Android applications, including the Android system architecture, security mechanisms, and classification of Android malware. Then, the authors analyze and summarize the current research status of malware detection from different aspects, including sample acquisition, data pre-processing, feature selection, machine learning algorithms, and the performance evaluation.

Kouliaridis et al. [12] summarized several papers that adopted different algorithms to detect malware, and quickly noted that a singular view of using static or dynamic analysis alone have proven to be unreliable as they can be easily evaded with code obfuscation and execution-stalling techniques respectively.

2.2   General Benchmarks

First and foremost, Drebin [16] makes up an important part of this study since all our malicious apps came from the Drebin study, making it a requisite benchmark for future comparisons. Drebin is a lightweight method for Android malware detection that works directly on the smartphone like an anti-virus software and identifies suspicious apps by name and attribute at the same time. It uses broad static analysis to collect features from 123,453 apps, with 5,560 of them being malware. As a pioneer, Drebin had a performance of a 94% accuracy score with few false alarms (false positives) of 1%, and explanations were provided for each malware detected, stating their properties - thus setting a very high bar for future studies. It was tested on five popular smartphones with an average runtime of 10 s per analysis [16].

Another high performing example is Yerima et al. [15] using Ensemble Learning on malware detection, promised to be high accuracy using 179 different features from diverse categories of malware behavior, emphasizing on robustness and diversity to malware problem solving. The experiment used a total of 6,863 Android applications that they got from McAfee's internal repository, out of which 2925 were malware and 3938 apps were benign. The best results that Yerima et al. has yielded is from combining Random Forest with Naïve Bayes, scoring an accuracy of 97.5%, with a false positive rate of around 2.3% and an AUC of 99.3%. However, our research does not use the AUC but instead calculates using the F-1 score to decide the relationship between precision and recall. Random Forest is used because randomness provides diversity in samples and robustness in speed of execution without having too much data processing. Interestingly, the Yerima et al. features did not exactly come from diverse sources as the study claimed, because it only made use of static analysis from permissions and API-calls. Judging from the results, it does seem like just crawling features from these two areas are more than enough.

Yang et al. came up with DroidMiner [17] that implemented one ensemble learning algorithm, namely the Random Forest algorithm, comparing its effectiveness against Naïve Bayes, Support Vector Machine (SVM), and Decision Tree. They evaluated 2400 malicious apps out of a corpus of over 77,000 apps, made up of 67,000 third party apps and 10,000 from Google Play. DroidMiner achieved the highest accuracy achieved on Random Forest with 95.3%. The other scores are 82.2% for Naïve Bayes, 86.7% for SVM and 92.4% for Decision Tree.

2.3 Collecting Features

Wang et al. came up with the top 40 most risky permissions [19], where the team had analyzed the risk of individual permissions and collaborative permissions by groups using machine learning techniques, and then performed feature ranking on them. Wang et al. reasoned that although Android enforces restrictions through a dual-party system, the Android system does not always require full declaration of permissions, while users are not always aware of the exact purpose of granting access to certain app functions [10, 19]. Apps can end up requesting for unnecessary permissions, resulting in over-privileged applications that often leave security loopholes that malware can quickly exploit. The results were classified using the Support Vector Machine (SVM), Decision Tree, and Random Forest techniques [19]. In addition, there were also other malware detection approaches which used various machine learning and deep learning algorithms based on permissions, API calls and other internal app features [30–37].

Comar et al. warned that for new-generation malware, the static detection method is no longer effective, known as zero-day malware [13, 14]. A zero-day malware (also known as next-generation malware) is a previously unknown malware for which specific antivirus software signatures are still unavailable. It is a vulnerability in software not known to the vendor, which can be exploited by hackers before the vendor becomes aware and patches a solution to fix it [14]. Therefore, apart from permission features, efforts should be made to venture into other avenues of features collection such as dynamic, ICC analysis, or other out-of-box areas as well.

Instead of simply going for inherent features of Android apps like permissions, API-calls, CPU usage and system calls, Munoz et al. [10] focused their study on identifying what they call indirect features or meta-data, mentioning that Google Play is also a fantastic repository of information for helping detect a malware, focusing on Application Category, Developer-related, Certificate-related features, and Social-related features.

Munoz et al. [10] collected a total of 48 features, and used Logistic Regression as their classifier, with the results showing that social-related features are not very useful. Some of the features categories showed high accuracy scores, but the precision, recall and F-1 are lackluster. On the other hand, developer-related and certificate-related features did show good promise. The study managed to greatly reduce their false negative rate but at the expense of their false positive rate, which they did not publish figures for.

2.4 ICC Analysis Using Intents and Intent-Filters

Apart from permissions, the Android system also uses intent and intent-filters as a mechanism for inter-process communication (ICC) between functions. The intent mechanism is predominantly for starting an activity, a service or sending a broadcast [6]. Explicit intents are normally safe and straightforward in its intention to access activities on an app, while implicit intents are not recommended as it contains inherent unsafe automatic app usage associations tied to them that may bypass the users' knowledge of app activity. Malicious apps can take advantage of this vulnerability to gain access to high security permissions through intent interception or intent spoofing.

Xu et al. [9] came up with the idea to trace malware by capturing ICC usage data from apps, and created a program named ICCDetector, which can tackle the problem of false positive and negative rates. They noted that Kirin [28] detects malwares by matching their required permissions against pre-defined security rules, while both DroidMiner [17] and DroidAPIMiner [7] build malware detection models based on API-related features. The weakness of these methods is that they treat the detected applications as standalone entities in Android platforms, assuming that the Android OS will keep separate apps mutually exclusive from each other, when in actual fact, resources could be shared through ICC means that is often overlooked.

3 Ensemble Learning Based Malware Detection for Android

3.1 System Architecture

The overall system architecture is shown as in Fig. 1.

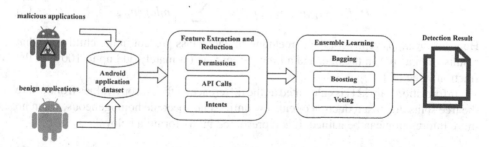

Fig. 1. Overall system architecture

In this work, we adopt the bucket of models [23] concept where a basket of algorithms is put together, the results are voted, and among all the accuracy scores, the best performing algorithm is chosen. The algorithms that we use in ensemble learning could be classified into two broad categories, one being ensemble learning models for bagging and boosting, and the other is a group of widely used machine learning algorithms such as Support Vector Machine (SVM), k-nearest neighbors (k-NN), etc. All of them will be put to a vote, which is also an ensemble algorithm, and all the algorithms, including the voting ensembles are sorted, and the top performing algorithm is chosen to ensure optimized results.

3.2 Decision Tree

We will first address the Decision Tree learning algorithm [20] as it is the basic function for most of the ensuing Ensemble Learning algorithms. Decision Tree generally uses greedy search as its searching strategy [20]. It has two criteria by which to split a tree to derive its results, namely the Gini Impurity or Entropy. By default, Python operates the Decision Tree classifier using the Gini Impurity if no further instructions are given. Using either does not seem to make a big difference in result in this particular study, as the accuracy scores of both criteria based on the dataset of this study reap about the results, with a difference of about 0.5%, which is insignificant.

The Gini Impurity [20] is a measure of the frequency of misclassified labels of randomly chosen samples in the branch. It is used to compute the impurities present in the partition dataset. It is defined as follows.

$$I_g(f) = \sum_{i=1}^{j} f_i(1 - f_i) = \sum_{i=1}^{j} \left(f_i - f_i^2 \right) = \sum_{i=1}^{j} f_i - \sum_{i=1}^{j} f_i^2 = 1 - \sum_{i=1}^{j} f_i^2 = \sum_{i \neq k} f_i f_k \tag{1}$$

Where f_i is the probability of an item with the label i being randomly chosen, while $(1 - f_i)$ is the probability of the labeling being a mistake. The Gini Impurity is the sum of f_i multiplied by $(1 - f_i)$, with i starting at 1 all the way till J, where J is the total number of classes or features within the set.

Entropy [21] is for calculating information gain, where it is defined as follows.

$$H(T) = I_E(p_1, p_2, ...p_n) = -\sum_{i=1}^{J} p_i log_2 p_i \tag{2}$$

Here, $p_1, p_2, ..., p_n$ represent the percentage of each class present in the child node that results from a split in the tree, and all the percentage ultimately add up to 100% or the fraction value of 1.

Information gain [21] is calculated as the difference of the entropy values from where the tree splits due to a reduction of entropy until values become homogeneous, when no more information can be gained. It is represented in the formula below.

$$IG(T, a) = H(T) - H(T/a) \tag{3}$$

It is important to note that the Decision Tree is not without limitations [20, 21]. It has problems expressing hard-to-learn concepts such as XOR, parity or multiplexer problems [22]. It also tends to be biased when using Entropy for information gain calculations, as it tends to favor attributes with more levels. It is very data sensitive, where a small change in the dataset can result in big changes in how the tree splits and therefore affecting the final prediction. Greedy search strategy is the Decision Tree's biggest flaw as it takes the most "convenient" close-by result and hence tends to return a favorable optimal local result but does not do a thorough and complete clean search through the entire tree, and hence does not always return the best optimal general result for the whole tree.

Due to this shortcoming of the Decision Tree algorithm, its accuracy and predictivity often suffers, especially when too many classes or features are involved, as the Decision Tree algorithm performs best when the trees are small. As such, it can have a problem of overfitting data. However, as mentioned, it works great as a base skeleton, and this study will build on the Decision Tree to improve its predictive via enhancements using various Ensemble Learning techniques. The three most popular methods for combining the predictions from different models currently are Bagging, Boosting and Voting.

3.3 Bagging

Bagging is fully known as Bootstrap Aggregation, which generally involves taking multiple samples from the training dataset and then training a model from each sample. Bagging generates multiple models using the same algorithm, using random sub-samples of the dataset drawn using the bootstrap sampling method from the original dataset, where some original examples may appear more than once and some not present in the sample. The final output prediction is averaged across the predictions of all of the sub-models.

Bagging performs best with base algorithms with high variance, and is excellent at reducing variance, thus stabilizing and improving the predictive performance. Unlike Decision Tree, Bagging uses more than one tree, and the user can either specify the maximum number of trees, or the algorithm will keep running until it runs off branches to split into. The samples of the training dataset are taken with replacement, which means the object is put back into the bag so that the number of samples to choose from is the same for every draw when constructing the model.

The three bagging models studied in this research are described as follows [18].

Bagged Decision Trees. The various bagging models are actually very similar to each other, and each can be said to be a level-up improvement of the other. Bagged Decision Trees is the most basic of the method. As its name suggests, it uses a Decision Tree as a base-estimator [18], and then does multi-sampling and can have multiple trees, and the results were combined using averaging to overcome the shortcoming of using a single tree. Decision trees that grow very deep tend to learn highly irregular patterns, and overfit their training sets. They may have low bias but end up with very high variance due to noise in the training data. Bagging is thus great for variance reduction without raising the bias.

Random Forest. Random forest [24] is an extension of bagged decision trees, and it does not train greedily when choosing the best split point in the construction of the tree, instead a random subset of features is considered for each split. This is also known as "feature bagging", and features that are deemed as strong predictors for output classification will be repeatedly chosen by most trees, thus causing correlations between trees.

Random Forest can deal with large numbers of training instances, missing values, and irrelevant features without running into problems. Random Forest deals with more than one tree and has multiple models. It reduces variance by averaging the predictions of a set of m trees with individual weight functions W_j, and can be represented by the following prediction function, which is similar to the K-Nearest Neighbor (KNN) algorithm but taking into account the number of trees and features used in the Random Forest [24, 25].

Extra Trees. Extra Trees does not mean that the algorithm involves using even more trees, but rather takes randomization up one notch from Random Forest. Instead of using the Gini Impurity, Entropy or feature calculation is used to decide a split in the tree, Extra Trees selects a random value for each feature under consideration based on the bootstrap sample, which is random sampling with replacement.

3.4 Boosting

The purpose of boosting algorithms is mainly for reducing bias and variance and turning weak learner algorithms into strong ones [26]. It achieves this by creating a sequence of models that attempt to correct mistakes of the models that came before in the sequence. Each model makes predictions which are weighted by their accuracy and results are combined to produce a final output prediction. The sequence starts with weights that are assigned according to the weak learner's accuracy. The weights are re-adjusted as misclassified samples gain weight and correct classifications lose weight, helping the algorithm to "learn its mistakes".

The two main algorithms often used in boosting techniques are Gradient Tree Boosting and AdaBoost, which are described further below.

Adaboost. AdaBoost, or Adaptive Boosting, begins by fitting a weak learner classifier on the original dataset and then fits additional copies of the same classifier on the same dataset, adjusting the weights of misclassified instances so that subsequent classifiers focus more on difficult cases.

Gradient Tree Boosting. Gradient Tree Boosting or Gradient Boosted Regression Trees (GBRT) is an accurate and effective off-the-shelf approach and is usually used with decision trees of a fixed size as base learners. It builds as an additive model in a forward stage-wise fashion, and instead of learning from errors like AdaBoost, GBRT optimizes its cost function by iteratively choosing samples that point in the negative gradient direction. When dealing with regression trees, the GBRT is fit on the negative gradient of the binomial or multinomial deviance loss function, using logistic regression as loss function. On the other hand, it recovers the Adaboost algorithm for exponential loss function.

3.5 Voting

Unlike Bagging and Boosting that build multiple models using the same algorithm, voting combines the results from multiple algorithms where the majority vote wins. It has the properties of error correction and predictive boosting.

There are generally two kinds of voting: the first is known as "Democratic Voting", where all members in the vote are assigned equal weights, and the other is "Weighted Voting" where significant members that are better performers are given more weights than poorer performers so that the predictive value will lean towards a classification that tends to choose the more "correct" answer. Both voting techniques are generally fine, but Kaggle [27] recommends using "3 Best vs the Rest" where higher weights are assigned to the top three performers compared to the rest, and the results are generally slightly better than the Democratic Voting technique.

4 Experimental Study

The experimental dataset consists of a total of 3618 features extracted from 4430 Android applications, with a 50% malicious and 50% benign split. The malicious apps were mostly from Drebin [16], while benign apps were directly downloaded from Google Play. The features come from various sources such as permissions, API calls, system calls (dynamic analysis) and ICC (inter-component communication). However, it should be noted that most dynamic analysis and ICC features have either very sparse data or have very rarely shared occurrences between apps.

The Extra Tree algorithm [29] has been used for feature reduction, which uses feature importance ranking scores to weed out unimportant features that have zero values or are not useful for telling apps apart. The dataset started out with 3618 features, and after feature reduction, only 567 are identified to be important.

4.1 Necessity of Using Multiple Machine Learning Algorithms

This section aims to show the necessity of using multiple algorithms over just using one. To make the experiments simple, the dataset has been randomly divided into three different sets containing different numbers of features, and each set is executed twice - once as a full dataset, and a second time after feature reduction, thereby creating 6 different scenarios to compare. Since the full dataset took a longer time to execute, the execution time has been included to show how long it takes, and the result is about the same as the one after feature reduction.

From Fig. 2, it can be clearly seen that from just using different numbers of features alone, the algorithm that has the highest accuracy differs, which indicates that one single algorithm is not always the best choice for every scenario. Thus, it is necessary to implement a basket of models using ensemble learning techniques.

In addition, we also observe that the full dataset with 3618 features has an exaggeratingly long execution time at 26745.15 s (about 7.4 h), which is a huge trade-off for the 1% increase in accuracy from the dataset with 800 features, so more features do not always help improve the performance. On the other hand, using feature reduction together with our basket of models allows us an 84.8 times improvement (from 26745.15 s to 315.43 s) in execution time efficiency, achieving roughly the same accuracy at 97.58%. Therefore, it is feasible to apply the ensemble learning technique, which can achieve similar accuracy with much less time overhead.

Feature Set	Best Algorithm & Accuracy	Exec. Time	Reduced Feature Set	Best Algorithm & Accuracy	Exec. Time
228 features	Gradient Boosting: 95.27%	40.29s	54 features	Extra Tree: 95.17%	48.94s
800 features	Weighted Voting: 96.62%	244.69s	151 features	Extra Tree: 96.84%	93.59s
3618 features	Extra Tree: 97.62%	26745.15s	567 features	Weighted Voting: 97.58%	315.43s

Fig. 2. Execution results by dataset

4.2 Performance Comparison of Different Algorithms

As shown in Fig. 3, all the algorithms listed in our basket of models have been applied to the dataset, and the results are sorted by their accuracy scores in descending order. It can be easily found that all the top performers are Ensemble Learning based approaches. The only exception is AdaBoost which falls behind Logistic Regression (which is not an ensemble learning based algorithm). Still, it performs better than most other non-ensemble algorithms. Therefore, we can conclude that ensemble learning based algorithms are the overall winners here.

At 97.73% accuracy, Weighted Voting is the best performing algorithm, while also boasting the highest recall score at 98.28% which is excellent with only 1.66% false negative rate. This means it managed to identify most of the malicious apps available in the dataset despite the fact that it contains members in the vote with low scores, but since the votes are weighted, chances are the weak votes have been compensated by the stronger votes, and hence being resilient to those errors.

3618 features, 567 reduced Algorithm	FN 10	FP 01	Accuracy	Precision	Recall	F1
VotingWeighted	1.66%	2.87%	97.73%	97.06%	98.28%	97.66%
VotingDemocracy	2.44%	2.64%	97.46%	97.26%	97.47%	97.37%
ExtraTree	2.88%	2.53%	97.30%	97.37%	97.01%	97.19%
GradientTreeBoosting	1.88%	3.79%	97.16%	96.14%	98.05%	97.09%
RandomForest	2.77%	3.10%	97.06%	96.79%	97.13%	96.96%
BaggedDecisionTree	2.77%	3.22%	97.01%	96.68%	97.13%	96.90%
LogisticRegression (Linear)	3.88%	3.79%	96.17%	96.06%	95.98%	96.02%
AdaBoost	5.43%	3.79%	95.39%	96.00%	94.37%	95.18%
SVC Radial	6.87%	2.87%	95.13%	96.89%	92.87%	94.84%
DecisionTreeEntropy	4.99%	6.55%	94.23%	93.32%	94.83%	94.07%
K Nearest Neighbour	6.87%	5.29%	93.92%	94.43%	92.87%	93.64%
DecisionTreeGini	5.43%	6.78%	93.90%	93.07%	94.37%	93.71%
GaussianNaiveBayesB	3.22%	39.20%	78.81%	70.40%	96.67%	81.47%

Fig. 3. Performance of ensemble learning based approach vs. single algorithm

5 Conclusion

In this paper, we propose a robust malware detection approach based on the ensemble learning technique. The experimental study showed that it can achieve high accuracy, recall and precision. Moreover, it is most interesting to note that through the experiments, it turns out that despite the boosting and error correcting nature of the majority voting based algorithms, they do not always guarantee the top results. They may be within the top 3–5 best performing algorithms, but depending on the dataset, bagging algorithms like Random Forest or Extra Trees still prevail, and Gradient Boosting on certain occasions.

As for the future direction, we would like to explore the adversarial attacks against the malware detectors, and how they could be coped with. Adversarial attacks have recently become a major threat to the malware detectors, as they could mutate or tamper with the dataset that the malware detectors are using. Consequently, the performance of the malware detectors will be severely degraded in the presence of adversarial attacks. Therefore, it would be valuable to do some research in how the adversarial attacks may impact the malware detectors, and how to address these attacks.

References

1. O'Dea, S.: Market share of mobile operating systems worldwide 2012–2021. https://www.sta tista.com/statistics/272698/global-market-share-held-by-mobile-operating-systems-since-2009/. Accessed 29 June 2021
2. Cisco. Midyear Security Report (2015). http://www.cisco.com/web/offers/pdfs/cisco-msr-2015.pdf
3. Trend Micro. A Look at Google Bouncer (2012). http://blog.trendmicro.com/trendlabs-sec urity-intelligence/a-look-at-google-bouncer/
4. QEMU. 2016. http://wiki.qemu.org/Main_Page
5. Stefanko, L.: Android Trojan drops in, despite Google's Bouncer. ESET, 22 September 2015–12:48 pm (2015). http://www.welivesecurity.com/2015/09/22/android-trojan-drops-in-despite-googles-bouncer/
6. Android Developer. Intents and Intent Filters. https://developer.android.com/guide/compon ents/intents-filters.html
7. Aafer, Y., Du, W., Yin, H.: DroidAPIMiner: mining API-level features for robust malware detection in Android. In: Proceedings of the 9th International ICST Conference on Security and Privacy in Communication Networks (Secure Comm), Sydney, NSW, Australia, September 2013, pp. 86–103 (2013). https://doi.org/10.1007/978-3-319-04283-1-6
8. Liu, K., Xu, S., Xu, G., Zhang, M., Sun, D., Liu, H.: A review of android malware detection approaches based on machine learning. IEEE Access **8**, 124579–124607 (2020)
9. Xu, K., Li, Y., Deng, R.H.: ICCDetector: ICC-based malware detection on android. IEEE Trans. Inf. Forensics Secur. **11**(6) (2016)
10. Munoz, A., Martin, I., Guzman, A., Hernandez, J.A.: Android malware detection from Google Play meta-data: selection of important features. IEEE CNS 2015 poster session (2015)
11. Android Developers. Manifest permission (2016). http://developer.android.com/reference/android/Manifest.permission.html
12. Kouliaridis, V., Kambourakis, G.: A Comprehensive survey on machine learning techniques for android malware detection. Information **12**, 185 (2021). https://doi.org/10.3390/info12 050185

13. Comar, P.M., Liu, L., Saha, S., Tan, P.-N., Nucci, A.: Combining supervised and unsupervised learning for zero-day malware detection. In: Proceedings of IEEE INFOCOM 2013 (2013)
14. PC Tools, Symantec. What is a Zero-Day Vulnerability?(2010). http://www.pctools.com/sec urity-news/zero-day-vulnerability/
15. Yerima, S.Y., Sezer, S., Muttik. I.: High accuracy android malware detection using ensemble learning. IET Inf. Secur. (2015). ISSN:1751-8717. Doi: https://doi.org/10.1049/iet-ifs.2014. 0099
16. Arp, D., Spreitzenbarth, M., Huebner, M., Gascon, H., Rieck, K.: Drebin: effective and explainable detection of android malware in your pocket. In: NDSS 2014, 23–26 February 2014, Internet Society, San Diego (2014). ISBN:1-891562-35-5
17. Kutyłowski, M., Vaidya, J. (eds.): ESORICS 2014. LNCS, vol. 8712. Springer, Cham (2014). https://doi.org/10.1007/978-3-319-11203-9
18. Scikit-Learn. Ensemble learning. http://scikit-learn.org/stable/modules/ensemble.html
19. Wang, W., Wang, X., Feng, D., Liu, J., Han, Z., Zhang, X.: Exploring permission-induced risk in android applications for malicious application detection. IEEE Trans. Inf. Forensics Secur. **9**, 1869–1882 (2014)
20. Lior Rokach, O. Maimon, 2008. Data Mining with Decision Trees: Theory and Applications, 2nd edn. World Scientific Pub Co Inc., Singapore (2007). ISBN: 978-9812771711
21. Witten, I., Frank, E., Hall, M.: Data Mining, pp. 102–103. Morgan Kaufmann. Burlington (2011). ISBN: 9780-12-374856-0
22. Gareth, J., Witten, D., Hastie, T., Tibshirani, R.: An Introduction to Statistical Learning, p. 315. Springer, New York (2015). https://doi.org/10.1007/978-1-4614-7138-7. ISBN 978-14614-7137-0
23. Zenko, B.: Is combining classifiers better than selecting the best one. Mach. Learn. **2004**, 255–273 (2004)
24. Hastie, T., Tibshirani, R., Friedman, J.: The Elements of Statistical Learning, 2nd edn., Springer, New York (2008). https://doi.org/10.1007/978-0-387-84858-7. ISBN:0-387-95284-5
25. Lin, Y., Jeon, Y.: Random forests and adaptive nearest neighbors (Technical report). Technical Report No. 1055. University of Wisconsin (2002)
26. Breiman, L.: Arcing [Boosting] is more successful than bagging in variance reduction. Bias, variance, and arcing classifiers. Technical Report (1996), Accessed 19 Jan 2015
27. Kaggle. Ensembling Guide. https://mlwave.com/kaggle-ensembling-guide/
28. Enck, W., Ongtang, M., Mcdaniel, P.: On lightweight mobile phone application certification. In: ACM Conference on Computer and Communications Security, pp. 235–245 (2009)
29. Scikit-Learn, Extra Tree Classifier. https://scikit-learn.org/stable/modules/generated/sklearn. ensemble.ExtraTreesClassifier.html
30. Li, W., Ge, J., Dai, G.: Detecting malware for android platform: an SVM-based approach. In: 2015 IEEE 2nd International Conference on Cyber Security and Cloud Computing, pp. 464–469. IEEE (2015)
31. Wang, Z., Cai, J., Cheng, S., Li. W.: DroidDeepLearner: identifying android malware using deep learning. In: 2016 IEEE 37th Sarnoff Symposium, pp. 160–165. IEEE (2016)
32. Monica, K., Li, W.: Lightweight malware detection based on machine learning algorithms and the android manifest file. In: 2016 IEEE MIT Undergraduate Research Technology Conference (URTC), pp. 1–3. IEEE (2016)
33. Li, W., Wang, Z., Cai, J., Cheng, S.: An android malware detection approach using weight-adjusted deep learning. In: 2018 International Conference on Computing, Networking and Communications (ICNC), pp. 437–441. IEEE (2018)
34. Su, X., Liu, X., Lin, J., He, S., Zhangjie, F., Li, W.: De-cloaking malicious activities in smartphones using HTTP flow mining. KSII Trans. Internet Inf. Syst. (TIIS) **11**(6), 3230–3253 (2017)

35. Li, W., Bala, N., Ahmar, A., Tovar, F., Battu, A., Bambarkar, P.: A robust malware detection approach for android system against adversarial example attacks. In: 2019 IEEE 5th International Conference on Collaboration and Internet Computing (CIC), pp. 360–365. IEEE (2019)
36. Su, X., Xiao, L., Li, W., Liu, X., Li, K.-C., Liang, W.: DroidPortrait: android malware portrait construction based on multidimensional behavior analysis. Appl. Sci. **10**(11), 3978 (2020)
37. Bala, N., Ahmar, A., Li, W., Tovar, F., Battu, A., Bambarkar, P.: DroidEnemy: battling adversarial example attacks for Android malware detection. Digit. Commun. Netw. (2021)

A Reverse Auction Based Efficient D2D Transmission Mechanism for Ubiquitous Power Terminals

Xingshen Wei[1(✉)], Yongjian Cao[1], Peng Gao[1], and Junxian Xu[2]

[1] Nanjing NARI Information and Communication Technology Co., Ltd., Nanjing, China
{weixingshen,caoyongjian}@sgepri.sgcc.com.cn
[2] Information and Communication Branch of State Grid Hebei Electric Power Co., Ltd., Shijiazhuang, China
xjx@he.sgcc.com.cn

Abstract. Cooperative download and broadcast among mobile devices over the hybrid base-station-to-device (B2D) and device-to-device (D2D) network has been proved to be an effective and efficient approach for video sharing among ubiquitous power terminals. However, incentive problem is arisen such that why would a mobile device be willing to broadcast video data to others at the cost of its own resources, e.g. bandwidth and energy. To address the incentive problem in wireless streaming, we propose a truthful sealed-bid reverse auction model in living streaming scenario where a group of users have synchronous playback offset. A logical central controller acts as the auctioneer, and streaming users act as bidders who download video data through cellular links and bid to sell the service of video data broadcast over the D2D links. Considering economic robust, we derive the relationship between the payment rule and the allocation rule in a truthful auction which guarantees each user to announce the state of resources truthfully. Based on these principles, we design a truthful auction mechanism which not only guarantees the smooth playing of individual user, but also minimizes the payment cost of the auctioneer. Finally, we demonstrate the effective and the economic robustness of our auction mechanism through extensive simulations.

Keywords: Incentive mechanism · Reverse auction · D2D transmission

1 Introduction

Recently, cooperations among individual mobile users (MUs) like ubiquitous power terminals over hybrid B2D/D2D networks have been extensively studied [1–7]. While the cellular interface provides long-range always-on B2D connections, the WiFi interface allows MUs to conduct short-range device-to-device (D2D) communications with high bandwidth and per-bit energy efficiency. For streaming service, some video requests could be responded by nearby MUs without incurring

G. Wang et al. (Eds.): UbiSec 2021, CCIS 1557, pp. 322–335, 2022.
https://doi.org/10.1007/978-981-19-0468-4_24

B2D traffic. However, these work do not consider the incentive problem such that why would a MU be willing to unicast/broacast data to others at the cost of its own resources. One approach to incentive mechanism is to provide monetary revenue for MUs that serve as relay nodes. As a result, there exists trades between a group of MUs for regulating the cooperations. Auction is one of the most popular form to deal with the trading interaction because of its economic robustness and easy to implement.

Auction mechanisms have been researched in many research topics in computer science to deal with the problems of individual interaction. In wired network based streaming system, auction schemes are applied to deal with the competition and optimization problem, such as video transmission and network resources allocation [8, 9]. Different with previous work, we propose an auction mechanism to incentivize individual MUs to share video data over the D2D network in a streaming system, where a group of co-located MUs are able to simultaneously receive video data via B2D and D2D connections. Due to the broadcast nature of the D2D network, several MUs can receive the same video data by overhearing in a single transmission. Therefore, previous auction-based incentive mechanisms designed for unicast scenario are not suitable for cooperative wireless streaming system.

In this work, we investigate incentive mechanism in a living streaming system where the playback offset of MUs are synchronous. We apply a sealed-bid reverse auction where a central controller acts as the auctioneer, and MUs act as bidders who may sell service of D2D broadcast to the auctioneer. A bidder announces a bid which reveals its evaluation on the energy consumption incurred by the D2D broadcast, and the auctioneer decides the scheduling of D2D transmission and the corresponding payment for each bidder. Two key design issues of auction mechanism are allocation rule and payment rule, which not only define rules of trading, but also affect behaviors of participating user. Specially, truthfulness is most critical for economic robustness such that a bidder can not get a larger profit by false-announcing its private resource state. Under the constraint for smooth playing of all bidders, we design an efficient auction mechanism which not only guarantees that MUs truthfully announce their resource state, but also incentivize MUs to broadcast video data over the D2D network.

The contributions of this work are summarized as follows.

- We design a truthful auction based incentive mechanism for cooperative wireless video streaming. The auction mechanism fall into sealed-bid reverse auction category. Through theoretical analysis, we establish the relationship between allocation rule an payment rule to achieve truthfulness.
- Under the constraints of truthfulness and smooth playback of MUs, we formulate an optimization problem to minimize the payment cost of the auctioneer. Then, we propose a polynomial algorithm for the auctioneer to decide a) the data scheduling over the D2D network, and b) the payment for each bidder, while maintaining the truthfulness and budget balance.
- Through extensive simulations, we demonstrate the effective and the economic robustness of our auction mechanism.

2 System Model

2.1 Network and Streaming Model

We consider a wireless streaming system as shown in Fig. 1, which consists of a streaming server, a base station (BS) and a group of mobile users (MUs). Each MU is able to download video data from the streaming server via the B2D cellular link and transmit data to other MUs via D2D links simultaneously. Let $\mathcal{N} = \{1, \cdots, N\}$ be the set of MUs, and r_i be the B2D download rate for each MU $i \in \mathcal{N}$. Similar to [3], we assume that each pair of MUs is one-hop reachable and the scheduling of D2D transmissions is determined by a logically central controller. Due to the interference, this implies that only one MU can transimit video data over the D2D network at one time. Considering the broadcast nature, all MUs are able to receive the data by overhearing in a D2D transmission. We apply a lossy D2D transmission model that all MUs broadcast video data with rate r^D and the loss ratio of D2D link from MU i to j are denoted as $p_{i,j}$.

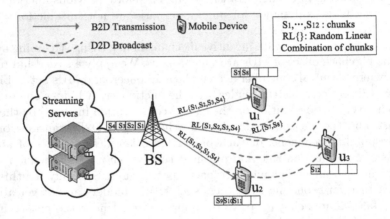

Fig. 1. Illustration of the wireless streaming system with network coding supported. In both B2D transmissions and D2D broadcast, chunks are coded with random coefficients.

Consider a typical live streaming scenario, where MUs are playing a video with synchronously playback offset. The video is divided into segments with equal length. Let $\mathcal{K} = \{1, \cdots, K\}$ be the set of segments. Each segment is further divided into S chunks. Same as the scheduling scheme of video delivery used in [3], time is divided into frames and the duration of a frame is equivalent to the duration of a segment. In frame k, all MUs are playing segment k, downloading segment $k + 2$ via B2D links and broadcasting segment $k + 1$ over the D2D network.

In addition, to facilitate the video distribution, we apply random linear network coding [10,11] over chunks of each segment for both B2D transmissions and D2D transmissions. More specifically, for each segment, coded chunks are

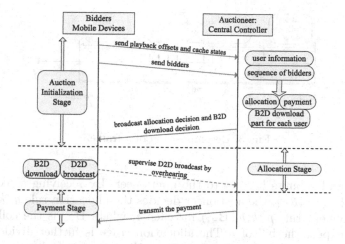

Fig. 2. Illustration of the process of the auction.

constructed by the linear combinations of all chunks of the segment, where the coefficients are randomly selected from a finite field. Since chunks are coded, there is no need to feedback in transmission process. Streaming server and MUs only have to generate a chunk with new coefficients for each transmission. We do not allow MUs broadcast chunks which are received via D2D links, since such re-broadcast will generate linearly dependent chunks and result in unnecessary energy costs. When finite field of coefficients is sufficiently large, each MU can recover the original segment with high probability once receiving S chunks of the segment.

2.2   Auction Model

Although MUs can receive chunks via both B2D and D2D links, the B2D transmission is more expensive than the D2D transmission in the term of both monetary and energy per bid. Meanwhile, the battery of mobile device is critical resource, and without favourable incentive mechanism, MUs are not willing to transmit chunks to others on the cost of their own resource. Therefore, the main objective is to incentivize individual MU broadcast over the D2D network.

We provide profits for D2D broadcast and employ a typical *reverse and sealed-bid* auction which is carried out periodically in each frame. In the reverse auction process, we consider a central controller that acts as the auctioneer, and a group of MUs act as bidders. The central controller could be the server of video service providers. The commodity is the service of D2D broadcast, and MUs bid for selling the service of broadcast over the D2D network in each frame. We divide the frame into three stages: auction initialization stage, allocation stage and payment stage, as shown in Fig. 2. Before frame k, each MU i has downloaded a_i^{k+1} chunks of segment $k+1$ via B2D links. At the auction initialization stage, MU i generates a bid b_i based on its valuation of energy consumption for D2D

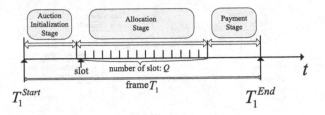

Fig. 3. Decomposition of a frame.

broadcast, and submits b_i, a_i^{k+1} to the auctioneer. By receiving a sequence of bids $\mathbf{B}_j = \{b_1, \ldots, b_N\}$, the auctioneer decides the allocation rule $q_i(k, b_i, \mathbf{B}_{-i})$ and the payment rule $p_i(k, b_i, \mathbf{B}_{-i})$ for each i, where $\mathbf{B}_{-i}$ is the collection of other bids expect the bid of i. The allocation stage is further divided into Q slots, which is the minimal unit for D2D transmission scheduling, as shown in Fig. 3. Based on the allocation rule and payment rule, chunks are transmitted over B2D and D2D links in the allocation stage, and the auctioneer provides payments to MUs in the payment stage finally. In the following, we introduce the main components in the reverse auction.

Valuation-The valuation is a function $f(E_i^k) : [0, 1] \to \mathbb{R}$, where E_i^k represents the remaining energy in percentage when MU i generates a bid in frame k. Battery is an important resource for mobile device, and troubles might be carried out in other services when battery is low. Therefore, we apply a monotone and decreasing valuation function with E_i^k. To simplify the computational complexity, we user $f(x) = 1 - x$ in this work.

Bid-The bid of bidder i is denoted by $b_i = (k, \hat{E}_i^k)$, where k represents frame, and $\hat{E}_i^k$ is the announced battery state. The real battery state of bidder i is denoted by $r_i = (k, E_i^k)$, which is the private information of bidder i.

Allocation Rule and Payment Rule-The allocation rule $q_i(k, b_i, \mathbf{B}_{-i})$ is a positive integer denoting the number of slots that are allocated to bidder i for D2D broadcast in frame k. The payment rule $p_i(k, b_i, \mathbf{B}_{-i})$ is the payment that the auctioneer provides for bidder i corresponding to the allocation rule. The payment can be either internal or monetary value, which can bring benefits to users in streaming service. In this following, we use $q_i(k, b_i)$ and $p_i(k, b_i)$ for shorter representations when there is no confusion.

Utility-The utility $u_i(q_i(k, b_i), p_i(k, b_i))$ is the profit that bidder i can get under the payment rule and the allocation rule in frame k, which is the payment offered by the auctioneer minus the cost for the D2D broadcast. We assume that the energy consumption for D2D broadcast is homogeneous for MUs, i.e. e_0 be the energy consumption for D2D broadcast per slot. If one bidder is allocated l slots for D2D broadcast, the cost $F(l, \hat{E}_i^k)$ can be presented as follows.

$$F(l, \hat{E}_i^k) = \begin{cases} \sum_{j=0}^{l-1} f(\hat{E}_i^k - je_0) & \text{if } \hat{E}_i^k \geq le_0 \\ +\infty & \text{otherwise} \end{cases} \tag{1}$$

And the utility is presented as:

$$u_i(q_i(k, b_i), p_i(k, b_i)) = p_i(k, b_i) - F(q_i(k, b_i), E_i^k) \tag{2}$$

3   Economic Robust and Problem Formulation

It is commonly believed that truthfulness and individual rationality are two important properties to provide economic robust for an auction. In wireless streaming scenario, bidders join and leave the system dynamically. In each frame, the only information involved in a bid $b_i = (k, \hat{E}_i^k)$ is the announced battery state $\hat{E}_i^k$. Truthfulness guarantees that bidders reveal their real battery state in auction process, and individual rationality guarantees that bidders are willing to broadcast video data over the D2D network. We first show the definitions of two property.

Definition 1 (Truthfulness). An auction $\mathcal{A} = (q, p)$ is truthfulness, if for any bidder i in any frame k, generating a bid that revealing its real battery state maximizes its own utility. For example, if the real battery state at frame k of bidder i is $r_i = (k, E_i^k)$, then for any bid that can be generated by bidder i, $b_i = (k, \hat{E}_i^k)$, we have:

$$u_i(q_i(k, r_i), p_i(k, r_i)) \geq u_i(q_i(k, b_i), p_i(k, b_i)) \quad \forall i \in \mathcal{N}; \quad \forall \hat{E}_i^k \in [0, 1] \tag{3}$$

Definition 2 (Individual Rationality). An auction $\mathcal{A} = (q, p)$ is individual rationality, if for any bidder i in any frame k, generating any bid b_i results in a non-negative utility, shown as the following.

$$u_i(q_i(k, b_i), p_i(k, b_i)) \geq 0, \quad \forall i \in \mathcal{N}; \quad \forall k \in \mathcal{K} \tag{4}$$

For the auctioneer carries out the auction process and have the objective to minimize the total payment for all bidders. The total payment cost of the auctioneer, denoted by $c(\mathcal{A})$, is represented as:

$$c(\mathcal{A}) = \sum_{k \in \mathcal{K}} \sum_{i \in \mathcal{N}} p_i(k, b_i). \tag{5}$$

The constraints contain two folds: the smooth playback for all bidders and the robustness of the auction mechanism, i.e., individual rationality and truthfulness. To achieve smooth playback, each bidder should receive at least S chunks of segment $k + 1$ at the end of frame k. Under the data scheduling described in Subsect. 2.1, bidders have downloaded some chunks of segment $k + 1$ via B2D links in the previous frame, i.e. $r_i t_F$ for bidder i, where r_i is the B2D data rate of i and t_F is the duration of the frame. Let $d_{i,j}^{k+1}$ be the number of chunks received by i from j over D2D network in frame k, then we have the constraint for smooth playing as follows.

$$\sum_{j \in \mathcal{N}} d_{i,j}^{k+1} + r_i t_F \geq S, \quad \forall i \in \mathcal{N}, k \in \mathcal{K}. \tag{6}$$

Under the allocation rule, the number of slots for D2D broadcast of bidder j is $q_j(k, b_j)$. Thus, the total number of coded chunks can be transmitted to bidder i is $r^D(1-p_{j,i})q_j(k,b_j)t_S$, where t_S is the duration of slot. In these coded chunks, at most $a_j^{k+1} = r_j t_F$ chunks are valid for decoding the original segment, since bidders only relay chunks received via B2D links. Then, we have the constraints for $d_{i,j}^{k+1}$ as

$$d_{i,j}^{k+1} \leq r_j t_F, \quad \forall i, j \in \mathcal{N}, k \in \mathcal{K}; \tag{7}$$

$$d_{i,j}^{k+1} \leq r^D(1 - p_{j,i})q_j(k, b_j)t_S, \quad \forall i, j \in \mathcal{N}, k \in \mathcal{K}. \tag{8}$$

Specially, the allocation rule is constrained by the transmission and interference model. Under the interference assumption described in Subsect. 2.1, only one bidder can broadcast video data over the D2D network in one slot. Then, we have the interference constraints as follows.

$$\sum_{i \in \mathcal{N}} q_i(k, b_i) \leq Q, \forall k \in \mathcal{K} \tag{9}$$

Thus, we formulate the optimization problem from auctioneer perspective as follows, where functions of allocation rule q and payment rule p are decision variables.

$$\min \quad c(\mathcal{A})$$
$$\text{s.t. } (3)(4)(6)(7)(8)(9). \tag{10}$$

4   Auction Design

4.1   Design of Allocation Rule and Payment Rule

We aim to design allocation rule $q(\cdot)$ and payment rule $p(\cdot)$ to form an economic robust auction with the properties of individual rationality and truthfulness. Since q and p is a function of bids $(b_i, \mathbf{B}_{-i})$ and a bid b_i of any bidder i is uniquely determined by the announced battery state $\hat{E}_i$, in the following we replace b_i by $\hat{E}_i$, i.e., $q_i(\hat{E}_i)$ denoted as the number of time slots for D2D broadcast of bidder i.

To achieve the individual rationality, we have:

$$p_i(\hat{E}_i) \geq F(q_i(\hat{E}_i), E_i) = q_i(\hat{E}_i)(1 - E_i) + \frac{q_i(\hat{E}_i)(q_i(\hat{E}_i) - 1)}{2}e_0. \tag{11}$$

On the other hand, truthfulness should guarantee that a bidder is not able to increase its utility by lying about the battery state. The basic principle to achieve truthfulness is that the payment for a bidder should be determined by the allocation result only, regardless of its own bid. Although the most famous Vickrey-Clarke-Groves (VCG) mechanism guarantees truthfulness while achieves a socially optimal solution, the calculation for the allocation/payment is NP-hard in general case [12–14]. Another truthful auction model for one-parameter agents is *Myerson Principle* [15], which is widely applied in auction design work [16,17]. Myerson principle point out that: (1) the payment for i is non-decreasing in b_i, and (2) the payment *charged* (or *paid* in reverse auction) is independent of b_i for a fixed $\mathbf{B}_{-i}$, e.g., the payment model formulated as follows when allocation rule has monotone property.

$$p_i(b_i, \mathbf{B}_{-i}) = b_i q_i(b_i, \mathbf{B}_{-i}) + \int_{b_i}^{+\infty} q_i(b_i, (B)_{-i}) du. \tag{12}$$

In wireless streaming scenario, the cost of a bidder is considered as the energy consumption for D2D broadcast. Under the constraint of individual rationality (11), the auctioneer should pay more for a bidder which announces a smaller $\hat{E}$ and win a slot for D2D broadcast. Intuitively, the auctioneer is willing to allocate more slots to the bidder with larger announced battery state, in order to minimize the total payment. Based on this we define the monotonicity of allocation rule.

Definition 3 *(Monotonicity of Allocation Rule). In any frame of the auction, for any bidder i, with the bids of other bidders $\mathbf{B}_{-i}$ is fixed. Consider two bids $b_i^1 = (\hat{E}_{i,1})$ and $b_i^2 = (\hat{E}_{i,2})$ of bidder i, where $\hat{E}_{i,1} \geq \hat{E}_{i,2}$. An allocation rule is monotone if*

$$q_i(\hat{E}_{i,1}) \geq q_i(\hat{E}_{i,2}) \tag{13}$$

Based on the monotone property and inspired by the Myerson principle, we design the payment rule in the following theorem to implement a truthful auction. Specially, considering that the variable of energy state in the announced bid is discrete instead of continuous, we extending the Myerson model to the discrete case, which will also simplify the calculation of allocation and payment rule.

Theorem 1. *An auction with allocation rule and payment rule (q, p) is truthful if (a) the allocation rule is monotone; and (b) the payment rule is represented as the following.*

$$p_i(\hat{E}_i) = q_i(\hat{E}_i)(1 - \hat{E}_i) + \frac{q_i(\hat{E}_i)(q_i(\hat{E}_i) - 1)}{2} e_0 + \sum_{k=1}^{\hat{E}_i/e_0} q_i(ke_0) e_0. \tag{14}$$

Proof. Due to the page limitation, we give the sketch of the proof.

For any bidder i and its real battery state E_i, an auction is truthfulness if and only if $u_i(q_i(E_i), p_i(E_i)) \geq u_i(q_i(\hat{E}_i), p_i(\hat{E}_i))$ for any $\hat{E}_i$ in $[0, 1]$.

Based on the definition of utility (2) and the above payment rule (14), we give the utility of bidder i under announced E_i and $\hat{E}_i$ respectively as follows.

$$u_i(q_i(E_i), p_i(E_i)) = p_i(E_i) - F(q_i(E_i), E_i) = \sum_{k=1}^{E_i/e_0} q_i(ke_0) e_0 \tag{15}$$

$$u_i(q_i(\hat{E}_i), p_i(\hat{E}_i)) = p_i(\hat{E}_i) - F(q_i(\hat{E}_i), E_i) = q_i(\hat{E}_i)(E_i - \hat{E}_i) + \sum_{k=1}^{\hat{E}_i/e_0} q_i(ke_0)e_0$$
(16)

Since bidder i are provided an additional payment $\sum_{k=1}^{\hat{E}_i/e_0} q_i(ke_0)e_0$, we can shown that the utility is maximum when i announces its real battery state.

(i): If bidder i announces a larger battery state, i.e., $\hat{E}_i \geq E_i$, then we have:

$$u_i(q_i(E_i), p_i(E_i)) - u_i(q_i(\hat{E}_i), p_i(\hat{E}_i)) \geq q_i(\hat{E}_i)(\hat{E}_i - E_i) - \frac{\hat{E}_i - E_i}{e_0} q_i(\hat{E}_i)e_0 = 0$$
(17)

where the inequality follows according to (15) and (16); and the monotonicity of allocation rule such that $q_i(\hat{E}_i) \geq q_i(ke_0)$ for any $E_i/e_0 + 1 \leq k \leq \hat{E}_i/e_0$.

(ii): If bidder i announces a smaller battery state, i.e., $\hat{E}_i \leq E_i$, similarly we have:

$$u_i(q_i(E_i), p_i(E_i)) - u_i(q_i(\hat{E}_i), p_i(\hat{E}_i)) \geq \frac{E_i - \hat{E}_i}{e_0} q_i(\hat{E}_i)e_0 - q_i(\hat{E}_i)(E_i - \hat{E}_i) = 0$$
(18)

This completes the proof.

4.2 Auction Algorithm

Section 4.1 provides a guideline for truthfulness in auction. However, to design a practical auction, the following two questions should be considered: (1) How to decide the allocation scheme, e.g. allocating slots in each frame to which bidders for D2D transmissions? (2) How to maintain the budget balance of the auctioneer for handling the auction process?

Deciding the Allocation Scheme. Under the design principle proposed in Theorem 1, the truthfulness guarantees that all bidders reveal their true battery state to the auctioneer. Therefore, if we follow the constraints that (a) the allocation rule is monotone; and (b) the corresponding payment rule as (14), then we can see E_i of any bidder i as known for the auctioneer.

The objective of the auction is minimizing the payment cost of the auctioneer, as shown in (10).

From the perspective of energy, for bidder i with battery state E_i, let $\overline{p_i(E_i)}$ be the payment per slots provided to bidder i. Based on (14), we have:

$$\overline{p_i(E_i)} = 1 - E_i + \left(\frac{q_i(E_i) - 1}{2} + \frac{\sum_{k=1}^{E_i/e_0} q_i(ke_0)}{q_i(E_i)}\right)e_0.$$
(19)

In frame k, to decode segment $k + 1$ for all MUs, the summation of the number of chunks should be received over D2D network is $NS - \sum_{i \in \mathcal{N}} a_i^{k+1}$, where a_i^{k+1} is the number of chunks have been downloaded via B2D links at the beginning of frame k. In our algorithm, the auctioneer allocate slot by slot, until all bidders can decoded the original segment or there is no slot for allocated. When the auctioneer allocates one slots for D2D broadcast, the value that the payment divides the number of chunks received over the D2D network should be minimized. Suppose the auctioneer have allocated first $l-1$ slot, and is deciding the allocation of slot l. Let $\tilde{a}_i^{k+1}$ be current number of chunks in j, and $\tilde{d}_{i,j}^{k+1}$ be number of chunks that bidder j have received from bidder i. By denoting $\Delta_{i,j}$ as the number of useful chunks that bidder j can receive if bidder i broadcast in the next slot, we have:

$$\Delta_{i,j} = \min\{S - \tilde{a}_j^{k+1}, r^D t_S(1 - p_{i,j}), a_i^{k+1} - \tilde{d}_{i,j}^{k+1}\} \tag{20}$$

Let Δ_i be the total number of chunks received over D2D network if bidder i broadcasts in the next slot, and p_i^c be the payment per chunks received over D2D network. Then, we have:

$$\Delta_i = \sum_{j \in \mathcal{N}} \Delta_{i,j} \tag{21}$$

$$p_i^c = \frac{\overline{p_i(E_i)}}{\Delta_i} = \frac{1 - E_i}{\Delta_i} + \left(\frac{q_i(E_i) - 1}{2} + \frac{\sum_{k=1}^{E_i/e_0} q_i(ke_0)}{q_i(E_i)}\right)\frac{e_0}{\Delta_i} \tag{22}$$

Notice that notation p_i^c is used to determine the allocation priorities, but not the actually payment. Therefore, we use $p_i^c = \frac{1-E_i}{\Delta_i}$ for approximation, which greatly simplifies the calculation while maintains the monotonicity of allocation rule. Based on this, we design a greedy allocation rule, which has the process as follows: initialize $\tilde{a}_i^{k+1}$ as a_i^{k+1} and $\tilde{d}_{i,j}^{k+1}$ as 0; calculate p_i^c for any bidder i based on (20), (21) and (22); find the bidder Alo with smallest p_i^c for D2D broadcast; update $\tilde{a}_i^{k+1} = \tilde{a}_i^{k+1} + \Delta_{Alo,i}^{k+1}$ and $\tilde{d}_{Alo,i}^{k+1} = \tilde{d}_{Alo,i}^{k+1} + \Delta_{Alo,i}^{k+1}$; repeat the above process until all bidders have cached S chunks or there is no slot to allocated.

Budget Balance. To maintain the budget balance, the auctioneer procures some virtual currency for providing convenience of D2D transmission at the beginning of each frame. Without loss of fairness, each mobile user is charge by

$$p^{ave} = \frac{\sum_{i \in \mathcal{N}} p_i(E_i)}{N}, \tag{23}$$

where $p_i(E_i)$ is derived by (14), and $q_i(E_i)$ is derived by the allocation rule described in Sect. 4.2.

Auction Algorithm in Auctioneer for Wireless Streaming. At the auction initialization stage of frame k, each bidder i sends the current cache state a_i^{k+1} to the auctioneer. After that, each mobile device i generates a bid b_i based on its real battery state E_i and submits b_i to the auctioneer. According to the auction mechanism described above, the auctioneer decides the allocation $q_i(E_i)$ and the payment $p_i(E_i)$ for each bidder i. Meanwhile, the auctioneer also derives p^{ave} and charges that from each bidders. The details of the algorithm are presented in Algorithm 1, which is executed periodically in each frame.

Algorithm 1. Auction Algorithm for Wireless Live Streaming

Input: $S, \mathcal{N}, Q, \{a_i^{k+1}\}, \{E_i\} \{r_{i,j}\}$
  1: $\tilde{a}_i^{k+1} \leftarrow a_i^{k+1}, \tilde{d}_{i,j}^{k+1} \leftarrow 0, q_i(E_i) \leftarrow 0$;
  2: **while** $\exists i, \tilde{a}_i^{k+1} \leq S$ and $\sum_{i \in \mathcal{N}} q_i(E_i) \leq Q$ **do**
  3:    $\Delta_{i,j}, \Delta_i, p_i^c \leftarrow$ according to equations (20), (21) and (22);
  4:    $Alo \leftarrow$ bidder index of the smallest p_i^c;
  5:    $q_{Alo}(E_{Alo}) \leftarrow q_{Alo}(E_{Alo}) + 1$;
  6:    $\tilde{a}_i^{k+1} = \tilde{a}_i^{k+1} + \Delta_{Alo,i}^{k+1}, \tilde{d}_{Alo,i}^{k+1} = \tilde{d}_{Alo,i}^{k+1} + \Delta_{Alo,i}^{k+1}$;
  7: **end while**
  8: **for** $k = 1$ to E_i/e_0 **do**
  9:    $q_i(ke_0) \leftarrow$ according to run line 1-7 with replacing E_i by ke_0;
 10: **end for**
 11: $p_i(E_i) \leftarrow$ according to equation (14);
 12: $p^{ave} \leftarrow \frac{\sum_{i \in \mathcal{N}} p_i(E_i)}{N}$;
 13: broadcast p^{ave} and (q, p) to all bidders;
 14: charge p^{ave} for each bidder;
 15: wait until the end of the frame (schedule the D2D transmission based on allocation rule q);
 16: send $p_i(E_i)$ payment for each bidder;

Theorem 2. *Algorithm 1 implements an truthful auction.*

Proof. The order of p_i^c affects the allocation result in Algorithm 1. Since $p_i^c = \frac{1-E_i}{\Delta_i}$ is decreasing with E_i, the number of slots allocated to user i is non-decreasing with E_i when other parameters are fixed. Therefore, the monotone with allocation rule is guaranteed. Based on Theorem 1, we can see that Algorithm 1 implements an truthful auction.

Theorem 3. *Algorithm 1 can run in $O(QEN^2)$, where Q is the number of slots in one frame and $E = 1/e_0$.*

Proof. The time complexity for calculating Δ_i is $O(N)$. Thus, it takes $O(N^2)$ time to find the smallest p^c. Considering the while loop (Line 2–7) and for loop (Line 8–10) in Algorithm 1, smallest p^c is calculated at most QE times. Therefore, the time complexity of Algorithm 1 is $O(QEN^2)$.

5   Simulation Results

To demonstrate the effectiveness of our proposed incentive mechanism, we consider the term of playback continuity of mobile users, which is the ratio between the duration of the video and the actual viewing time of the video. When video is smoothly played, the ratio is 1; and otherwise it is less than 1 because of rebufferring to download enough data. When the data rate of B2D links are limited and not adequate to receive enough chunks for decoding the original video, playback continuity indicates the degree of cooperation between mobile users. On the other hand, to verify the economic efficiency of the proposed auction

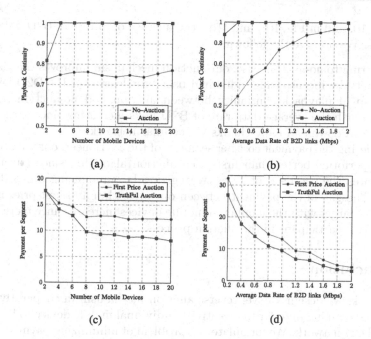

Fig. 4. The comparisons in term of **playback continuity/payment per segment** with the variation of **the number of mobile devices** and **the average data rate of B2D links**.

mechanism, we consider the term of payment per frame, which is the total payment that the auctioneer should provide during one frame. Since the payment is collected from all mobile users participated in the wireless streaming service, the total payment is the cost of the auctioneer and also indicates the economic efficiency of all participator.

In auction based incentive mechanism, two mainly parameters that affect the playback continuity and the payment are the number of mobile devices and the average data rate of B2D links. The number of mobile devices affects the cooperation opportunities via D2D transmission, and the average data rate of B2D links affects the number of chunks downloaded by each mobile devices via cellular links. In the following simulation results, we vary one parameter and fix another, and present the average results of 20 times for each parameter setting.

Live streaming scenario. First, we consider a group of users have synchronous playback offset of a video. We present the results in Fig. 4, where Fig. 4(a) and 4(b) present the comparison in term of playback continuity between auction case and no-auction case with the variation of the number of mobile devices and the data rate of B2D links; and Fig. 4(c) and 4(d) present the comparison in terms of payment per segment between our auction algorithm and first-price auction mechanism with the variation of these parameters. The first-price auction mechanism is a trivial untruthful auction such that the payment for the winner is the bid of itself. In Fig. 4(a) and 4(c), the number of mobile devices is 10, and in Fig. 4(b) and 4(d), the average data rate of B2D links is set as 1 Mbps. We observe the following:

- Comparing to no-auction case, our auction mechanism improves the playback continuity by incentivizing individual user broadcast over the D2D network. The gap of playback continuity between auction and no-auction becomes smaller with the average data rate of B2D links increasing since each mobile device can download more chunks via cellular network.
- Considering the payment cost per segment of the auctioneer, our auction algorithm performs better than first-price auction algorithm since truthfulness eliminates the overhead of users strategizing by announcing unreal battery state. The gap of the payment between our algorithm and first price auction becomes larger with the number of mobile devices increase, since more mobile device are participant in the auction process.

6 Conclusion

In this work, we design a novel reverse auction mechanism in cooperative wireless video streaming in order to incentivize individual mobile device to broadcast over the D2D network. We formulate the problem of minimizing payment cost of the auctioneer in the auction mechanism, and transform the optimization problem into functions design problem for payment rule and allocation rule. Then, we derive the relationship between allocation rule and payment rule to achieve truthfulness, and design the corresponding transmission scheduling algorithm over the D2D network. Finally, we demonstrate the effectiveness and economic robustness of our proposed auction mechanism though extensive simulations.

Acknowledgements. This work is supported by the science and technology project of State Grid Corporation of China "Research and application of dynamic access control technology for power Internet of things based on business scenarios" (Grand No. 5700-202013189A-0-0-00).

References

1. Seferoglu, H., Keller, L., Cici, L., Le, A., Markopoulou, A.: Cooperative video streaming on smartphones. In Proceedings of the Allerton (2011)
2. Keller, L., Le, L., Cici, B., Seferoglu, H., Fragouli, C., Markopoulou, A.: MicroCast: cooperative video streaming on smartphones. In: Proceedings of the ACM MobiSys (2012)
3. Abedini, N., Sampath, S., Bhattacharyya, R., Paul, S., Shakkottai, S.: Realtime streaming with guaranteed QoS over wireless D2D networks. In: Proceedings of ACM MobiHoc (2013)
4. Chen, Y.C., Towsley, D., Khalili, R.: MSPlayer: multi-source and multi-path video streaming. IEEE J. Select. Areas Commun. **34**(8), 2198–2206 (2016)
5. Chen, L., Shen, C., Zhou, P., Xu, J.: Collaborative service placement for edge computing in dense small cell networks. IEEE Trans. Mobile Comput. **20**(2), 377–390 (2021)

6. Chen, C., Berry, R.A., Honig, M.L., Subramanian, V.G.: The impact of unlicensed access on small-cell resource allocation. IEEE J. Select. Areas Commun. **38**(4), 685–696 (2020)
7. Qu, Z., Ye, B., Tang, B., Guo, S., Lu, S., Zhuang, W.: Cooperative caching for multiple bitrate videos in small cell edges. IEEE Trans. Mob. Comput. **19**(2), 288–299 (2020)
8. Chu, X., Zhao, K., Li, Z., Mahanti, A.: Auction-based on-demand P2P min-cost media streaming with network coding. IEEE Trans. Parallel Distrib. Syst. **20**(12), 1816–1829 (2009)
9. Wu, C., Li, Z., Qiu, X., Lau, F.C.M.: Auction-based P2P VoD streaming: incentives and optimal scheduling. ACM Trans. Multim. Comput. Commun. Appl. **85**(1), 1–22 (2021)
10. Katti, S., Rahul, H., Hu, W., Katabi, D., Médard, M., Crowcroft, J.: XORs in the air: practical wireless network coding. In: Proceedings of ACM SIGCOMM (2006)
11. Ho, T., Médard, M., Koetter, R., Karger, D.R., Effros, M., Shi, J., Leong, B.: A random linear network coding approach to multicast. IEEE Trans. Inf. Theory **52**(10), 4413–4430 (2006)
12. Vickrey, W.: Counterspeculation, auctions, and competitive sealed tenders. J. Fin. **16**(1), 8–37 (1961)
13. Clarke, E.H.: Multipart pricing of public goods. Public Choice **11**, 17–33 (1971). https://doi.org/10.1007/BF01726210
14. Groves, T.: Incentives in teams. Econometrica **41**(4), 617–631 (1973)
15. Myerson, R.B.: Optimal auction design. Math. Oper. Res. **6**, 58–73 (1981)
16. Zhao, J., Chu, X., Liu, H., Leung, Y.-W., Li, Z.: Online procurement auctions for resource pooling in client-assisted cloud storage systems. In: Proceedings of IEEE INFOCOM (2015)
17. Hajiesmaili, M.H., Deng, L., Chen, M., Zongpeng, L.: Incentivizing device-to-device load balancing for cellular networks: an online auction design. IEEE J. Select. Areas Commun. **35**(2), 265–279 (2017)

A Fine-Tuning Strategy Based on Real Scenes in Gait Identification

Xianggang Zhang[1]([✉]) [iD], Jing Zeng[1], and Guoyu Wang[2] [iD]

[1] University of Electronic Science and Technology of China, Chengdu 611731, China
csxgzhang@uestc.edu.cn
[2] West China Second University Hospital, Sichuan University,
Chengdu 610041, China

Abstract. Many medical studies have shown that human gait has individuality. As a biometric technology, gait can be used for human identity recognition. Gait has many valuable features in human recognition, such as not easy to forge, not to touch and not disturbed. However, the gait recognition technology based on inertial sensor is difficult to be applied to the actual scene. The reason is that models, algorithms and parameters are generated from specific training data sets, most of which come from the laboratory. So they can't adapt to the real and unrestricted situation. This paper aims to explore the method of gait recognition model to quickly adapt to different real scene. Firstly, a network model for gait recognition was designed based on convolutional neural network (CNN), including model structure and parameters. Secondly, in gait identification using mobile phones, the most frequently changed scenes are motion mode and placement position. The movement patterns (such as walking on a flat road and going upstairs) and sensor placement will bring different gait characteristics. In this paper, we explored which parts of the model realized the extraction and recognition of these features. The scene features of this paper mainly included: movement patterns and sensor placement position. Further, based on the hypothesis of motion combination, we studied the directionality of model transfer. Experiments showed that some layers of the model were closely related to identity recognition, while others were not related to identity recognition. Based on this conclusion, only fine tuning the relevant layer could obtain similar accuracy and shorten convergence time. Secondly, the direction of transfer could also affect the recognition accuracy.

Keywords: Gait · Person identification · Convolutional neural network · Transfer learning

1 Introduction

Due to the popularity of portable smart devices (such as mobile phones), the security of smart devices and their private data has attracted wearer's close attention. Therefore, establishing a more comprehensive identification mechanism is

G. Wang et al. (Eds.): UbiSec 2021, CCIS 1557, pp. 336–350, 2022.
https://doi.org/10.1007/978-981-19-0468-4_25

becoming an urgent need. For example, when the mobile phone is lost, the owner hope that the mobile phone can automatically lock or protect it.

Medical and psychological research showed that everyone's gait had unique features. Gait recognition refers to person identity recognition based on gait features. It has the characteristics of not easy to forge, non-contact recognition, implicit and so on. Gait has become a new biometric for person identity recognition. At present, gait-based identification technology mainly includes two categories: one is based on video data; The other is based on wearable sensors.

This paper studies gait identification technology based on acceleration sensors. Specifically, in this paper, we collected the signal of the inherent acceleration sensor of the mobile phone and established a gait identification application based on the acceleration signal. We used it as a supplement to other person identificaiton technologies in order to strengthen privacy protection on mobile phone. However, in the process of achieving this overall goal, there is a difficult problem, that is, the recognition model and algorithm generated by specific training data can not adapt to the changing real scene. For example, the used environment of our mobile phones is constantly changing, such as wearer's movement, road conditions and the placement of mobile phones. There is a large gap in data from different environments. A model based on a kind of data does not work effectively in another environment. Moreover, it is difficult to train a high-precision recognition model suitable for various environments according to various data.

Therefore, the idea of this paper is that the recognition model can quickly adapt to the changing environment. For example, users with mobile phones are sometimes walking, sometimes going upstairs and downstairs, and sometimes running. The recognition model needs to quickly generate the recognition model of the new environment from the general recognition model. For another example, the mobile phone will be placed in different parts of the body by the user, sometimes in the hand, sometimes at the waist, and sometimes in the trouser pocket. The method of this paper is to find out the relationship between the model and environmental variables. When environmental variables change, the general model adopts transfer learning technology to realize rapid adaptation.

These environment variables should be easy to monitor. This paper will mainly study two scene elements, namely wearer's movement pattern and placement position of the sensors. In this paper, we will study which part of the recognition model plays a key role of person identification in changing scenes. Then, the corresponding parts of the recognition model are quickly adjusted according to the changing environmental characteristics, so as to quickly adapt to different scenarios even if there are only small samples.

The main chapters of this paper are as follows. The related works are introduced in the second part. A gait recognition model based on CNN is designed in the third part. In the fourth part, we explore which parts of the model extract and recognize the gait features brought by placement and activity patterns. Based on these findings, some optimized transfer strategies could be designed. At the same time, based on the composition of motion, the transfer direction of the model can also improve the convergence speed of the model. The last part is the conclusion.

2   Related Works

From the beginning of the 21st century, gait identification based on wearable sensors has been studied by many scholars. The gait recognition systems using acceleration sensors are mainly based on three class of technologies. Namely: (1) similar matching; (2) classification based on machine learning; (3) Deep Neural Network.

The method of similarity matching was usually based on distance measurement or correlation measurement. In this method, the collected gait data were compared with the stored gait template. Then the user's identity was recognized according to the score of similarity.

The similarity measurement of gait data include: histogram similarity, Manhattan distance [1], Euclidean distance [6], correlation coefficient [4], Tanimoto distance [3] and Hamming distance [28], cosine distance [2]. In some literatures, some advanced measurement methods are introduced. They include: dynamic time warping (DTW), Derivative algorithm based on DTW [9], Cyclic Rotation Metric CRM [26], cycle matching using the fusion of multiple similarity scores of Min rule [32], a statistical Measure of Similarity (MOS) [37], fuzzy finite state machine rules [14], Jaccard distance [11], sparse-code collection (CSCC) [34], weighted voting scheme [13], Geometric Template Matching [38], Box approximation geometry [36], weighted Pearson correlation coefficients [33], curve aligning [16], computational theory of perceptions [14], statistical significance analysis [37], Gaussian membership functions [14], and etc.

The recognition algorithms based on machine learning are the classification process. Machine learning methods usually use gait features to train recognition models. Then the training recognition models are used for classification prediction. At present, most of the methods based on machine learning are supervised learning, and some advanced algorithms in unsupervised learning are also used for gait recognition. But they need experimental verification. Machine learning methods in gait recognition include: KNN (nearest neighbour) [30], support vector machines (SVM) [29], decision trees (DT) [35], random forests [25,31], neural networks [18], hidden Markov model (HMM) classifier [22,27], Gaussian mixture model (GMM) classifier [10], logistic regression [17], Bayesian network classifiers [23]. Other advanced methods are also mentioned, such as Linear Discriminant Analysis (LDA) [15], I-vector approach [7], principal component analysis (PCA) [12,21], Fisher discriminant analysis [20], Gradient-Boosted Trees [39], spare-code collection [34], Gaussian Mixture Model-Universal Background Model GMM-UBM [19] etc.

Compared with the former two, the research of gait identification based on deep neural network is relatively less. The main research is as follows. Dehzangi Omid and etc. designed a deep convolutional neural network (DCNN) learning to extract discriminative features from the 2D expanded gait cycles and jointly optimized the identification model [40]. Gadaleta, Matteo presented a system named IDNet. IDNet was the first system that exploited a deep learning approach as universal feature extractors for gait recognition, and that combined classification results from subsequent walking cycles into a multi-stage decision making framework [41].

3   Proposed Approach

3.1   Structure of Network HIR-Net

In our convolution network model (HIR-Net), a five-layer convolution network structure was adopted. Each layer contained one-dimensional convolution and Activation Function (Relu). The first three layers were appended the maximum pooling. The last layer was appended batch regularization and dropout operation. Finally, the final recognition was carried out through a full connection layer. The convolution layers were used to extract deep spatial and temporal features. The structure of the model was shown in Fig. 1 and the model parameters were shown in Table 1.

Table 1. HIR-net model hyper-parameters

Parameter	Value	Parameter	Value
CNN kernel number	96-256-384-384-256	Optimization method	Adam
CNN kernel size	7	Regularization coefficient	0.0001
Network layers	5	Initial learning rate	0.001
Pooling size	2	Beta_1	0.9
Dropout value	0.5	Beta_2	0.999
Batchsize	128	Epsilon	1E–08

3.2   Transfer Strategies of HIR-Net Model

Generally, the first convolutional layer of the CNN model extracts small scale features. There are equivariant representations between different layers. So the extracted features from the deeper convolution layer are closely related to large scale features. The extracted features from the deeper convolution layer are closely related to specific tasks.

The wearer's movement mode and placement of cellphone are the most common factors affecting gait characteristics. In this paper, we tried to find out which layers got the features related to person identification in various states. The detailed processes were explained in the section experiment.

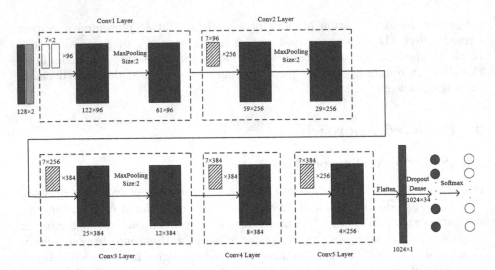

Fig. 1. Stucture of architecture

4   Experiments

4.1   Data Acquisition and Preprocessing

(1) Tester and Environment

The age distribution of 34 testers was between 22 and 27 years old. There were 18 males and 16 females. The height and weight of male were 163 cm–181 cm and 52 kg–82 kg respectively. The height and weight of women were 150 cm–169 cm and 43 kg–58 kg respectively. Pants were sports pants or jeans. The test environment is indoor. Four Android mobile phones (Huawei glory V8, oppo find5, red rice Note1, Meizu pro5) were selected for the data-collecting devices. The data acquisition time was 1 min.

(2) Normalization and Filtering

The original data obtained from the accelerometer were the x-y-z triaxial acceleration. The original data were normalized in G (one acceleration of gravity). The formula 1 took the acceleration of X axis as an example. $OAccx_i$ was originalrunning, going upstairs data and $Accx_i$ was normalized data.

$$Accx_i = \frac{OAccx_i}{9.8\,m/s^2}g \tag{1}$$

(3) Organization of Data

In order to avoid the difference of X-Y-Z axis data caused by orientation of the phones, two kinds of direction independent features were adopted in this paper. They were defined in formula 3 and formula 4. $Acc_i = (Accx_i, Accy_i, Accz_i)$ was the acceleration data of the i-th sampling, which including X-Y-Z axis data. $Accg_i = (Accgx_i, Accgy_i, Accgz_i)$ was the gravitational acceleration data of the i-th sampling, which including X-Y-Z axis data. $Accu_i = (Accux_i, Accuy_i, Accuz_i)$ was the wearer's acceleration data of the i-th sampling, which including X-Y-Z axis data. $Accux_i, Accuy_i, Accuz_i$ are defined in formula 4. The data, inputing to model, contained two dimensional components, which were $< Acct_i, Accp_i >$

$$Acct_i = \sqrt{Accx_i^2 + Accy_i^2 + Accz_i^2} \qquad (2)$$

$$Accp_i = Accxu_i \times Accxg_i + Accyu_i \times Accyg_i + Acczu_i \times Acczg_i \qquad (3)$$

$$Accux_i = Accx_i - Accgx_i, Accuy_i = Accy_i - Accgy_i, Accuz_i = Accz_i - Accgz_i \qquad (4)$$

(4) Data segmentation

The collected data were time series data with a long period of time. In sample preparation, we used sliding window to segment time series data. In the following chapter, we would determine the size of sliding window by experiments. The size of the sliding window is 128 sample points.

4.2 Test Method

Firstly, the data domain was divided into source domain and target domain. In each test, we first trained the model on the source domain, and then transfered the model from the source domain to the target domain. In order to find the layer which has the strongest correlation with the specific environmental factors in the network model, the parameters of some layers were fixed while other layers could be fine tuned. Then, according to the convergence rate and accuracy of the model, the layers with strongest correlation to the specific environmental factors were found out.

4.3 Transfering on Movement Pattern

A person's movement pattern (such as walking or running) is randomness and individual. In daily living, movement patterns always change. The dataset in this section contains four movements, i.e. walking, running, going upstairs and going downstairs. We took the gait data collected during the walking as the source domain dataset and the data collected from the other three movement patterns as the target domain dataset. The data set of the source domain contained the data collected from 34 subjects when they walk, and the data set of the target domain contained the data collected from 34 subjects when they run, went upstairs and went downstairs. The collection environment was indoor. The sensors were placed at the waist. The comparison of experimental elements between source domain and target domain was listed in Table 2. The goal of the experiment was to find the layers which had the strongest correlation with person identificaiton in changing movement pattern.

Firstly, the model was trained in the source domain dataset. Then the model was tranfered to the target domain dataset. In Fig. 2, Fig. 3, and Fig. 4, the notion $finetune\_X+$ represents the parameters of all layers were imported from the source domain model and the parameters of layers before X were fixed in the target training. i.e.: The parameters of layers after X (including layer X) would be tuned in the target training. Such as, $finetune\_4+$ indicates that the parameters of layer 1, layer 2 and layer 3 were imported from the source domain model and fixed during the training on the target domain. The parameters of the latter layers would be tuned in the target training. The notion $base\_mode$ represents retraining the model in the target domain dataset from parameters initialized randomly.

The belows can be seen from Fig. 2, Fig. 3, and Fig. 4. Firstly, when the source domain model was directly used for prediction on the target data set, the prediction performance was very poor. As shown in curve notion $finetune6+$.

Secondly, the method based on transfer learning can better adapt to different movement patterns and converged faster. As can be seen from Fig. 2, Fig. 3, and Fig. 4, the performance of curve notion as $base\_modal$ was poor.

Third, $finetune\_1+$, $finetune\_2+$, $finetune\_3+$ have very similar performance. Therefore, we believed that the small-scale features extracted from the first two layers had little relationship with identity recognition under different motion modes. The features related to identity recognition mainly were the further combination of the previous features. The three layers and the back layers of the model got the identity features in different motion modes.

Therefore, when the model needs to switch between different motion models, the transfer strategy of fixing the first two layers can be adopted. This fine tuning strategy would not reduce the recognition rate, and could shorten the convergence time.

Table 2. Data set of transfering on movement patterns

Data sets	Labels	Activity	Location
Souce domain data	Person's ID	Walking	Waist
Target domain data 1	Person's ID	Run	Waist
Target domain data 2	Person's ID	Unstair	Waist
Target domain data 3	Person's ID	Downstair	Waist

4.4   Transfering on Placement of Mobile Phone

The mobile phone are often placed in different positions of the body. For example, mobile phones are sometimes held by hand, sometimes put on the waist, and sometimes put in the trouser pocket. Therefore, it is very meaningful to study the model to quickly adapt to the data collected from different placement.

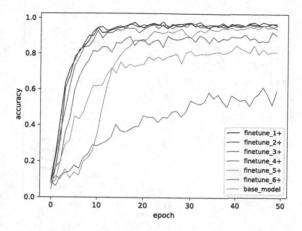

Fig. 2. Fine tune on running data

In this paper, we used four placement positions (waist, upper arm, trouser pocket and hand). The source domain dataset contains data collected from the phone on waist. The target domain dataset contains data collected from phones placed in the other three locations (i.e. upper arm, trouser pocket and hand). Both the source domain dataset and the target domain dataset contain data collected from 34 subjects when walking. The comparison of experimental elements between the source domain dataset and the target domain dataset was listed in Table 3.

Table 3. Data set of transfering on placed position

Data sets	Labels	Activity	Location
Souce domain data	Person's ID	Walking	Waist
Target domain data 1	Person's ID	Walking	Upper arm
Target domain data 2	Person's ID	Walking	Trouser pocket
Target domain data 3	Person's ID	Walking	Hand

From Fig. 5, Fig. 6, and Fig. 7, we could get similar results. Firstly, when the source domain model was directly used for prediction on the target data set, the prediction performance was very poor. As shown in curve notion $finetune6+$.

Secondly, the method based on transfer learning can better adapt to different placement position. As can be seen from Fig. 5, Fig. 6, and Fig. 7, the performance of curve notion as $base\_modal$ was not the best ones.

Thirdly, $finetune\_1+$, $finetune\_2+$, $finetune\_3+$ have very similar performance. Therefore, we believed that the small-scale features extracted from the first two convolution layers had little relationship with identity recognition. When the parameters of the first two layers were fixed, the migrated model could achieve similar performance. The features related to identity recognition

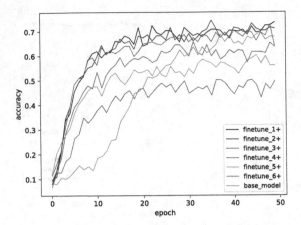

Fig. 3. Fine tune on upstairs data

are mainly the further combination of previous features. The third layer and the back layers of the model obtain the identity features. As can be seen from the figure, if we chosed to fix the first two layers, we could obtain good performance in most cases.

Therefore, when the model needs to adapt to the data collected from different positions, the transfer strategy of fixing the first two layers can be adopted. This fine tuning strategy would not reduce the recognition rate, and could shorten the convergence time.

4.5   Transfering Based on Motion Composition

Firstly, if the acceleration data was directly input into the model trained with different position data, the recognition rate was very low. This conclusion could be seen from the Table 4.

Secondly, from the perspective of human physiological structure and behavior, the movement of different parts of the human body is related to each other. For example, hand motion can be regarded as a combination of waist motion and arm motion relative to the waist. Therefore, we believed that the data collected from the hands contained the characteristics of the waist data. We tested this hypothesis from two aspects.

In this paper, we inputed the waist data into the hand model to test its accuracy. At the same time, we inputed the hand data into the waist model for accuracy test. We compared the above two accuracy rates. Because the hand motion includes the waist motion, the recognition rate obtained by inputting the waist data into the hand model was higher than that obtained by inputting the hand data into the waist model.

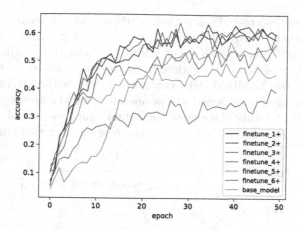

Fig. 4. Fine tune on downstairs data

Table 4. The data set of different parts are directly input into the trained model

	Model from uparm data	Model from waist data	Model from hand data
Data from uparm	92.43%	21.42%	19.32%
Data from waist	20.58%	94.53%	7.58%
Data from hand	10.08%	5.04%	91.57%

We used the waist data to fine tune the hand model (i.e. the hand model was transfered to the waist model) to test the accuracy. At the same time, we used the hand data to fine tune the waist model (i.e. the waist model was transfered

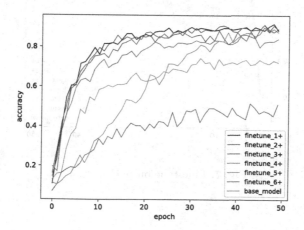

Fig. 5. Fine tune on hand data

to the hand model) to test the accuracy. Furthermore, we compared the above two accuracy rates. The results were shown in the Fig. 8 and Fig. 9. As can be seen from the figure, the effect of migrating from the handheld model to the waist model was better than that from the waist model to the handheld model. Because the handheld data contains the characteristic information of waist data, the convergence speed was accelerated and the accuracy was higher; On the contrary, the waist data does not contain some details of the handheld data and lacks corresponding features, so the reverse migration effect was poor.

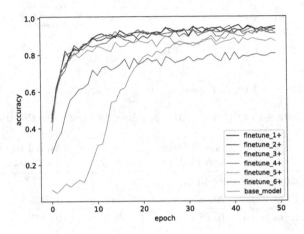

Fig. 6. Fine tune on uparm data

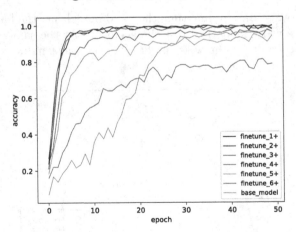

Fig. 7. Fine tune on pocket data

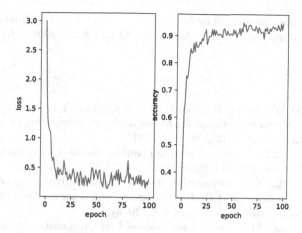

Fig. 8. Transfering from hand to waist

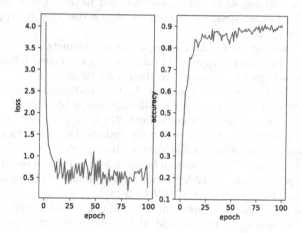

Fig. 9. Transfering from waist to hand

5   Conclusion

The automatic feature extraction ability of convolutional neural network is more suitable for extracting hidden personality features from gait data. In order to make the recognition model quickly adapt to a variety of data sets, in this paper, we explored the rapid adaptation technology based on fine tuning. We explored which parts of the model extracted and identified gait features related to placement and activity patterns. Based on these findings, some optimized fine tuning strategies could be designed. At the same time, based on the superposition of motion, the transfer direction of the model could also improve the convergence speed and accuracy of the model.

Acknowledgments. Supported by Department of Science and Technology of Sichuan Province. The Funding numbers are 2020YFS0083 and 2021YJ0081.

References

1. Ngo, T.T., Makihara, Y., Nagahara, H., Mukaigawa, Y., Yagi, Y.: Orientation-compensative signal registration for owner authentication using an accelerometer. lEICE Trans. Inf. Syst. 97(3), 541–553 (2016)
2. Zhong, Y., Deng, Y.: Sensor orientation invariant mobile gait biometrics. In: International Joint Conference on Biometrics, IJCB (2014)
3. Subramanian, R., et al.: Orientation invariant gait matching algorithm based on the Kabsch alignment. In: IEEE International Conference on Identity, Security and Behavior Analysis (ISBA 2015), pp. 1–8 (2015)
4. Sprager, S., Juric, M.B: Inertial sensor-based gait recognition: a review. Sensors 15(9), 22089–22127 (2015)
5. Johnston, A.H., Weiss, G.M.: Smartwatch-based biometric gait recognition. In: 2015 IEEE 7th International Conference on Biometrics Theory, Applications and Systems (BTAS), pp. 1–6 (2015)
6. Gafurov, D., Snekkkenes, E.: Arm swing as a weak biometric for unobtrusive user authentication. In: 2008 International Conference on Intelligent Information Hiding and Multimedia Signal Processing, pp. 1080–1087 (2008)
7. San-Segundo, R., Cordoba, R., Ferreiros, J., D'Haro-Enriquez, L.: Frequency features and GMM-UBM approach for gait-based person identification using smartphone inertial signals. Pattern Recogn. Lett. 73(April 1), 60–67 (2016)
8. Szegedy, C., et al.: Going deeper with convolutions. In: Proceedings of the IEEE Conference on Computer Vision and Pattern Recognition (2015)
9. Muaaz, M., Mayrhofer, R.: Orientation independent cell phone based gait authentication. In: Proceedings of the 12th International Conference on Advances in Mobile Computing and Multimedia, pp. 161–164 (2014)
10. Lu, H., Huang, J., Saha, T., Nachman, L.: Unobtrusive gait verification for mobile phones. In: Proceedings of the 2014 ACM International Symposium on Wearable Computers, pp. 91–98 (2014)
11. Damaševičius, R., Maskeliūnas, R., Venčkauskas, A., Woźniak, M.: Smartphone user identity verification using gait characteristics. Symmetry 8(10), 100 (2016)
12. Sprager, S., Zazula, D.: Impact of different walking surfaces on gait identification based on higher-order statistics of accelerometer data. In: 2011 IEEE International Conference on Signal and Image Processing Applications (ICSIPA), pp. 360–365 (2011)
13. Sun, B., Wang, Y., Banda, J.: Gait characteristic analysis and identification based on the iPhone's accelerometer and gyrometer. Sensors 14(9), 17037–17054 (2014)
14. Trivino, G., Alvarez-Alvarez, A., Bailador, G.: Application of the computational theory of perceptions to human gait pattern recognition. Pattern Recogn. 43(7), 2572–2581 (2010)
15. Lin, B.-S., Liu, Y.-T., Yu, C., Jan, G.E., Hsiao, B.-T.: Gait recognition and walking exercise intensity estimation. Int. J. Environ. Res. Public Health 11(4), 3822–3844 (2014)
16. Sun, H., Yuao, T.: Curve aligning approach for gait authentication based on a wearable accelerometer. Physiol. Meas. 33(6), 1111 (2012)

17. Primo, A., Phoha, V.V., Kumar, R., Serwadda, A.: Context-aware active authentication using smartphone accelerometer measurements. In: Proceedings of the IEEE Conference on Computer Vision and Pattern Recognition Workshops, pp. 98–105. Springer, New York (2014)
18. Mondal, S., Nandy, A., Chakraborty, P., Nandi, G.C.: Gait based personal identification system using rotation sensor. J. Emerg. Trends Comput. Inf. Sci. **3**(2), 395–402 (2012)
19. San-Segundo, R., Echeverry-Correa, J.D., Salamea-Palacios, C., Lutfi, S.L., Pardo, J.M.: I-vector analysis for gait-based person identification using smartphone inertial signals. Pervasive Mob. Comput. **38**, 140–153 (2017)
20. Kobayashi, T., Hasida, K., Otsu, N.: Rotation invariant feature extraction from 3-D acceleration signals. In: 2011 IEEE International Conference on Acoustics, Speech and Signal Processing (ICASSP), pp. 3684–3687 (2011)
21. Sprager, S., Zazula, D.: A cumulant-based method for gait identification using accelerometer data with principal component analysis and support vector machine. WSEAS Trans. Signal Process. **5**(11), 369–378 (2009)
22. Nickel, C., Brandt, H., Busch, C.: Benchmarking the performance of SVMs and HMMs for accelerometer-based biometric gait recognition. In: 2011 IEEE International Symposium on Signal Processing and Information Technology (ISSPIT), pp. 281–286 (2011)
23. Watanabe, Y.: Influence of holding smart phone for acceleration-based gait authentication. In: 2014 Fifth International Conference on Emerging Security Technologies, pp. 30–33 (2014)
24. Gafurov, D., Helkala, K., Søndrol, T.: Biometric gait authentication using accelerometer sensor. J. Comput. **1**(7), 51–59 (2006)
25. Frank, J., Mannor, S., Pineau, J., Precup, D.: Time series analysis using geometric template matching. IEEE Trans. Pattern Anal. Mach. Intell. **35**(3), 740–754 (2012)
26. Gafurov, D., Bours, P.: Improved hip-based individual recognition using wearable motion recording sensor. In: Security Technology, Disaster Recovery & Business Continuity-International Conferences, pp. 179–186 (2010)
27. Nickel, C., Busch, C.: Does a cycle-based segmentation improve accelerometer-based biometric gait recognition?. In: 2012 11th International Conference on Information Science, Signal Processing and their Applications (ISSPA), pp. 746–751 (2012)
28. Hoang, T., Choi, D., Nguyen, T.: Gait authentication on mobile phone using biometric cryptosystem and fuzzy commitment scheme. Int. J. Inf. Secur. **14**(6), 549–560 (2015). https://doi.org/10.1007/s10207-015-0273-1
29. Ren, Y., Chen, Y., Chuah, M.C., Yang, J.: User verification leveraging gait recognition for smartphone enabled mobile healthcare systems. IEEE Trans. Mob. Comput. **14**(9), 1961–1974 (2014)
30. Sprager, S., Juric, M.B: An efficient HOS-based gait authentication of accelerometer data. IEEE Trans. Inf. Forensics Secur. **10**(7), 1486–1498 (2015)
31. Zeng, Y., Pande, A., Zhu, J., Mohapatra, P.: WearIA: wearable device implicit authentication based on activity information. In: 2017 IEEE 18th International Symposium on A World of Wireless, Mobile and Multimedia Networks (WoW-MoM), pp. 1–9 (2017)
32. Gafurov, D., Snekkenes, E., Bours, P.: Improved gait recognition performance using cycle matching. In: 2010 IEEE 24th International Conference on Advanced Information Networking and Applications Workshops, pp. 836–841 (2010)

33. Ren, Y., Chen, Y., Chuah, M.C., Yang, J.: Smartphone based user verification leveraging gait recognition for mobile healthcare systems. In: 2013 IEEE International Conference on Sensing, Communications and Networking (SECON), pp. 149–157 (2013)
34. Zhang, Y., Pan, G., Jia, K., Lu, M., Wang, Y., Wu, Z.: Accelerometer-based gait recognition by sparse representation of signature points with clusters. IEEE Trans. Cybern. **45**(9) 1864–1875 (2014)
35. Kwapisz, J.R., Weiss, G.M., Moore, S.A.: Cell phone-based biometric identification. In: 2010 Fourth IEEE International Conference on Biometrics: Theory, Applications and Systems (BTAS), pp. 1–7 (2010)
36. Samà, Al., Ruiz, F.J., Agell, N., Pérez-López, C., Català, A., Cabestany, J.: Gait identification by means of box approximation geometry of reconstructed attractors in latent space. Neurocomputing **121**(Dec. 9), 79–88 (2013)
37. Bächlin, M., Schumm, J., Roggen, D., Töster, G.: Quantifying gait similarity: user authentication and real-world challenge. In: International Conference on Biometrics, pp. 1040–104 (2009)
38. Frank, J., Mannor, S., Precup, D.: Activity and gait recognition with time-delay embeddings. In: AAAI, pp. 1581–1586 (2010)
39. Preuveneers, D., Joosen, W., et al.: Improving resilience of behaviometric based continuous authentication with multiple accelerometers. In: IFIP Annual Conference on Data and Applications Security and Privacy, pp. 473–485 (2017)
40. Dehzangi, O., Taherisadr, M., ChangalVala, R.: IMU-based gait recognition using convolutional neural networks and multi-sensor fusion. Sensors **17**(12), 2735 (2017)
41. Gadaleta, M., Rossi, M.: IDNet: smartphone-based gait recognition with convolutional neural networks. Pattern Recogn. **74**, 25–37 (2018)

An Online Automated Anti-anti-virus Method

Li Ma[1], Huihong Yang[1], Yiming Chai[2], Jiawen Fan[1], and Wenyin Yang[1]([✉])

[1] Foshan University, Foshan 528000, China
cswyyang@fosu.edu.cn
[2] Beijing Normal University - Hong Kong Baptist University United International College,
Zhuhai 519000, China

Abstract. In offensive and defensive exercises, the security detection side (red team) conducts simulated real network attacks from various entry points to the maximum extent in limited time without affecting the operation of the enterprise. And defense detection side (blue team), always represented the enterprise, conducts the defense based on the existing security measures to the best. Anti-anti-virus technology is significant and commonly used by the red team, to save the virus Trojan from being checked by antivirus software. However, most of existing anti-anti-virus methods are offline and complicated to develop on the site. This paper proposed an online automated anti-anti-virus method and introduced the design and implementation of an online anti-anti-virus tool in Python based on Flask Framework. Testing results show that the virus files processed by this tool can bypass much mainstream security software such as Velvet, 360, and Tencent Computer Control and it can achieve a low detection rate of 21.73%.

Keywords: Anti-anti-virus · Payload generation · Flask · Offensive and defensive · Python

1 Introduction

Malicious codes lurking in banks, enterprise intranets, or critical information infrastructures probably bring huge losses to the organization, even the society. Network attack and defense exercise is beneficial to test the ability of various departments to find and coordinate the disposal of security risks when encountering network attacks and is of great significance to improve the network security emergency response mechanism and improve the technical protection ability.

The offensive and defensive exercises are conducted between the red team (security detection side) and the blue team (defense detection side). The red team conducts simulated real network attacks from various entry points to the maximum extent in limited time without affecting the operation of the enterprise. The blue team, always representing the enterprise, conducts the defense based on the existing security measures to the best.

Anti-anti-virus technology [1, 2] is significant and commonly used by the red team, in-network offensive and defensive exercises, to save the virus Trojan from being checked

G. Wang et al. (Eds.): UbiSec 2021, CCIS 1557, pp. 351–362, 2022.
https://doi.org/10.1007/978-981-19-0468-4_26

by antivirus software. It is highly difficult to implement the anti-anti-virus technology for the red team members because it involves several obscure technologies, such as disassembly, reverse engineering, system vulnerabilities, which leads to low attack efficiency.

The fundamental principle of anti-anti-virus technology is to destroy the existing virus features while ensuring the original function of the Trojan horse virus working normally, so as to keep the Trojan horse virus away from antivirus software detection and killing. The common anti-anti-virus methods include: modification of feature code, adding junk instructions, adding shell, memory anti-anti-virus, secondary compilation, and separation anti-anti-virus [3].

However, most of these methods are offline and complicated to develop. Besides, most of existing anti-anti-virus tools just have single function. In order to improve the efficiency of the red team in the offensive and defensive exercises, developing an integrated and automated anti-anti-virus tool is of great significance.

This paper puts forward an online automated anti-anti-virus method and implements an online anti-anti-virus tool in Python based on Flask Framework, with comprehensive functions. Experiments show that the virus files processed by this tool can bypass the security software such as Velvet, 360, and Tencent Computer Control [4]. This tool can achieve a low detection rate of 21.73%.

The rest of the paper is structured as follows. Related research works are discussed in Sect. 2. Section 3 introduces the details of online automatic anti-anti-virus method. Next, we introduce the design and implementation of online automatic anti-anti-virus system in Sect. 4. Section 5 includes the testing results and analysis. Finally, we conclude in Sect. 6.

2   Related Work

Anti-anti-virus technology, a.k.a. kill-free technology, of whose fundamental purpose is to destroy the existing virus features while ensuring the original function of the Trojan horse virus is normal, so that the Trojan horse virus can avoid detection and killing by antivirus software.

In 1987, Andreas Lüning and Kai Figge released their first anti-virus product on Atari ST. Anti-virus technology has also slowly started to evolve, and the number of malicious samples captured has increased rapidly in the early 1990s, and up to about 5 million in 2007. The change in malicious samples has driven the development of antivirus software [5]. In the following, some common methods are described.

2.1   Modify Feature Code

The feature code can be understood as a blacklist of anti-virus software [6]. For the current anti-virus technology, there are two ideas of feature code modification free: the first one is an original method that modifies or removes the feature value that will be recognized by the anti-virus software; the second one is to modify a particular area of the file which is inspected and matches the characteristics of the virus database, thus achieving the deception of anti-virus software. This technique can bypass static detection.

2.2　Adding Junk Instruction

Adding junk instructions to avoid killing means adding some useless code, such as several if-and-else judgments, before performing the real function. Therefore the antivirus software thinks it is executing the normal function. The fundamental idea of this technique is to "maintain stack balance", which can both disrupt the execution order of the program and prevent decompiling. This technique is characterized by its versatility and effectiveness, and it is often used to bypass dynamic detection.

2.3　Adding Shelling

Adding shelling is achieved by obfuscating and encrypting or compressing the code. So that when the shelled program is executed, the shell program is executed first, and then a shelled program releases the original program into memory for execution. This technique can bypass static detection and kill.

2.4　Anti-anti-virus Based on Memory

Anti-anti-virus based on memory means that malicious code is loaded into memory and executed in memory, so as to avoid detection. Its principle is the same as that of file anti-anti-virus, both of which use techniques such as irrelevant context swap and equivalent statement replacement to achieve the purpose of avoiding killing.

2.5　Secondary Compilation

Secondary compilation, like shellcode obfuscation [7], encrypts the shellcode in various ways before execution and then decrypts it when it is executed [8]. This technique can bypass most of the static detections.

2.6　Anti-anti-virus Based on Separation

Anti-anti-virus based on separation means that the malicious code is placed on a remote server, and the executable file requests the malicious code on the remote server and executes it, thus bypassing static detection.

3　Detail of Online Automatic Anti-anti-virus Method

To achieve online automatic no-kill, there are two key phases: pre-detect of Antivirus software process, and anti-anti-virus payload generation. The design details of these two techniques are as follows.

3.1 Antivirus Software Pre-detect

Since none anti-anti-virus tool can guarantee to bypass all antivirus software forever, quickly analyzing whether a process contains an antivirus process based on the process information is significant preparation work. Before each anti-anti-virus process, users can analyze the target computer processes to discover the presence of antivirus software. Getting known the existence of antivirus software in the target machine, helps to customize a particular anti-anti-virus payload.

Antivirus software pre-detect function can be performed as the following process (see Fig. 1): Because the query conducted by email is common, the process should check if the email is activated firstly. If yes, users can query the antivirus software by the process information on a query page. After the back-end obtains the user input data, it first extracts all the process names by regular matching, then queries them one by one in the "avprocess" table, and finally returns the query results to the front-end, outputting the antivirus software contained in the process list.

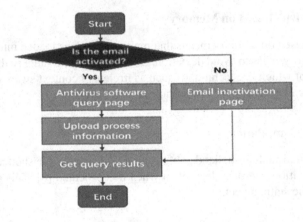

Fig. 1. Antivirus software pre-detect flow chart

3.2 Anti-anti-virus Payload Generation

To be a synthetic anti-anti-virus payload, the generation should integrate obfuscation and coding of payload, code generation, obfuscation, encryption, packaging, bundling, and automatic jumping to download link functions [9]. Anti-anti-virus payload can be generated in advance using Metasploit framework [10] or Cobalt Strike [11]. Shellcode file can be modified and change the file extension name to ".txt", and output the file in a selected format to specified URL address. Anti-anti-virus payload generation flow diagram is shown in Fig. 2.

During the process of anti-anti-virus payload generation, there are three key techniques: handling the content of payload files in.txt format, generating executable files and the design of loader memory calling code. The detail of each step of these techniques are introduced in the following:

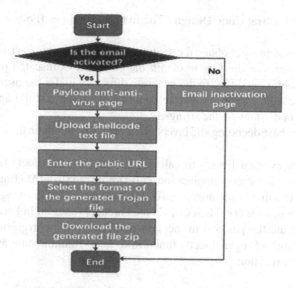

Fig. 2. Payload anti-anti-virus business flow chart

Handling the Content of Payload Files in.txt Format. The main steps are as follows:

(1) Read the contents of the file and use the "binascii" library to re-translate the hexadecimal numbers, turning the hexadecimal strings into strings of the corresponding byte types.
(2) Use the UUID library to convert the string into a UUID value.
(3) Perform string inversion, base64 encoding, hex encoding, and obfuscating strings.
(4) Perform XOR iso-encryption on the strings and output the key.txt key file to the user directory.

Generate. exe Executable File. The main steps are as follows:

(1) Judge the format of the address entered by the user, splice the download address and the four.txt file names generated above to generate three strings to achieve the contents of the file on the remote server.
(2) Splice the four strings together with the memory call code, and output the spliced contents to a randomly named file to be saved in the user directory.
(3) The back-end calls the system command to obfuscate the file using the "pyminifier" library, generating random strings to replace variable names and function names in the code, modifying the indentation, and obfuscating the imported library names.
(4) Call pyarmor library for secondary obfuscation and encryption of the file, and compile the.py file into a dynamic link library file after obfuscating it into a.c file.
(5) Use pyinstaller to package all the files and finally generate the exe executable file in the dist directory.

Loader Memory Calling Code Design. The main steps are as fFollows:

1) Use the requests library to obtain the contents of the str1. txt, str2. txt and str3.txt files, splice the contents of the files to obtain the complete obfuscated paylaod strings, and save the obfuscated files to the generate directory under the user directory.
2) Use the requests library to obtain the contents of the key.txt file and perform xor dissimilarity operations on the strings.
3) Hex decoding, base decoding and inversion of the string to obtain the original payload string.
4) Import ctypes external library to call windll, call VirtualAlloc() function in kernel32 for dynamic memory application, call UuidFromStringA() function in Rpcrt4 to write UUID value to memory, UUID will be automatically recognized as corresponding data in memory. Then call CreateThread() function in kernel 32 to create a thread, execute the payload in memory and realize the corresponding function, finally use WaitForSingleObject() function to keep running state and wait for the end of thread execution.

After successfully generating the.exe file, call the "zipfile" library to compress the str1.txt, str2.txt, str3.txt, key.txt, and exe files packaged into a.zip archive file, and save to the user download directory. Route automatically jumps to the link of download, the user can click to download.

4   Implementation of Online Automatic Anti-anti-virus System

We design a system mainly to implement the online automatic anti-anti-virus, for the red team in network offensive and defensive exercises. The system includes four main functions: user information management, antivirus software query, anti-anti-virus payload generation, and antivirus software information base management.

System users can be divided into normal users and administrators. Ordinary users can use anti-anti-virus payload generation and antivirus software query function after activating mailbox. The administrator also assigned user management and antivirus information base management functions. Figure 3 shows the flow chart of this system. The system is implemented on the Flask Framework.

4.1   Antivirus Software Query Module

The user executes "tasklist /v" on the target machine to get the process list information, copy and paste the information into the text box and click to identify. After the back-end obtains the user input data, it first extracts all the process names by regular matching, then queries them one by one in the "avprocess" table, and finally returns the query results to the front-end, outputting the antivirus software contained in the process list. The query result interface is shown in Fig. 4.

The core code segment is as follows:

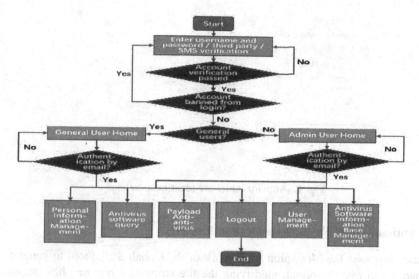

Fig. 3. Flow chart of the system

```
# Route processing section
  if request.method == 'POST':
    task_text = request.form['tasklist']
    tasklist = get_proc(task_text)
    result_liist = []
    for task in tasklist: # Loop query avprocess table
      software =
  AVprocess.query.filter_by(av_process=task).first()
      if software is not None:
        result_liist.append(software)

    return render_template('avscan/appscan.html',
result_liist=result_liist) # Return the query results
# Regular match for all process names
def get_proc(tasks):
  if tasks:
    pattern = re.compile(".+\.exe",re.I)
    result = pattern.findall(tasks)
    if result:
      tasklist = list(set(result))
      return tasklist
  return None
```

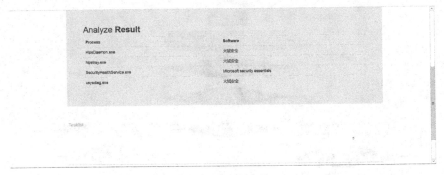

Fig. 4. Antivirus software identification page

4.2 Anti-anti-virus Payload Generation Module

The user first uses the Metasploit framework or the Cobalt Strike tool to generate the payload file in python format, modifying the file string to a one-line hexadecimal \x format string, removing other redundant characters, as shown in Fig. 5. Then modify the file suffix to.txt.

Fig. 5. Example of shellcode

The submission page is shown in Fig. 6. The user only needs to upload the processed txt file, fill in the public download address used to separate the no-kill, select the generated file format, and then click the button to upload, and the file will be automatically uploaded to the directory named after the user's username. The backend gets the data and processes the txt file content and the public download address separately. The core code segment is as follows:

The anti-anti-virus effect is shown in Fig. 7.

```
select = request.form.get('comp_select')
    filename = myfile.save(request.files['bin'])
    filepath =
    current_app.config['UPLOADED_MYFILE_DEST']+'\\'+filename
    url1 = request.form.get('url1') # Get user upload infor-
mation
    user_path = current_app.config['UPLOADED_MYFILE_DEST'] +
'\\' + current_user.username + '\\'
    if not allowed_file(filename):
      os.remove(filepath)
      flash('Wrong format of files. Please upload.txt file! ')
      return render_template('upload/up-
load_wtform.html',data=data)
      flash('Uploaded successfully~')
      shellcode = read_file(filepath)
      generate_pices(shellcode, user_path)
      py_file = generate_py(url1, user_path)
      generate_exe(py_file, user_path)
      process_file = to_zip()
    return redirect(url_for('upload.uploaded_file',file-
    name=process_file))
    # Return to download links
  except Exception as e:
    print(e)
    flash('Wrong format of files. Please upload.txt file! ')
```

Fig. 6. Upload page

4.3 Antivirus Software Information Base Management Module

The antivirus information base management module adds, deletes, and changes the "avprocess" and "avurl" tables. When new antivirus-related information is collected,

Fig. 7. The effect of anti-anti-virus

the administrator can add the information about the antivirus software, related processes and official website information through this module. You can also modify and delete the previously added antivirus software information. The operation page is shown in Fig. 8 and the core code segment is as follows:

```
# Return to all antivirus software information
av_list = AVurl.query.all()
return render_template('avlist.html', userlist=user_av)
# Add antivirus information
# Related Processes
for i in av_process:
new_av_data = AVprocess(av_name=av_name, av_process=i )
db.session.add(new_av_data)
db.session.commit()
# 相关url
new_av_data = AVurl(av_name=av_name, av_url=av_url)
db.session.add(new_av_data)
db.session.commit()
# Modify antivirus-related information
user_data = AV.query.filter_by(id=request.form['id']).first()
user_data.confirmed1 = request.form['confirmed1']
user_data.role_id = request.form['role_id']
user_data.phone = int(request.form['phone'])
db.session.commit()
# Delete antivirus related information
proc_data = Avprocess.query.get(av_process)
db.session.delete(proc_data)
db.session.commit()
url_data = Avurl.query.get(av_name)
db.session.delete(url_data)
db.session.commit()
```

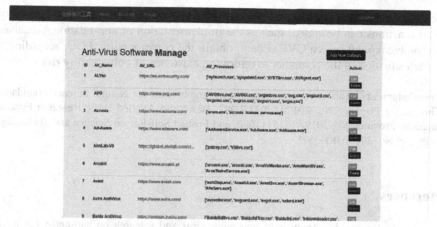

Fig. 8. Antivirus software information base management webpage

5 System Testing

The system was tested in many ways, including unit test, non-functional test and functional test respectively. The non-functional test includes page testing and stress testing.

In the unit test, the corresponding test cases were used to test, and the test results all met the expectations.

In the page test, the page layout was reasonable, the switching was smooth, and no bugs affecting customer experience were found.

In the stress test, the program crashed under high concurrency.

In the functional test, the system can achieve all functions completely.

Test results show that the virus files processed by the system can bypass security software such as Velvet, 360, and Tencent Computer Control and on the personal computer and only 15 antivirus software issued warnings among 69 antivirus software detections by Virustotal [12], with a low detection rate of 21.73%.

6 Conclusions

This paper proposed an online automatic anti-anti-virus method and a design and implementation of a system for anti-anti-virus. This system, with comprehensive functions, is mainly designed for the attack teams to exploit vulnerabilities in security vendors' protection devices in live network attack and defense drills. Pre-detection of Antivirus software process and anti-anti-virus payload generation are important phrases in this automatic anti-anti-virus method. System testing results show that the virus detection rate is low. This tool promoted the development of the red team and the blue team technology, in line with the trend of the development of network security tools.

In the future work, the concurrency ability will be increased, and more security-related functions can be added, such as the implementation of non-relational database based on breakpoint search CVE code to obtain the corresponding POC, according to the patch situation of the computer to return the existence of vulnerability risks.

Acknowledgments. This work was supported by grants from the Natural Science Foundation of Guangdong Province No. 2018A0303130082, Basic and Applied Basic Research Fund of Guangdong Province No. 2019A1515111080, and Foshan Self-Raised Science and Technology Plan Project No. 2018AB003691.

References

1. Long, Z., Baixue, L.: Analysis of poisonivy virus and research on anti-anti-virus methods. In: 2020 IEEE 3rd International Conference on Automation, Electronics and Electrical Engineering (AUTEEE), pp. 413–417. IEEE, Shenyang (2020)
2. Yifu, C., Ping, W.: Practice and exploration of php webshell anti-antivirus technology. Commun. Technol. **53**(12), 3078–3086 (2020)
3. Jia-Xi, H.U., Wang, Y.J., Xue, Z.: Research of anti-anti-virus and anti-virus technology under new situation. Communications Technology (2017)
4. Chen, B., Ren, Z., Yu, C., Hussain, I., Liu, J.: Adversarial examples for CNN-based malware detectors. IEEE Access **7**(99), 54360–54371 (2019)
5. Lu, Q., Wang, Y.: Detection technology of malicious code based on semantic. Multimed. Tools App. **76**(19), 19543–19555 (2016). https://doi.org/10.1007/s11042-015-3228-7
6. Jingjing, G.: China's cybersecurity industry urgently needs talent training. China Inf. World **04**, 38–41 (2018)
7. Ntantogian, C., Poulios, G., Karopoulos, G., Xenakis, C.: Transforming malicious code to ROP gadgets for antivirus evasion. IET Inf. Secur. **13**(6), 570–578 (2019)
8. Hedrick, M.R., Holman, J.: Stegarmory: offensive cyber security software for embedding shellcode in images (2021). (Preprint)
9. Li, L., Wei, L.: Automatic XSS detection and automatic anti-anti-virus payload generation. In: 2019 International Conference on Cyber-Enabled Distributed Computing and Knowledge Discovery, pp. 71–76. IEEE, Guilin (2019)
10. Raj, S, Walia, N.K.: A study on metasploit framework: a pen-testing tool. In: 2020 International Conference on Computational Performance Evaluation (ComPE), pp. 296–302. IEEE (2020)
11. Chen, L., Chunqiang, L., Guowei, Q.: Research on intruder countermeasures based on cobalt strike and office vulnerabilities. Cyberspace Secur. **9**(1), 56–61 (2018)
12. Huang, H., et al.: A large-scale study of android malware development phenomenon on public malware submission and scanning platform. IEEE Trans. Big Data **7**(2), 255–270 (2018)

Research on Bandwidth Reservation Algorithm of Teaching Resources in Cloud Computing Environment

Hongling Chen[1], Zhiwen Liao[2(✉)], and Qin Liu[3]

[1] Computer Engineering Technical College, Guangdong Polytechnic of Science and Technology, Zhuhai 519090, China
[2] Artificial Intelligence College, Zhuhai City Polytechnic, Zhuhai 519090, China
[3] College of Computer Science and Electronic Engineering, Hunan University, Changsha 410082, China
gracelq628@hnu.edu.cn

Abstract. The main purpose of education cloud application is to deploy teaching resources to the cloud and realize the elastic access of teaching resources. However, because of the concentration of teaching activities, it will lead to the lack of network bandwidth at sometimes, which will affect the normal teaching; On the other hand, when teaching activities are not carried out, the network bandwidth is idle again, resulting in low utilization of network bandwidth. In order to solve this problem, this paper proposes Bandwidth Reservation Algorithm based on Static Timeslot (BRAST) for teaching resources in cloud computing environment. BRAST aims at maximizing the number of successful reservation requests, and takes the network bandwidth size and effective time as constraints. Experiments show that the success ratio of non-bandwidth reservation algorithm (NBRA) is much lower, and the success ratio is 40%–50% lower than that of BRAST.

Keywords: Cloud computing · Bandwidth reservation · Resource reservation · Elastic access · Software defined networking · Teaching resources

1 Introduction

At present, cloud computing technology has been applied to the field of education, and the Internet has a fuller interpretation and support for the storage and utilization of educational resources. This paper is the thinking and exploration of the application scheme of cloud teaching resources under the cloud computing environment.

Education cloud service refers to a cloud computing platform that uses virtualization, load balancing, distributed storage and other technologies to deeply integrate various resources, platforms and applications [1]. It meets the needs of educational users to complete teaching, learning, scientific research, management and social communication through various information terminals in the form of rental or free services, so as to release educational information to obtain teaching resources, carry out teaching interaction, count educational information and data, form scientific decision-making, implement educational evaluation, carry out collaborative scientific research and other activities.

The teaching resources in the education cloud are called cloud teaching resources. It is a digital teaching resource deployed through the cloud computing platform, mainly including all kinds of network media materials, network test bank, network courseware, network courses, teaching cases, FAQs, resource directory index, literature, etc. [2]. The teaching work based on cloud resources mainly applies teaching resources flexibly and in real time by uploading and downloading teaching resources on the cloud platform. However, the cloud platform often causes congestion when accessing the cloud resource server to download teaching resources in peak hours, on the other hand a large amount of idle bandwidth occurs during off peak hours. In view of this, this paper proposes a cloud resource reservation service model, which can enable users to complete the customization and reservation of required resources before using resources, so that resources can be cached to the local server in advance by using idle bandwidth before being used, in this way users can obtain and use resources more effectively.

The bandwidth reservation was first used to reserve bandwidth for real-time applications, such as video conferencing [3–5]. Recently, the bandwidth reservation is also used in high-performance networks for long-distance big data transmission [6, 7]. Software defined networking (SDN) [8] separates the control layer from the data layer. Under the unified view, the control layer can arrange the network and provide customized services for specific applications. OpenFlow [9] provides a standard protocol for control layer controlling equipment. Based on SDN, advance reservation is widely used in optical networks to reserve routing and wavelength assignment (RWA) [10, 11] for specific applications. Reserving bandwidth for applications can not only ensure the quality of service of the network, but also make overall use of network resources and improve resource utilization.

2   System Structure and Bandwidth Reservation Process

The bandwidth reservation function of cloud computing teaching resources needs the support of the network management system. This paper uses the SDN controller to obtain the network topology and traffic information, and calculates the bandwidth routing based on the topology and traffic. In addition to the reservation function, teaching resource management in cloud computing environment can also retrieve resources, that is, obtain the resource list of cloud resource storage server or local storage server; it can also use the resource management function to delete expired resources in the local storage server to save storage space. The specific cloud computing teaching resource management architecture is shown in Fig. 1.

In Fig. 1, it includes six functional entities: cloud resource application, bandwidth reservation server, SDN controller, switches, cloud resource storage server and local storage server. In cloud resource application, resource retrieval and resource management directly obtain the resource list or operate resources from the cloud resource storage server or local server without going through the bandwidth reservation server. After the user submits the resource reservation request, the resource reservation module selects to download teaching resources from the cloud resource storage server to the local storage

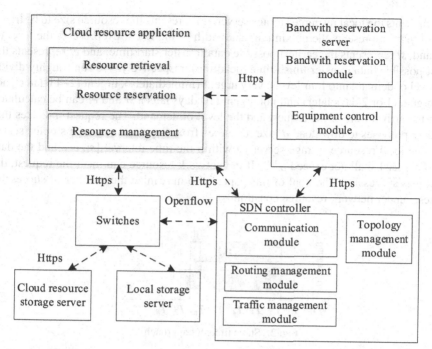

Fig. 1. Cloud computing teaching resource management architecture

server at an appropriate time according to degree of urgency and the objective function. Next, the process of the bandwidth reservation is described in detail:

Step 1: the user logs in to the browser to access the cloud resource application interface, and makes a resource reservation request required for teaching activities on the reservation page.

Step 2: after receiving the resource reservation request, the bandwidth reservation server first makes admission control from the perspective of the management layer. If allowed, the bandwidth reservation module then makes admission control from the perspective of the network layer which is based on the topology management module and traffic management module of the SDN controller. If the network can provide the routing path of the required bandwidth, it accepts the request. If not, it rejects the request.

Step 3: when the transmission time arrives, the equipment control module sends a command to the communication module of the SDN controller.

Step 4: the communication module sends resource reservation commands to the corresponding switches to reserve bandwidth for the bandwidth reservation request.

Step 5: the teaching resource data stream is transmitted from the cloud resource storage server to the local storage server along the routing path of reserved bandwidth.

3 Bandwidth Reservation Model

This paper defines the set of bandwidth reservation requests as $R = \{(v_s, v_d, d, b^{\max}, l, [st, et])\}$, in which v_s represents the cloud resource storage server,

v_d represents the local resource storage server, d represents the resource size to be transmitted, b^{max} represents the maximum bandwidth of the LAN, l represents the level of demand, st represents the earliest possible data transfer start time, and et represents the latest possible data transfer finish time (deadline), respectively. We can roughly divide the level of demand into four levels: very urgent (immediately), urgent (2–4 h later), not too urgent (1 or 2 days later) and not urgent (10 days later). st and et can be calculated from the arrival time of the request and the level of demand. The request indicates that the user proposes to download d size resources from the cloud resource storage server v_s to the local resource storage server v_d within the time interval $[st, et]$, and the data transfer speed shall not exceed b^{max}. If the network resource can meet the request, the request is successful. The goal of this paper is to maximize the number of successful requests under network resource constraints.

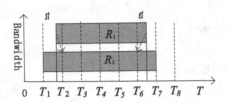

Fig. 2. Static timeslot approach

The education network model is defined as a directed graph $G(V, E, B)$, where V represents nodes, including terminals and switches, E represents the links and B represents the available bandwidth matrix of the links. This paper uses static timeslot approach to manage resources. The static timeslot approach divides time into equidistant time intervals, which are also called time granularity. In the static timeslot approach, t is defined to save the ordered sequence of time points constituting the timeslots. Assuming that the time that users can reserve is from the current time to the future time, as shown in Fig. 2, the distance between dotted lines is called time granularity, which is the minimum length of time divided. There are a total of 8 timeslots in T, i.e., $\{(0, T_1), (T_1, T_2), (T_2, T_3), (T_3, T_4), (T_4, T_5), (T_5, T_6), (T_6, T_7), (T_7, T_8)\}$. When the request R_1 arrives, the reservation system will reduce the earliest possible data transfer start time st upward and the latest possible data transfer finish time et downward respectively to the closest integer multiples of the time granularity, i.e., T_2 and T_6. The algorithm verifies whether the resource requirements of R_1 can be met within the timeslots. If the request R_1 is successfully accommodated, the actual transmission time of R_1 is recorded, and reserve the bandwidth for R_1 within these timeslots. Here, a two-dimensional matrix $AvailableBW[|E|, |T|]$ is defined to represent the available bandwidth of each link in the timeslots. When $t_0 = 0$, the available bandwidth of the link is equal to the physical bandwidth of the link. $AvailableBW$ saves the available bandwidth at different timeslots and is the main credential for resource reservation. For R_1, there may be multiple time intervals containing multiple timeslots to provide the resources required by R_1. In this paper, these time intervals that meet the resource requirement are called time window WL, that is $WL = \{(T_2, T_3), (T_2, T_4), (T_2, T_5), (T_2, T_6), (T_3, T_4), (T_3, T_5), \cdots\}$. That is, for an ordered sequence of time points TS, which contains n time points, the number of time intervals contained in the time window TW is C_n^2. The algorithm verifies whether R_1 can be satisfied in one time interval in turn. Once the time interval satisfying the required resource of R_1 is found, the algorithm exits.

4 Algorithm Design

Figure 3 presents the pseudo code of the Bandwidth Reservation Algorithm based on Static Timeslot (BRAST). In algorithm 1, the requests are first sorted in ascending order according to the size of required resources. This is because the goal of this paper is to maximize the number of successful requests. Therefore, processing requests with small required resources first is conducive to increasing the success ratio.

Lines 2 to 28 process the sorted requests in turn. In Line 3, a symbol bit is set to identify whether there is a legal time interval satisfying the required bandwidth. Once found, BRAST breaks from this request and continue with the next request, as shown in lines 25 to 27.

Line 4 calculates the overlapped timeslots T of r, the index of time points in T is *low* and *high*.

Lines 5 to 24 calculate whether there is a path satisfying the required resources in each time interval of the time window list WL.

Lines 7 to 9 judge whether the current time length is less than the minimum time internal length. If not, it will directly enter the next time internal.

Line 10 calculates the required bandwidth, and line 11 prunes the edges less than the required bandwidth from the topology.

Lines 12 to 19 calculate the path and save the current path and time interval, and set flag $= 1$ to exit the current time interval.

5 Simulation

Generally, Monday to Friday is the normal teaching time. At this time, resources are downloaded frequently, which is easy to form a bandwidth bottleneck and affect the normal teaching. According to the degree of demand, the reservation system reserve the required bandwidth for resource download in advance, and download teaching resources when the transmission time arrives, which can reduce the bandwidth pressure of teaching week and ensure the teaching quality. Next, we verify the performance of the proposed bandwidth reservation algorithm based on static timeslot BRAST and the non-bandwidth reservation algorithm NBRA.

As shown in Fig. 4, as the number of requests increases and the bandwidth remains unchanged, the success ratio of both algorithms decreases. When compared BRAST and NBRA, we can observe that BRAST can achieve 40% higher success ratio than NBRA.

Figure 5 shows the success ratio of both the algorithms when the percentage of available bandwidth to physical bandwidth increases. With the increase of the percentage of available bandwidth to physical bandwidth, the success ratio of BRAST grows until 1, while NBRA grows much lower. The success ratio of BRAST is at most 50% higher than that of NBRA.

Algorithm 1 Bandwidth Reservation Algorithm based on Static Timeslot (BRAST)

GIVEN: $G(V, E, B)$

INPUT: $R, T, AvailableBW$

OUTPUT: ARL, accommodated requests list containing successful requests accommodated with resources.

1:   Sort the requests in R in increasing order;

2:   for each $r \in R$ do

3:   | $flag = 0$;

4:   | Initialize the overlapped timeslots T of r, the index of time points in T is low and $high$;

5:   | for $low \leq i < high$ do

6:   | | for $i < j \leq high$ do

7:   | | | if $T_j - T_i < \dfrac{d}{b^{max}}$ do

8:   | | | | continue;

9:   | | | end if

10: | | | $bw_m = \dfrac{d}{T_j - T_i}$;

11: | | | Prune edges with available bandwidth in time interval (T_i, T_j) less than bw_m;

12: | | | $[path, dis] \leftarrow Dijkstra(G, AvailableBW, v_s, v_d)$;

13: | | | if $dis = +\infty$ do

14: | | | | continue;

15: | | | end if

16: | | | $AR \leftarrow (r, path, bw_m, [T_i, T_j])$

17: | | | Insert AR into accommodated requests list ARL;

18: | | | $flag = 1$;

19: | | | break;

20: | | end for

21: | | if $flag == 1$

22: | | | break;

23: | | end if

24: | end for

25: | if $flag == 1$

26: | | continue;

27: | end if

28: end for

Fig. 3. The pseudo code of BRAST

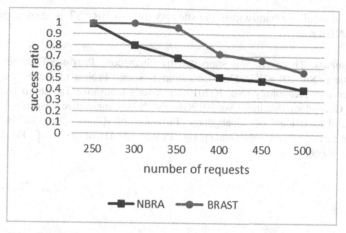

Fig. 4. Success ratio as the number of requests increases

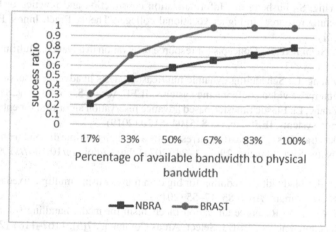

Fig. 5. Success ratio as the ratio of available bandwidth increases

In conclusion, the use of resource reservation in advance can greatly improve resource availability and solve the uncertain factors caused by resource bottleneck.

6 Conclusions

This paper studies the bandwidth reservation mechanism based on SDN of teaching resources in cloud computing environment, including the research of architecture and resource reservation algorithm. This paper designs the bandwidth reservation algorithm based on static timeslot to maximize the number of resource download requests. The simulation results show that the success ratio of BRAST can reach 100% in a certain environment. The success ratio of NBRA is 40% lower than that of BRAST with the increase of the number of requests. In the case of the number of requests remains unchanged and the increase of available bandwidth, the success ratio of BRAST is at most 50% higher than that of NBRA.

Acknowledgments. This work was supported by Guangdong Province Educational Science Planning Project (No. 2019GXJK272), Education Research Project of Guangdong Polytechnic of Science and Technology (No. JG201922), Young Innovative Talents in Department of Education of Guangdong Province (No. 2019GKQNCX043), Innovative Research.

Team in Universities of Guangdong Province of China (No. 2021KCXTD079), Scientific research project of Guangdong Provincial Department of Education (No. 2018GWQNCX039).

References

1. Lingling, S.: Research on construction of cloud computing teaching resources open sharing platform. Electr. Test **22**, 72–73 (2020)
2. Lina, Z., Ying, S., Fusheng, L.: Informatization construction and practice of high quality digital teaching resources in higher vocational colleges. Theory Pract. Innov. Entrepren. **8**, 87–88 (2021)
3. Wolf, L.C., Steinmetz, R.: Concepts for resource reservation in advance. Multim. Tools Appl. **4**(3), 255–278 (1997)
4. Liao, Z., Zhang, L.: Scheduling dynamic multicast requests in advance reservation environment for enterprise video conferencing systems. IEEE Access **8**, 76913–76928 (2020)
5. Liao, Z., Zhang, L.: Elastic timeslot-based advance reservation algorithm for enterprise video conferencing systems. IEEE Access **8**, 5104–5120 (2019)
6. Zuo, L.: Data transfers using bandwidth reservation through multiple disjoint paths of dynamic HPNs. J. Netw. Syst. Manage. **29**(3), 1–24 (2021). https://doi.org/10.1007/s10922-021-095 85-w
7. Hou, A., et al.: Bandwidth scheduling for big data transfer using multiple fixed node-disjoint paths. J. Netw. Comput. Appl. **85**: 47–55 (2017)
8. Soltanian, A., et al.: Resource allocation mechanism for media handling services in cloud multimedia conferencing. IEEE J. Select. Areas Commun. **37**(5), 1167–1181 (2019)
9. McKeown, N., et al.: OpenFlow: enabling innovation in campus networks. ACM SIGCOMM Comput. Commun. Rev. **38**(2), 69–74 (2008)
10. Lu, W., Zhu, Z.: Dynamic service provisioning of advance reservation requests in elastic optical networks. J. Lightwave Technol. **31**(10), 1621–1627 (2013)
11. Mahala, N., Thangaraj, J.: Resource allocation with advance reservation using artificial neural network in elastic optical networks. Soft. Comput. **25**(11), 7515–7525 (2021). https://doi.org/10.1007/s00500-021-05710-8

An Edge-Cloud Collaborative Object Detection System

Lei Xu and Dingkun Yang(✉)

Jiangsu Electric Power Information Technology Co. Ltd., Nanjing 210000, China

Abstract. Edge computing system usually consists of the lightweight neural network to preprocess the video stream, and then transmits the intermediate data to the cloud for video analysis, which not only ensures the real-time performance of video processing but also greatly reduces the WAN bandwidth consumption. However, many existing edge processing systems sacrifice video processing accuracy to reduce intermediate transmission volume or reduce processing delay. Therefore, the leveraging of accuracy and latency places a challenge on how to deploy the network on the edge device and set the pre-processing parameters. This paper builds a real-time video stream processing system, then tries to achieve the balance between the cost and benefit of edge preprocessing by designing a dynamic configuration algorithm for optimal preprocessing deployment to achieve low latency, low transmission, and high precision real-time video processing.

Keywords: Edge computing · Video analytics · Object detection · Neural networks · Scheduling problem · Random rounding

1 Introduction

Recent years have seen great advances in neural networks [1,2]. Deeper layers and more complicated parameters of these networks facilitate timely and precise responses to common queries such as object detection. Due to the complexity of these networks, traditionally, they are deployed at the cloud servers.

However, with the advent of auto-driving and other detection tasks which require low latency and high accuracy, the transmission rate over the WAN has become a common bottleneck in such tasks [2].

Many object detection tasks use an edge-cloud collaborative architecture [3–5]. However, because the computational power of edges is far less than that of servers, it is impossible to deploy complex neural networks on them. Many research efforts have been devoted to improving edge-assisted object recognition.

Here are several techniques that current research adopts:

(1) Split the neural network [6], deploy the first half at the edges and pre-process before transferring the intermediate data to the cloud to continue.
(2) Reduce the parameters and the number of layers while ensuring a certain accuracy of the network, making it less complicated for edge deployment.

G. Wang et al. (Eds.): UbiSec 2021, CCIS 1557, pp. 371–378, 2022.
https://doi.org/10.1007/978-981-19-0468-4_28

To achieve both high accuracy and low latency, the cloud-edge collaborating system proposed in this paper deploys lightweight networks at the edge to identify the first k of the most probable classifications for each object to choose the keyframes, and then uploads these candidate frames to the cloud as intermediate results for further processing.

To accomplish these goals, how to efficiently complete the scheduling of requests while adjusting various parameters of the edge neural network becomes a core challenge in this system.

In our system, each surveillance camera is ingesting a live video, which needs to be uploaded to the edge for pre-processing. The intermediated results will be analyzed by the cloud then. This system considers the deployment of the neural network jointly with the parameter settings and the scheduling of tasks to ensure a lower transmission and higher accuracy.

After building the system, the paper proposes a joint scheduling-deployment problem, which considers regulating the number of layers and other parameters of the neural network deployed on edges and the routing of requests, making video analytics with higher accuracy in a shorter response time.

To solve the problem, the paper proposes a gradient descent random rounding method and tests the outcomes with some simulated experiments.

The rest of the paper is organized as follows: the second section introduces the edge-cloud system model and a formal formulation of the deployment-scheduling problem; the third section illustrates the gradient descent random rounding algorithm. The fourth section includes simulated experiments of different scales and compares the results obtained by our algorithm against other methods. And the last section summarizes the paper.

2 System Model

This paper uses the following model for the edge-cloud collaborative video analytics. Consider the scenario in Fig. 1, where a number of surveillance devices(for example, cameras) $S = s_1, s_2, ..., s_m$ are ingesting videos and the stream of each camera s stream needs to be analyzed before t_s. These cameras can be connected to a number of edge servers with varying capacities $E = e_1, e_2, ..., e_n$. Since each of these edge servers e has a fixed downlink bandwidth, uplink bandwidth and computational resource R_e, only a small fraction of the camera requests can be processed simultaneously on one edge. Our goal is to maximize the accuracy of the video processing while meeting the latency requirements of all devices. This requires a feasible deployment of different neural networks on each edge and a careful routing of all requests to the edges.

As is shown in Fig. 1, due to the low computational power of the edge servers, they are unable to run complex neural networks. Therefore, we choose to deploy lightweight neural networks with fewer layers and operations on these edges (e.g., the mobilenet [7], simplified vgg16 [8], etc.). However, their accuracy is also relatively low. To ensure the accuracy of the results, after preprocessing with the edge servers, we pick out all the candidate frames for a more complex

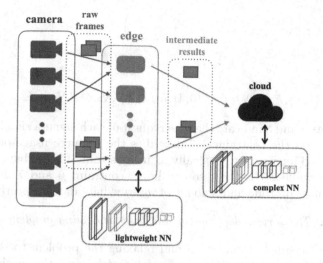

Fig. 1. System model

network in the cloud. Since the network deployed at the edge will filter out frames that are unlikely to contain a target object, the amount of intermediate results will be far less than the original, which ensures that the WAN bandwidth does not affect the overall delay.

In order to describe the real-world scenario in mathematical model, we take two aspects: the accuracy goal and the resource (including time, computational capacity and bandwidth, transmission rate) into consideration separately. First, we mode the accuracy with a function of the top k parameter and the layers as well as the numbers of operations in each network. Then, we use the frame rate, parameter k and bandwidth to determine the transmission rate and overall latency, along with the resource usage in edges.

We take the overall accuracy of the system as an optimization goal and use decision variable m_e and k_e to control the MACC and parameter k of the network deployed on edge e, f_s to decide the frame rate for each camera s, $x_{s,e}$ to control whether the request of camera s is routed to edge e and formulate the problem as follows:

$$\max \sum_{e \in E} \sum_{s \in S} x_{s,e} \left(c - c_1 \alpha_1^{k_e} - c_2 \alpha_2^{m_e} - c_3 \alpha_3^{f_s} \right) \tag{1}$$

$$\text{s.t. } x_{s,e} \leq \chi_{s,e}, \forall s \in S, \forall e \in E, \tag{2}$$

$$\sum_{e \in E} x_{s,e} = 1, \forall s \in S \tag{3}$$

$$b_s \cdot f_s \cdot x_{s,e} \leq B, \forall e \in E, s \in S \tag{4}$$

$$\alpha_4 m_e \sum_{s \in S} x_{s,e} \leq R_e, \forall e \in E \tag{5}$$

$$\sum_{e \in E} \left(c_4 - c_5 \alpha^{k_e} \right) f_s \cdot x_{s,e} \cdot \left(\frac{1}{b_e} + \frac{1}{v_{cloud}} \right) + m_e \cdot c_6 \cdot x_{s,e} \leq t_s, \forall s \in S \quad (6)$$

$$\sum_{s \in S} x_{s,e} \left(c_4 - c_5 \alpha^{k_e} \right) f_s \leq D_e, \forall e \in E \quad (7)$$

$$\text{var. } x_{s,e} \in \{0,1\}, k_e \in N^*, f_s \in (0,1], m_e \in N^*, \forall s \in S, \forall e \in E \quad (8)$$

Constraints 2 and 3 indicate that the request of each camera should be routed to one edge. And the contraint 4–7 describes the resource usage on each edge shouldn't exceed its capacity. Typically, B in constraint 4 is the bandwidth limit of each edge, while R_e is the resource limit, contraint 6 and 7 describes the limited transmission time and amount of intermediate data respectively.

Theorem 1. *The service deployment and task scheduling problem is NP-hard.*

Proof. We can begin by simplifying and relaxing the problem to the following form by assuming that m and k are fixed for each edge, this problem can be reduces to a multidimensional knapsack problem (MNP) [9], so it is at least NP-hard, thus it is difficult to obtain an exact optimal solution in polynomial time.

3   Algorithm

Similar to MNP, the main difficulty of this problem also lies in the existence of integers constrained variables. To address this problem, we shall transform the integer programming problem into a convex optimization problem before applying the gradient descent method to solve the problem. Finally we round all variables to integers with a random rounding method.

3.1   Gradient Descent

First, we use a simple trick to relax the problem into a convex one.

We can find that in constraints (5) and (6), the parameter k appears on the exponent form, which makes the function concave and hard to solve using algorithms for convex optimization. If the parameter k_e is enumerated for each network on edge e, the search space would be $5|E|$. To transform the problem's constraints into convex functions, we can adjust the data transfer function into $D' = c_4' + c_5' \cdot k$, where $c_5' = -c_5 \alpha^3 \ln \alpha$, $c_4' = c_4 - c_5 \alpha^3 + 3c_5 \alpha^3 ln\alpha$, to get the relaxed version of constraint (5*) and (6*).

For such problems, an optimal solution can be obtained using the Lagrange multiplier method [10]. The Lagrange multiplier method can transform inequalities and equation constraints into the object of convex optimization problems, and then obtain the final results using the gradient descent method:

Algorithm 1: Gradient Descent Algorithm

---

1 **for** *current solution* $\hat{\Omega} = \left(\hat{x}_{s,e}, \hat{m}_e, \hat{k}_e, \hat{f}_s \right)$ **do**

2      $\beta = \mathrm{argmin}_{h \geq 0}(\Omega + hd)$

3   Update $\hat{\Omega} = \hat{\Omega} + \beta d$

After multiple iterations, the results will converge, thus terminated the algorithm. After this, we can obtain an optimal solution to this convex optimization problem.

3.2 Random Rounding

Now we have relaxed the variables $x_{s,e}$ and m_e, k_e to continuous forms, so we round the decision variable $x_{s,e}$ according to probability:

Algorithm 2: Random Rounding Algorithm

---

1 **for** *every camera s* **do**

2   Let $E' = E$;

3   **for** *every edge e* **do**

4   set $x_{s,e} = 1$ with the probability of $\frac{\hat{x}_{s,e}}{\sum_{j \in E'} x_{s,j}}$

5          $E' = E' - \{e\}$

6   **if** $x_{s,e} = 1$ **then**

7   **for** *every* $e \in E'$ **do**

8   set $x_{s,e} = 0$

9   break

10 **for** *every edge e* **do**

11   set $m_e = \frac{R_e}{\alpha_4 \sum_{s \in S} x_{s,e}}$

12      $k_e = \left\lfloor \hat{k}_e \right\rfloor$;

Lines 1–9 determine the request scheduling for each camera based on probability and guarantee for each camera, the probability that each server e handles the request at the probability of $\hat{x}_{s,e}$. Lines 10–12 determine m_e for each edge server based on the scheduling results, and finally downward integer gives the value of the parameter k_e.

4 Experiments and Analysis

To verify the performance of the algorithm, we perform several simulations at different scales, and compares the results obtained by this algorithm and three other algorithms, namely:

1. Fixed deployment method: deploy low (40%), median (40%) and high (20%) performance neural networks on all edges and decided the routing with simplex method.
2. linear programming method: the optimization objective and all the constraints of the problem are approximated into a linear plan for solving.
3. Simple greedy method: prioritize the scheduling of the camera's video processing requests to edges with the most remaining resources.

In order to simulate the real situation, in both experiments at different scales, we ensured that each camera be covered by 3–4 edges and use generated traces for bandwidths and resources. We use the 2014videotestset for processing.

4.1   Experiment Result

To make the experimental results more reliable, we conducted experiments of 4 different scales: 20, 200, 400, 1000 and 2000 cameras. The results of our algorithm in comparison with those of the control methods are as follows.

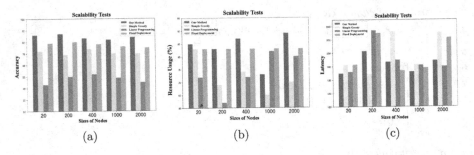

(a)   (b)   (c)

Fig. 2. Comparison of algorithms

As is shown in Fig. 2a, our algorithm yields a relatively better result than control methods. It is 12% to 26% more accurate than the results of the naive greedy method and more accurate than the results of the LP method by 49% to 76%. It is also higher than the fixed deployment method by 6% to 12%.

By Fig. 2b we can see that the deployment yielded by our method has a higher resource usage rate than the simple greedy method by 12% to 26%, and is higher than that LP method by 49% to 76%, and higher than the fixed deployment method by 6% to 12%.

Figure 2c shows that the average overall latency achieved by our method is at most 20% higher than the naive greedy method, while the minimum latency is 19% lower than it. Our latency is 5% higher than the that of the LP method at most and the minimum latency is 14% lower. Also, the average latency of our algorithm is 7% more than the fixed deployment method, and the minimum latency is 16% less than it.

4.2   Tail Analysis

In addition to comparing accuracy and server resource utilization in large-scale experiments, we also performed some comparisons of tail data, Fig. 3a shows the average, median and mode of the 100 requests with the lowest precision.

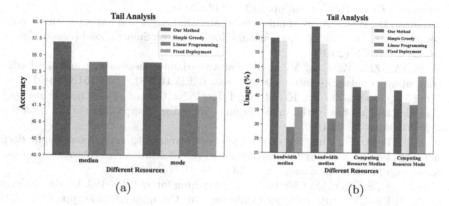

Fig. 3. Tail comparison of algorithms

Figure 3b shows the bandwidth of the 10 servers with the lowest resource utilization rate. 10 edge servers with the lowest resource utilization have bandwidth utilization of 5%, 86.9% and 72% higher than the control algorithms. The rate of utilization of computing resources was 112%, 114% and 86%, respectively higher than that of three other algorithms.

Our method considers both parameter configuration and the requests routings, the tail results also improved.

5   Conclusion

In conclusion, this paper proposes an edge-assisted video processing system and formulates a network deployment, request routing problem based on that system. We then design a novel gradient descend and random rounding algorithm for this problem as well as conduct some simulated experiments.

This system adjusts various parameters of the neural network on the edge server, adds preprocess module on the nearby edge to reduce the transmission over WAN to the cloud, allowing for maximum processing accuracy while ensuring that requests are completed on time. It was also demonstrated in the experiments that the system and its decision algorithm can achieve good results in a short period of time.

In all, this paper proposes a novel solution in face of the challenge of low latency and high accuracy demands in real-time video analytics.

References

1. Ren, S., He, K., Girshick, R., et al.: Faster R-CNN: towards real-time object detection with region proposal networks. IEEE Tans. Pattern Anal. Mach. Intell. **39**(6), 1137–1149 (2016)
2. Gidaris, S., Komodakis, N.: Object detection via a multi-region and semantic segmentation-aware CNN model. In: Proceedings of the IEEE International Conference on Computer Vision, pp. 1134–1142 (2015)
3. Varghese, B., Wang, N., Barbhuiya, S., et al.: Challenges and opportunities in edge computing. In: 2016 IEEE International Conference on Smart Cloud (SmartCloud), pp. 20–26. IEEE (2016)
4. Wang, A., Zha, Z., Guo, Y., et al.: Software-defined networking enhanced edge computing: a network-centric survey. Proc. IEEE **107**(8), 1500–1519 (2019)
5. Yang, S., Gong, Z., Ye, K., et al.: EdgeCNN: Convolutional neural network classification model with small inputs for edge computing. arXiv preprint arXiv:1909.13522 (2019)
6. Kim, J., Park, Y., Kim, G., et al.: SplitNet: learning to semantically split deep networks for parameter reduction and model parallelization. In: International Conference on Machine Learning, pp. 1866–1874. PMLR (2017)
7. Howard, A., Sandler, M., Chu, G., et al.: Searching for mobilenetv3. In: Proceedings of the IEEE/CVF International Conference on Computer Vision, pp. 1314–1324 (2019)
8. Tammina, S.: Transfer learning using VGG-16 with deep convolutional neural network for classifying images. Int. J. Sci. Res. Publ. **9**(10), 143–150 (2019)
9. Martello, S., Monaci, M.: Algorithmic approaches to the multiple knapsack assignment problem. Omega **90**, 102004 (2020)
10. Donato, M.B.: The infinite dimensional Lagrange multiplier rule for convex optimization problems. J. Funct. Anal. **261**(8), 2083–2093 (2011)

Author Index

Printed in the United States
by Baker & Taylor Publisher Services